D1712596

American Casebook Series
Hornbook Series and Basic Legal Texts
Nutshell Series

of

WEST PUBLISHING COMPANY
P.O. Box 43526
St. Paul, Minnesota 55164
January, 1984

ACCOUNTING

Faris' Law and Accounting in a Nutshell, approximately 392 pages, 1984 (Text)

Fiflis, Kripke and Foster's Teaching Materials on Accounting for Business Lawyers, 3rd Ed., approximately 784 pages, 1984 (Casebook)

Siegel and Siegel's Accounting and Financial Disclosure: A Guide to Basic Concepts, 259 pages, 1983 (Text)

ADMINISTRATIVE LAW

Davis' Cases, Text and Problems on Administrative Law, 6th Ed., 683 pages, 1977 (Casebook)

Davis' Basic Text on Administrative Law, 3rd Ed., 617 pages, 1972 (Text)

Davis' Police Discretion, 176 pages, 1975 (Text)

Gellhorn and Boyer's Administrative Law and Process in a Nutshell, 2nd Ed., 445 pages, 1981 (Text)

Mashaw and Merrill's Introduction to the American Public Law System, 1095 pages, 1975, with 1980 Supplement (Casebook)

Robinson, Gellhorn and Bruff's The Administrative Process, 2nd Ed., 959 pages, 1980, with 1983 Supplement (Casebook)

ADMIRALTY

Healy and Sharpe's Cases and Materials on Admiralty, 875 pages, 1974 (Casebook)

Maraist's Admiralty in a Nutshell, 400 pages, 1983 (Text)

Sohn and Gustafson's Law of the Sea in a Nutshell, approximately 250 pages, 1984 (Text)

AGENCY PARTNERSHIP

Fessler's Alternatives to Incorporation for Persons in Quest of Profit, 258 pages, 1980 (Casebook)

Henn's Cases and Materials on Agency, Partnership and Other Unincorporated Business Enterprises, 396 pages, 1972 (Casebook)

Reuschlein and Gregory's Hornbook on the Law of Agency and Partnership, 625 pages, 1979, with 1981 pocket part (Text)

Seavey's Hornbook on Agency, 329 pages, 1964 (Text)

Seavey and Hall's Cases on Agency, 431 pages, 1956 (Casebook)

Seavey, Reuschlein and Hall's Cases on Agency and Partnership, 599 pages, 1962 (Casebook)

Selected Corporation and Partnership Statutes and Forms, 556 pages, 1982

Steffen and Kerr's Cases and Materials on Agency-Partnership, 4th Ed., 859 pages, 1980 (Casebook)

Steffen's Agency-Partnership in a Nutshell, 364 pages, 1977 (Text)

AMERICAN INDIAN LAW

Canby's American Indian Law in a Nutshell, 288 pages, 1981 (Text)

Getches, Rosenfelt and Wilkinson's Cases on Federal Indian Law, 660 pages, 1979, with 1983 Supplement (Casebook)

ANTITRUST LAW

Gellhorn's Antitrust Law and Economics in a Nutshell, 2nd Ed., 425 pages, 1981 (Text)

Gifford and Raskind's Cases and Materials on Antitrust, 694 pages, 1983 (Casebook)

LAW SCHOOL PUBLICATIONS—Continued

ANTITRUST LAW—Continued

Oppenheim, Weston and McCarthy's Cases and Comments on Federal Antitrust Laws, 4th Ed., 1168 pages, 1981 (Casebook)

Posner and Easterbrook's Cases and Economic Notes on Antitrust, 2nd Ed., 1077 pages, 1981, with 1982–83 Supplement (Casebook)

Sullivan's Hornbook of the Law of Antitrust, 886 pages, 1977 (Text)

See also Regulated Industries, Trade Regulation

ART LAW

DuBoff's Art Law in a Nutshell, approximately 290 pages, 1984 (Text)

BANKING LAW

Lovett's Banking and Financial Institutions in a Nutshell, 409 pages, 1984 (Text)

White's Teaching Materials on Banking Law, 1058 pages, 1976, with Case and Statutory Supplement (Casebook)

BUSINESS PLANNING

Epstein and Scheinfeld's Teaching Materials on Business Reorganization Under the Bankruptcy Code, 216 pages, 1980 (Casebook)

Painter's Problems and Materials in Business Planning, 2nd Ed., approximately 1035 pages, 1984 (Casebook)

Selected Securities and Business Planning Statutes, Rules and Forms, 485 pages, 1982

CIVIL PROCEDURE

Casad's Res Judicata in a Nutshell, 310 pages, 1976 (text)

Cound, Friedenthal and Miller's Cases and Materials on Civil Procedure, 3rd Ed., 1147 pages, 1980 with 1984 Supplement (Casebook)

Ehrenzweig, Louisell and Hazard's Jurisdiction in a Nutshell, 4th Ed., 232 pages, 1980 (Text)

Federal Rules of Civil-Appellate-Criminal Procedure—West Law School Edition, 343 pages, 1983

Hodges, Jones and Elliott's Cases and Materials on Texas Trial and Appellate Procedure, 2nd Ed., 745 pages, 1974 (Casebook)

Hodges, Jones and Elliott's Cases and Materials on the Judicial Process Prior to Trial in Texas, 2nd Ed., 871 pages, 1977 (Casebook)

Kane's Civil Procedure in a Nutshell, 271 pages, 1979 (Text)

Karlen's Procedure Before Trial in a Nutshell, 258 pages, 1972 (Text)

Karlen, Meisenholder, Stevens and Vestal's Cases on Civil Procedure, 923 pages, 1975 (Casebook)

CIVIL PROCEDURE—Continued

Koffler and Reppy's Hornbook on Common Law Pleading, 663 pages, 1969 (Text)

McBaine's Cases on Introduction to Civil Procedure, 399 pages, 1950 (Casebook)

Park's Computer-Aided Exercises on Civil Procedure, 2nd Ed., 167 pages, 1983 (Coursebook)

Shipman's Hornbook on Common-Law Pleading, 3rd Ed., 644 pages, 1923 (Text)

Siegel's Hornbook on New York Practice, 1011 pages, 1978 with 1981–82 Pocket Part (Text)

See also Federal Jurisdiction and Procedure

CIVIL RIGHTS

Abernathy's Cases and Materials on Civil Rights, 660 pages, 1980 (Casebook)

Cohen's Cases on the Law of Deprivation of Liberty: A Study in Social Control, 755 pages, 1980 (Casebook)

Lockhart, Kamisar and Choper's Cases on Constitutional Rights and Liberties, 5th Ed., 1298 pages plus Appendix, 1981, with 1983 Supplement (Casebook)—reprint from Lockhart, et al. Cases on Constitutional Law, 5th Ed., 1980

Vieira's Civil Rights in a Nutshell, 279 pages, 1978 (Text)

COMMERCIAL LAW

Bailey's Secured Transactions in a Nutshell, 2nd Ed., 391 pages, 1981 (Text)

Epstein and Martin's Basic Uniform Commercial Code Teaching Materials, 2nd Ed., 667 pages, 1983 (Casebook)

Henson's Hornbook on Secured Transactions Under the U.C.C., 2nd Ed., 504 pages, 1979 with 1979 P.P. (Text)

Murray's Commercial Law, Problems and Materials, 366 pages, 1975 (Coursebook)

Nordstrom and Clovis' Problems and Materials on Commercial Paper, 458 pages, 1972 (Casebook)

Nordstrom and Lattin's Problems and Materials on Sales and Secured Transactions, 809 pages, 1968 (Casebook)

Nordstrom, Murray and Clovis' Problems and Materials on Sales, 515 pages, 1982 (Casebook)

Nordstrom's Hornbook on Sales, 600 pages, 1970 (Text)

Selected Commercial Statutes, 1379 pages, 1983

Speidel, Summers and White's Teaching Materials on Commercial and Consumer Law, 3rd Ed., 1490 pages, 1981 (Casebook)

Stockton's Sales in a Nutshell, 2nd Ed., 370 pages, 1981 (Text)

Stone's Uniform Commercial Code in a Nutshell, 507 pages, 1975 (Text)

Uniform Commercial Code, Official Text with Comments, 994 pages, 1978

LAW SCHOOL PUBLICATIONS—Continued

COMMERCIAL LAW—Continued

UCC Article 8, 1977 Amendments, 249 pages, 1978

UCC Article 9, Reprint from 1962 Code, 128 pages, 1976

UCC Article 9, 1972 Amendments, 304 pages, 1978

Weber and Speidel's Commercial Paper in a Nutshell, 3rd Ed., 404 pages, 1982 (Text)

White and Summers' Hornbook on the Uniform Commercial Code, 2nd Ed., 1250 pages, 1980 (Text)

COMMUNITY PROPERTY

Mennell's Community Property in a Nutshell, 447 pages, 1982 (Text)

Verrall and Bird's Cases and Materials on California Community Property, 4th Ed., 549 pages, 1983 (Casebook)

COMPARATIVE LAW

Barton, Gibbs, Li and Merryman's Law in Radically Different Cultures, 960 pages, 1983 (Casebook)

Glendon, Gordon, and Osakwe's Comparative Legal Traditions in a Nutshell, 402 pages, 1982 (Text)

Langbein's Comparative Criminal Procedure: Germany, 172 pages, 1977 (Casebook)

COMPUTERS AND LAW

Mason's An Introduction to the Use of Computers in Law, approximately 200 pages, 1984 (Text)

CONFLICT OF LAWS

Cramton, Currie and Kay's Cases-Comments-Questions on Conflict of Laws, 3rd Ed., 1026 pages, 1981 (Casebook)

Scoles and Hay's Hornbook on Conflict of Laws, Student Ed., 1085 pages, 1982 (Text)

Scoles and Weintraub's Cases and Materials on Conflict of Laws, 2nd Ed., 966 pages, 1972, with 1978 Supplement (Casebook)

Siegel's Conflicts in a Nutshell, 469 pages, 1982 (Text)

CONSTITUTIONAL LAW

Engdahl's Constitutional Power in a Nutshell: Federal and State, 411 pages, 1974 (Text)

Lockhart, Kamisar and Choper's Cases-Comments-Questions on Constitutional Law, 5th Ed., 1705 pages plus Appendix, 1980, with 1983 Supplement (Casebook)

Lockhart, Kamisar and Choper's Cases-Comments-Questions on the American Constitution, 5th Ed., 1185 pages plus Appendix, 1981, with 1983 Supplement (Casebook)—reprint from Lockhart, et al. Cases on Constitutional Law, 5th Ed., 1980

CONSTITUTIONAL LAW—Continued

Manning's The Law of Church-State Relations in a Nutshell, 305 pages, 1981 (Text)

Miller's Presidential Power in a Nutshell, 328 pages, 1977 (Text)

Nowak, Rotunda and Young's Hornbook on Constitutional Law, 2nd Ed., Student Ed., 1172 pages, 1983 (Text)

Rotunda's Modern Constitutional Law: Cases and Notes, 1034 pages, 1981, with 1983 Supplement (Casebook)

Williams' Constitutional Analysis in a Nutshell, 388 pages, 1979 (Text)

See also Civil Rights

CONSUMER LAW

Epstein and Nickles' Consumer Law in a Nutshell, 2nd Ed., 418 pages, 1981 (Text)

McCall's Consumer Protection, Cases, Notes and Materials, 594 pages, 1977, with 1977 Statutory Supplement (Casebook)

Selected Commercial Statutes, 1379 pages, 1983

Spanogle and Rohner's Cases and Materials on Consumer Law, 693 pages, 1979, with 1982 Supplement (Casebook)

See also Commercial Law

CONTRACTS

Calamari & Perillo's Cases and Problems on Contracts, 1061 pages, 1978 (Casebook)

Calamari and Perillo's Hornbook on Contracts, 2nd Ed., 878 pages, 1977 (Text)

Corbin's Text on Contracts, One Volume Student Edition, 1224 pages, 1952 (Text)

Fessler and Loiseaux's Cases and Materials on Contracts, 837 pages, 1982 (Casebook)

Freedman's Cases and Materials on Contracts, 658 pages, 1973 (Casebook)

Friedman's Contract Remedies in a Nutshell, 323 pages, 1981 (Text)

Fuller and Eisenberg's Cases on Basic Contract Law, 4th Ed., 1203 pages, 1981 (Casebook)

Hamilton, Rau and Weintraub's Cases and Materials on Contracts, approximately 950 pages, 1984 (Casebook)

Jackson and Bollinger's Cases on Contract Law in Modern Society, 2nd Ed., 1329 pages, 1980 (Casebook)

Keyes' Government Contracts in a Nutshell, 423 pages, 1979 (Text)

Reitz's Cases on Contracts as Basic Commercial Law, 763 pages, 1975 (Casebook)

Schaber and Rohwer's Contracts in a Nutshell, 2nd Ed., approximately 409 pages, 1984 (Text)

Simpson's Hornbook on Contracts, 2nd Ed., 510 pages, 1965 (Text)

COPYRIGHT

See Patent and Copyright Law

LAW SCHOOL PUBLICATIONS—Continued

CORPORATIONS

Hamilton's Cases on Corporations—Including Partnerships and Limited Partnerships, 2nd Ed., 1108 pages, 1981, with 1981 Statutory Supplement and 1984 Supplement (Casebook)

Hamilton's Law of Corporations in a Nutshell, 379 pages, 1980 (Text)

Henn's Cases on Corporations, 1279 pages, 1974, with 1980 Supplement (Casebook)

Henn and Alexander's Hornbook on Corporations, 3rd Ed., Student Ed., 1371 pages, 1983 (Text)

Jennings and Buxbaum's Cases and Materials on Corporations, 5th Ed., 1180 pages, 1979 (Casebook)

Selected Corporation and Partnership Statutes, Regulations and Forms, 556 pages, 1982

Solomon, Stevenson and Schwartz' Materials and Problems on the Law and Policies on Corporations, 1172 pages, 1982 with 1983 Supplement (Casebook)

CORPORATE FINANCE

Hamilton's Cases and Materials on Corporate Finance, approximately 882 pages, 1984 (Casebook)

CORRECTIONS

Krantz's Cases and Materials on the Law of Corrections and Prisoners' Rights, 2nd Ed., 735 pages, 1981, with 1982 Supplement (Casebook)

Krantz's Law of Corrections and Prisoners' Rights in a Nutshell, 2nd Ed., 384 pages, 1983 (Text)

Popper's Post-Conviction Remedies in a Nutshell, 360 pages, 1978 (Text)

Robbins' Cases and Materials on Post Conviction Remedies, 506 pages, 1982 (Casebook)

Rubin's Law of Criminal Corrections, 2nd Ed., 873 pages, 1973, with 1978 Supplement (Text)

CREDITOR'S RIGHTS

Bankruptcy Code and Rules, Law School Ed., 438 pages, 1984

Epstein's Debtor-Creditor Law in a Nutshell, 2nd Ed., 324 pages, 1980 (Text)

Epstein and Landers' Debtors and Creditors: Cases and Materials, 2nd Ed., 689 pages, 1982 (Casebook)

Epstein and Sheinfeld's Teaching Materials on Business Reorganization Under the Bankruptcy Code, 216 pages, 1980 (Casebook)

Riesenfeld's Cases and Materials on Creditors' Remedies and Debtors' Protection, 3rd Ed., 810 pages, 1979 with 1979 Statutory Supplement and 1981 Case Supplement (Casebook)

CRIMINAL LAW AND CRIMINAL PROCEDURE

Cohen and Gobert's Problems in Criminal Law, 297 pages, 1976 (Problem book)

Davis' Police Discretion, 176 pages, 1975 (Text)

Dix and Sharlot's Cases and Materials on Criminal Law, 2nd Ed., 771 pages, 1979 (Casebook)

Federal Rules of Civil-Appellate-Criminal Procedure—West Law School Edition, 343 pages, 1983

Grano's Problems in Criminal Procedure, 2nd Ed., 176 pages, 1981 (Problem book)

Israel and LaFave's Criminal Procedure in a Nutshell, 3rd Ed., 438 pages, 1980 (Text)

Johnson's Cases, Materials and Text on Substantive Criminal Law in its Procedural Context, 2nd Ed., 956 pages, 1980 (Casebook)

Kamisar, LaFave and Israel's Cases, Comments and Questions on Modern Criminal Procedure, 5th ed., 1635 pages plus Appendix, 1980 with 1983 Supplement (Casebook)

Kamisar, LaFave and Israel's Cases, Comments and Questions on Basic Criminal Procedure, 5th Ed., 869 pages, 1980 with 1983 Supplement (Casebook)—reprint from Kamisar, et al. Modern Criminal Procedure, 5th ed., 1980

LaFave's Modern Criminal Law: Cases, Comments and Questions, 789 pages, 1978 (Casebook)

LaFave and Scott's Hornbook on Criminal Law, 763 pages, 1972 (Text)

Langbein's Comparative Criminal Procedure: Germany, 172 pages, 1977 (Casebook)

Loewy's Criminal Law in a Nutshell, 302 pages, 1975 (Text)

Saltzburg's American Criminal Procedure, Cases and Commentary, 2nd Ed., 1193 pages, 1984 (Casebook)

Uviller's The Processes of Criminal Justice: Investigation and Adjudication, 2nd Ed., 1384 pages, 1979 with 1979 Statutory Supplement and 1983 Update (Casebook)

Uviller's The Processes of Criminal Justice: Adjudication, 2nd Ed., 730 pages, 1979. Soft-cover reprint from Uviller's The Processes of Criminal Justice: Investigation and Adjudication, 2nd Ed. (Casebook)

Uviller's The Processes of Criminal Justice: Investigation, 2nd Ed., 655 pages, 1979. Soft-cover reprint from Uviller's The Processes of Criminal Justice: Investigation and Adjudication, 2nd Ed. (Casebook)

Vorenberg's Cases on Criminal Law and Procedure, 2nd Ed., 1088 pages, 1981 (Casebook)

LAW SCHOOL PUBLICATIONS—Continued

**CRIMINAL LAW AND CRIMINAL PRO-
CEDURE**—Continued

See also Corrections, Juvenile Justice

DECEDENTS ESTATES

See Trusts and Estates

DOMESTIC RELATIONS

Clark's Cases and Problems on Domestic
Relations, 3rd Ed., 1153 pages, 1980
(Casebook)

Clark's Hornbook on Domestic Relations,
754 pages, 1968 (Text)

Krause's Cases and Materials on Family
Law, 2nd Ed., 1221 pages, 1983 (Casebook)

Krause's Family Law in a Nutshell, 400
pages, 1977 (Text)

Krauskopf's Cases on Property Division at
Marriage Dissolution, 250 pages, 1984
(Casebook)

EDUCATION LAW

Alexander and Alexander's The Law of
Schools, Students and Teachers in a Nut-
shell, approximately 395 pages, 1984
(Text)

Morris' The Constitution and American Education, 2nd Ed., 992 pages, 1980 (Casebook)

EMPLOYMENT DISCRIMINATION

Player's Cases and Materials on Employment
Discrimination Law, 2nd Ed., approximately 675 pages, 1984 (Casebook)

Player's Federal Law of Employment Discrimination in a Nutshell, 2nd Ed., 402
pages, 1981 (Text)

See also Women and the Law

**ENERGY AND NATURAL RESOURCES
LAW**

Rodgers' Cases and Materials on Energy
and Natural Resources Law, 2nd Ed., 877
pages, 1983 (Casebook)

Selected Environmental Law Statutes, 768
pages, 1983

Tomain's Energy Law in a Nutshell, 338
pages, 1981 (Text)

See also Environmental Law, Oil and Gas,
Water Law

ENVIRONMENTAL LAW

Bonine and McGarity's Cases and Materials
on the Law of Environment and Pollution,
approximately 892 pages, 1984 (Casebook)

Findley and Farber's Cases and Materials on
Environmental Law, 738 pages, 1981,
with 1983 Supplement (Casebook)

Findley and Farber's Environmental Law in
a Nutshell, 343 pages, 1983 (Text)

ENVIROMENTAL LAW—Continued

Hanks, Tarlock and Hanks' Cases on Environmental Law and Policy, 1242 pages,
1974, with 1976 Supplement (Casebook)

Rodgers' Hornbook on Environmental Law,
956 pages, 1977 (Text)

Selected Environmental Law Statutes, 768
pages, 1983

See also Energy and Natural Resources Law,
Water Law

EQUITY

See Remedies

ESTATES

See Trusts and Estates

ESTATE PLANNING

Kurtz' Cases, Materials and Problems on
Family Estate Planning, 853 pages, 1983
(Casebook)

Lynn's Introduction to Estate Planning, in a
Nutshell, 3rd Ed., 370 pages, 1983 (Text)

See also Taxation

EVIDENCE

Broun and Meisenholder's Problems in Evidence, 2nd Ed., 304 pages, 1981 (Problem book)

Cleary and Strong's Cases, Materials and
Problems on Evidence, 3rd Ed., 1143
pages, 1981 (Casebook)

Federal Rules of Evidence for United States
Courts and Magistrates, 327 pages, 1983

Graham's Federal Rules of Evidence in a
Nutshell, 429 pages, 1981 (Text)

Kimball's Programmed Materials on Problems in Evidence, 380 pages, 1978 (Problem book)

Lempert and Saltzburg's A Modern Approach to Evidence: Text, Problems, Tran-
scripts and Cases, 2nd Ed., 1296 pages,
1983 (Casebook)

Lilly's Introduction to the Law of Evidence,
486 pages, 1978 (Text)

McCormick, Elliott and Sutton's Cases and
Materials on Evidence, 5th Ed., 1212
pages, 1981 (Casebook)

McCormick's Hornbook on Evidence, 3rd
Ed., Student Ed., approximately 1006
pages, 1984 (Text)

Rothstein's Evidence, State and Federal
Rules in a Nutshell, 2nd Ed., 514 pages,
1981 (Text)

Saltzburg's Evidence Supplement: Rules,
Statutes, Commentary, 245 pages, 1980
(Casebook Supplement)

**FEDERAL JURISDICTION AND PROCE-
DURE**

Currie's Cases and Materials on Federal
Courts, 3rd Ed., 1042 pages, 1982 (Casebook)

LAW SCHOOL PUBLICATIONS—Continued

**FEDERAL JURISDICTION AND PROCE-
DURE**—Continued

Currie's Federal Jurisdiction in a Nutshell,
2nd Ed., 258 pages, 1981 (Text)

Federal Rules of Civil-Appellate-Criminal
Procedure—West Law School Edition,
343 pages, 1983

Forrester and Moye's Cases and Materials
on Federal Jurisdiction and Procedure,
3rd Ed., 917 pages, 1977 with 1981 Supplement (Casebook)

Redish's Cases, Comments and Questions on
Federal Courts, 878 pages, 1983 (Casebook)

Vetri and Merrill's Federal Courts, Problems
and Materials, 2nd Ed., approximately
250 pages, 1984

Wright's Hornbook on Federal Courts, 4th
Ed., Student Ed., 870 pages, 1983 (Text)

FUTURE INTERESTS

See Trusts and Estates

**HOUSING AND URBAN DEVELOP-
MENT**

Berger's Cases and Materials on Housing,
2nd Ed., 254 pages, 1973 (Casebook)—
reprint from Cooper et al. Cases on Law
and Poverty, 2nd Ed., 1973

See also Land Use

IMMIGRATION LAW

Weissbrodt's Immigration Law and Procedure in a Nutshell, approximately 337
pages, 1984 (Text)

INDIAN LAW

See American Indian Law

INSURANCE

Dobbyn's Insurance Law in a Nutshell, 281
pages, 1981 (Text)

Keeton's Cases on Basic Insurance Law, 2nd
Ed., 1086 pages, 1977

Keeton's Basic Text on Insurance Law, 712
pages, 1971 (Text)

Keeton's Case Supplement to Keeton's Basic
Text on Insurance Law, 334 pages, 1978
(Casebook)

Keeton's Programmed Problems in Insurance Law, 243 pages, 1972 (Text Supplement)

York and Whelan's Cases, Materials and
Problems on Insurance Law, 715 pages,
1982 (Casebook)

INTERNATIONAL LAW

Henkin, Pugh, Schachter and Smit's Cases
and Materials on International Law, 2nd
Ed., 1152 pages, 1980, with Documents
Supplement (Casebook)

INTERNATIONAL LAW—Continued

Jackson's Legal Problems of International
Economic Relations, 1097 pages, 1977,
with Documents Supplement (Casebook)

Kirgis' International Organizations in Their
Legal Setting, 1016 pages, 1977, with
1981 Supplement (Casebook)

Weston, Falk and D'Amato's International
Law and World Order—A Problem Oriented Coursebook, 1195 pages, 1980,
with Documents Supplement (Casebook)

Wilson's International Business Transactions
in a Nutshell, 2nd Ed., 476 pages, 1984
(Text)

INTERVIEWING AND COUNSELING

Binder and Price's Interviewing and Counseling, 232 pages, 1977 (Text)

Shaffer's Interviewing and Counseling in a
Nutshell, 353 pages, 1976 (Text)

INTRODUCTION TO LAW

Dobbyn's So You Want to go to Law School,
Revised First Edition, 206 pages, 1976
(Text)

Hegland's Introduction to the Study and
Practice of Law in a Nutshell, 418 pages,
1983 (Text)

Kelso and Kelso's Studying Law: An Introduction, approximately 585 pages, 1984
(Coursebook)

Kinyon's Introduction to Law Study and Law
Examinations in a Nutshell, 389 pages,
1971 (Text)

See also Legal Method and Legal System

JUDICIAL ADMINISTRATION

Carrington, Meador and Rosenberg's Justice
on Appeal, 263 pages, 1976 (Casebook)

Nelson's Cases and Materials on Judicial
Administration and the Administration of
Justice, 1032 pages, 1974 (Casebook)

JURISPRUDENCE

Christie's Text and Readings on Jurisprudence—The Philosophy of Law, 1056
pages, 1973 (Casebook)

JUVENILE JUSTICE

Fox's Cases and Materials on Modern Juvenile Justice, 2nd Ed., 960 pages, 1981
(Casebook)

Fox's Juvenile Courts in a Nutshell, 3rd Ed.,
approximately 290 pages, 1984 (Text)

LABOR LAW

Gorman's Basic Text on Labor Law—Unioni-
zation and Collective Bargaining, 914
pages, 1976 (Text)

Leslie's Labor Law in a Nutshell, 403 pages,
1979 (Text)

Nolan's Labor Arbitration Law and Practice
in a Nutshell, 358 pages, 1979 (Text)

LAW SCHOOL PUBLICATIONS—Continued

LABOR LAW—Continued

Oberer, Hanslowe and Andersen's Cases and Materials on Labor Law—Collective Bargaining in a Free Society, 2nd Ed., 1168 pages, 1979, with 1979 Statutory Supplement and 1982 Case Supplement (Casebook)

See also Employment Discrimination, Social Legislation

LAND FINANCE

See Real Estate Transactions

LAND USE

Hagman's Cases on Public Planning and Control of Urban and Land Development, 2nd Ed., 1301 pages, 1980 (Casebook)

Hagman's Hornbook on Urban Planning and Land Development Control Law, 706 pages, 1971 (Text)

Wright and Gitelman's Cases and Materials on Land Use, 3rd Ed., 1300 pages, 1982 (Casebook)

Wright and Webber's Land Use in a Nutshell, 316 pages, 1978 (Text)

See also Housing and Urban Development

LAW AND ECONOMICS

Goetz' Cases and Materials on Law and Economics, 547 pages, 1984 (Casebook)

Manne's The Economics of Legal Relationships—Readings in the Theory of Property Rights, 660 pages, 1975 (Text)

See also Antitrust, Regulated Industries

LAW AND MEDICINE—PSYCHIATRY

Cohen's Cases and Materials on the Law of Deprivation of Liberty: A Study in Social Control, 755 pages, 1980 (Casebook)

King's The Law of Medical Malpractice in a Nutshell, 340 pages, 1977 (Text)

Shapiro and Spece's Problems, Cases and Materials on Bioethics and Law, 892 pages, 1981 (Casebook)

Sharpe, Fiscina and Head's Cases on Law and Medicine, 882 pages, 1978 (Casebook)

LEGAL HISTORY

Presser and Zainaldin's Cases on Law and American History, 855 pages, 1980 (Casebook)

See also Legal Method and Legal System

LEGAL METHOD AND LEGAL SYSTEM

Aldisert's Readings, Materials and Cases in the Judicial Process, 948 pages, 1976 (Casebook)

LEGAL METHOD AND LEGAL SYSTEM—Continued

Bodenheimer, Oakley and Love's Readings and Cases on an Introduction to the Anglo-American Legal System, 161 pages, 1980 (Casebook)

Davies and Lawry's Institutions and Methods of the Law—Introductory Teaching Materials, 547 pages, 1982 (Casebook)

Dvorkin, Himmelstein and Lesnick's Becoming a Lawyer: A Humanistic Perspective on Legal Education and Professionalism, 211 pages, 1981 (Text)

Fryer and Orentlicher's Cases and Materials on Legal Method and Legal System, 1043 pages, 1967 (Casebook)

Greenberg's Judicial Process and Social Change, 666 pages, 1977 (Coursebook)

Kempin's Historical Introduction to Anglo-American Law in a Nutshell, 2nd Ed., 280 pages, 1973 (Text)

Kimball's Historical Introduction to the Legal System, 610 pages, 1966 (Casebook)

Mashaw and Merrill's Introduction to the American Public Law System, 1095 pages, 1975, with 1980 Supplement (Casebook)

Murphy's Cases and Materials on Introduction to Law—Legal Process and Procedure, 772 pages, 1977 (Casebook)

Reynolds' Judicial Process in a Nutshell, 292 pages, 1980 (Text)

See also Legal Research and Writing

LEGAL NEGOTIATION

Edwards and White's Problems, Readings and Materials on the Lawyer as a Negotiator, 484 pages, 1977 (Casebook)

Williams' Legal Negotiation and Settlement, 207 pages, 1983 (Coursebook)

LEGAL PROFESSION

Aronson's Problems in Professional Responsibility, 280 pages, 1978 (Problem book)

Aronson and Weckstein's Professional Responsibility in a Nutshell, 399 pages, 1980 (Text)

Mellinkoff's The Conscience of a Lawyer, 304 pages, 1973 (Text)

Mellinkoff's Lawyers and the System of Justice, 983 pages, 1976 (Casebook)

Pirsig and Kirwin's Cases and Materials on Professional Responsibility, 4th Ed., approximately 650 pages, 1984 (Casebook)

Schwartz and Wydick's Problems in Legal Ethics, 285 pages, 1983 (Casebook)

Selected Statutes, Rules and Standards on the Legal Profession, 249 pages, 1984

Smith's Preventing Legal Malpractice, 142 pages, 1981 (Text)

LEGAL RESEARCH AND WRITING

Cohen's Legal Research in a Nutshell, 3rd Ed., 415 pages, 1978 (Text)

LAW SCHOOL PUBLICATIONS—Continued

LEGAL RESEARCH AND WRITING—
Continued

Cohen and Berring's How to Find the Law, 8th Ed., 790 pages, 1983. Problem book by Foster and Kelly available (Casebook)

Cohen and Berring's Finding the Law, 8th Ed., Abridged Ed., 556 pages, 1984 (Casebook)

Dickerson's Materials on Legal Drafting, 425 pages, 1981 (Casebook)

Felsenfeld and Siegel's Writing Contracts in Plain English, 290 pages, 1981 (Text)

Gopen's Writing From a Legal Perspective, 225 pages, 1981 (Text)

Mellinkoff's Legal Writing—Sense and Nonsense, 242 pages, 1982 (Text)

Rombauer's Legal Problem Solving—Analysis, Research and Writing, 4th Ed., 424 pages, 1983 (Coursebook)

Squires and Rombauer's Legal Writing in a Nutshell, 294 pages, 1982 (Text)

Statsky's Legal Research, Writing and Analysis, 2nd Ed., 167 pages, 1982 (Coursebook)

Statsky's Legislative Analysis: How to Use Statutes and Regulations, 2nd Ed., 217 pages, 1984 (Text)

Statsky and Wernet's Case Analysis and Fundamentals of Legal Writing, 2nd Ed., 441 pages, 1984 (Text)

Teply's Programmed Materials on Legal Research and Citation, 334 pages, 1982. Student Library Exercises available (Coursebook)

Weihofen's Legal Writing Style, 2nd Ed., 332 pages, 1980 (Text)

LEGISLATION

Davies' Legislative Law and Process in a Nutshell, 279 pages, 1975 (Text)

Nutting and Dickerson's Cases and Materials on Legislation, 5th Ed., 744 pages, 1978 (Casebook)

Statsky's Legislative Analysis: How to Use Statutes and Regulations, 2nd Ed., 217 pages, 1984 (Text)

LOCAL GOVERNMENT

McCarthy's Local Government Law in a Nutshell, 2nd Ed., 404 pages, 1983 (Text)

Michelman and Sandalow's Cases-Comments-Questions on Government in Urban Areas, 1216 pages, 1970, with 1972 Supplement (Casebook)

Reynolds' Hornbook on Local Government Law, 860 pages, 1982 (Text)

Stason and Kauper's Cases and Materials on Municipal Corporations, 3rd Ed., 692 pages, 1959 (Casebook)

Valente's Cases and Materials on Local Government Law, 2nd Ed., 980 pages, 1980 with 1982 Supplement (Casebook)

MASS COMMUNICATION LAW

Gillmor and Barron's Cases and Comment on Mass Communication Law, 4th Ed., approximately 1100 pages, 1984 (Casebook)

Ginsburg's Regulation of Broadcasting: Law and Policy Towards Radio, Television and Cable Communications, 741 pages, 1979, with 1983 Supplement (Casebook)

Zuckman and Gayne's Mass Communications Law in a Nutshell, 2nd Ed., 473 pages, 1983 (Text)

MILITARY LAW

Shanor and Terrell's Military Law in a Nutshell, 378 pages, 1980 (Text)

MORTGAGES

See Real Estate Transactions

NATURAL RESOURCES LAW

See Energy and Natural Resources Law, Environmental Law, Oil and Gas, Water Law

OFFICE PRACTICE

Hegland's Trial and Practice Skills in a Nutshell, 346 pages, 1978 (Text)

Strong and Clark's Law Office Management, 424 pages, 1974 (Casebook)

See also Legal Interviewing and Counseling, Legal Negotiation

OIL AND GAS

Hemingway's Hornbook on Oil and Gas, 2nd Ed., Student Ed., 543 pages, 1983 (Text)

Huie, Woodward and Smith's Cases and Materials on Oil and Gas, 2nd Ed., 955 pages, 1972 (Casebook)

Lowe's Oil and Gas Law in a Nutshell, 443 pages, 1983 (Text)

See also Energy and Natural Resources Law

PARTNERSHIP

See Agency—Partnership

PATENT AND COPYRIGHT LAW

Choate and Francis' Cases and Materials on Patent Law, 2nd Ed., 1110 pages, 1981 (Casebook)

Miller and Davis' Intellectual Property—Patents, Trademarks and Copyright in a Nutshell, 428 pages, 1983 (Text)

Nimmer's Cases on Copyright and Other Aspects of Law Pertaining to Literary, Musical and Artistic Works, 2nd Ed., 1023 pages, 1979 (Casebook)

POVERTY LAW

Brudno's Poverty, Inequality, and the Law: Cases-Commentary-Analysis, 934 pages, 1976 (Casebook)

LAW SCHOOL PUBLICATIONS—Continued

POVERTY LAW—Continued

LaFrance, Schroeder, Bennett and Boyd's Hornbook on Law of the Poor, 558 pages, 1973 (Text)

See also Social Legislation

PRODUCTS LIABILITY

Noel and Phillips' Cases on Products Liability, 2nd Ed., 821 pages, 1982 (Casebook)

Noel and Phillips' Products Liability in a Nutshell, 2nd Ed., 341 pages, 1981 (Text)

PROPERTY

Aigler, Smith and Tefft's Cases on Property, 2 volumes, 1339 pages, 1960 (Casebook)

Bernhardt's Real Property in a Nutshell, 2nd Ed., 448 pages, 1981 (Text)

Boyer's Survey of the Law of Property, 766 pages, 1981 (Text)

Browder, Cunningham and Smith's Cases on Basic Property Law, 4th Ed., approximately 1368 pages, 1984 (Casebook)

Bruce, Ely and Bostick's Cases and Materials on Modern Property Law, approximately 1000 pages, 1984 (Casebook)

Burby's Hornbook on Real Property, 3rd Ed., 490 pages, 1965 (Text)

Burke's Personal Property in a Nutshell, 322 pages, 1983 (Text)

Chused's A Modern Approach to Property: Cases-Notes-Materials, 1069 pages, 1978 with 1980 Supplement (Casebook)

Cohen's Materials for a Basic Course in Property, 526 pages, 1978 (Casebook)

Cunningham, Whitman and Stoebuck's Hornbook on the Law of Property, Student Ed., approximately 928 pages, 1984 (Text)

Donahue, Kauper and Martin's Cases on Property, 2nd Ed., 1362 pages, 1983 (Casebook)

Hill's Landlord and Tenant Law in a Nutshell, 319 pages, 1979 (Text)

Moynihan's Introduction to Real Property, 254 pages, 1962 (Text)

Phipps' Titles in a Nutshell, 277 pages, 1968 (Text)

Uniform Land Transactions Act, Uniform Simplification of Land Transfers Act, Uniform Condominium Act, 1977 Official Text with Comments, 462 pages, 1978

See also Housing and Urban Development, Real Estate Transactions, Land Use

REAL ESTATE TRANSACTIONS

Bruce's Real Estate Finance in a Nutshell, 292 pages, 1979 (Text)

Maxwell, Riesenfeld, Hetland and Warren's Cases on California Security Transactions in Land, 3rd Ed., approximately 710 pages, 1984 (Casebook)

REAL ESTATE TRANSACTIONS—Continued

Nelson and Whitman's Cases on Real Estate Transfer, Finance and Development, 2nd Ed., 1114 pages, 1981, with 1983 Supplement (Casebook)

Osborne's Cases and Materials on Secured Transactions, 559 pages, 1967 (Casebook)

Osborne, Nelson and Whitman's Hornbook on Real Estate Finance Law, 3rd Ed., 885 pages, 1979 (Text)

REGULATED INDUSTRIES

Gellhorn and Pierce's Regulated Industries in a Nutshell, 394 pages, 1982 (Text)

Morgan's Cases and Materials on Economic Regulation of Business, 830 pages, 1976, with 1978 Supplement (Casebook)

Pozen's Financial Institutions: Cases, Materials and Problems on Investment Management, 844 pages, 1978 (Casebook)

See also Mass Communication Law, Banking Law

REMEDIES

Dobbs' Hornbook on Remedies, 1067 pages, 1973 (Text)

Dobbs' Problems in Remedies, 137 pages, 1974 (Problem book)

Dobbyn's Injunctions in a Nutshell, 264 pages, 1974 (Text)

Friedman's Contract Remedies in a Nutshell, 323 pages, 1981 (Text)

Leavell, Love and Nelson's Cases and Materials on Equitable Remedies and Restitution, 3rd Ed., 704 pages, 1980 (Casebook)

McCormick's Hornbook on Damages, 811 pages, 1935 (Text)

O'Connell's Remedies in a Nutshell, 364 pages, 1977 (Text)

York and Bauman's Cases and Materials on Remedies, 3rd Ed., 1250 pages, 1979 (Casebook)

REVIEW MATERIALS

Ballantine's Problems

Black Letter Series

Smith's Review Series

West's Review Covering Multistate Subjects

SECURITIES REGULATION

Hazen's Hornbook on The Law of Securities Regulation, approximately 520 pages, 1984 (Text)

Ratner's Securities Regulation: Materials for a Basic Course, 2nd Ed., 1050 pages, 1980 with 1982 Supplement (Casebook)

Ratner's Securities Regulation in a Nutshell, 2nd Ed., 322 pages, 1982 (Text)

Selected Securities and Business Planning Statutes, Rules and Forms, 485 pages, 1982

LAW SCHOOL PUBLICATIONS—Continued

SOCIAL LEGISLATION

Brudno's Income Redistribution Theories and Programs: Cases-Commentary-Analyses, 480 pages, 1977 (Casebook)—reprint from Brudno's Poverty, Inequality and the Law, 1976

Hood and Hardy's Workers' Compensation and Employee Protection Laws in a Nutshell, 274 pages, 1984 (Text)

LaFrance's Welfare Law: Structure and Entitlement in a Nutshell, 455 pages, 1979 (Text)

Malone, Plant and Little's Cases on Workers' Compensation and Employment Rights, 2nd Ed., 951 pages, 1980 (Casebook)

See also Poverty Law

TAXATION

Dodge's Federal Taxation of Estates, Trusts and Gifts: Principles and Planning, 771 pages, 1981 with 1982 Supplement (Casebook)

Garbis and Struntz' Cases and Materials on Tax Procedure and Tax Fraud, 829 pages, 1982 with 1984 Supplement (Casebook)

Gunn's Cases and Materials on Federal Income Taxation of Individuals, 785 pages, 1981 with 1983 Supplement (Casebook)

Hellerstein and Hellerstein's Cases on State and Local Taxation, 4th Ed., 1041 pages, 1978 with 1982 Supplement (Casebook)

Kahn's Handbook on Basic Corporate Taxation, 3rd Ed., Student Ed., 614 pages, 1981 with 1983 Supplement (Text)

Kahn and Gann's Corporate Taxation and Taxation of Partnerships and Partners, 2nd Ed., approximately 1300 pages, 1984 (Casebook)

Kragen and McNulty's Cases and Materials on Federal Income Taxation, Vol. I: Taxation of Individuals, 3rd Ed., 1283 pages, 1979 with 1983 Supplement (Casebook)

Kragen and McNulty's Cases and Materials on Federal Income Taxation, Vol. II: Taxation of Corporations, Shareholders, Partnerships and Partners, 3rd Ed., 989 pages, 1981 with 1983 Supplement (Casebook)

McNulty's Federal Estate and Gift Taxation in a Nutshell, 3rd Ed., 509 pages, 1983 (Text)

McNulty's Federal Income Taxation of Individuals in a Nutshell, 3rd Ed., 487 pages, 1983 (Text)

Posin's Hornbook on Federal Income Taxation of Individuals, Student Ed., 491 pages, 1983 (Text)

Rice's Problems and Materials in Federal Estate and Gift Taxation, 3rd Ed., 474 pages, 1978 (Casebook)

Rice and Solomon's Problems and Materials in Federal Income Taxation, 3rd Ed., 670 pages, 1979 (Casebook)

TAXATION—Continued

Rose and Raskind's Advanced Federal Income Taxation: Corporate Transactions—Cases, Materials and Problems, 955 pages, 1978 (Casebook)

Selected Federal Taxation Statutes and Regulations, 1255 pages, 1983

Sobeloff and Weidenbruch's Federal Income Taxation of Corporations and Stockholders in a Nutshell, 362 pages, 1981 (Text)

TORTS

Christie's Cases and Materials on the Law of Torts, 1264 pages, 1983 (Casebook)

Green, Pedrick, Rahl, Thode, Hawkins, Smith and Treece's Cases and Materials on Torts, 2nd Ed., 1360 pages, 1977 (Casebook)

Green, Pedrick, Rahl, Thode, Hawkins, Smith, and Treece's Advanced Torts: Injuries to Business, Political and Family Interests, 2nd Ed., 544 pages, 1977 (Casebook)—reprint from Green, et al. Cases and Materials on Torts, 2nd Ed., 1977

Keeton, Keeton, Sargentich and Steiner's Cases and Materials on Torts, and Accident Law, 1360 pages, 1983 (Casebook)

Kionka's Torts in a Nutshell: Injuries to Persons and Property, 434 pages, 1977 (Text)

Malone's Torts in a Nutshell: Injuries to Family, Social and Trade Relations, 358 pages, 1979 (Text)

Prosser and Keeton's Hornbook on Torts, 5th Ed., Student Ed., approximately 1052 pages, 1984 (Text)

Shapo's Cases on Tort and Compensation Law, 1244 pages, 1976 (Casebook)

See also Products Liability

TRADE REGULATION

McManis' Unfair Trade Practices in a Nutshell, 444 pages, 1982 (Text)

Oppenheim, Weston, Maggs and Schechter's Cases and Materials on Unfair Trade Practices and Consumer Protection, 4th Ed., 1038 pages, 1983 (Casebook)

See also Antitrust, Regulated Industries

TRIAL AND APPELLATE ADVOCACY

Appellate Advocacy, Handbook of, 249 pages, 1980 (Text)

Bergman's Trial Advocacy in a Nutshell, 402 pages, 1979 (Text)

Binder and Bergman's Fact Investigation: From Hypothesis to Proof, approximately 350 pages, 1984 (Coursebook)

Goldberg's The First Trial (Where Do I Sit?) (What Do I Say?) in a Nutshell, 396 pages, 1982 (Text)

Hegland's Trial and Practice Skills in a Nutshell, 346 pages, 1978 (Text)

LAW SCHOOL PUBLICATIONS—Continued

TRIAL AND APPELLATE ADVOCACY—Continued

Hornstein's Appellate Advocacy in a Nutshell, approximately 270 pages, 1984 (Text)

Jeans' Handbook on Trial Advocacy, Student Ed., 473 pages, 1975 (Text)

McElhaney's Effective Litigation, 457 pages, 1974 (Casebook)

Nolan's Cases and Materials on Trial Practice, 518 pages, 1981 (Casebook)

Parnell and Shellhaas' Cases, Exercises and Problems for Trial Advocacy, 171 pages, 1982 (Coursebook)

Sonsteng, Haydock and Boyd's The Trialbook: A Total System for Preparation and Presentation of a Case, Student Ed., approximately 400 pages, 1984 (Coursebook)

TRUSTS AND ESTATES

Atkinson's Hornbook on Wills, 2nd Ed., 975 pages, 1953 (Text)

Averill's Uniform Probate Code in a Nutshell, 425 pages, 1978 (Text)

Bogert's Hornbook on Trusts, 5th Ed., 726 pages, 1973 (Text)

Clark, Lusky and Murphy's Cases and Materials on Gratuitous Transfers, 2nd Ed., 1102 pages, 1977 (Casebook)

Gulliver's Cases and Materials on Future Interests, 624 pages, 1959 (Casebook)

Gulliver's Introduction to the Law of Future Interests, 87 pages, 1959 (Casebook)—reprint from Gulliver's Cases and Materials on Future Interests, 1959

McGovern's Cases and Materials on Wills, Trusts and Future Interests: An Introduction to Estate Planning, 750 pages, 1983 (Casebook)

TRUSTS AND ESTATES—Continued

Mennell's Cases and Materials on California Decedent's Estates, 566 pages, 1973 (Casebook)

Mennell's Wills and Trusts in a Nutshell, 392 pages, 1979 (Text)

Powell's The Law of Future Interests in California, 91 pages, 1980 (Text)

Simes' Hornbook on Future Interests, 2nd Ed., 355 pages, 1966 (Text)

Turrentine's Cases and Text on Wills and Administration, 2nd Ed., 483 pages, 1962 (Casebook)

Uniform Probate Code, 5th Ed., Official Text With Comments, 384 pages, 1977

Waggoner's Future Interests in a Nutshell, 361 pages, 1981 (Text)

WATER LAW

Getches' Water Law in a Nutshell, approximately 400 pages, 1984 (Text)

Trelease's Cases and Materials on Water Law, 3rd Ed., 833 pages, 1979, with 1984 Supplement (Casebook)

See also Energy and Natural Resources Law, Environmental Law

WILLS

See Trusts and Estates

WOMEN AND THE LAW

Kay's Text, Cases and Materials on Sex-Based Discrimination, 2nd Ed., 1045 pages, 1981, with 1983 Supplement (Casebook)

Thomas' Sex Discrimination in a Nutshell, 399 pages, 1982 (Text)

See also Employment Discrimination

WORKERS' COMPENSATION

See Social Legislation

FACT INVESTIGATION
FROM HYPOTHESIS TO PROOF

By

David A. Binder
Professor of Law
University of California, Los Angeles

and

Paul Bergman
Senior Lecturer in Law
University of California, Los Angeles

AMERICAN CASEBOOK SERIES

WEST PUBLISHING CO.
ST. PAUL, MINN., 1984

COPYRIGHT © 1984 By WEST PUBLISHING CO.
50 West Kellogg Boulevard
P.O. Box 43526
St. Paul, Minnesota 55164
Printed in the United States of America

Library of Congress Cataloging in Publication Data

Binder, David A.
  Fact investigation.
  (American casebook series)
  1. Evidence (Law)—United States. I. Bergman, Paul,
1943–   II. Title. III. Series.
KF8935.B5 1984   347.73'6   84–3676
                     347.3076

ISBN 0–314–81258–X

Binder & Bergman Fact Invest. ACB

To Andrea

*

Preface

This book attempts to fill a few gaps of long standing in legal education. At trial, the substantive rules of law invoked depend upon what facts the factfinder believes have been proven. Yet, to our knowledge, law school courses and scholarly texts have never systematically considered the process by which litigators gather, analyze and use evidence to prove facts.

In substantive law courses, facts are given and doctrinal discussions follow. True, through hypotheticals an instructor may change the facts, but these changes are designed merely to facilitate doctrinal analysis. Like their predecessors, the new facts too are a given. Law school evidence courses are no exception. Despite fleeting reference to the concept of relevance, evidence courses focus almost exclusively upon rules that exclude relevant evidence and the policies that underlie such rules. Finally, even clinical courses such as trial advocacy and interviewing pay little attention to a conceptual analysis of how facts are proved. Most trial advocacy courses emphasize effective presentation of evidence found in witness statements. As in substantive law courses, the information with which the students work is a given. In interviewing courses, the focus is typically not on the evidentiary significance of the questions asked, but rather is upon the forms of questions and the interpersonal skills useful in motivating clients and witnesses to reveal information. Thus, many students may be excused for graduating from law school thinking that facts are like starving trout, ready to be reeled in at the drop of a question or two.

Experienced litigators, by contrast, tend to have far fewer misconceptions about the ease of gathering evidence to prove facts. For one thing, they understand that no one can reel in facts. At most, one can gather evidence from which facts can be proved. Second, they recognize that, far from lurking near the surface, items of evidence tend to lay on the murky bottom, hidden beneath layers of abstract legal principles, uncertain memory, people's desires to remain silent and competition fostered by the adversary system. As a result, litigators spend most of their time trying to peel away layers to gather evidence which might prove favorable facts.

Given the distance between litigators' activities and the coverage of legal education, gaps in the wall of legal education are apparent.

To fill those gaps, we offer a limited but we think important kind of mortar. We focus on disputes that are litigated in a formal setting in which the parties are at odds with respect to past happenings. In so doing, we recognize that one may have great difficulty gathering evidence unless one has a basic understanding of how facts are proved. To build such an understanding, we endeavor to provide a conceptual description of the thought processes which people use, whether consciously or subconsciously, in deciding disputed questions of fact.

The book is a blend of the theoretical and the practical. No less than the law of evidence or the law of torts, the processes by which people think about evidence are complex and demand close conceptual analysis. At the same time, for us theory cannot be divorced from practice. Since lawyers play a major role in resolving and litigating disputes, a theoretical understanding of the proof of facts is not sufficient. Lawyers must also understand how people describe events and how the use of interpersonal skills may affect those descriptions. Similarly, lawyers must analyze abstract legal issues in factual terms, marshal evidence according to those issues and record information in some meaningful way. In writing this book, our attention has never been far from these "practical" skills. We hope that our use of numerous examples and sample dialogues, as well as the hypothetical case of *Phillips v. Landview* which unfolds through many chapters, underlines our concern for both practical and intellectual understanding.

We hope too that our book stimulates among both law teachers and practicing litigators greater study of the proof of facts.

DAVID A. BINDER
PAUL BERGMAN
LOS ANGELES, CA

February, 1984

Acknowledgments

There were those who insisted that this book could not be written. Unfortunately, they were wrong. We gratefully acknowledge the contributions of many scholars, colleagues and students, whose ideas and phrases we have shamelessly incorporated. To the extent we have been able to, their contributions are memorialized either in footnotes or in the names of characters who populate the many examples scattered through the text. To those whose contributions are unnoted, especially students with whom we have discussed many of our ideas, we assure you that you are not unremembered, but perhaps just lucky.

Among those who read drafts of various chapters, we especially want to thank Patrick Patterson, Carrie Menkel-Meadow, Al Moore, Susan Gillig, Gary Palm, Sue Bryant, Michael Wolfson, Marsha Diedrich, Jerry Lopez, Ken Graham, Steve Yeazell and Melinda Binder. While, and even after he was our colleague, Paul Boland contributed many useful ideas. Over a period of three or four years we were assisted by excellent student research assistants, including Dorothy Shubin, Sara Deubner, Steve Ellis, Mary Royce and Allison Graves. Kim Bobby and Pat Truscello labored long and magnificently in the absence of word processors. We used many of the same words that were used earlier by William Shakespeare and William Faulkner, though of course we used the words in different order. While we accept ultimate responsibility for the entire book, readers who find errors may want to keep the above names in mind should they ever contemplate publication.

We wish also to thank our publisher, which stoutly supported us and refused suggestions of some readers to publish the book only in Swedish.

Finally, what can one say about Kenny Hegland?

*

Summary of Contents

*

Table of Contents

PART IV. UNEARTHING EVIDENCE

Table of Cases

References are to pages.

*

FACT INVESTIGATION
FROM HYPOTHESIS TO PROOF

*

Part I

INTRODUCTION

Chapter 1

THE IMPORTANCE OF FACT INVESTIGATION

1. INTRODUCTION

Whether lawyer or law student, you are certainly familiar with the ancient complaint that "law school doesn't prepare you for what lawyers actually do." Based largely on the study of appellate cases, legal education typically fosters the impression that the primary function of litigators is to understand legal rules and their policy underpinnings in order to construct appropriate "legal arguments" regarding the application of old rules or the need to formulate new ones. Indeed, traditional legal study inherently suggests that if one understands the relationship between values, social policies, and the application of legal principles, one fully understands the law and its operation.[1]

While this view may be useful, it certainly does not present a complete picture of how lawyers, clients and the legal system function. After all, substantive rules are not self-activated. They are triggered by evidence which proves, to the degree of certainty required, that certain facts exist to which the rules in turn can be applied.[2] The triggering mechanism itself relies on lawyers to present evidence in such a way as to convince a factfinder that facts occurred which render a given substantive rule applicable or inapplicable. And it is through fact investigation that lawyers amass and shape the evidence

1. Whether the relationship between values and substantive legal principles is adequately explored in current legal education is the subject of much debate. See R. Cramton, "The Current State of the Law Curriculum" 32 J.Legal Ed. 321, 330–331 (1982); K. Klare, "The Law-School Curriculum in the 1980s: What's Left?" 32 J.Legal Ed. 336, 339–341 (1982); F. Michelman, "The Parts and the Whole: Non-Euclidean Curricular Geometry" 32 J.Legal Ed. 352, 352–353 (1982).

2. For a further discussion of this proposition, see Chapter 2, pp. 10–11 infra.

presented at trial. Thus, the gathering and shaping of evidence is as central to the operation of the law as is the application of rules once the facts are determined. Indeed, this gathering and shaping forms the basis from which a factfinder decides whether or not to invoke a given rule.

Ferreting out evidence may not be the most publicized or romanticized aspect of litigation. But in the main, it is what litigators "actually do." [3]

2. CENTRAL ROLE OF FACT INVESTIGATION

Several reasons account for litigators' spending the bulk of their time on fact investigation. Obviously, if a dispute proceeds to trial, the evidence introduced by the parties will control which substantive principles determine the parties' rights. But regardless of trial, effective fact investigation is the underpinning for most of the other major tasks litigators undertake. For example, if one is not aware of the evidence that is likely to be introduced at trial, one can neither adequately counsel a client nor effectively negotiate regarding a case's substantive merits.

Moreover, because of a modern trend toward "notice pleading," pleadings no longer serve to inform a litigant of what facts an adversary relies upon. In a civil case, a defendant may know little more after reading a complaint than that he or she allegedly drove negligently and caused an unspecified amount of damages. The defendant's response may consist in essence of, "I did not. Anyway, you drove worse." In criminal cases defendants are usually charged only in the language of a statute.[4] In response, prosecutors typically hear nothing more than "not guilty." [5] Thus, in almost every case, if one is to find out much about an adversary's version of what happened, one must do so through investigation.

Furthermore, modern discovery rules encourage litigators to engage in comprehensive fact investigation prior to trial. In civil cases

3. See, e.g., "See Them in Court," TWA Ambassador Magazine 20 (Nov. 1982). In a survey of practicing lawyers in Chicago, "the legal skill they rated most important was fact-gathering, and only sixteen percent . . . said they'd learned *that* one in law school." (emphasis in original).

4. Under the Federal Rules of Criminal Procedure, it is generally sufficient that an indictment set forth the offense in the words of the statute so long as the language clearly sets forth all the elements of the offense intended to be pun-

ished. See 8 *Moore's Federal Practice* (2nd Ed.) Criminal Rules § 7.04.

5. Under the Federal Rules of Criminal Procedure affirmative defenses, such as not guilty by reason of insanity, are usually asserted by motion subsequent to the time the plea is entered. See 8 *Moore's Federal Practice* (2nd Ed.) Criminal Rules § 12.04. Moreover, when the defendant's plea is limited to "not guilty," a defendant need not specify which elements of the prosecutor's case are actually in dispute.

one can, among other things, send written interrogatories to adverse parties, depose potential witnesses and compel the production of documents. Ideally, at least in civil cases, discovery provisions make it possible "for the parties to obtain the fullest possible knowledge of the issues and facts before trial." [6] Though many attorneys resist discovery requests, the policy behind thorough fact investigation is clear.

Finally, most trials do not center on disputes over applicable substantive rules. Frequently, the parties largely agree on the substantive rules which govern a case. Where they differ is in their versions of the facts. Hence, litigators tend to spend a proportionately greater percentage of their time researching evidence to prove facts than they do researching law.

3. HISTORICAL FACTS

What is the nature of the "evidence" that occupies so many of a litigator's billable hours? Litigators resemble historians, and litigation is largely a process of re-creating historical events. Because the applicability of a substantive law is primarily dependent on a party's ability to prove historical facts that trigger the effect of that law, evidence in most cases concerns what happened in the past.

A brief example illustrates our point that most cases principally involve contests over historical events, not over substantive rules. Assume that a plaintiff brings an action for rescission based on false statements in the sale of a used Hutmobile. The defendant denies making any false statements. The applicable substantive law is that of fraudulent misrepresentation, and neither party is likely to argue that a change in that substantive law is required. But the law of fraudulent misrepresentation can be applied only if the factfinder first believes the plaintiff's evidence concerning false statements knowingly made by the defendant. The result will be determined according to whose version of past events is believed.

The critical influence of past events is evident even in cases seeking prospective relief. Assume that in the same suit for rescission, the plaintiff asks for an injunction preventing the defendant from making fraudulent misstatements in the future. The court's determination of whether the plaintiff is entitled to injunctive relief will depend in substantial part on whether the plaintiff's evidence as to what happened in the past is believed.

6. Hickman v. Taylor, 329 U.S. 495, 501, 67 S.Ct. 385, 388, 91 L.Ed. 451 (1947).

4. TRUTH AND THE ADVERSARY SYSTEM

The lawyer's role as an identifier, selector, and marshaller of evidence is not accidental. That role grows out of our system of dispute resolution. We do not resolve disputes by tying rocks to litigants, throwing them into pools and then giving verdicts according to whether a litigant sinks or swims. Rather, we resolve disputes primarily through settlement or trial. If a dispute is resolved through settlement, the parties' perceptions of the likely result at trial will greatly influence the terms of the settlement. If a dispute is resolved through trial, the factfinder's perception of the evidence largely dictates the result. In either circumstance, a lawyer's gathering and selecting evidence greatly affects the outcome of most disputes.

Moreover, we do not, because we cannot, force litigants to take factfinders back in time to actual events to demonstrate what really happened. Instead, under our adversary system, we ask the parties to present their competing stories, from which we hope truth emerges.

The parties' stories consist largely of verbal re-creations of past events.[7] Yet, a verbal re-creation can never be more than an abstraction of an actual event. The testimony of an eyewitness that "the defendant fired the gun" is not, and can never be, the equivalent of the actual event.

The inherent limitation of words in re-creating the past is poetically illustrated by John Fowles in *Daniel Martin*. In complaining that movies create their own pasts, he dramatically points out:

> Under the tyranny of the eye, that glutton for frontiers, this is the prime alienation of the cinema; always inherent in the theater, yet obscured there because of different performances and productions of the same text. But the final cut allows no choice, no more than the one angle; no creative response, no walking around, no time for one's own thought. In the very act of creating its own past, the past of the scenario and the past of the shooting, it destroys the past of the mind of each spectator.
>
> Images are inherently fascistic because they overstamp the truth, however dim and blurred, of the real past experience; as if, faced with ruins, we must turn architects, not archeologists. The word is the most imprecise of signs. Only a science-obsessed age could fail to comprehend that this is its great virtue, not its defect. What I was trying to tell Jenny in Hollywood was that I would murder my past if I tried to evoke it on camera; and it is precisely

7. The availability of real or documentary evidence should not be seen as an exception to our system's reliance on verbal testimony. Real or documentary evidence is rarely self-admissible. Verbal testimony of a witness is almost always necessary before this type of evidence is admitted.

because I can't really evoke it in words, can only hope to awaken some analogous experience in other memories and sensitivities, that it must be written.[8]

Words tend to become an even less accurate portrayal of the past when they are uttered by witnesses. We are not cameras, able to observe, absorb and recall all that occurs in our presence. What we observe, remember and state is greatly influenced by such matters as our individual abilities, the nature of our settings, personal biases, expectations, and the skills of attorneys who extract our stories.[9]

Because one cannot usually return in a time machine to show a trier of fact "what really happened," investigations do not produce "facts." They produce evidence, from which the trier of fact will resolve the parties' factual dispute(s) by deciding the *probable facts.*

Out of necessity, then, our system of justice is content with less-than-complete truth based on admittedly imperfect evidence. That is not to say that ours is a system of injustice, or that trials are inappropriate ways of settling disputes. It is to say that case investigation is a vital aspect of nearly all litigation. And one must recognize and attempt to deal with the foregoing deficiencies if trials are to come close to producing "truth."

For litigators, who are charged in an adversary system with representing clients, the reliance on evidentiary probabilities is critical. With objective truth unattainable, and the adversary system in place, one zealously attempts to ferret out and shape evidence so that a factfinder finds to be true facts which trigger a favorable legal result.[10]

5. NORMATIVE FACTS AND LEGISLATIVE FACTS

Although the evidence which triggers a legal result usually focuses on proof of historical events, this is not always the case. Sometimes, disputes also involve what might be termed "normative facts"

8. J. Fowles, *Daniel Martin,* p. 90, Copyright © Little, Brown and Company (Signet Ed.1978).

9. See generally B. Frank & J. Frank, *Not Guilty* (1957); P. Wall, *Eye-Witness Identification in Criminal Cases* (1965); G. Williams, *The Proof Of Guilt* (3rd ed. 1963); Fishman & Loftus, "Expert Psychological Testimony on Eyewitness Identification," 4 Law & Psych.Rev. 87 (1978); Note, "Did Your Eyes Deceive You? Expert Psychological Testimony on the Unreliability of Eyewitness Identification," 29 Stan.L.Rev. 969 (1977).

10. Whether the adversary system, with its emphasis on the role of the zeal-

ous advocate, perhaps obscures too much truth is, of course, subject to much debate. In general see M. Frankel, *Partisan Justice* (1978); M. Freedman, *Lawyer's Ethics in an Adversary System* (1975); D. Luban "The Adversary System Excuse," in Luban (Editor) *The Good Lawyer* (1983); V. Held "The Division of Moral Labor and The Role of the Lawyer," in Luban (Editor) *The Good Lawyer;* M. Schwartz, *Lawyers and the Legal Profession* pp. 3–165 (1979); L. Fuller, "The Adversary System," *Talks on American Law* 30–43 (H. Berman, Ed.1961).

and/or "legislative facts." In such cases, factfinders are called upon not only to determine what occurred in the past in relation to the parties, but also to determine the criteria to be used in judging the past events.

When "normative facts" are involved a factfinder, after determining what happened—the historical facts—evaluates what happened according to his or her perception of a community standard of reasonable, expected or proper behavior. For example, if in a negligence case a factfinder determines that a parent was driving a seriously ill child to a hospital at a speed of 70 m.p.h. when the parent collided with another car, that factual determination alone does not resolve the case. The factfinder must still decide whether, governed by normative standards, the parent was acting "unreasonably." Similarly, in a commercial dispute, a factfinder may, after deciding when notice of breach was given, need to evaluate whether a purchaser of goods gave notice of a breach of warranty within a reasonable time.[11]

In cases in which one argues for a change in substantive law, one may introduce evidence to establish "legislative facts." To the extent a change arguably rests on the nefarious social consequences of existing law, and the nirvana that new law would bring, one is sometimes permitted to present evidence regarding the asserted social consequences of changing the law. In evaluating this evidence, the factfinder decides whether on balance a change in the law is desirable. The factfinder's judgment is similar to judgments legislators make. Hence, the term "legislative facts." [12]

From the standpoint of fact investigation, the importance of "normative facts" and "legislative facts" is that they extend the scope of investigation beyond the historical events concerning the parties. One may additionally have to search for evidence about community standards (be they, e.g., standards for people in emergency situations or for commercial practices) or about likely social consequences.[13]

This book does not address specifically investigative concerns relating to normative facts and legislative facts. Its focus is on those

---

11. For a further discussion of normative facts, see Bohlen, "Mixed Questions of Law & Fact," 72 U.Penn.L.R. 111, 113–114 (1923); 2 Harper & James, *The Law of Torts* 936–965 (1956).

12. For further discussion of legislative facts, see McCormick on Evidence 759, 766 (2d ed. 1972); K. Karst, "Legislative Facts in Constitutional Litigation," 1960 Sup.Ct.Rev. 75, 99–100, 109; K. Davis, *Admin.Law Treatise* § 15.3 at 353 (1958).

13. The categories of historical, normative and legislative facts are in some sense artificial. To some degree, all historical facts are normative and legislative. A rule of law, which is primarily an embodiment of selected historical facts, reflects previous normative and legislative judgments that those facts should trigger a legal result. For example, the rule of law establishing what facts constitute a breach of contract reflects a judgment that people ought to be held accountable for agreements they have made.

cases in which the outcome depends upon the factfinder's determination of historical events concerning the parties. One reason for this focus is that historical facts are the primary subject of dispute in the majority of litigated cases. Second, so far as we can tell, the techniques one uses to pursue normative and legislative facts are similar to those used in pursuit of historical facts.

6. OUR OBJECTIVE

This is a book about how one thinks about and elicits evidence. We do not focus primarily on legal rules which delineate the boundaries of proper investigation—e.g., discovery rules. Nor do we attempt to identify particular pieces of evidence important in different types of disputes. Finally, we do not address techniques for telling stories at trial.

Rather, our intent is to develop principles of factual analysis and case investigation that apply to the full range of litigated disputes. Whether one tries a dog-bite case or a class action concerning the use of dogs in medical experiments (when one might truly find a case "on all fours!"), we believe the principles to be valid. We have tried to analyze the proof of facts with the same care with which other writers have analyzed substantive subjects such as torts and contracts. With what types of evidence does one prove historical facts? How does one determine the probative worth of evidence? How does one identify potential evidence which either strengthens or detracts from probative worth? What types of evidence affect credibility? By what methods may one most effectively elicit and record evidence? By addressing ourselves to such questions from a variety of perspectives—civil and criminal, plaintiff and defendant—we have tried to develop generally applicable principles for thinking about evidence and investigation.

To convey our ideas, we divide this book into four parts. Part One focuses on the objectives one pursues when investigating a case. Part Two explores how one might evaluate the probative worth of the evidence already in a file. As you will see, evidence often does not prove what one at first blush thinks it does. In Part Three, we discuss how one might go about identifying additional evidence to look for by building hypotheses about what evidence might exist if a client's version of facts were correct. Lastly, in Part Four, we turn to the process of actually extracting evidence from witnesses. Focusing mainly on oral interrogation, we examine methods of eliciting evidence one has identified as potentially important.

Chapter 2

INVESTIGATORY OBJECTIVES

One's law office is momentarily quiet. A client has just left, after telling a story which presents problems so serious that litigation seems inevitable. Just as inevitably, before the case can come to trial one will have to learn much more about the client's case through that aspect of lawyering termed "fact investigation." After all, an initial interview provides all the information one needs to assure success for a client about as often as one is dealt a laydown hand in gin rummy.

Fact investigation itself has many facets, including learning which legal issues an adversary truly disputes; searching for information that, while perhaps not technically admissible at trial, has negotiation value; probing the background of potential triers of fact. Without denying or belittling the importance of such facets, perhaps the most important purpose of investigation is to unearth persuasive evidence on behalf of one's own client, and to learn the evidence an adversary is likely to introduce if a case proceeds as far as trial.

Yet, in our experience, the term "evidence" provides little guidance regarding the specific information one should pursue. On the one hand, the term is too broad. Evidence may be direct or circumstantial; it may go to substantive issues or to credibility; it may be admissible or inadmissible. In short, advising one simply to "learn the evidence" is no more helpful than advising one to "buy low and sell high." The advice is fine, but without some specification the term "evidence" is too broad for use.

On the other hand, it is futile to attempt to catalog specific items of evidence one ought to seek in particular types of cases. Evidence that may be highly significant in one automobile accident case may not be of the slightest concern in another.

9

Therefore, this text identifies general categories of evidence we believe sufficiently broad to be pursued in all cases, and also sufficiently concrete to provide guidance. Pursuit of these general categories will, we hope, significantly assist your reaching the goal of learning the evidence each side will probably introduce should a case actually proceed to trial. To enable you to understand the reasons we identify certain categories as important, we first describe what usually occurs at trial.

1. WHY TRIALS OCCUR

Usually, a lawsuit is filed because of a dispute about what occurred on some prior occasion(s)—a dispute, that is, about "historical facts." The plaintiff contends that in the past certain events occurred which make the defendant, under applicable substantive law, obligated to perform a particular act. In civil cases, plaintiffs typically contend that because of certain prior events—e.g., defendant made and breached a contract; defendants issued a false securities prospectus—defendant owes the plaintiff certain obligations—e.g., payment of money, conveyance of certain property. In criminal cases, the plaintiff typically contends that the defendant previously committed some act forbidden by substantive law and therefore must pay a fine or go to prison.

The defendant, on the other hand, typically disputes one or more of the plaintiff's factual contentions. The defendant asserts that since the "historical facts" did not occur as the plaintiff alleges, the substantive law imposes no obligation upon him or her. Thus, by way of response, the defendant may contend that, e.g., no contract was made or breached, no false securities prospectus was issued, or no conduct violative of the criminal law occurred. Accordingly, asserts the defendant, the substantive law imposes no duty to pay money or perform any other act.

Whenever the parties present the court with conflicting contentions about past happenings, a trial—taking testimony from witnesses—is almost always necessary. Absent occurrences such as settlement, the sustaining of a demurrer without leave to amend, or the granting of a motion for summary judgment, a case with conflicting factual contentions must proceed to trial. Trial is necessary because a court can apply the substantive law to determine the rights and obligations of the parties *only after* "(f)irst it finds the facts . . . ." [1] As Jerome Frank noted, "If you scrutinize a legal rule, you will see that it is a conditional statement referring to facts. Such a rule . . . say(s), in effect 'If such and such fact exists, then this

1. J. Frank, Courts on Trail 3 (Athenum Ed. 1970).

or that legal consequence should follow.' It . . . say(s), for example, 'If a trustee, for his own purposes, uses money he holds in trust, he must repay it.' " [2]

In sum, trials are necessary to resolve disputed questions of historical fact. The court must first determine what occurred in the past—the historical facts—before it can apply the substantive law to decide the parties' rights and obligations.[3] In turn, the court must receive evidence of what occurred, before it can decide what "in fact" occurred. Indeed, as has been suggested, perhaps "lawsuits are misnamed: They should be called 'fact suits.' " [4]

2. PRESENTATION OF EVIDENCE IN STORY FORM

At trial, after a jury has been impaneled and the lawyers have presented their opening statements, each party presents its case through witnesses whose evidence emerges in story form. A witness' story is a description of what he or she heard, saw or otherwise perceived. From the perspective of a factfinder, a story is a tale of the type your parents told or read to you when you were a child; it is a narration of what happened "once upon a time." Like any good tale, it is not confined to major happenings. Thus, it is not confined to descriptions such as, "A small engine pulled a long line of cars up a steep hill," [5] "Oswald shot Kennedy," or "Jesse James robbed the bank." Rather, in a story, the various events—e.g., Oswald shot Kennedy—are typically surrounded by various contextual details such as where, when, and how the events occurred.

Moreover, like any genuine tale, a story is typically not a description of a single moment in time. It usually narrates a series of events that happened over time; it has a beginning, a middle, and an end.

From our perspective, a story at trial is a description of the details of a series of interrelated incidents arranged according to their time relationship.[6] In other words, a story is a detailed, chronological narration of interrelated events with a beginning point, connecting points and a termination point. It normally focuses on substantively critical events and surrounds such events with details of happenings that came before and after.

2. Ibid at 14.

3. Remember in some cases one will also need to offer evidence about normative or legislative facts.

4. See note 1, supra, at 32.

5. *The Little Engine That Could*, as retold by Waddy Piper.

6. Story need not be so defined. What story means and what it means to think, talk and act in story form are questions central to many disciplines. See e.g., R. Schank and R. Abelson, *Scripts, Plans, Goals and Understanding* (1977); R. Barthes, *Introduction to Structural Analysis of Narrative, Image, Music, Text* (1977); W.J.T. Mitchell, *On Narrative* (1980); D. Porter, *The Emergence of the Past* (1981).

In addition to the stories of individual witnesses, a second type of story emerges at trial: The overall story of each litigant. In most cases an individual witness' story is not presented in isolation. Rather, the witnesses for each side, although relating their individual stories, usually also provide the events and details that make up a larger overall story. This overall story—the party's story—is, in the main, no different from the stories of the individual witnesses. The overall story too is a description of the details of interrelated incidents arranged according to their time relationship.[7] In sum, at trial, a party's evidence is usually presented through the stories of individual witnesses that dovetail into the party's overall story.

This story form of presentation is used at trial largely because there is no other realistic choice. A story is the basic way that people in our society explain to each other what they have observed.[8] The story provides a sequence of events and accompanying details which clarify exactly what happened. Think back to the last time that you related an interesting event to a friend, or had one related to you. Did the description of the happening include some details of events that preceded and succeeded the major event as well as details surrounding the major event itself? Probably it did, and the story became all the more real and comprehensible because of that sequence and accompanying details.

The effect of a detailed sequence can be illustrated with a short example. Assume you are told only that, "Marsha was hurt in a market." You cannot have any accurate image of what happened to Marsha. Indeed, there may be as many images as there are readers. Now, insert the kinds of details found in a story: "Marsha was over in the Spend and Save Market on Migwore Ave. She was pushing a cart slowly down an aisle past the produce section when both her feet went a couple of feet in the air and she fell on her tailbone; the cart fell on top of her. She was unconscious and was taken by ambulance to the hospital." This sequence and the accompanying details provide a clearer image of what happened, and make more believable the conclusion that Marsha was hurt.[9]

Additionally, a story provides clarity by putting events in chronological order. The sequential order affects the overall picture that emerges. For example, the following two descriptions of what occurred on a certain occasion give quite different pictures:

 1. John went into a bar, had a double martini, got into his car, drove a block and hit a lightpole.

---

7. See Webster's Third New International Dictionary (unabridged) 2253 (1961).

8. W. Bennett and M. Feldman, *Reconstructing Reality In The Courtroom* 7 (1981).

9. R. Nesbett and L. Ross, *Human Inference: Strategies and Shortcomings of Social Judgment* (1980).

2. John got into his car, drove a block, hit a lightpole, went into a bar and had a double martini.

As the example illustrates, the story's sequential order clarifies the significance of specific events. The evidence of drinking the martini before the collision is far more likely to link the driver with negligence than the evidence of a martini following the collision.

3. EVIDENCE SUPPORTING THE CLIENT'S CASE AND CHALLENGING THE ADVERSARY'S CASE: AFFIRMATIVE AND REBUTTAL EVIDENCE

As your intuition suggests, a witness' story is not simply a narration of all relevant events and details the witness knows; nor is it merely a description of events and details the witness believes are important. Rather, under a lawyer's guidance, the story typically focuses on the events and details which the lawyer believes important. The events and details which become evidence are largely those a lawyer selects to persuade a factfinder that the client should prevail.

The need for persuasion is, of course, implicit in our system of trial. Recall that a trier of fact can never see what actually happened. The disputed occurrence(s) is already history. Furthermore, no witness can tell the factfinder what actually happened. Even under the best of circumstances, no one is able to perceive, record, recall and convey all that occurred in one's presence.[10] Finally, the factfinder must reach its decision on the basis of opposing verbal stories, perhaps reconstituted through pre-trial interviews and usually selectively elicited in court. As a consequence, with objective reality unavailable, lawyers have a genuine need to present testimony that persuades the factfinder that the client's version is closer to the truth than is the adversary's.

To persuade factfinders that events occurred in a particular manner, each side focuses the stories of its witnesses on those events and details which support its version of what happened, and on those which tend to undermine the adversary's version. This text refers to the evidence through which a party establishes its version of what happened as *affirmative evidence*. It refers to evidence through which a party undermines the adversary's affirmative evidence as *rebuttal evidence*. In most cases, despite the fact that the plaintiff has the burden of proof, both plaintiffs and defendants present affirmative as well as rebuttal evidence. It is this process of each side at-

---

10. See generally B. Frank & J. Frank, *Not Guilty* (1957); P. Wall, *Eye-Witness Identification In Criminal Cases* (1965); G. Williams, *The Proof Of Guilt* (3d ed. 1963); E. Loftus, *Eyewit-ness Identification* (1979); Note, "Did Your Eyes Deceive You? Expert Psychological Testimony on the Unreliability of Eyewitness Identification," 29 Stan.L. Rev. 969 (1977).

tempting both to prove its case and to rebut the adversary's case that one must understand if one is to comprehend what occurs at trial.

What is the "case" that a party attempts to prove at trial? A case is a party's version of substantively critical events. No matter what a party's overall story, substantive law, by requiring the proof of certain specific elements, isolates specific events encompassing these elements and makes proof or disproof of these events vital. For example, in a story in an action for breach of contract, one critical event encompassed in the plaintiff's version is the alleged making of the contract. Thus, in presenting affirmative and rebuttal evidence, each side usually orchestrates its story toward proving or disproving what happened at substantively critical moments.

Parties' stories at trial are not, however, limited to describing events which are substantively critical. Because an adversary typically offers a competing version of those events, each party wants to make its story as persuasive as possible. As a result, stories told at trial typically feature affirmative and rebuttal evidence of the following types:

(1) *"Before" and "after" evidence.* This consists of events and details which occurred before and after the substantively critical events. From evidence of surrounding events, one hopes a factfinder will infer that the substantively critical events occurred as one contends they did.

(2) *Explanatory evidence.* Most affirmative and rebuttal evidence is descriptive, consisting of what happened before, during and after the substantively critical moments. Explanatory evidence is offered to prove *why* the substantively critical events occurred as one contends they did. While explanations of a variety of events are contained in stories, explanatory evidence usually focuses on motives or other reasons that produced the substantively critical events.

(3) *Credibility evidence.* Credibility evidence affects the believability of stories and the witnesses who tell them.

(4) *Emotional evidence.* Emotional evidence is to some degree psychological; it acts on the heart as well as on the mind. It may cause a factfinder to react emotionally in favor of the good people (née "guys") or against the bad people to reach a result felt to be morally, not merely legally, just.

Each of these features of stories at trial will be developed further. As you will come to appreciate, these categories are not water-tight. A piece of evidence may often fit into more than one category. For example, in a prosecution for bank robbery, the prosecutor may uncover evidence that the defendant had a desperate need of money to support a drug habit. Evidence of "desperate need" explains why the defendant committed the robbery; it occurred at a point in time before the robbery; and it may cause the factfinder to react emotionally toward the defendant. However, we identify the categories because they often constitute separately identifiable aspects of stories, and we hope our listing of them furthers your understanding of the persuasive role that specific pieces of evidence play.[11] But for now, it is enough that you understand that no matter which of the above categories a piece of evidence fits into, it is encompassed within affirmative or rebuttal evidence.

The following example briefly illustrates what we mean by affirmative and rebuttal evidence. Assume that Bruce Chartoff is charged with murdering his girlfriend, Pat Truscello. Chartoff pleads not guilty, and also pleads an affirmative defense of not guilty by reason of insanity. At trial, Kim Bobby, a prosecution witness, testifies that she saw Chartoff stab Truscello. Bobby provides affirmative evidence for the prosecution. The evidence tends to prove the prosecution's version of what happened—that Chartoff stabbed the victim. Similarly, defense witness Diedrich testifies that Harold Evans, not the defendant, stabbed Truscello. Diedrich provides affirmative evidence for the defendant. So too does Dr. Boland, who testifies that at the time of the stabbing, Chartoff was legally insane.

Testimony by a prosecution witness that Dr. Boland is not a psychiatrist is rebuttal evidence. It calls into question the evidence of insanity, but it does not prove affirmatively Chartoff's sanity. In like manner, testimony that Bobby's view of the scene at the time the stabbing occurred was obstructed by a large truck constitutes rebuttal of the prosecution's evidence.

Admittedly, the line between affirmative and rebuttal evidence is hazy at times. If one party calls a witness who directly contradicts evidence given by a witness for an opposing party, the contradicting evidence may be regarded as both affirmative and rebuttal evidence. For example, Chartoff's testimony that he did not stab Truscello is both affirmative evidence (it helps to prove Chartoff's version of what happened) and rebuttal evidence (it challenges Bobby's evidence). However, although evidence may on occasion constitute both affirmative and rebuttal evidence, the distinction is an important one.

For one thing, usually a party's rebuttal evidence does not (except, perhaps, very indirectly) establish its version of what happened. In the Chartoff case, a defense witness offered evidence that at the time of the stabbing a truck passed between witness Bobby and the victim, Truscello. This is strictly rebuttal evidence, for it does not

---

11. The story features we have identified are not etched in stone. They grow out of our experiences and that of many colleagues and attorneys. However, we certainly recognize that our list of features may not be complete, and that others may categorize evidence in different ways.

establish that Chartoff did not stab Truscello. Thus, one reason for the distinction is to make one aware of the need to look for both affirmative and rebuttal evidence during investigation.

A second reason for the distinction grows out of the realities of trial. One might think, because of the burden of proof, that in most cases a plaintiff's task during trial is to prove its case to a sufficient standard, and a defendant's task is to raise doubts concerning that case. By the same token, when a defendant pleads an affirmative defense, one's thought may be that the defendant's task is to prove that affirmative defense, and the plaintiff's task is to raise doubts concerning it. But neither of these conceptions is adequate. As every experienced trial lawyer knows, one is not solely in a defensive posture merely because the adversary has the burden of proof on an issue. At trial each party, irrespective of the burden of proof, tries affirmatively to establish its own version of what happened. For the party not having the burden of proof, this is the legal equivalent of the axiom that "the best defense is a good offense."

That each party usually presents affirmative evidence, regardless of the burden of proof, is responsive to the way in which factfinders decide cases. When deciding cases, factfinders too usually resemble historians: they try to reconstruct history to learn "what really happened." Because of this, they typically expect a party to do more than poke holes in the opponent's story. The expectation is that if a party's claim is correct, then regardless of the burden of proof the party ought to be able to present evidence of the correctness of that claim.[12]

In the above hypothetical, for example, the factfinder probably would expect the prosecution to do more to attack the affirmative defense of insanity than impeach Dr. Boland. It would probably expect the prosecution to establish affirmatively that Chartoff was sane.

Awareness of this factfinder expectation will help guide one's actions during investigation. The need to present affirmative evidence should impel one to begin the search for affirmative evidence as early as possible. By contrast, viewing one's role as limited to rebuttal might incline one to delay looking for evidence until after one was fully aware of an adversary's evidence. In many cases, however, one does not learn much of the adversary's evidence until very late, indeed often as late as trial. Accordingly, even when one does not

12. We cannot document this factfinder expectation for you. And certainly it is not always met; in some criminal cases defendants do sit mute (or simply try to poke holes in the prosecution's case), relying on the burden of proof. However, our notion that this expectation is a real one, and that attorneys try to meet it, is based on our own experiences as well as discussions with numerous trial attorneys, judges and jurors. See also S. Goldberg, *The First Trial In A Nutshell* 394, 395 (1982).

have the burden of proof on an issue, one usually cannot think about investigation simply in terms of rebuttal. Rather, one must continually think in terms of developing both affirmative and rebuttal evidence.

To solidify your understanding of affirmative and rebuttal evidence, we illustrate how such evidence is embedded in testimony during trial. We do so through a hypothetical which also illustrates how a trial is normally organized and the sequence through which each side usually presents its evidence. The case is an action brought by a general contractor, Red Homes, against an electrical sub-contractor, Tiny Watts. Homes alleges that he and Watts entered into an oral contract whereby Watts agreed to do all the electrical installation in a 10-unit housing tract being built by Homes on Circuit Court for a fee of $100,000. Homes contends that he performed his part of the contract, that Watts breached the agreement and that Homes was damaged. Homes alleges damages of $15,000, the difference between the contract price and the market price. In his answer, Watts denies each of Homes' allegations; Watts also asserts, by way of affirmative defense, that Homes failed to mitigate damages.

As in almost all trials Homes, the plaintiff, presents his case first. In presenting Homes' case (technically called the plaintiff's case-in-chief), plaintiff's counsel will elicit testimony from witnesses whose stories focus on events and details tending to prove each disputed substantive element. Thus, Homes' counsel will call witnesses whose stories focus on evidence tending to show: (a) Homes and Watts entered into a contract, (b) Homes performed his part of the contract, (c) Watts breached the contract, and (d) Homes suffered $15,000 damages.

In all likelihood, however, Homes' counsel will not limit the witnesses' stories to evidence directly proving the foregoing elements. In addition, Homes' counsel will probably have the witnesses relate events and details which tend to buttress the witnesses' credibility. Furthermore, the witnesses' stories may include events surrounding the substantively critical ones, as well as explanatory evidence and emotional evidence. Altogether, the testimony provides Homes' affirmative evidence; it is the testimony through which Homes affirmatively presents his version of what happened.

Analyze the affirmative evidence in the following excerpt from the direct testimony of Red Homes, the first witness called by Homes' counsel, Ana Turney:

Q: Mr. Homes, what is your business?

A: I'm a developer and general contractor. I've been in the business for 25 years.

Q: In June of last year, were you engaged in a building project on Circuit Court?

A: Yes. It was a 10-unit housing tract I was developing; I was both the developer and general contractor.

Q: Are you acquainted with Tiny Watts?

A: I am.

Q: When did you first meet him?

A: It was about five years ago. He did the electrical work in connection with a condominium project on Line Ave.

Q: Was Mr. Watts the electrical sub-contractor on that job?

A: Yes, he was.

Q: Other than the Line Ave. project, did he ever do any other work for you?

A: Yes. On two or three other projects that I can recall; he always worked as an electrical sub-contractor.

Q: Was his work on each of these projects satisfactory?

A: Yes, it was.

Q: Did you ever discuss a housing project on Circuit Court with Mr. Watts?

A: I did.

Q: Where and when did this discussion take place?

A: We actually first discussed this project on June 10th of last year, at the Chatam restaurant. We had lunch together. Before that we had talked briefly on the phone to arrange the meeting, but June 10th was our first real discussion.

Q: Why do you remember the date?

A: Because it was my birthday.

Q: Was anyone else present at this discussion?

A: Yes, my friend, Harriet Fish, was there.

Q: Where were the three of you seated?

A: In a booth; Harriet was sitting between Watts and me.

Q: Please tell us what was said by you and Mr. Watts concerning the project.

A: Well, I had previously sent Mr. Watts a letter requesting his bid on the electrical work for the Circuit Court project, along with the project plans and specifications. Mr. Watts mentioned that he had reviewed the materials, and that he was interested in the job and thought he could do it for $115,000. We went over his cost breakdown and over various areas in which cost savings could be achieved. Mr. Watts finally agreed the job could be done for $100,000, and I told him the job was his.

Q: Could you tell us as best as you can remember how you arrived at the figure of $100,000?

A: I remember we talked a lot about the amount of labor that would be required to do the job on each unit. As we reviewed the labor costs, Mr. Watts discovered that his estimate was based on a 12-unit project, instead of the 10-unit project we were actually building. Mr. Watts stated that that difference alone would save $10,000.

Q: Were any other savings discussed?

A: I mentioned that I thought his figures for flexible conduit were too high. I said, "Look, Tiny. We've had a good relationship in the past. You know I run my job on time—you'll be able to get your people in and out on schedule. Will you do the job for $100,000?"

Q: How did Mr. Watts reply?

A: He said, "O.K., I think I can come out all right at $100,000. I'll do it." He said he was real glad to have the job because work had been slow.

Q: Did he say anything else?

A: Yes, he said he had to have $10,000 in order to get started.

Q: Did Mr. Watts say anything about when the $10,000 should be paid?

A: No, not at that time.

Q: Was there any discussion of when Mr. Watts would begin work?

A: I told him that foundations and framing were scheduled for completion in about three months, and that he could anticipate beginning work in about that time and finishing within five months.

Q: What happened next?

A: By this time, we had finished our meal. Mr. Watts then ordered a bottle of wine and proposed a toast to the success of the project.

Q: When was your next contact with Mr. Watts concerning . . . .

[Portion of testimony in which Homes relates Watts' subsequent refusal to work on the project omitted]

Q: And after that discussion with Mr. Watts, what happened?

A: I contacted three other electrical sub-contractors. One was not available for two months. Another wanted $125,000 to do the job. Finally, Sparky Voltz agreed to do the job for $115,000.

Q: Did you employ Ms. Voltz to do the job for that price?

A: Yes.

Q: Did you attempt to get Ms. Voltz to do the job for less than $115,000?

A: Yes. We had a meeting in her office. It was exactly one week after my last conversation with Mr. Watts. A messenger had taken the plans and specs to Voltz three days before our meeting.

Q: Was anyone other than you and Ms. Voltz present at this meeting?

A: Yes, her job superintendent, Barb Wire, was there.

Q: What was said concerning the price of the job?

A: I asked her to do the job for $100,000, and told her that Watts had been willing to do it for that amount. Ms. Voltz said that Watts' contract did not matter, that her price was $120,000. I told her that my maximum was $115,000. She and Wire left the room for a few minutes, and then Ms. Voltz returned and said she could do the job for $115,000.

[Plaintiff offers written contract with Voltz, which is received in evidence.]

Q: Did Ms. Voltz complete the work?

A: Yes.

Q: Why did you contact only three potential sub-contractors to do the job?

A: I needed somebody immediately. I couldn't delay the project and keep the other subs waiting.

Q: Did you pay Ms. Voltz for the work she performed?

A: Yes, I gave her five separate checks totalling $115,000. [Plaintiff offers five cancelled checks, which are received in evidence.]

Note first, that the evidence is in story form. Homes does not simply testify that he and Watts had a contract which was breached. Instead, Homes tells the factfinder that he had known Watts about five years and that Watts had previously done some electrical work for Homes. Prior to June 10th, Homes had sent Watts a letter requesting that Watts bid on the electrical work for the Circuit Court project, and had then arranged, by phone, to lunch with Watts at the Chatam restaurant. On the 10th, at the Chatam, in the presence of Harriet Fish, Homes and Watts went over some cost figures, and ulti-

mately Watts agreed to do the job for $100,000. When Watts re-
neged (omitted from the testimony), Homes contacted three other
sub-contractors, one of whom was unavailable. He then hired Sparky
Voltz, who gave the lowest bid of $115,000. In terms of the defini-
tion of a story, Homes' testimony includes a sequence of events relating to the contract for the Circuit Court project—e.g., the letter requesting a bid, the phone call to arrange lunch, the lunch and the
hiring of Voltz. In terms of details, only the events of June 10 and
the meeting with Voltz received major treatment.

Consider now the portions of this story which provide affirmative
evidence on the substantive issues. One issue is whether the parties
entered into a contract. Clearly Homes' testimony regarding Watts'
actual agreement to do the job on the 10th provides evidence on this
point. Watts' alleged statement, "OK, I think I can come out all
right at $100,000, I'll do it," constitutes evidence that an agreement
was made. Similarly, the testimony that at the lunch, Watts admitted previously reviewing project plans and specifications is evidence
that an agreement may have been made. Electrical sub-contractors
who review plans and specifications for potential construction
projects are more likely to enter contracts to do such work than persons who do not conduct such reviews. In addition, there are a great
number of other events and details in Homes' story which provide
evidence that the parties came to an agreement on the 10th. List as
many of these as you can find. Similarly, list those events and details tending to prove that Homes had been damaged in the amount
of $15,000.

Homes' affirmative evidence concerning a substantively critical
event, formation of the contract, features at least one item of explanatory evidence. Homes testifies that when Watts agreed to do the
job for $100,000, Watts remarked that he was "real glad to have the
job because work had been slow." Since Watts arguably accepted
the job at below prevailing market rates, evidence that work had been
slow explains why he might have done so. A factfinder is more likely
to accept Homes' version that Watts did accept the job for $100,000 if
it is given a reason why Watts accepted.

The power of explanatory evidence grows out of its symbiosis
with our most basic thought processes. We think in terms of cause-
and-effect and are impressed when we are told not only what events
happened, but why they happened. Notions of cause-and-effect are
developed through childhood. The child who does not understand
why parents get angry when "washable" paint spills on the carpet
understands the anger when the cost of new carpeting is made clear.
And these notions are equally strong in adulthood. A report on the
stock market's daily activities is hardly complete without some
description of factors that contributed to its rise or fall. It is this

ingrained sense of cause-and-effect on which Homes seeks to capitalize by offering explanatory evidence about Watts' acceptance of the job.

Other portions of the story provide affirmative evidence of Homes' credibility. Homes' testimony that he is a developer and a general contractor with 25 years of experience is calculated to stamp him as a trustworthy, reliable witness. Similarly, the testimony regarding Homes' recollection of the date of the agreement aids Homes' credibility. People do not normally remember the precise dates of events; however, here Homes' remembering is made plausible by the testimony that it was his birthday. Read the testimony again; what other events and/or details constitute affirmative evidence of Homes' credibility?

At the conclusion of Homes' testimony, after he has been cross-examined, Homes' counsel calls the remainder of her witnesses. Each witness, through his or her story, provides affirmative evidence to support Homes' version of the facts. When these witnesses are examined and cross-examined, Homes' case-in-chief is complete.

It is now Watts' turn to present his version of the case. During Watts' case-in-chief, Watts' counsel is not limited, as was Homes' counsel, to producing affirmative evidence. Rather, Watts' counsel may include in the stories of Watts' witnesses both affirmative and rebuttal evidence, as we next illustrate.

Below are excerpts from the direct testimony of three defense witnesses; each witness is questioned by Watts' attorney, Vi Tummin. Please examine these excerpts, with particular attention to those portions of the witnesses' stories which constitute affirmative and rebuttal evidence.

Alice Graham

Q: What is your occupation?

A: I'm a waitress at the Chatam restaurant.

Q: Please look around the courtroom, and tell us if there is anyone seated here that you recognize.

A: Sure. I know Red (pointing to the plaintiff) and I've seen that gentleman there (indicating defendant Watts).

Q: Do you recall ever seeing these two gentlemen together?

A: Yes, they were at lunch together at the Chatam one day last summer. Harriet Fish, Mr. Homes' friend, was also present.

Q: Can you be any more specific about the date of that lunch?

A: Not really. It was a weekday, and I think it was before I took my vacation in July.

Q: How do you happen to remember that occasion?

A: Red is a pretty regular customer—he comes in for lunch about twice a week. Around that time, my husband and I were interested in buying a house. Red had been showing me plans and sketches of some houses he was planning to build, and I remember that he was going over those plans with the other gentleman (indicating defendant) when they were having lunch.

Q: Did you actually wait on Mr. Homes and Mr. Watts on that occasion?

A: Yes.

Q: Were you able to hear any part of their conversation?

A: Not too much—we're usually pretty busy at lunch. I did hear them saying something about electrical costs, and I heard the figure $100,000.

Q: Do you remember who mentioned the figure of $100,000?

A: No, I'm sorry. I can't remember.

Q: Do you remember whether you served them any wine at the meal?

A: Yes, I do. They did have a bottle of wine.

Q: How is it you are able to recall that they had a bottle of wine?

A: I was really surprised. Red never has anything to drink with his meal, and he ordered the bottle of wine.

Q: At what point during the lunch did Mr. Homes order the wine?

A: It was immediately after they sat down, before I took their orders.

Q: Are you sure the wine was ordered before the meal?

A: Yes.

Q: Did Mr. Homes or anybody else at the table order any other wine during the lunch?

A: No, I'm pretty sure that was the only bottle.

Note that Ms. Graham's testimony, like that of Red Homes, is elicited in story form. Moreover, she is a classic rebuttal witness. Graham's testimony that the bottle of wine was ordered prior to the meal, not after it, rebuts Homes' testimony. Homes' testimony that Watts ordered a bottle of wine at the end of the discussion and then proposed a toast to the success of the project is affirmative evidence; it provides the basis for an inference that an agreement had been reached. Graham's testimony calls into question the accuracy of Homes' affirmative evidence. However, it is not affirmative evidence for Watts, since Homes' purchase of a bottle of wine prior to the discussion does not provide the basis for an inference that an agreement was not reached.

There is also evidence in Graham's story which supports her credibility. Her testimony concerning why she remembers a bottle of wine having been ordered is an example of such evidence. Can you find another example of credibility evidence?

Now consider the evidence of two additional defense witnesses, Juan Chu and Betty Ohms. Please read their testimony, and then be prepared to identify which portions of their stories constitute:

    a. affirmative evidence,

    b. rebuttal evidence,

    c. evidence that might be considered both affirmative and rebuttal evidence,

    d. credibility evidence.

Juan Chu

Q: What is your occupation?

A: I am an electrical sub-contractor, licensed by the State. I am the current president of the Electrical Subcontractors Association.

Q: Do you specialize in any particular kind of work?

A: Yes, I work almost exclusively on new home construction and home remodels.

Q: Do you know the plaintiff in this action, Red Homes?

A: I do.

Q: Did you have any conversation with him during the summer of last year?

A: Yes, I did.

Q: When and where did this conversation take place?

A: It was the week just before the July 4th holiday. He came to my office.

Q: Had you ever met Mr. Homes before this meeting?

A: Yes. I've met him at two or three golf tournaments sponsored by the Electrical Subcontractors Association. I remember on one occasion we played together in the same foursome.

Q: Directing your attention again to the conversation you had with Mr. Homes during the week before the Fourth of July, can you tell us what happened?

A: I was reading over my mail when my secretary told me that Mr. Homes had come to see me, so I went to the reception room and bade him enter my office. He told me he was building a 10-unit housing project and that he needed an electrical sub-contractor. He had brought some plans and specifications, and he asked if I'd be interested in looking them over.

Q: Did Mr. Homes mention where the project was?

A: I believe he said it was on Circuit Court.

Q: How is it that you are able to remember this conversation?

A: For a couple of reasons, actually. It's very unusual for a general contractor to come to a sub's office to discuss a job. Also, I remember Mr. Homes seemed quite nervous and upset. He kept saying he had not yet been able to get anybody to do the electrical subcontracting.

Q: Now, after he brought out the plans and specifications . . . . .

Betty Ohms

Q: Ms. Ohms, what is your occupation?

A: I am the Executive Secretary of the Electrical Subcontractors Association.

Q: How long have you held that position?

A: Well, I've been with the Association for twenty-two years, the last fifteen as the Executive Secretary.

Q: What are your duties as Executive Secretary?

A: I am responsible for the budget, maintaining membership lists, public relations, and liaison with contractors who are hiring subs.

Q: So if a contractor needed an electrical sub-contractor, he or she might contact you?

A: Yes, it's one of my main functions. The subs keep me up to date on when they're available, what jobs they're doing, and the like.

Q: Has Red Homes ever contacted you, seeking to hire an electrical sub-contractor?

A: Sure, Mr. Homes has contacted me a number of times in the past.

Q: And has he hired subs whom you have referred to him?

A: Yes, he's told me so.

Q: Do you recall a conversation with Mr. Homes in August of last year?

A: I do. He called up and said he needed an electrical sub-contractor to work on a project of his.

Q: Did he mention the name of that project?

A: Yes, the Circuit Court project, I believe.

Q: Please tell us what was said in that conversation.

A: Well, he said he needed someone who could start in about a week, and who was available for at least three months. I mentioned the name of Dee Fuse. I told Mr. Homes that Dee had taken over her father's business about four months earlier, and that she could really use the work. Her father, Ray, had been killed in an automobile accident, and her mother was badly hurt in the same accident. I reminded him that Dee herself was a licensed sub, and that she had worked in her father's business for a long time, on jobs for Mr. Homes even. I told him that she might give him a good price, since she was available and, especially with her mother's injuries, really needed the work.

Q: How did Mr. Homes reply?

A: He said that he knew Dee, and that she did good work, but that he just didn't want to get involved with someone who was having all those personal problems.

Q: Then what happened?

A: I told him I'd check my files, if he could hold on. He said, "Forget it. I'll handle it on my own." He hung up.

The testimony of Chu and Ohms, together with that of any other witnesses Watts may call, constitutes the defendant's case-in-chief, and defendant then "rests." At this point, Homes, as plaintiff, has a chance to present more evidence. This phase of the case is commonly called plaintiff's rebuttal. As the term suggests, the main purpose of this phase is to rebut the defendant's case. The plaintiff can rebut both the defendant's affirmative evidence and the defendant's rebuttal evidence. For instance, to rebut Watts' rebuttal evidence, Homes might produce evidence that Alice Graham (Watts' rebuttal witness) is biased in Watts' favor.

Moreover, at this stage, the plaintiff is not limited to rebuttal evidence. Affirmative evidence to disprove an affirmative defense is permitted. Thus, during rebuttal, Homes may present affirmative evidence disproving Watts' affirmative defense of failure to mitigate. For instance, Homes might produce an electrical sub-contractor to testify that Homes contacted him about the Circuit Court project, and attempted to get him to do the job for less than $115,000.

When the plaintiff's rebuttal case is concluded, the defendant would generally be given another chance as well, creatively called defendant's surrebuttal. Usually, in this phase the defendant is limited to producing rebuttal evidence.

Thereafter, depending on the parties' endurance and ingenuity, and the trial judge's patience, the parties may be given additional opportunities to rebut each other's evidence. These later phases of the case are formally called "surrebuttal." When all the evidence is in, final arguments are made. If there is a jury, it is normally given its instructions by the trial judge, and it retires to consider its verdict.

Following post-judgment motions and conclusion of the appeal process the case would probably be concluded. At this point the heirs of Watts and Homes meet and shake hands at the former site of the Circuit Court project, long since demolished in favor of a Video Pizza Center.

Let us summarize the types of evidence each party typically presents during trial through a chart. The chart illustrates the nature and flow of evidence in most trials. For the sake of clarity, we have annotated the chart with references to *Homes v. Watts.*

1. *Plaintiff's case-in-chief*

Plaintiff's affirmative evidence to prove its cause(s) of action.

[E.g., Prove Watts' breach of contract and Homes' damages.]

2. *Defendant's case-in-chief*

(a) *Defendant's affirmative evidence to disprove the plaintiff's cause(s) of action.*

[E.g., Prove no breach of contract by Watts and no damages to Homes.]

(b) *Defendant's rebuttal evidence to call into question affirmative evidence in plaintiff's case-in-chief.*

(c) *Defendant's affirmative evidence to prove affirmative defense(s).*

[E.g., Prove no mitigation of damages by Homes.]

3. *Plaintiff's Rebuttal Case*

(a) *Plaintiff's rebuttal evidence to call into question affirmative evidence in defendant's case-in-chief.*

(b) *Plaintiff's affirmative evidence to disprove affirmative defense(s).*

[E.g., Prove efforts by Homes to mitigate damages.]

> 4. *Defendant's Surrebuttal Case*
>
> *Defendant's rebuttal evidence to call into question evidence in plaintiff's rebuttal case.*

5. *Potential Surrebuttal*

Like any chart, this one pictures reality to the same extent that "I Love Lucy" depicts the lives of ordinary people. At trial, the order of testimony is influenced by a variety of factors, including lawyer strategy, congested court calendars and the schedules of witnesses. As a result, plaintiffs and defendants do not necessarily introduce their respective affirmative and rebuttal evidence strictly at the times indicated on the chart. Moreover, a plaintiff may anticipate an affirmative defense (e.g., review Homes' direct testimony regarding his hiring of Voltz), or introduce rebuttal evidence during cross-examination of defense witnesses. Similarly, defense counsel may introduce affirmative evidence to disprove an element of the plaintiff's case through cross-examination during plaintiff's case-in-chief. However, the fact remains that regardless of when it comes out, the evidence of both sides consists of affirmative and rebuttal evidence.

4. EMOTIONAL EVIDENCE

To this point, our discussion of *Homes v. Watts* has focused primarily on evidence that has some "tendency in reason" [13] to prove or disprove either a disputed substantive point or the credibility of a witness. Certainly, all evidence introduced at trial must have some rational relationship to one of the foregoing matters. But evidence often plays a second, more important, and perhaps less acknowledged role. Some evidence tends to cause the factfinder to react emotionally, or psychologically, towards or against a party. For example, a fact such as the wealth of a defendant often influences the amount of damages awarded to a plaintiff. The defendant's wealth, of course, has no logical relationship to the amount of injury the plaintiff suffered. The plaintiff's damages, regardless of the type of injury—loss of spouse, loss of business, loss of limb—bear no connection to the defendant's financial status.

As we discuss in ensuing chapters, particularly in those cases where the "rational" evidence seems closely balanced, evidence having a tendency to evoke feelings of sympathy or hostility often has a persuasive impact. Where the evidence tends to invoke feelings of

---

13. See Federal Rules of Evidence, Rule 401.

sympathy or hostility in a factfinder, the factfinder may arrive at its verdict based largely on those feelings, though it believes both the result and the process through which the result was reached to be highly "rational."

In this light, consider the testimony of Betty Ohms in *Homes v. Watts* regarding Homes' rejection of Dee Fuse as a replacement for Watts. Is there any part of this testimony which might evoke an emotional response in a judge or juror?

5. INVESTIGATORY OBJECTIVES

Thus far, we have explained why trials occur, why evidence is presented in story form and how each party's case usually consists of evidence supporting its version together with evidence undermining the adversary's version. From this description of the trial process, we draw our list of the principal investigatory objectives. The objectives are to learn the following:

    1. The events and details which make up each side's probable story, and therefore the events and details which will make up the individual stories of each side's probable witnesses.

    2. The events and details in the stories which constitute each side's affirmative evidence and rebuttal evidence, including events and details which (a) explain why the substantively critical events occurred; (b) affect credibility; and (c) may have emotional impact.

As you will see, effective pursuit of these goals requires substantial knowledge, insight and skill. The stories one seeks are not simply those that each party's witnesses would relate voluntarily, in response to questions such as "What happened?" If an investigation is confined to learning the stories that witnesses would tell spontaneously, the investigation will inevitably be incomplete. Even the non-existent ideal witness, who has perfect perception and recollection, who wants to be helpful and who is scrupulously honest, cannot be relied upon to supply all the evidence that might be useful at trial. Witnesses often omit relevant data because they do not understand all that is legally salient. Furthermore, many legally significant pieces of information are not revealed spontaneously because they are recalled only as a result of specific probing questions.[14] And, of course, many witnesses who know of helpful information will not voluntarily divulge it because they are hostile to the side requesting that information. Antitrust and medical malpractice cases, for example, illustrate situations in which evidence helpful to the plaintiff fre-

---

    14. J. Marshall, K. Marquis and S. Oskamp, "Effects of Kind of Question and Atmosphere of Interrogation on Accura-cy and Completeness of Testimony," 84 Harv.L.Rev. 1620, 1629 (1971).

quently resides within the knowledge of witnesses who are friendly to the defendant and hostile to the plaintiff.

To develop stories containing all relevant events and details known to witnesses, one must have an understanding of legal issues, an awareness of existing evidence, and a clear conception of the additional evidence it would be useful to develop. This conception, awareness and understanding together with the ability to motivate people to talk and to stimulate memories with probing questions, are the abilities needed to pursue effectively the investigatory objectives. It is to the development of these abilities that this text is directed.

Before we turn, however, to pursuit of the objectives, consider two additional points about the development of complete stories. First, recognize that not all of the evidence developed in a thorough investigation will necessarily be introduced at trial. As noted earlier, at trial one usually selects the evidence to be presented in a way that will tell the most persuasive story. One therefore emphasizes some details and events, omits others, and elicits the selected events and details in a particular order. Nonetheless, if one is to have an adequate basis for choosing what evidence to present, the investigation must endeavor to develop whatever the witnesses know.

Second, the development of complete stories envisions that one purposefully sets out to learn from each person not only evidence helpful to one's client, but also evidence that may be helpful to the adversary. At first glance, this advice might appear heretical to one's client. But in our opinion, the advice is supported by both ethical and practical considerations. On the ethical level, a conscious decision not to probe for harmful evidence may prevent one from discharging ethical duties as a counselor. Clients should be advised to follow a particular course of action only after they have been made aware of the likely consequences.[15] If one does not learn the evidence available to the adversary prior to trial, there may be an inadequate basis for advising the client of the likely outcome at trial.

This ethical duty to seek out harmful evidence is supported by practical considerations (and isn't it refreshing when ethics accord with practicality?). First, knowledge of harmful evidence prior to trial allows one to be prepared to rebut it. Second, some witnesses may be impressed by one's interest in all aspects of a case, not just those that may favor one's client. Even if the witness is called to testify by the adversary, the positive impression one made during investigation may incline the witness' testimony somewhat in the client's direction. Finally, remember that even if one uncovers harmful evidence, one usually will have no ethical duty to present it at trial.[16]

15. See ABA Code of Professional Responsibility, EC 7–5 and 7–8.

16. But see ABA Code of Professional Responsibility, DR 7–102. Regarding

The purposeful pursuit of harmful evidence is not, however, without its risks. Questioning may uncover evidence the adversary has overlooked. For example, if one uncovers harmful evidence during a deposition when the adversary lawyer is present, one may alert the adversary to such evidence. Moreover, even if the harmful evidence is produced at an informal interview, out of the adversary's presence, there is some possibility that the witness will report the evidence to the other side, or even blurt it out on the stand. Realistically, this kind of disclosure does not occur often. On the other hand, what does occur quite often is that the lawyer who consciously avoids discovery of harmful evidence learns for the first time at trial what the adversary has known all along.

Our discussion of specific investigatory objectives has stressed the need to learn each side's affirmative and rebuttal evidence and the stories in which such evidence is likely to be immersed. These goals omit a number of commonly stated pre-trial objectives. Omitted are tasks such as the following: securing documents, pinning witnesses down, corroborating the client's story, identifying (and perhaps narrowing) the disputed issues, and ensuring that evidence is admissible.[17]

Certainly, each of these tasks is an important part of pre-trial discovery. Each will be discussed in various parts of this text. However, we have not listed these tasks as discrete investigatory objectives because, in the main, we see them as subsidiary to learning the stories and the evidence within them. Accordingly, in order to focus on what we see as the primary investigatory goals, we have chosen to integrate these subsidiary objectives into our discussion of the primary goals.

Now let us turn your attention to the process by which the major objectives are translated into specific topics for investigation.

the special duties of the public prosecutor or other government lawyers to reveal evidence, see DR 7–103(B) and EC 7–13.

17. There are also some commonly stated goals of investigation that we exclude entirely. They include learning an adversary's leverage points for purposes of negotiation, and investigating a factfinder. Our "explanatory evidence" for the omissions is that our central focus is on proof of facts.

*

Part II

ANALYZING THE EVIDENCE ON HAND

Chapter 3

ANALYSIS: THE PREREQUISITE TO INQUIRY

---

1. THE NEED TO ANALYZE EVIDENCE ON HAND AND EVIDENCE TO BE DEVELOPED

Assume that Tiny Watts has come into your law office. He hands you a complaint indicating that Red Homes is suing him for $15,000 for an alleged breach of contract. After hearing his story, you file an answer denying liability and asserting an affirmative defense of failure to mitigate damages. You now need to decide what to do with the case. You undoubtedly are aware that you need additional evidence. However, you may be less aware of how to develop this additional evidence. Do you notice a deposition or send out interrogatories? Do you contact witnesses informally? Do you pursue the denial of liability, or the affirmative defense? Do you call the lawyer for the other side and ask for an explanation of the adversary's version?

All of these questions are probably premature. Whatever the investigative tool one uses, investigation consists primarily of inquiry—obtaining information from someone (or some thing). As discussed in Chapter 2, an investigation cannot be limited to broad questions such as, "What happened?" The inquiry must include more specific probing questions. But, in turn, this requires that before one proceeds very far with an investigation, one thinks through the specific factual areas to probe. Hence, a prerequisite to any decision about what step to take next is identification of the specific information one needs.

However, identification of the specific information one should look for is itself subject to a prerequisite. One cannot know what additional evidence one needs until one is aware of the evidence already on hand. For example, Watts' attorney cannot meaningfully analyze what additional evidence is needed on the issue of Homes' failure to mitigate damages without first analyzing the evidence on this issue that already exists. Similarly, Watts' counsel cannot identify potential evidence which might rebut Homes' contention that a contract was entered into until he or she learns what evidence Homes has on this issue.

The process by which one analyzes the evidence on hand (the existing evidence) and then determines what additional evidence is needed (the potential evidence) involves a good deal of thought. The evidence on hand cannot be determined simply by listing the evidence gleaned from a client or witness interview. In addition, one needs at least to analyze the probative value of the evidence. Often, the probative value of an item of evidence depends on the strength of inferences that may rationally be drawn from that evidence. Until one has subjected evidence to inferential reasoning, one cannot know what evidence "exists." For instance, a prosecutor may have evidence that a defendant's fingerprints were found on the murder weapon. But how strongly does the evidence link the defendant with the murder? Does it prove beyond a reasonable doubt that the defendant held the weapon? Even if it does, does it prove or tend to prove when he held it, whether or not he held it voluntarily, whether or not he alone held the weapon, or the purpose for which the weapon was held? These questions indicate the frequent gap between the evidence on hand and its probative value.

Moreover, this analytical process must be carried out periodically. Once existing evidence has been analyzed and potential additional evidence identified, investigation gets under way. But as new evidence is learned, that new evidence must in turn be analyzed together with the earlier evidence, and, in light of the total evidence on hand, potential additional evidence again identified. Thus, the analytic process is a cyclical one in which potential evidence is identified, obtained and evaluated, and then used as the basis for identifying further potential evidence. This analytic process is the subject of Chapters Four through Eight.

The above discussion demonstrates why it was premature to consider specific investigatory steps at the conclusion of the Watts interview. Investigation is a process of reasoning before it is a series of discrete tasks.

By and large, once one has identified potential evidence, one then chooses the investigatory vehicles (e.g., deposition or informal interview) that will most likely enable one to ferret it out. It would be wonderful if some system, such as "Depose one, interview two," could be devised. However, such mechanical advice is better left to instructional books on how to dance or how to knit. Litigated disputes are too varied to permit any such step-by-step approach. The actual investigatory steps one takes depend on a host of variables, such as:

1. One's knowledge of applicable law;

2. Legal issues known to be in dispute;

3. Evidence known before an inquiry begins;

4. The potential evidence needed;

5. The accessibility of witnesses, documents, and other evidence;

6. The time available;

7. The clients' desires and financial (and emotional) resources.

Moreover, unlike almost every other area of litigation, the conduct of fact investigation is virtually free of fixed procedural rules. For example, there are no rules on whether interrogatories must precede or follow depositions.[1] When embarking on the investigation of a case, one can follow whatever lawful methods might be successful. If this means that one is unlikely to make an obvious mistake, it also means that it is harder to do what is obviously right. Compare, for example, the attorney as investigator with the attorney as a pleader of an initial claim for relief. In the latter role, the attorney's product must conform to a hierarchy of rules, ranging from the contents of the claim to the dimensions and opacity of the paper on which it is typed. Once the attorney knows those rules, successful drafting of a claim for relief is nearly automatic. In the role of investigator, on the other hand, one does not have the comfort of fixed rules to fall back on. We hope, however, that the process we suggest for identifying specific topics of investigation will provide you with a basis for making intelligent decisions.

2. THE NEED TO RECORD THE ANALYSIS

As we have suggested, the process of analyzing existing evidence and identifying potential topics of investigation is one that requires thought and analysis. For reasons discussed below, it also requires one other element: recordation.

The analytic process produces categories of existing evidence and potential evidence. The evidence in these categories is not, however, static. As an investigation continues, some potential evidence becomes existing evidence; other potential evidence is discarded; new potential evidence is identified. Moreover, the categories of existing and potential evidence each contain subcategories of affirmative evi-

---

1. However, in complex litigation, an order of discovery may be established by the court. See *Manual for Complex Litigation* § 1.50 (5th ed. 1982).

dence and rebuttal evidence. In each of these subcategories, there may also be explanatory evidence, credibility evidence and emotional evidence. An analysis involving this sort of complexity should not be trusted to one's memory, unless one also has the capacity to memorize the London telephone directory. The analysis should be recorded in an organized fashion, and the record should be periodically updated as an investigation continues.

The need to record and periodically update one's investigatory analysis is heightened by the realities of litigation and law office practices. One such reality is time. Since the pretrial phase of a case may take many years, one may be beguiled into thinking that an unlimited time for investigation exists. But that is simply not true. Albert Einstein postulated, and scientists have confirmed, that speed of travel affects time. There is even a phrase for it: "space time." Litigation, too, plays tricks with time; it may be referred to as "litigation time." Rarely is there a smooth, even flow of activity and information during the pretrial stage of litigation. Rather, this stage is usually characterized by flurries of frenzied activity, separated by long intervals of inactivity. For example, there may be a great deal of activity around the time initial pleadings are filed, as the parties file motions of various kinds. Then, the case may lie dormant for months, when suddenly interrogatories are served. After another interval, a series of depositions is taken. To investigate properly in the face of litigation time, one must be able to pick up an investigatory analysis quickly, where it had been left months earlier. Thus, the need for recording and periodic updating.

Litigation time also affects the time available to discuss a case with witnesses. One does not have years to discover evidence known to a witness. If one did, the need for recording the specific evidence to be sought might not be as great. Information missed during a first interview could be obtained during a second, or maybe during a fifth. However, whether formal or informal discovery methods are used, one frequently has but one meaningful opportunity to learn information from a witness. If a witness' deposition has been taken, a court frequently will not permit an additional deposition of that witness. Courts are loathe to subject people to the inconvenience and expense of multiple formal discovery unless good cause to do so is shown. Similarly, if one interviews a witness informally, the witness is often reluctant to meet again. Even friendly witnesses (who after all may have no financial stake in the outcome) will usually find better things to do with their time than repeatedly discuss a lawsuit with an attorney. Arranging for one interview is difficult enough; encores are unlikely. Further, if a witness who has already been interviewed later remembers evidence that was not revealed at the interview, the witness typically will not call the lawyer to report it.

Hence, those seemingly endless pretrial years may well boil down to only one chance at meaningful investigation. If one has not prepared a careful analysis of the evidence one seeks prior to contacting a witness, one may miss much potential evidence.

Litigation time is also, unfortunately, unpredictable. The pretrial portion of some lawsuits is measured not in years, but in weeks. For example, criminal cases are often tried within a month or two of a defendant's indictment. Then, one does not have even the illusion of a long period of time to allow investigatory thoughts to bubble up. Rather, one needs a complete list of the potential evidence readily at hand so that complete interviews can be undertaken quickly. Thus, in "short cause" cases as well, a recorded analysis assists an efficient investigation.

For most lawyers, litigation time also tends to be very crowded. Those long intervals between activities on a case are not devoted to quiet contemplation. Rather, they are filled with frenzied flurries in connection with other cases. Statistics on attorney stress tell us that these flurries often occur simultaneously: an attorney is served with three sets of interrogatories from three different cases the same day. It is difficult to shift one's train of thought between cases without derailing. Law practice is a modern day juggling act. Again, a written investigatory analysis, periodically updated, is the best method of moving from one case to another while staying on track.

A final characteristic of litigation time is that it is frequently fractionalized. One tends to learn information during investigation the way weight comes off during a diet—a little bit at a time. One witness, at time A, may give one a needed piece of information. Perhaps, at time B, one will get a related piece from another witness. For example, assume it is relevant to know how many times the boy cried, "Wolf!" Perhaps Burridge heard him cry "Wolf!" twice, and he so indicates during an interview. But one cannot be certain that Burridge supplied complete information. Burridge indicates that Sherr, who is presently out of town, may have heard the boy cry "Wolf!" on other occasions. Therefore, one will at least have to talk to Sherr, and perhaps to others as well. Because evidence so often comes in piecemeal fashion, a systematic way of retaining it is necessary.

Two additional factors, not directly related to litigation time, also militate in favor of recording investigatory analyses. One is the reality of law office practice. At various stages of a case, including its investigation, one is frequently either a delegator or delegatee of certain tasks. An associate, who has only at most a nodding acquaintance with a case, often will have to be updated to prepare for a deposition, to prepare interrogatories, or to make a court appearance. It is far too time consuming, inefficient and ineffective for the lawyer with full knowledge (even assuming such knowledge could be retained in one's head) to provide a comprehensive oral update on the state of the evidence. Moreover, the way most litigation files are currently kept, such an update cannot be obtained readily from a review of the file. Most files do not contain a systematic update of evidence on hand and evidence to be sought. For example, answers to interrogatories, containing evidence on a variety of disparate issues, lie idly in a file. Rarely are those answers separated out according to the issues to which they relate.[2] Thus, without a written update in a file, there is little hope of delegating work effectively.

Finally, new attorneys in particular need to record their analyses periodically to overcome, in part, the "roller coaster" effect of many investigations. New lawyers are especially prone to dramatic shifts in attitudes as new information is received. If a helpful piece of information is learned, all is right with the world and the client is a candidate for sainthood. But when negative information comes in, the client is a rotter of the first ilk and medical school suddenly seems more appealing. These swings of mood make it difficult to pursue an orderly investigation. Yet, an investigator must be like a ship's captain. One eye must always be on the horizon. Even as particular pieces of information are processed, one must stay aware of what one is ultimately seeking to prove. Recording information helps keep one's eye on the horizon; it focuses one on the overall state of the evidence. And it may spare some emotional trauma.

3. A SYSTEM TO RECORD THE ANALYSIS: AN OVERVIEW

This chapter has stressed the importance of recording and periodically updating existing evidence and potential additional evidence. This section provides an overview of one system of recording this information. The system will be elaborated upon in Chapters Four through Eight.

The system consists of five outlines. Cumulatively, they allow one to keep track of the events and details which make up each party's probable story as those stories unfold during investigation. In addition, they allow one to record and update one's analysis of the events and details in those stories which make up each party's then-existing affirmative and rebuttal evidence. Finally, they allow one to record and update an analysis of potential additional affirmative and rebuttal evidence that may be sought on behalf of one's own client. Below is a brief description of each of these outlines.

---

2. For an example of this point see J. Kelner & F. McGovern, *Successful Litigation Techniques* § 7.01 (1981).

a. Story Outline

The story outline lists in chronological sequence the events which comprise the story of each party. It identifies portions of the stories which agree and those which are in conflict. Also, it indicates gaps in the chronology which may need to be filled. This outline is described in Chapter 4.

b. Outline of Client's Existing Affirmative Evidence

This outline lists the client's existing affirmative evidence according to substantive legal issues. It "marshals" the affirmative evidence by listing each item of evidence under the substantive legal element which it helps to prove (or in a defendant's case, to disprove). Also included in this outline is the adversary's existing rebuttal evidence. The adversary's rebuttal evidence is listed opposite the affirmative evidence which it appears to rebut. This outline is discussed in Chapters 5, 6 and 7.

c. Outline of Adversary's Existing Affirmative Evidence

This outline is the converse of the previous one. It marshals the adversary's existing affirmative evidence, and also includes one's own rebuttal to that evidence. This outline too is discussed in Chapters 5, 6 and 7.

d. Outline of Client's Potential Affirmative Evidence

Like the two previous outlines, this outline also is structured according to substantive legal elements. Below each substantive element one lists the potential affirmative evidence which may prove (or, in a defendant's case, disprove) that element. This outline is discussed in Chapter 10.

e. Outline of Client's Potential Rebuttal Evidence

This outline, too, is structured according to substantive legal issues and it in effect builds upon the outline described in "c." This outline consists of the adversary's existing affirmative evidence, with potential rebuttal for one's client listed opposite that evidence. This outline is discussed in Chapter 10.

Please note that we do *not* recommend that one outline the adversary's potential affirmative and potential rebuttal evidence. It is enough to plan the investigation of a client's case. However, in a particular case, one may want to prepare this type of outline.

4. SOME PERSPECTIVES ON THE OUTLINE SYSTEM

The outline system developed in this text is intended, above all, to be of practical benefit. Lest one believe that the system is intractable and mechanically complete, a few words of caution are in order.

First, the outline system described here is not the only one which might be used. Lawyers use different outline systems to record their evidentiary analyses.[3] Our system does, we believe, incorporate the general theory and method that most lawyers who use a system adopt in recording their analyses. Moreover, it is a system which most lawyers and law students can readily learn to use.

A system which recommends the preparation of five different outlines may seem at first blush unduly onerous. One may fear that time spent in preparing outlines will detract from other important pretrial activities, such as talking to witnesses and eating meals regularly. However, such fears are unfounded. Five outlines rather than one are prepared primarily for the sake of convenience. The outlines, other than the story outline, conceivably could be reduced to one, as they all marshal evidence according to the legal issues. However, most cases are sufficiently complex that the attempt to combine in a single outline both parties' affirmative, rebuttal and potential evidence would create chaos. Except in very simple cases, it would turn an outline into something resembling the planning map for D-Day.

Moreover, in a real sense the outlines are not an added layer of duty. They are based on the reasoning process one should employ when thinking about cases. The time spent in thought should be there anyway. The outlines are a way of preserving the fruits of those thoughts.[4] Moreover, if one concentrates on the analysis and leaves the recordation to paralegals and computers, even greater time savings will result.[5]

Complete frankness compels us to state that, especially the first few times, use of the outlines may eat up time the way an Indy racing car eats up gas. But if one does not have enough gas, perhaps it is because one is digging too many dry wells. Experience suggests that once one learns the system, time savings result. Time is saved when one knows when and where to drill for information.

3. For an example of one such system see L. Pretty, "Enter the Microcomputer in Litigation Support," VI ABTL Report (Association of Business Trial Lawyers) No. 1 (June 1983).

4. In final preparation for trial, lawyers often marshall their evidence in a trial notebook. See T. Mauet, *Fundamentals of Trial Techniques* § 1.3

(1980); K. Hegland, *Trial and Practice Skills in a Nutshell* 140–143 (1978). The system described in this text can be seen as simply the ongoing preparation of that part of a trial notebook which marshalls the evidence according to the issues.

5. For a discussion of the use of paralegals and computers in preparing the outlines, see Chapter 10, p. 206, infra.

Second, recognize the limits of the outline system. Even diligent preparation of the outlines does not guarantee that all evidence which could be useful at trial will be found somewhere in the outlines. Certainly, the outline system will help you analyze evidence in the way a trier of fact is likely to evaluate it. But the outline system does not create evidence; it is a way of recording evidence. Practically speaking, one cannot record every piece of· evidence which one learns or thinks might might be potentially useful. Indeed, that level of detail might well drown the outlines. Moreover, in some situations it may not be clear in which outline, if any, an item of evidence should be placed. One must exercise discretion and adapt the outlines to the circumstances of each case. As the various outlines are discussed, some of the factors that may assist your use of discretion will be explored.

Finally, recognize that the system is something of an idealized one: most lawyers, it is fair to say, do not use a system like that described in this text.[6] However, it is also fair to say that the litigation system is not without its critics. There is general agreement that the pretrial process is slow, wasteful, often unproductive and therefore too costly. In addition, there is much criticism that at trial, attorneys are not sufficiently prepared and skilled. One likely reason for these criticisms is that lawyers do not prepare cases as well as they should. That, in turn, may result from their failure to know how to investigate. The outline system above cannot solve all of the problems in the litigation system. But it can provide a substantial step toward thorough preparation.

5. A HYPOTHETICAL PROBLEM: PHILLIPS v. LANDVIEW ET AL.

In order to integrate a conceptual analysis of investigation with a practical approach, and to bring continuity to the text, many of the remaining chapters examine principles of investigation in the context of a hypothetical case. In this chapter, you will be given only sparse information concerning the case. As the investigation unfolds in later chapters, additional information will be provided as it becomes relevant. At different times, the case will be analyzed from the standpoint of both plaintiff's attorney and defense counsel. Since the case involves allegations of fraud, raising the potential for a criminal prosecution, investigatory principles in criminal as well as in civil cases will be discussed.

The case assumes that initial interviews have taken place and that formal appearances have been entered by both parties. Plaintiff has filed a complaint and defendant has filed a responsive pleading; both

6. But see note 2, supra.

parties are ready to begin investigation. You are undoubtedly aware that often a good deal of investigation takes place before formal court proceedings begin. In fact, ethical considerations and legal requirements may compel an attorney to investigate a client's claims before filing allegations based on those claims.[7] However, we begin at a convenient point, with formal proceedings already underway. By and large, at whatever point investigation occurs, the principles which apply are the same.

The case is entitled James Phillips and Joan Randolph-Phillips, Plaintiffs v. Landview Corporation and Soil Engineers, Inc., Defendants. It is pending in local state court.

In the complaint, the plaintiffs, purchasers of two one-acre lots, seek damages and rescission from the seller, Landview Corporation. Also sued is Soil Engineers, Inc., a corporation. This company prepared a soil inspection report on the tract in which the two parcels are located.

---

7. See, for example, Fed.R.Civ.P. Rule 11; C. Wright and A. Miller, *Federal Practice and Procedure: Civil* § 1333 (1969); Cf. ABA Code of Professional Responsibility DR 7–102 and EC 7–4.

Chapter 4

STORY OUTLINES

---

1. INTRODUCTION

Lawyers, judges and jurors tend to assess cases in two ways. In one way, testimony is analyzed in the context of specific legal issues to be proved or disproved. All evidence bearing on a particular element is "marshalled", and then a decision is reached as to whether or not the element has been proved. In the other way of thinking about cases, the overall credibility of the respective parties' stories is assessed by testing for significant gaps, internal inconsistencies, and the like. Of course, in any individual case, both kinds of reasoning may occur simultaneously.

The outline system incorporates both modes of thought. The outlines other than the story outline respond to a "marshal the evidence" type of reasoning. The story outline focuses on the credibility of the respective parties' overall stories.

This chapter discusses the purposes of a story outline, and illustrates the initial preparation of such an outline in the context of *Phillips v. Landview Corp., et al.* Following the illustration, the component parts of the outline are analyzed. Finally, you are asked to complete the initial preparation of the outline.

2. BRIEF DESCRIPTION OF STORY OUTLINES

A story outline lists, in chronological order, the events that comprise both parties' overall stories. Depending upon factors discussed later in the chapter, an outline may also contain details pertaining to various events. Within an outline, one notes conflicts in the parties' respective stories and also gaps in those stories. The story outline is periodically updated and expanded as new information is learned.

3. PURPOSES OF STORY OUTLINES

Various considerations support the preparation of story outlines. First, a story outline helps overcome a tendency during investigation to examine credibility almost exclusively in terms of individual witnesses and individual items of evidence. For instance, is Mary likely to be a believable witness given that she has given conflicting versions about the color of a traffic light? Is her story that she could see the color of the light from a distance of 150 yards believable?

But the concept of credibility is not confined to individual considerations. A factfinder also assesses the credibility of a party's overall story. If this story lacks credibility, the testimony of the individual witnesses who provide it may be disregarded. Therefore, in preparing a case, one must be aware of each party's overall story. Taken as a whole, does an overall story ring true? Is it internally consistent? Is it plausible? Since a factfinder will probably ask such questions, one must also ask them prior to trial. Story outlines, which contain the combined stories of the parties, provide one with a basis for assessing overall credibility.[1]

Story outlines also help keep evidentiary details in perspective. Because evidence is often received in piecemeal fashion, its evidentiary significance may become lost or overstated in relation to an overall story. In a story outline one lists evidence in the context of surrounding events, and one therefore has an opportunity to assess realistically its overall significance.

Moreover, an investigator's goal is to pursue potentially important evidence, not to follow all possible evidentiary leads. Yet, for a variety of reasons, one may stray from time to time from the path of sensible pursuit. Information may be sought not necessarily because it appears important, but merely because it is readily obtainable. Conversely, information may be sought because the evidentiary source lives in Tahiti. If a client suggests a possible source of information, one may pursue that source simply to demonstrate diligence. Or, one may attempt to prove the truth of an insignificant point only because an obnoxious opponent claims it is not true. An investigation need not remain doggedly fixed on a set story. Indeed, especially early on, one may not even be certain of one's story. But too many stray paths waste precious investigatory resources. Story outlines focus on main paths, and therefore provide a perspective for sensing when one may be going astray.

In addition to providing a perspective for assessing overall story credibility and evaluating the significance of acquired and potential evidence, story outlines serve another general function. They identi-

---

1. For a detailed discussion of credibility, see Chapter 8.

fy areas for further investigation. Because an outline contains the major events comprising both parties' stories, it often indicates gaps and conflicts in the stories. In the event of a gap in a witness' story, one is apprised of the need for further evidence. If there is a conflict, one realizes the need either to develop additional evidence to resolve it or to bolster the credibility of the client's version. Thus, because a story outline arranges stories chronologically and places individual evidentiary items in the context of a total narrative, it serves to alert one to the need for additional evidence.

Finally, a story outline has something of a "reservoir" function. Of course, one wants to focus an investigation on important evidence. But how does one know whether certain tidbits are important? After all, we have all grown up with detective stories in which the important clue was given to us in the first five minutes, only to be forgotten because at the time it did not seem important. In litigation, too, there is a risk that evidence will be lost because its importance depends on information developed subsequently. Frankly, no outline system can eliminate this risk. If every evidentiary detail is included in an outline, it will become so bloated that it becomes useless. However, the story outline at least provides one with a place to keep alive evidence which is part of a story, even if it does not immediately seem to help prove or disprove any substantive legal element. Thus, while no guarantee is possible, a story outline does preserve some evidence that otherwise might be forgotten.

4. INITIAL PREPARATION OF STORY OUTLINES

By the time one is ready to prepare a story outline, one has already received some information about a case. Perhaps one has interviewed a client, spoken to one or more witnesses, and reviewed some documents. If the case is at issue, the file may consist of initial pleadings, a memorandum of law, a memorandum to the file detailing information given by the client during an interview, some handwritten notes of telephone conversations with the witnesses and opposing counsel, some reports and a few letters. Although it is relatively early, one can begin a story outline. Below are some of the documents in the file of plaintiffs' counsel in *Phillips v. Landview*. After you review these documents, we illustrate the initial preparation of a story outline that might be prepared, based on the information in these documents.

Memo to File

To: File
From: Jerry Mason
Re: Phillips v. Landview
Date: June 1

This memorandum summarizes facts learned from James and Joan Phillips in an interview conducted on May 27. The Phillipses bought two parcels of land from Landview on September 22 of last year. Their intention was to build homes on both lots and sell them. They first heard about the land when a friend gave them a brochure. Subsequently, they learned that the land was subject to landslides and that as a result the cost of building homes on the lots would be prohibitive. Each lot is a one acre parcel; each was purchased at a cost of $75,000. Eighty percent financing was provided by Last Federal Savings & Loan. The parcels are located in the northern section of a hundred acre development in Campion Hills. Landview told the clients that there is nothing wrong with the lots and that Landview has a report to prove it.

The negotiations for the lots took place in July and August of last year. Salesman Guy Lotz met with them on several occasions. He showed them homes that were already built, and vacant parcels particularly suitable for building. The clients were shown through most of the development, except the west section. The purchase agreement was signed on August 31, and title passed on September 22. During the negotiations, Lotz made no mention of any slide problems. On one occasion, in mid-August, Lotz stated that a recreation center was to be built in the development, and he showed the Phillipses sketches of the center. Lotz stated that the center would include a pool and a jacuzzi, a meeting room, tennis courts, a gym and an equestrian center. Lotz said he was uncertain when the center would be built, that it had to do with when enough lots were sold. Nonetheless, it definitely would be completed within 18 months, and anyone who lived in the development would be eligible for membership. The Phillipses were very impressed by the plans for the recreation center.

A few months after they bought the parcels, the Phillipses were told by Paul Lade, a vice-president with Landview, that the recreation center might not be built.

After the purchase, the Phillipses contacted an architect, Woody Garvey, to draw up plans for a house on one of the parcels. Garvey did so, at a cost of $10,000. Garvey projected that the cost of building the house would be $80,000. When the plans were submitted to the Building Department, it refused to issue a permit. The refusal was on the basis that the plans for the foundation did not take into account potential landslide conditions in Campion Hills. The Department stated any foundation had to be supported by caissons. That was in early March—around March 12. On March 13, the Phillipses met with Paul Lade, who said there were no landslide problems in the area and that the Building Department had never before refused to issue a building permit. The Phillipses went back to the Building Department and spoke with Inspector Bill Knott. Knott said that within the past month, two permits had been denied because plans did not make adequate provision for possible soil slippage. Knott mentioned that on March 5, a Department employee, Henry Aldridge, had observed signs of slippage on parcels 35 and 36 of the south section of the development. The Phillipses then spoke with Woody Garvey, the architect, who said that caissons would increase the cost of each dwelling by approximately $20,000. Thereafter, the Phillipses tried to arrange a joint meeting with Knott, Garvey, and Paul Lade of Landview. However, Lade did not appear at the meeting.

The Phillipses indicated that if Landview refuses to resolve the situation through a reasonable settlement, we should file suit.

Notes re Telephone Call

June 3

Florence Darrow, attorney for Landview, called me back today. Pursuant to my request, Darrow had spoken to Lade regarding the Phillipses claim. Darrow says that, according to Lade, no one has ever been denied a building permit in the Campion Hills development, and Landview is totally unaware of any problem with soil slippage. Also, Landview had purchased the development from a previous developer, Landlocked Inc., and at the time of the purchase had paid for a soil engineering study by Soil Engineers Inc. That study indicated that there were no problems anywhere in the development with soil slippage. Darrow says that the Building Department should not require caissons but that the issue was a matter between the Building Department and the Phillipses. With regard to the recreation center, Darrow said it was uncertain whether it would be built. Lotz did show sketches of the proposed center but is certain that he made no promises that the center would be built.

Notes re Telephone Call

June 15

Received telephone call from Joan Phillips. She has gotten report from Alex Stein, a licensed soil engineer hired by the Phillipses to inspect their Campion Hills property. He reported that there are definite soil slippage problems on their property, and that the Building Department is correct in requiring caissons. She will send report. Stein's bill is $500.00.

Review the following outline that one might begin to prepare based on these memoranda and note a few of its physical features. There are columns for "Events," "Gaps," and "Conflicts." Within the "Events" column, individual events are separated by blank spaces. The purpose of these spaces is to allow the story to be filled in as more information is learned. Those lawyers with memory typewriters (or those with speedy scissors and mounds of cellophane tape) may not need to leave such spaces. Arrows are sometimes used to indicate uncertainty as to when in the time sequence a certain event occurred. The names of persons who supply information, as well as any documents which contain this same information, are listed inside parentheses following events. This data is very handy, since as a file builds, one will be grateful if a person or document which serves as a source for information can be quickly located.

In addition to noting the outline's physical features, please keep in mind the following questions. Why is much of the information in the memoranda not included in the event column? To what extent are gaps and conflicts more apparent in the outline than they are in the memoranda? Why is some information included in the outline even though it is not "evidence" in the sense that it would be admissible at trial? The discussion which follows the outline will address such questions through an examination of each of the three outline columns.

STORY OUTLINE—PHILLIPS v. LANDVIEW

Gaps	Events	Conflicts
Date? Both clients?	Learn of property from friend; brochure (Cl.—memo of 6/1)	
↑		
Meetings with Lotz *re* Negotiation How many? When? Details?	Mid-August meeting with Lotz re recreation center—center to be completed within 18 months (Cl.—memo of 6/1)	No promise to build (Darrow—phone note re Lotz 6/3)
↓	No mention of soil problems (Cl.—memo of 6/1)	
Details?	August 31—Purchase agreement (Cl.—memo of 6/1)	
Get deed	Sept. 22—Title passes (Cl.—memo of 6/1)	
↑		
# of meetings? When? Details?	Contacts with Architect (Cl.—memo of 6/1)	

Gaps	Events	Conflicts
↓		
Date? $10,000 paid?	Plans drawn up (Cl.—memo of 6/1)	
When? By whom? To whom? Get plans	Plans submitted to Building Dept. (Cl.—memo of 6/1)	
Confirm with Aldridge—hearsay	March 5. Henry Aldridge observes slippage on parcels 35 & 36 in South section (Cl.—memo of 6/1)	
Date? Details?	March 12? Plans rejected by Building Department because plans don't include caissons (Cl.—memo of 6/1)	
	March 13. Meeting with Lade; Lade says no landslide problems and no previous refusal by Building Dept. to issue a permit (Cl.—memo of 6/1)	

5. THE EVENTS COLUMN

You may be surprised by how much information in Mason's file is omitted from the events column. For example, no mention is made of the statement in the June 1st memorandum that "the clients were shown through most of the development, except the west section." The exclusion of this information points to a distinction which is central to fact investigation. The distinction relates to the elusive line between conclusions and evidence.

Admittedly, the distinction between conclusions and evidence is not always clear. In fact, distinguished scholars have suggested that the term "evidence" cannot be meaningfully defined.[2] However, advocates are concerned not with definitional niceties, but with the discovery of persuasive proof. And that discovery depends, in part, upon one's abilities to recognize conclusions and to probe for evidence that underlies them. This distinction between conclusions and underlying evidence is one that is repeatedly stressed in this book. Unless

---

2. See C. Wright and K. Graham, 22 *Federal Practice and Procedure* § 5163 at 28 (1978).

one can recognize the difference between conclusions and evidentiary detail, one will often be unable to marshal evidence, to define issues for further investigation, to question witnesses for details or to perform a host of other investigatory tasks.

Return to the statement that the Phillipses were shown through most of the development. This statement may, in some epistemological sense, be regarded as evidence. But it should not be regarded as such by a trial attorney. How many times were the Phillipses shown around Campion Hills? Exactly what portion(s) of the property were they shown on each occasion? When, with respect to the other events, did the tour(s) take place? What property is in the west section and why did the Phillipses not see it? These are but a few of the myriads of questions that could be raised. We do not suggest that all of them must be answered before this general conclusion becomes sufficiently definite to be regarded as evidence. But the questions do serve to point out how conclusory the statement in the file actually is.

Thus, conclusory statements are not part of the events column because they do not adequately describe what really happened. If one knows only that the Phillipses were "shown around" some unspecified portion of the Campion Hills development, the description is too vague to provide a sense of what specific happenings are of evidentiary significance. Recall that a story at trial contains the events and details that make up a party's affirmative and rebuttal evidence. Conclusory statements obfuscate the affirmative and rebuttal evidence, and therefore do not belong in the events column.

If one thinks of a continuum of information, ranging from excruciatingly specific detail to ultimate conclusion, then the conclusory end is one category of information that is not included in the events column. Likewise, the other end of the spectrum—excruciating detail—is usually equally unwelcome. Too many details may bury the narrative. Moreover, details which do have special significance can be included in those outlines which marshal evidence. A story outline should serve primarily as an overview of the competing overall versions of historical events, and it should not be littered with minute detail.

The events column should focus, therefore, on the specific events which comprise each party's overall version of what happened. It should contain all the events one learns during the investigation without regard to whether a given event might be included in the story told at trial. So constructed, the events column will aid the outline's reservoir function, and also will provide a basis for assessing a story's overall credibility. Since all events are included, those that seem unimportant will be preserved in case they later become important. And since many details are omitted, overall story credibility can still be assessed.

Like most rules in this area, the rule against detail in the events column is far from absolute. Its application requires judgment. The more important one believes a detail to be, the more one may want to include it. For example, in the outline above, Lotz's statement that the recreation center would be built within 18 months was well nigh irresistible. It appears to be an important detail in the overall story. Also, where stories are in conflict, one is more likely to list the details of each party's version. Further, some details may be included pursuant to the outline's "reservoir" function. The events column is a good place to put details which do not comprise affirmative and rebuttal evidence but which one's instinct whispers may in the future be important. Hence, details there will be. However, any details should be subsidiary to the events which compromise the overall story. Remember, to the extent specific details constitute affirmative and rebuttal evidence, they will be picked up in the evidence marshalling outlines.

Although one may state with confidence that the events column houses all of the events in each party's story, one cannot state with equal confidence what constitutes an event. Unfortunately, the term "event" is no more capable of precise definition than the term "evidence." Return to the memorandum statement that the Phillipses were shown around a portion of Campion Hills. Thoroughly de-conclusioned and undetailed, that statement might be, "Lotz escorted the Phillipses to parcels 53, 54 and 55 on August 26." But is this one event, or three separate events? If Lotz and the Phillipses reviewed some documents while on the tour, would that review be a separate event? Or, in a criminal case, a defendant may be arrested, searched at the scene of the arrest, questioned at the scene and questioned again at the police station. Is this one event—an arrest; or is it a series of events? A precise answer is neither possible nor necessarily desirable. A story outline is but a means to an end. Events should be listed in a way that helps one understand what led up to and followed the moments of substantive importance.

If the distinction between an "event" and a "conclusion" is troubling, the distinction between an "event" and a "detail" is no less so. If Lotz and the Phillipses returned to the main sales office after touring the three sections of Campion Hills and reviewed a set of model building plans, is that review a separate event, or a detail of what occurred in the office? Again, the question is without an answer in the abstract. In the context of a particular case, one simply tries to organize evidence in a way that is helpful.

a. Non-Events

The classification of events and details is further complicated because some parts of a story involve "non-events": they are neither events nor details. Therefore, they do not fit into a neat chronology even though they form part of the story. Examples of such non-events include the following:

1. *Non-Occurrences.* One often notes things that did *not* happen. In *Phillips*, for example, the plaintiffs contend that prior to the purchase no statement concerning land slippage was ever made. In a criminal homicide case in which the defense is self-defense, part of the prosecution's story might be that at no time did the victim have a weapon. In neither case is there a separable event that can be pinpointed on a time line.

2. *Mental State.* Evidence of mental states such as intent and sanity is relevant in a wide variety of civil and criminal cases. Thus, a criminal defendant may in some instances be guilty only if she or he acted with a specific intent. In a civil employment discrimination case, the employer's intent may be of import. And in *Phillips*, if the Phillipses seek damages based on a fraud theory, they will have to produce evidence of defendant's scienter. A mental state is not an observable, objective event, although it usually needs to be chronologically located in a story.

3. *Conditions That Exist Over Time.* In many cases, relevant evidence may consist of conditions that existed over a period of weeks or years. In *Phillips*, the existence of a landslide condition may have existed for some time; if so, it existed continuously. In a negligence action, a litigant may claim pain has persisted over a five year period. Neither condition can be neatly inserted into a chronology.

These categories of non-events are neither exhaustive nor mutually exclusive. One may need to show that a mental state existed over a period of time, or that a particular mental state never occurred. For example, in a criminal case, the defense may want to show that the defendant had no intent to commit a crime.

Whenever one is faced with non-events, one must frankly recognize that compromise is needed. Important "non-events" can simply be placed in the events column at some sensible point. There are other options as well. For example, even if there is no direct evidence of a mental state or of a non-occurrence, events constituting circumstantial evidence of it can be chronologically located. Or, if a condition exists for a lengthy period, perhaps the event marking its beginning can be located and annotated in some way to show its continuation. In addition, the evidence-marshalling outlines are available for listing non-events as well as events and details constituting circumstantial evidence of them. Thus, the outline system is a flexible one, and in the context of a specific case one will usually be able to outline all important evidence in a meaningful way.

b. Sources

A final issue concerning the events column relates to sources of information. If one has doubts concerning the credibility of a source, or the source cannot supply information in the form of admissible evidence, one may be uncertain whether to include the information in the events column. In the partial story outline based on the memoranda in Mason's file, recall that a listed event was Henry Aldridge's observation of slippage on parcels 35 and 36. The Phillipses' report of what Aldridge observed may be inadmissible hearsay, yet that event is included in the event column. As with earlier uncertainties, one must exercise judgment when deciding whether to list inadmissible evidence in a story outline. In this situation, perhaps the event was listed because the point was an important one. Moreover, its listing was accompanied by a notation in the gap column that the event must be confirmed with Aldridge. The notation serves as a reminder that, in its present form, the information is perhaps inadmissible.

A similar exercise of judgment is called for when a source is uncertain of a fact, or for some other reason may lack credibility. In *Phillips*, assume that the Phillipses' statement to Mason, as reflected in the memorandum, was, "Knott isn't sure, but he thinks Aldridge observed some slippage in lots 35 and 36." Or, assume that the information was supplied not by the Phillipses, but by an individual listed in the Guinness Book of World Records as holder of the record for most perjury convictions. In each of these situations, one is uncertain as to the reliability of the evidence. All one can do is make some judgment whether to include the evidence in the event column, based on factors such as (1) the importance of the evidence, (2) how uncertain the source is, (3) how uncertain one is of the source (perhaps the source holds only second place in the Guinness book) and (4) the existence of other supporting evidence. Even if one includes evidence which is inadmissible or filled with uncertainty, the infirmity should be noted in the gap column. Judgment in an individual case is the ultimate guide.

6. THE GAPS COLUMN

As one lists the events which comprise each party's potential story, one will inevitably become aware of gaps in those stories. The events column in the *Phillips* outline, for example, indicates that the purchase agreement was entered into on August 31, and that title passed on September 22. But did any relevant events occur between these two dates? A review of the events column itself will often reveal gaps that may need to be filled in with other events.

There are other types of gaps that are not easily revealed in the events column. The principal function of the gaps column is to remind one of areas for further investigation. If you recall the transfer of information from the file to the story outline in *Phillips,* you will remember that much information in the memoranda consisted of conclusions, not distinct events. Those conclusions, for reasons stated in section 5, are not listed in the events column. Yet, the conclusions furnish a guide to the probable events, and perhaps their approximate place in the chronology. It is useful, therefore, to remind oneself that the conclusions need to be pierced and transformed into actual events. The gaps column provides a place for this reminder.

An example of this use of the gaps column is found in Mason's outline. According to the June 1 memorandum, the Phillipses had some meetings with Lotz, and perhaps with other Landview officials as well, in the weeks before they took title to the parcels. That information is too conclusory to be listed in the events column. However, the gaps column serves as a place where the conclusion of "meetings" is noted in its approximate relation to other events. A review of this portion of the gaps column would remind Mason that he must investigate the conclusory information to determine its component events and details.

The gaps column is also useful when one is aware of an event, but is unaware of important details concerning the event. The gaps column then serves as a reminder that more details are needed. In *Phillips,* Mason had information that on March 12, the Building Department rejected the plans because they did not provide for slippage. This event is quite properly listed in the events column. But the significance of the event may be affected by numerous other details. What type of caissons will be required? Who in the Building Department rejected the plans? What precisely did the person say when rejecting the plans? Mason's gaps column listed only the need for "details." In another case, especially the absent-minded among us may want to jot down specific details that they would like to know.

There are other situations in which one may find the gaps column useful. The column is simply a convenient spot for noting a variety of needed factual details. The details may be those that would convert a bit of inadmissible hearsay into admissible evidence, or perhaps make admissible a copy of a writing in conformity with an exception to the Best Evidence Rule. Or, the details may be of the type that make more credible an already admissible evidentiary event, such as additional facts supporting a witness' opportunity to observe. In all these situations, the gaps column enables one to note missing pieces of the parties' stories.

7. THE CONFLICTS COLUMN

The third section of the story outline is the conflicts column. As you know, we suggest that the events in both parties' stories be meshed in the events column into one chronological sequence. In most cases, although usually the stories will coincide to some degree, there will be conflicts between the parties' versions.[3] The conflicts column is an area where such conflicts can be noted as a reminder for further investigation.

The possibility of one other potential form of conflict should be noted: conflict within a party's own version. For example, Mr. Phillips may have one version of a meeting with Bill Knott of the Building Department, and Mrs. Phillips may have a different version of that same meeting. Or, due to poor memory, mendacity or schizophrenia, Mr. Phillips may supply different versions of the same event. The event—the meeting with Knott—can be listed in the events column, and the existence of conflicting versions noted in the conflicts column.

Needless to say, parties can be quite ingenious when it comes to creating conflicting versions of events. Party A claims an event happened, but party B denies its occurrence. (The conflict which appears in the *Phillips* outline is of this type.) Or, party A claims an event happened, and party B claims it happened as well, except at a different time with, therefore, different meaning. Or, party B admits that an event occurred, but contends it happened in a different way. Or, there may be permutations of these conflicting versions. Whatever the conflict, it should be noted in the margin as a reminder for further investigation. Typically, during investigation one will either resolve an apparent conflict or, if it cannot be resolved, attempt to produce evidence supporting the client's version.

8. FLEXIBILITY

Our comments concerning the specific attributes of the three columns are not intended to lock one into a particular style of preparation. One should be flexible so that an outline accomplishes the purposes for which it is being prepared. The amount and the variety of details listed, the extent to which events are separated and even the types of notes listed in the gap column should be allowed to vary depending upon one's predilections and the circumstances in a given case. There is no rule which, if not strictly followed, will doom an outline. If one understands the reasons a story outline is prepared, and grasps the principles set forth in this chapter, a story outline that aids investigation should result.

An example of flexibility concerns our suggestion that the stories of both parties be combined in one outline. To the reasons already

3. There are of course cases in which the litigants are in total agreement as to what happened, but cannot agree on the legal significance of what occurred. But in the majority of cases, in which there are factual disputes between the parties, the conflicts column will generally be used.

given in support, we might add that in most cases, the parties agree about more events than they disagree. Therefore, combining information in one outline will usually result in less writing and will sharpen one's sense of the competing versions. However, some may adhere to our suggestions concerning the gaps and conflicts columns while maintaining a separate events column for each party's story. Others may want to include a "conclusion" column as well. If one is more comfortable with other methods, one may follow them and still be consistent with the suggestions in this chapter.

Moreover, one need not generally be anxious about omission of an event or detail. Although the five outlines are discussed sequentially, in practice they are prepared contemporaneously. Thus, if an important fact is omitted from the story outline, there is an excellent chance that it will show up in one of the other outlines. Like the U.S. Constitution, the outline system too is one of checks and balances.

The flexibility carries through to the process of updating a story outline. How often an outline is updated must be left to individual judgment. Similarly, whether one updates by preparing entirely new pages, or by interlineating and crossing out, is a matter of choice.

9. STORY OUTLINE EXERCISE

Now that you have some understanding of the story outline, consider how you might go about completing the initial phase of the *Phillips v. Landview* outline. What specific events can be included in the event column? For example, do the meeting with Knott, the Phillipses' discussion with Garvey about a price increase, and the arranging of a joint meeting with Knott, Garvey and Lade constitute specific events to be included in the event column? How about Landview's purchase of Campion Hills from Landlocked and Landview's obtaining a report from Soil Engineers? Where, if anywhere, do these go?

Think also for a moment about the gap and conflict columns. Is the statement by Lade that the Department had never refused to issue permits in conflict with Knott's story? What else might you want to know in determining whether a conflict exists? Is Lade talking about what "in fact" has occurred or something else?

Following your mental ruminations, please complete the story outline begun on pages 49–50.

Chapter 5

THE SUBSTANTIVE STRUCTURE FOR THE EVIDENCE–MARSHALLING OUTLINES

1. INTRODUCTION

This chapter discusses the substantive law framework for the evidence-marshalling outlines explored in Chapters 6–8. To review, those outlines are the following:

    a. Outline of client's existing affirmative evidence and opponent's existing rebuttal evidence.

    b. Outline of opponent's existing affirmative evidence and client's existing rebuttal.

    c. Outline of client's potential affirmative evidence.

    d. Outline of client's potential rebuttal evidence.

As mentioned in Chapter 3, each of the four outlines has a common base: each is structured according to applicable legal elements. The outlines will eventually become very different, in large part because the existing or potential evidence which fills each outline will be different. However, since each outline is built on the same substantive structure, it makes sense to examine that structure before we describe how to adorn it with evidence.

It is not coincidental that four of the five outlines marshal evidence according to substantive legal elements. The substantive elements determine the parameters of the stories the parties tell at trial. Whether eliciting testimony through direct or cross-examination, one edits and refines witnesses' stories principally so that they present the most persuasive evidence on the specific substantive elements one seeks to prove or disprove.

Despite this attempt to focus on specific substantive elements, affirmative and rebuttal evidence relating to any element is necessarily sprinkled throughout the witnesses' stories. Because witnesses testify in story form, and because generally the next witness cannot testify until the testimony of previous witnesses has concluded, evidence related to any particular element is likely to come out in piecemeal fashion. Some of the evidence may emerge in one part of a witness' story and some in another. Some evidence may come from one witness, and some from other witnesses. Some evidence may be elicited on direct, and some on cross. Some may be elicited during the case-in-chief, and some during rebuttal. For these reasons, one cannot during witness testimony directly marshal evidence according to substantive elements. Rather, one must be content with a presentation that leaves the evidence on a given issue spread throughout disparate parts of the testimony.

However, once the testimony is complete, and the time for decision-making arises, the evidence usually is then explicitly marshalled according to legal issues. During closing argument, lawyers identify each disputed legal issue, and then pluck the evidence that relates to each from different parts of the overall stories. They spell out which items of evidence in the various witness' stories tend to prove or disprove a given substantive element.[1]

Even if lawyers do not marshal evidence around specific issues during argument, judges and jurors are bound to do so when a case is submitted to them.[2] The way in which factfinders approach decisions is exemplified by the following typical jury instruction given in malicious prosecution cases:

> In order to return a verdict for damages in an action for malicious prosecution, each of the following elements must be established by a preponderance of the evidence:
>
> (1) That the defendant initiated or procured the arrest or prosecution of the plaintiff,
>
> (2) That the criminal proceeding against the plaintiff terminated in his favor,
>
> (3) That the defendant acted without probable cause in initiating or procuring the arrest or prosecution of the plaintiff, and

---

1. For an example of this marshalling concept during the closing argument, albeit at a somewhat conclusory level, see T. Mauet, *Fundamentals of Trial Techniques* 313 (1980). See also L. Smith, *Art of Advocacy—Summation* § 5.08 (1978). This is not, however, the exclusive mode of argument. Typically, arguments also analyze the parties' respective stories.

2. Cf. Comment, "Memory, Magic, and Myth: The Timing of Jury Instructions," 59 Oregon L.Rev. 451 (1981). The author advocates use of preliminary pretrial jury instructions.

(4) That the defendant acted with malice.[3]

This instruction tells the jurors to examine the evidence in relation to each issue, keeping in mind who has the burden of proof and the necessary degree of proof for the burden to be met. If jurors are to carry out such instructions, their only logical choice is to marshal evidence according to the issues. This marshalling applies with equal force in judge-tried cases, since jury instructions reflect the reasoning process a judge would use.

In sum, grouping affirmative and rebuttal evidence around distinct legal issues is at the heart of trial. It makes sense, therefore, to investigate cases in a way that encourages one to marshal evidence according to legal issues. The four non-story outlines help one do just that.

Our emphasis on the need to marshal evidence should not obscure the role of related factors that influence the factfinder's decision. Recall that a party's overall story is important, for it colors the attitude with which a factfinder views the credibility of individual items of evidence. And remember, a factfinder's judgment may be swayed by emotional evidence. All the logical arguments in the world are of no avail to a prosecutor when a jury, swayed by sympathy, finds a defendant not guilty. But whatever role these factors may play in the final decision, at the investigatory stage marshalling evidence around legal issues is the most effective way of analyzing evidence on hand and pursuing potential evidence. When an investigation concludes, the marshalled evidence depicts as accurately as possible most of the evidence that will be produced at trial.

2. FOCUS ON THE ELEMENTS OF THE APPLICABLE LEGAL THEORIES

The legal issues a factfinder considers in deciding a case depend primarily on what causes of action or affirmative defenses are stated in the pleadings, developed in the course of investigation and subsequently advanced at trial. These causes of action and affirmative defenses provide the parameters of the outlines' structures. The causes of action and defenses are not esoteric abstractions. They are of the type that have occupied much of your law school career. The causes of action and defenses may be common law or statutory, legal or equitable, civil or criminal. Typical causes of action are negligence, breach of contract, and robbery; typical affirmative defenses are failure to mitigate damages and alibi. In any given case the substantive structure of both parties' outlines focuses on the same causes of action and affirmative defenses, since each party attempts

---

3. BAJI *California Jury Instructions* Civil § 6.92, compiled and edited by P. Richards (6th ed. 1977).

during investigation to develop both affirmative and rebuttal evidence.

However, one cannot organize evidence effectively in an evidence-marshalling outline if one does no more than label causes of action and affirmative defenses. A cause of action or an affirmative defense is merely a label that attaches to the grouping together of one or more elements. For example, when the elements of a false statement, knowingly made, with intent to defraud, reasonable reliance, and damages, come together, the cause of action for intentional fraud results. Or, when the elements of taking property of another, with the intent permanently to deprive the other of possession, through force or fear, come together, a robbery results. Similarly, when the elements of a confidential relationship between plaintiff and defendant, the defendant's exercise of influence over the plaintiff, and the plaintiff's intent to defraud are combined, the affirmative defense of duress results.

If one attempted to marshal evidence according only to the label attached to a particular cause of action or affirmative defense, it would be akin to trying to construct a house without plans. Just as one needs to focus on plans to know what materials to purchase for the house, so one needs to focus on individual elements to know what evidence to pursue.

The focus on distinct elements is an inherent part of what goes on at a trial. If one has the burden of proving a cause of action or an affirmative defense, then one must prove each element, or lose. When a judge rules on the admissibility of a particular item of evidence, the judge normally determines admissibility according to the particular element the evidence is offered to prove, not according to a cause of action as a whole. Moreover, an item of evidence relevant to one element may be totally irrelevant to another. Because a trial requires one to segregate evidence according to elements, one must do the same during investigation. Therefore, one needs to structure evidence-marshalling outlines according to the elements of each potential cause of action or affirmative defense.

There is no fixed method of outlining the elements of any substantive theory. Sometimes evidence suggests that an element itself needs to be broken down. In two breach of contract cases in which the disputes center on the making of a contract, the only issue in one might be whether the parties ever signed the contract, and in the other whether there was a valid offer. In the latter case, the element of "making of the contract" may be broken down into the sub-elements of offer and acceptance. The breaking down of elements into sub-elements has the effect of localizing evidence around points in dispute. However, the breaking down should be done only if the facts suggest it would be helpful.

Interestingly, especially in civil cases in jurisdictions where "notice pleading" is the norm, even after initial pleadings are filed, the elements of the pleaded theories may not be self-evident. For example, a complaint may state causes of action for breach of contract and negligence without identifying the separate elements of each.[4] Hence, if one is unfamiliar with those elements, a few moments of legal research are a prerequisite to making up the substantive structure.

Although substantive outlines are organized primarily around the legal elements of substantive theories, they are by no means necessarily confined to such elements. A wide variety of other issues may be added to the substantive elements in an outline, even though they are not part of a substantive legal theory. For example, there may be issues in a case of whether an opponent is a corporation, and thus amenable to suit as such; or whether the amount of damages is sufficient to confer jurisdiction on a court. These types of issues are often important, though they are technically not part of the applicable causes of action or affirmative defenses. A glance through the headnotes of any law reporter volume will demonstrate how often these additional elements are significant. Therefore, when evidence suggests that there are such elements in a case, they should be outlined along with the relevant substantive theories.

3. STATE EACH THEORY SEPARATELY

The need to outline causes of action and affirmative defenses according to their distinct elements also militates in favor of separately outlining each different cause of action or defense. This seems obviously true when the causes of action are so distinct that different labels attach to them. In such situations, totally different elements will have to be proved. Thus, in *Phillips v. Landview*, if plaintiffs were to allege the causes of action of fraud and breach of contract, the elements of each are so distinct that certainly a separate section of the outline should be devoted to each. The same is true, however, when the elements are more similar. Again, in *Phillips*, plaintiffs might allege intentional fraud and negligent misrepresentation. Despite the similarity of the elements of each cause of action, each may be separately outlined even though for some elements the identical proof will be used. On those occasions, one need only incorporate by reference under one element evidence marshalled under that same element in a different cause of action.

4. See generally, 2A *Moore's Federal Practice* §§ 8.13, 8.14 (1983).

The value of separately stating causes of action applies equally in criminal cases. The prosecution may allege one traditional cause of action—e.g., kidnapping. It may also, in many states, allege the closely related crime of kidnapping with bodily injury. The crimes are nearly identical, but the additional element of bodily harm requires its own proof.

Perhaps surprisingly, we also suggest that when two theories of relief, or affirmative defenses, carry the same general legal label, one also consider separate structures. For example, if one brings suit based on breach of contract, one might pray for both damages and injunctive relief. Even though in some sense there is but one cause of action, the plaintiff will be faced with different legal elements to prove. The breach of contract theory rests on the elements of the making of a contract, breach by defendant, plaintiff's performance and damages. The injunctive theory rests on these same elements plus an additional one—for example, an inadequate remedy at law.

In sum, whether one must prove different causes of action or affirmative defenses to get the same relief, or prove additional elements within the same cause of action to obtain different relief, each cause of action and affirmative defense may be separately outlined according to its distinct elements.

Because the term "cause of action" is subject to different meanings, we hereafter refer to each group of separately stated elements as a theory of relief. And, in order to avoid repetition, we encompass within the term "theory of relief" possible theories of affirmative defense. Admittedly, our suggested classification of theories of relief may not be conceptually pure. On the other hand, attempts at conceptual purity often create confusion in the real world. Scholars have long debated the definition of a "cause of action," with the frequent result of abstract scholarship: muddle.[5] Whether a cause of action seeking damages for breach of contract is conceptually different from one seeking injunctive relief by reason of that same breach, is not the critical question. One's client is in a different position if a jury awards damages than if a court grants injunctive relief. Therefore, it behooves one to consider any theory of relief which depends on proof of different elements as a separate substantive theory, and to marshal evidence accordingly.

4. STATE THEORIES OF RELIEF IN FACTUAL TERMS

Next, consider how individual elements might be stated.

5. B. Witkin, 3 *California Procedure,* Pleading § 23 (2d ed. 1971).

a. Convert Elements to Factual Terms

In setting forth the elements, one describes each in factual terms. Recall that the applicability of any substantive rule depends primarily upon a factual determination of what happened in the past. A litigant does not prove directly that certain substantive law is applicable. Rather, one introduces evidence which proves facts, and those facts in turn trigger the substantive law. Thus, one does not prove negligence, breach of contract or robbery. Instead, one introduces evidence to prove facts: that Manny drove 85 m.p.h., that Moe signed an agreement to buy a car, that Jack took money at gunpoint from Jill. Since one proves facts, it follows that one should list the elements to be proved in factual terms.

Moreover, by stating elements in factual terms, one ensures that investigation focuses on the particular evidence needed in each case. In their substantive law aspect, many cases are alike: the law governing one breach of contract case is typically identical to that governing another. Yet, like snowflakes, fingerprints and recipes for Caesar salad dressing, no two legal disputes are factually identical. The law may be the same, but the facts that trigger the substantive result are likely to be quite different. In one breach of contract case, the alleged agreement may involve 12,000 gold widgets, while in another the alleged agreement may involve 12,001 silver widgets. To be sure that during investigation one gathers evidence with the particular facts of a case in mind, it again makes sense to tailor the substantive structure so it reflects the facts of a specific case.

By way of illustration, assume that Tinkers sues Evers, claiming he loaned Evers $10,000; that Evers promised to repay by Groundhog Day; and that Evers failed to repay. Evers claims the loan did not have to be repaid until the first February 29 following the making of the agreement, and that he already repaid $5,000. Since one theory of relief applicable to this claim is breach of contract, the substantive structures both for Tinkers and for Evers should include this theory. If their attorneys stated the elements of breach of contract in legal terms only, both structures would look like this:

Breach of Contract
Making of Agreement

Performance

Breach

Damages

There is some advantage to such a structure. It could be prepared in advance and pulled out whenever a breach of contract case entered the office. But its advantage is also its disadvantage. The statement of elements fails to distinguish the *Tinkers v. Evers* case from any other breach of contract case. The structure focuses attention on abstract legal conclusions such as "performance," instead of on the facts of the particular case. Moreover, even though both structures correctly identify the same theory, they totally fail to recognize the parties' opposite factual contentions. Such structures do not guide an investigation; they leave it strictly to chance.

Contrast the structure in *Tinkers v. Evers* when the elements of breach of contract are stated in factual terms. The structures of the parties would look like this:

Breach of Contract

Tinkers' Structure   Evers' Structure

1. Tinkers agreed to loan $10,000 to Evers and Evers agreed to repay by Groundhog Day.

2. Tinkers loaned $10,000 to Evers.

3. Evers failed to repay the loan by Groundhog Day.

4. Tinkers is out $10,000.

1. Tinkers agreed to loan $10,000 to Evers and Evers agreed to repay by the next February 29.

2. No issue that Evers received $10,000.

3. Evers repaid $5,000 before Groundhog Day.

4. Evers owes nothing to Tinkers.

Consider first the plaintiff's structure. Each element is stated in factual terms applicable to this particular dispute. All elements are included, even though the second element is not contested by the defendant, and the fourth does not require any evidence beyond that encompassed by the first three. The second element is included because, absent a stipulation, plaintiff will have to introduce evidence on it to avoid a nonsuit. With regard to the fourth element, as in most other areas, the outline system is flexible. One may list the fourth element, and indicate beneath it that no separate evidence is required. (In other words, it follows from evidence that $10,000 was loaned and not paid back when due that plaintiff is out $10,000). Or, the element could be omitted. We include it here because of our belief that one should always keep in mind the elements which will control the admissibility of evidence.

Now consider the defendant's structure. It tailors the elements according to Evers' specific factual posture. Moreover, it includes an element on which defendant is not likely to offer proof (Element # 2), merely as a reminder of that element. However, in many cases defendants dispute only certain elements of plaintiffs' theories. Defendants' outlines could certainly omit reference to non-disputed elements.

b. Identify Possible Alternative Factual Hypotheses

In many cases, a party may have more than one factual hypothesis to prove an element of a given theory. Since one states elements in factual terms, one may want to make a separate factual statement for each hypothesis.

Please re-examine *Tinkers v. Evers*. Tinkers had but one factual hypothesis for the manner in which Evers breached the contract: Evers failed to repay by Groundhog Day. Because of that, Tinkers' attorney stated the element of breach in only one way, since there was but one way Evers could have breached the contract.

Let us alter the facts a bit to bring into play the possibility of alternative factual hypotheses. Assume Tinkers is a homeowner for whom Evers built a room addition. After Evers completed the job and had been paid, Tinkers discovered several defects and sued for breach of contract. Tinkers claims that Evers breached in a variety of ways: improperly sealing the roof; using wallboard instead of plaster; failing to install a staircase leading to the second story addition. Since each hypothesis would tend to prove Evers' breach, Tinkers' counsel may identify each separately to target investigation on each.

Alternative factual hypotheses are also possible in criminal cases. For example, assume defendant is charged with vehicular manslaughter, in that defendant struck and killed someone while driving a car in a grossly negligent manner. The prosecution may have alternative factual hypotheses which might prove gross negligence: defendant's excessive speed; defendant's driving while scanning the skies for Halley's Comet; and defendant's failure to have a steering wheel in the car.

As is true with separately stating distinct legal theories, one usually should list distinct factual hypotheses separately. The separate stating allows one to marshal evidence for each hypothesis.

When an element is stated according to separate factual hypotheses, we suggest that in outlining a given legal theory one state an element as many times as one has factual hypotheses. Thus, in the criminal gross negligence case, the theory that defendant committed vehicular manslaughter may be structured as follows:

1. On January 1 at 2:00 A.M. defendant was driving a 1932 Hutmobile.

2. Defendant drove with gross negligence in that:

    (a) Defendant was driving at least 75 m.p.h. on a residential street;

    (b) While defendant was driving he was scanning the skies for Halley's Comet; and/or

(c) Defendant was driving a car that did not have a steering wheel.

3. Victim was killed when struck by defendant's 1932 Hutmobile.

4. Defendant's gross negligence was the proximate cause of victim's death in that:

(a) Defendant could have stopped before striking victim had he not been driving 75 m.p.h.;

(b) Defendant could have stopped before striking victim had he been watching the road; and/or

(c) Defendant could have avoided the victim had the Hutmobile been equipped with a steering wheel.

In this example, note that within the outline of one cause of action, the elements of both gross negligence and proximate cause are stated factually and separately.

c. State Theories From Opposing Perspectives

In *Tinkers v. Evers*, we illustrated how the elements of a claim for relief (i.e., "breach of contract") may be phrased to reflect each party's evidentiary perspective. For example, the element "Making of the Agreement" was phrased one way to reflect Tinkers' version, and another way to reflect that of Evers. The ability to state issues in factual terms that reflect each party's contentions is an important one. One needs that ability in order to keep track of each party's evidence as an investigation progresses. To keep track of one's existing and potential affirmative evidence, one states the elements of applicable claims for relief according to one's client's version. To keep track of the adversary's rebuttal to one's existing affirmative evidence, one adopts this same perspective.

Conversely, to keep track of an adversary's existing affirmative evidence, and one's existing and potential rebuttal, one states the elements of applicable claims for relief according to the adversary's version.

How one uses the outlines to track the evidence of both parties will be explored in Chapters 6, 7 and 8. For now, it is sufficient that one understands why one needs to be able to state elements in factual terms from differing perspectives. An example of how one incorporates opposing perspectives into each evidence-marshalling outline may bring additional clarity.

In *Tinkers v. Evers*, Tinkers' counsel will incorporate elements phrased according to Tinkers' version in the outline of Tinkers' existing affirmative evidence and the outline of Tinkers' potential affirmative evidence. And in the outline of Evers' existing affirmative evidence and the outline of Tinkers' potential rebuttal, Tinkers' counsel will state the elements according to Evers' version of what happened.

The converse, of course, applies to Evers' counsel. Evers' counsel will incorporate elements phrased according to Evers' version in two outlines (the outlines of Evers' existing and potential affirmative evidence) and according to Tinkers' version in the other two outlines (the outlines of Tinkers' existing affirmative evidence and Evers' potential rebuttal).

The principles apply with equal vigor in criminal cases. Assume a defendant on trial for murder asserts the affirmative defense of alibi, contending that she was hunting penguins in Kansas at the time the murder occurred in Milwaukee. In the appropriate outlines, both defense counsel and the prosecutor would state this defense in factual terms from *each* party's perspective: "On the day of the murder, defendant was hunting penguins in Kansas;" and, "On the day of the murder, defendant was not hunting penguins in Kansas."

In the alibi hypothetical, the prosecutor and the defense counsel will probably state the prosecution and defense perspectives in identical terms. This similarity will be due, in part, to the fact that "alibi" consists only of a single element, and in part to an assumption that through pretrial discovery, the prosecution normally learns just what the defendant's alibi is.[6]

But this similarity in stating an adversary's perspective may not occur, at least until the time for trial nears. In most cases, especially before discovery is complete, one will know much more about one's own case than about an adversary's. Therefore, one may not be able to state with accuracy the factual contentions from an opponent's perspective. Return to *Tinkers v. Evers.* Recall that according to the defendant's structure of the breach of contract theory, defense counsel indicated no contest of the issue that Evers received $10,000. But if defendant has filed only a general denial, and little discovery has taken place, Tinkers' counsel may not be aware of Evers' position. Therefore, when outlining the defendant's position, Tinkers' counsel might leave this element blank. By doing so, Tinkers' counsel has clearly flagged an area in which more information is needed. Or, Tinkers' counsel may speculate that Evers will deny receiving $10,000, thereby alerting himself or herself to potentially important information in stories. There is no objectively correct answer. The purpose of the outlines is to aid investigation, and they can always be amended.

6. See Fed.Rules Crim.Proc. Rule 12.1.

d. Stating a Defendant's Perspective: An Aside

Special considerations sometimes apply to the preparation of outlines from the defendant's perspective. At trial, defendants are normally counter-punchers. Plaintiffs usually have to state each theory of relief on which they rely, and then to succeed on each theory they must prove each element. Defendants, on the other hand, usually focus on attempting to disprove selected elements. Outlines of the defense perspective, therefore, are normally more limited.

Return to *Tinkers*. In the defendant's version, Evers attempted to disprove only some elements of Tinkers' theory. For example, there was no attempt to disprove Evers' receipt of $10,000.

In other cases, a defendant might not attempt to disprove *any* element of a plaintiff's theory. In *Tinkers*, defendant may have premised the defense entirely on the statute of limitations. In this situation, Evers might not even bother to outline the plaintiff's theory of relief. Rather, Evers' structure would consist only of an outline of the elements of the statute of limitations, cast in factual terms. If the loan were oral, the defendant's outline might look like this:

Statute of Limitations
Plaintiff did not file suit within 2 years of Groundhog Day.

When defendants do try to disprove an element of a plaintiff's theory, the defense version of the element is typically stated from an affirmative perspective. This is because, as noted in Chapter 2, at trial defendants typically try to establish affirmatively their own versions of what happened. Defendants may be counterpunchers, but they do punch. Thus, if a plaintiff claims, "Defendant went to the beach," and defendant disputes this claim, defendant will typically do more at trial than proclaim, "You're wrong." Such a position would merely result in the defendant's use of rebuttal evidence to call into question plaintiff's evidence.

In addition, through affirmative evidence, defendants usually offer their own versions. That affirmative version may take two forms. Its more limited form is no more than a simple denial: "I did not go to the beach." Defense evidence that the defendant is allergic to sand would constitute affirmative evidence supporting such a simple denial.

In its more expansive form, a simple denial produces a story resembling an affirmative defense. It is similar to an affirmative defense because it embodies facts beyond those included in the factual statements of the elements of plaintiff's theory. In the beach hypothetical, the expansive defense version might be, "I went to the movies." Hence, the complete affirmative version to counter plaintiff's theory, "Defendant went to the beach," is, "I did not go to the beach. I went to the movies."

Consider now in *Tinkers* how one might structure the defendant's perspective in a situation in which a defendant has an affirmative version of what occurred. Assume that Evers admits receiving $10,000 from Tinkers, but contends the money was a gift, not a loan. The outline of Tinkers' theory might reflect both the more limited and the more expansive versions of the defendant's position. The structure for the more limited version might look like this:

Evers' Theory: No Breach of Contract

    1. Evers did not agree to repay $10,000 to Tinkers by Groundhog Day.

    2. No issue of performance.

    3. No issue of breach.

    4. No issue of damages.

In its more expansive form, the structure of Evers' version would look like this:

Evers' Theory: Gift

    1. Tinkers intended to give $10,000 to Evers.

    2. Tinkers gave $10,000 to Evers.

The reason one may want to prepare both structures is very practical. Even if Evers is ultimately unable to convince the factfinder that a gift was made, Evers still might be able to produce affirmative evidence to support the more limited version that he did not agree to repay by Groundhog Day. If Evers had evidence that Tinkers did not make a demand for repayment around Groundhog Day, and that Tinkers maintained a personal calendar for important dates, yet failed to note that a loan to Evers was due on Groundhog Day, this evidence would indicate that Tinkers did not believe that Evers had agreed to repay the $10,000 by that date. From Tinkers' lack of belief, the factfinder could infer that in fact Evers had not agreed to repay by Groundhog Day. Yet, that evidence would not, except very indirectly, prove that a gift was made. Hence, although one might be tempted to outline only the gift theory, since proof of gift negates the plaintiff's theory, preparation of separate structures reminds one that defendant does have two ways to win.

So far, the discussion has considered Evers' perspective only in the context of Tinkers' claim of breach of contract. But it may be dangerous for defense counsel to limit defense theories merely to those that respond to theories initially pleaded by a plaintiff. This is particularly a danger in civil cases, in which pleadings can be rather freely amended. One may identify a number of theories of defense which respond to theories of relief stated in an initial pleading, only later to be served with entirely new theories of relief in an amended pleading or at a pretrial conference. Since defendants cannot generally compel plaintiffs to identify theories by any set pretrial point,[7] defense counsel often must speculate to some extent. In *Tinkers*, for example, defense counsel should at least consider the possibility that plaintiff will later plead fraud. Perhaps wise defense counsel will disregard an initial pleading long enough to identify plaintiff's other potential theories of relief, and then consider potential theories of defense.

e. An "Aside" to Plaintiff's Counsel

The foregoing description of outlining a defendant's perspective emphasizes the earlier point that a lack of information may create difficulty in outlining an adversary's structure. Defendants typically limit their proof to certain elements of plaintiffs' theories, though that proof may take the form of rebutting plaintiffs' evidence and/or offering affirmative evidence in the limited or expanded forms. Plaintiffs yearn to avoid the Scylla of investigating defense claims that are not made and the Charybdis of overlooking those that are. Hence, like defense counsel, plaintiffs' counsel too must often speculate as to possible contentions the defense might make, and attempt to uncover those contentions through discovery.[8]

5. BEGINNING THE SUBSTANTIVE STRUCTURE

This section begins a substantive structure that might be used in *Phillips v. Landview*. In order to illustrate the principles in this chapter, we provide additional data about the case, which is contained in two memoranda from the file of Florence Darrow, defense counsel for Landview. We then draft the outlines that plaintiffs' counsel, Mason, might prepare for the theory of "Fraud-Concealment" from the Phillipses' and from Landview's perspectives. Finally, we ask you to do additional drafting.

a. Additional Data Re Phillips v. Landview

Memo to File

To: File
From: Florence Darrow
Re: Landview, et al. adv. Phillips
Date: July 13 (approximately ten months after the Phillipses' purchase of two lots)

7. As discussed in Chapter 17, in civil cases "contention interrogatories" may enable one to identify an adversary's theories, whether or not they are pleaded. Moreover, many local court rules provide for mandatory pretrial conferences in civil cases, at which the parties must reveal any theory on which they will rely at trial. See, e.g., Local Rules for United States District Court for the Southern District of California, Rule 235 (1983).

8. See note 7, supra.

This memo summarizes my discussion of this date with Paul Lade. The Phillipses have served Lade with a complaint on behalf of Landview Corp. The plaintiffs are James and Joan Phillips, and Landview and Soil Engineers are named as co-defendants. The Phillipses bought two lots from Landview last September, in the Campion Hills development. The Phillipses now complain that the lots are subject to landslides, and that this fact was concealed from them.

Lade states that since our conversation a month ago, there have been a few reports of soil slippage on some of the Campion Hills lots in the south and west portions of the development. However, Lade is definite that prior to our conversation, no one at Landview knew anything about soil problems. He has now learned that the building department has refused to issue a building permit for some plans which did not account for problems of soil slippage. Lade showed me a report from Soil Engineers, dated two years before the purchase by the Phillipses. My review of that report seems to bear out Lade's claim that no one at Landview was aware of soil problems.

With regard to the recreation center, Lade insists no representations were made that the center would be completed. He told me that the secretary in the sales office, Bob Farrell, remembers talking with the Phillipses and some friends of theirs around the middle of October, about a month after they bought their lots. Farrell remembers that the Phillipses were showing their friends around Campion Hills, and that the Phillipses pointed to a section of the relief map and said that some day a recreation center might be built in that area. The Phillipses seemed not to be counting on the building of the recreation center. Farrell's statement confirms Lotz's assertion that he made no promises that a recreation center would be built.

I told Lade that we would file an answer denying liability and a cross-complaint for indemnity against Soil Engineers.

Memo to File

To: Florence Darrow
From: F. Lee Nizer
Re: Landview, et al. adv. Phillips—
         Analysis of Complaint
Date: July 15 (two days after July 13 memo)

Hope you had a wonderful holiday in the Falklands. In the meantime, this memo will bring you up-to-date on the Landview matter.

The complaint by the Phillipses asserts two causes of action against our client, Landview, and a cause of action against a co-defendant, Soil Engineers. Landview has been sued on the theories of fraud-misrepresentation and fraud-concealment. The cause of action against Soil Engineers is for negligence. Plaintiff seeks recission plus $10,500 or, in the alternative, damages according to proof. Punitive damages according to proof are also sought.

Plaintiff has not alleged a cause of action for negligent misrepresentation; might they amend?

Based on your conversation with Lade (refer to your Memo of July 13), and my discussions with Lotz and with Melba Belli, attorney for Soil Engineers, I have prepared and filed an answer denying any liability. No affirmative defenses appear applicable. I have also prepared and filed a cross-complaint against Soil Engineers, on an indemnity theory.

b. Initial Preparation of Substantive Structure

The structure of the theory of relief based on fraud-concealment that plaintiffs' attorney, Mason, prepared is below. This structure would appear both in the outline of plaintiffs' existing affirmative evidence, and the outline of plaintiffs' potential affirmative evidence. It is based on the information available to Mason thus far in the case.

Phillipses' Theories of Relief (Partial) [Prepared by Mason, plaintiffs' lawyer]

1. *General*

    A. Landview is a corporation authorized to do business in this State.

    B. Soil Engineers is a corporation authorized to do business in this State.

    C. Soil Engineers is a licensed soil engineer.

2. *Theory One: Fraud (Non-Disclosure of Material Fact)*

    A. When Landview sold lots 70 and 71 to the Phillipses, the land was subject to slides.

    B. When it sold lots 70 and 71 to the Phillipses, Landview was aware that the land was subject to slides.

    C. When it sold lots 70 and 71 to the Phillipses, Landview did not disclose that the land was subject to slides.

    D. Landview failed to disclose that lots 70 and 71 were subject to slides with the intent to induce the Phillipses to buy the lots.

    E. Had the Phillipses been aware that lots 70 and 71 were subject to slides, they would not have bought them.

    F. The Phillipses have suffered damages of at least $40,000 because they must install caissons in order to secure a building permit—other consequential damages?

    G. Punitive damages according to:

        (1) Financial strength of Landview;

        (2) Landview's knowing concealment (See 2–C);

        (3) Other?

Mason, of course, must also prepare a structure of this same theory of relief from Landview's perspective. This structure would appear in Mason's outline of Landview's existing affirmative evidence, and Mason's outline of the Phillipses' potential rebuttal. Below is the structure prepared by Mason of Landview's perspective.

Landview's Theory—No Fraudulent Concealment

1. *No Failure to Disclose a Material Fact*

A. Lots 70 and 71 were not subject to soil slippage when they were sold to the Phillipses.

B. Landview was not aware of any soil slippage on Lots 70 and 71 when they were sold to the Phillipses.

C. Reliance?

D. Accuracy of claimed damages—actual and punitive?

Mason is not alone, of course, in preparing structures of the concealment theory of relief. Darrow, too, will be busily preparing the same structures. We have not included those structures, since they would generally track those prepared by Mason. Recall, however, that the structures may not be identical. Information known to Darrow, but not to Mason, would be reflected only in Darrow's structures. For example, assume that Darrow had talked with an expert who had advised her that the cost of caissons would be no more than $10,000 per lot, and that Mason was unaware of this factual defense to damages. The damages portion of Mason's structure of the defense perspective would retain damages as a questionable item. The damages portion of Darrow's structure of the defense perspective, by contrast, would state, "Plaintiffs' damages do not exceed $20,000, the cost of caissons for both lots." As discovery continues, each party would probably learn the other's factual contentions, and the structures would probably grow more similar.

Please note also that even though Mason's structure is incomplete as to certain elements, it still serves as a reminder of areas where Mason lacks information of defendant's factual theories. When Mason puts question marks next to the elements of reliance and damages, Mason cannot help but be aware that he needs to discover what factual contentions Landview will make as to those elements.

Finally, be aware that one's lack of knowledge concerning factual contentions is not confined to the opponent's case. Sometimes one is not even aware of one's own factual theories. In *Phillips*, plaintiffs' complaint includes a cause of action against Soil Engineers for negligence. However, Mason has, on the data given, no factual basis to support a theory that Soil Engineers was negligent. How was Soil Engineers negligent? Did Soil Engineers improperly test the soil? If so, how? Did it fail to inspect all of the Campion Hills development? Until Mason has some factual support for the contention that Soil Engineers was negligent, the structure of a negligence theory would necessarily be incomplete. Assuming that Mason has no data beyond that given in Chapter 4, what arguments can be made that Mason violated ethical duties by suing Soil Engineers for negligence and opened both himself and his clients to an action for malicious prosecution?

6. SUBSTANTIVE STRUCTURE EXERCISES

a. *Prepare a Structure*

We have illustrated two structures prepared by Mason, plaintiffs' attorney, relating to the theory that Landview defrauded the Phillipses by intentionally failing to disclose that the lots bought by them were subject to soil slippage. Based on the data provided, Mason has other theories of possible fraud. Primary among these is the theory that Landview defrauded the Phillipses when it represented to them, through Lotz, that a recreation center would be built within 18 months. You may be asked to prepare a structure of this theory, from one or more of the following perspectives:

1. As attorney for the Phillipses, prepare a structure from the Phillipses' perspective;

2. As attorney for the Phillipses, prepare a structure from Landview's perspective;

3. As attorney for Landview, prepare a structure from Landview's perspective;

4. As attorney for Landview, prepare a structure from the Phillipses' perspective.

Although by this time you have reviewed memoranda prepared in the law offices of both Mason and Darrow, for the purpose of this exercise limit yourself to the memoranda prepared by the party to which you are assigned. Thus, plaintiffs' counsel should base their structures on the memoranda set forth in Chapter 4 (pp. 46–48) and defense counsel on those set forth in this chapter (pp. 71–73). The Phillipses must prove that Lotz was an authorized agent of Landview. Where applicable, include in your structures the element of agency.

b. *Questions for Discussion*

1. The legal theory of concealment in Mason's structure is based on the factual hypothesis that Landview knew of soil slippage and did not disclose it. Do the memoranda in Chapter 4 suggest another factual hypothesis for concealment? Are there any facts that suggest that Landview did more than merely fail to disclose, that it actively attempted to conceal the condition of the soil? If such facts exist,

consider how you might draft a structure based on this factual hypothesis.

2.   Does the following portion of Mason's memorandum of June 1 suggest a factual hypothesis for affirmative misrepresentation: "Salesman Guy Lotz met with them (the Phillipses) on several occasions.   He showed them homes that were already built and vacant parcels particularly suitable for building?"   If so, consider how you might draft a structure based on this factual hypothesis.

Chapter 6

ANALYSIS OF EXISTING AFFIRMA-TIVE EVIDENCE: USING GENERALIZATIONS

At the start of Chapter 3, we pointed out that one cannot figure out what evidence to pursue unless one first analyzes the evidence on hand. This analysis, we warned, "involves a good deal of thought." This chapter, then, gives you a good deal.[1]

1. DIRECT AND CIRCUMSTANTIAL EVIDENCE

Consider first the distinction between direct and circumstantial evidence. How one analyzes evidence is very different, depending upon whether evidence is direct or circumstantial.

Rule No. 1. All evidence is either direct or circumstantial. *Rule No. 2.* There is no such thing as direct evidence. Lest one think that these two rules are contradictory, some explanation is in order.

Direct evidence is evidence which proves or disproves, without the need for an inference, an element which a party must establish.[2] Circumstantial evidence is evidence which, if believed, permits one to infer the existence of another fact. The inferred fact may be an element which must be proved or disproved, or the inferred fact may be one which does not itself prove such an element, but rather proves a fact which permits a further (second) inference to prove such an ele-

1. Many of the insights for this chapter were contributed by our colleague William W. Graham while he was teaching at UCLA Law School during 1978–80. For his contributions we are extremely grateful.

2. See, e.g., R. Lempert and S. Saltzburg, *A Modern Approach to Evidence* 150 (2d Ed.1982); McCormick, *Evidence* 434 (Cleary Ed.1972). Remember, one often attempts to prove or disprove elements which are not technically part of a claim for relief. Such an element might be the fact that a party is a corporation.

ment.[3] Theoretically, the chain of inferences from the circumstantial evidence to the element may be quite extensive. In practice, if an item of offered evidence is so remotely connected to an element that an extensive chain of inferences is required to establish the relationship, a court is likely either to rule that the evidence's probative value is outweighed by the time it would take to prove it [4] or perhaps even that the evidence is irrelevant.

These abstract principles may be clarified by an example. Assume that Ivy Haddit is charged with robbery. The indictment charges that on August 4th she took property belonging to Ida Lefter by the use of force or fear. At trial, Lefter testifies as follows:

Q (D.A.): Do you recognize anyone seated in this courtroom as the person you saw around 9:00 P.M. on August 4th?

A: Yes, I do. That woman over there (sneering, and pointing to Haddit).

Q: Where did you first see her?

A: She was walking towards me, holding a pair of brown oxford shoes in her hands.

Q: And then what happened?

A: She pulled a large knife out of her purse, pointed it at me, and told me to take the shoelaces out of my shoes and give them to her.

Q: What color were those shoelaces?

A: Each was purple and orange, to match my shoes.

Q: How did you respond?

A: I was so frightened; I did just what she told me to.

Lefter's testimony provides direct evidence. If her testimony is believed, her testimony proves most of the elements of the crime of robbery: (1) identity of the culprit; (2) taking of property; and (3) taking through the use of force or fear. No inference is necessary to establish a relationship between Lefter's testimony and these elements.

Suppose, however, that Lefter could not recognize her assailant. To prove the element of identity of the culprit, the prosecution offers the testimony of Hy Stander, who testifies that around 9:15 P.M. on August 4th, one-half block from the point at which Lefter was robbed, he saw Haddit seated at a bus stop lacing a pair of brown oxfords with purple and orange shoelaces. Stander's testimony provides evidence that Haddit was the culprit, but it does so circumstantially. Lacing shoes is not an element of robbery. However, the factfinder may infer that the orange and purple laces in Haddit's pos-

3. Fed.Rules of Evidence Rule 104(b).   4. Fed.Rules of Evidence Rule 403.

session were the same ones taken from Lefter and that therefore Haddit is the lady who lifted Lefter's laces.[5]

Similarly, evidence relating to Stander's credibility would be circumstantial evidence. For example, evidence introduced by Haddit that Stander had previously told the police that he had seen Haddit at the bus stop around midnight would be circumstantial evidence. Evidence of the inconsistent statement would not directly disprove any element of the prosecution's theory. However, it would provide the basis for an inference that Stander is uncertain about the incident and that the accuracy of the remainder of his testimony might be suspect.[6]

As mentioned above, one may occasionally attempt to use an extensive chain of inferences to prove an element. Assume that the prosecutor in Haddit offers the testimony of a police officer to the effect that when Haddit was arrested around 10:00 P.M. on August 4th, Haddit did not have a knife but she had a band-aid on one finger. Defense counsel objects that evidence of the band-aid is irrelevant. The prosecutor responds, "Your Honor, from the fact of the band-aid on defendant's finger, we may infer that she had an injury to that finger. We may further infer that such injury was a cut. From the fact that the defendant had a cut finger, we may infer that the cut was made by a knife. From this fact, we may infer that defendant had been in possession of a knife. From this, we may infer that she was in possession of a knife at a fairly recent time and from that infer she had a knife at the time Lefter was robbed." Each inference may be logically possible, so there may be some minimal relevance to the band-aid evidence. However, in view of the lengthy chain of inferences required to get from the evidence (band-aid) to the element (force—use of a knife), a court is likely to rule that the evidence is irrelevant or that any possible relevance is outweighed by considerations of time and prejudice. Whoever wrote the famous lines that begin, "For the want of a nail . . . ," would never have been able to introduce them in evidence in a court of law.

Thus, the distinction between direct and circumstantial evidence seems clear enough—the latter requires at least one inference to prove or disprove an element, the former does not. Why then did we initially state that there is no such thing as direct evidence? We did so primarily to emphasize that in reality all evidence is subject to the frailties of circumstantial evidence. Because a factfinder is confront-

---

5. Return for a moment to Lefter's testimony. Does it furnish direct evidence of the element of robbery which consists of "intent to permanently deprive" Lefter of her laces?

6. In some jurisdictions, evidence of Stander's previous statement might be admissible as a hearsay exception. See, e.g., West's Ann.Cal.Evid.Code § 1235. Even so, the evidence would remain circumstantial.

ed not with reality, but rather with a witness' verbal re-creating of reality, a factfinder's acceptance even of direct evidence requires inferences. When Lefter testifies, "She is the woman who took my shoelaces at knifepoint," the factfinder must make inferences before it can accept Lefter's testimony. It must infer that Lefter observed the incident well enough to tell about it, that she is able to remember it, that she is sincere in reporting it, and that words to Lefter have the same meaning as they do for the factfinder—e.g., Lefter does not belong to a cultural group whose word for "cooked spaghetti" is "knife." [7] However, even though direct evidence does depend on these sorts of inferences, the rules of evidence still regard it as direct evidence. It is up to the opponent of the evidence to demonstrate through cross-examination that one or more of those inferences cannot be drawn in a particular case.

Although there is a logical distinction between direct and circumstantial evidence, the law does not value one more highly than the other. This may surprise those who have been raised in front of television lawyers who scream, "It's nothing but a bunch of circumstantial evidence." Nevertheless, direct and circumstantial evidence are equally admissible to prove an element. Moreover, in any case, circumstantial evidence might be of more probative value than direct evidence. "There is still no man who would not accept dog tracks in the mud against the sworn testimony of a hundred eye-witnesses that no dog had passed by." [8] Thus, the need to distinguish direct from circumstantial evidence is not based on the fact that one type of evidence is necessarily more persuasive than the other. Instead, it is based on one's need to recognize that circumstantial evidence proves elements only through means of inferences.

In order to aid your understanding of the difference between direct and circumstantial evidence, consider a second hypothetical. Bauman sues Warren for breach of contract. Bauman's version is that on October 4th Warren promised to install a 300 square foot brick patio in Bauman's backyard for $2,000 and that thereafter Warren breached. Warren denies entering into a contract with Bauman; Warren's version is that the parties never reached a final agreement.

At trial, Bauman's lawyer examines Bauman, M. Schwartz and R. Maxwell. Bauman testifies that on October 4th, in a telephone conversation with Warren, Warren agreed to install a 300 square foot patio in Bauman's yard for the sum of $2,000. Bauman also testifies that when Bauman came home from work on October 11th, a large stack of bricks was standing in the driveway but that the next day

7. See C. Wright and K. Graham, 22 *Federal Practice and Procedure: Evidence* § 5162, at 16 (1978).

8. W. Prosser, *The Law of Torts* 212 (4th Ed.1971).

the bricks were gone. Bauman's testimony concludes with the statement that Warren never installed the patio.

M. Schwartz testifies that on October 10th, Warren ordered and picked up from Schwartz' brickyard enough bricks to cover 300 square feet. Maxwell testifies to being a city building inspector and that on October 7th Warren told Maxwell that Warren had a contract to install a brick patio at 1052 Hanley (Bauman's address) and asked if a building permit was required. List which portions of the testimony of Bauman, Schwartz and Maxwell provide direct and which provide circumstantial evidence of the elements of "breach of contract."

The distinction between direct and circumstantial evidence is critical to case investigation. If one has direct evidence, one need not analyze it in order to determine what element it establishes. With direct evidence, one's analysis is focused principally on the credibility of the evidence and its source. Credibility is discussed in detail in Chapter 8.

With circumstantial evidence, one is concerned, of course, with its credibility. But one must also be concerned with analyzing exactly what element the evidence proves and with what degree of certainty it proves that element. Making this analysis during investigation is the key to determining the probative value of existing evidence, identifying potential affirmative evidence, and identifying potential rebuttal evidence. For example, if analysis shows that the link between circumstantial evidence and an element is weak, one knows more precisely what evidence is on hand and is better able to identify potential evidence that might strengthen the link.

The need to analyze circumstantial evidence during investigation is heightened by the fact that most evidence one uncovers and later introduces at trial is circumstantial. If one were to "add up" evidence presented at trials, typically the vast majority of it would be circumstantial. Indeed, for lovers of the famed Miller Analogy Test, usually direct evidence is to circumstantial as the tip of an iceberg is to its mass.

One reason that circumstantial evidence predominates is consistent with the story form of testimony. Often, substantively critical events are but moments in time—the exchange of words in an oral contract case, the flash of a gun in a homicide case. Yet, if one is to persuade the factfinder that one's version of the substantive moment in time is accurate, one must usually be able to relate a multitude of events and details that occurred before, during and after the critical moment. When surrounding events and details are consistent with those comprising the critical elements, the factfinder is more likely to be persuaded. Evidence of surrounding events and details is, by definition, circumstantial.

The second factor accounting for the predominance of circumstantial evidence concerns credibility of witnesses. Typically, facts are disputed because witnesses disagree about what they saw, heard, read or did. To succeed at trial, one attempts to persuade the factfinder that one's evidence is more credible than one's opponent's. Yet, credibility cannot be established by direct evidence. Even if it is permitted, a witness' testimony that he or she speaks the truth has little persuasive force since it is the witness' credibility that is in question. Furthermore, no other person has the capacity to actually determine that the witness accurately observed, recalled and reported the evidence the witness provides. Accordingly, credibility usually must be established or attacked through circumstantial evidence.

A final factor bearing on the importance of circumstantial evidence concerns the types of elements that often need to be established. Elements such as intent and knowledge must generally be proved by circumstantial evidence. Facts such as these are not observable except perhaps by the person whose state of mind is in issue. Credible direct evidence, therefore, is not available and resort to circumstantial evidence is essential.

Thus, at this point at least, direct evidence may be temporarily set aside. It requires little analysis since no inferences are needed to link such evidence with legal elements. We turn, then, to the analysis of circumstantial evidence.

2. GENERALIZATIONS: THE LINK BETWEEN CIRCUMSTANTIAL EVIDENCE AND ELEMENTS

Given that most evidence is circumstantial, and that circumstantial evidence proves elements only through inferences, the importance of inferential reasoning to factfinding is apparent. If in medieval times there was "trial by combat," then today we have "trial by inference."

The question that irresistibly comes to one's mind is, on what basis are inferences made? Inferences are made from premises assumed to be true. When one adopts a premise that a given proposition is true, one is able to use existing evidence to infer another fact. For example, if one adopts a premise that roses usually bloom in the spring, one may infer from the evidence that roses were in bloom that it was springtime. A simple graphic illustrates the link between evidence, premise and conclusion:

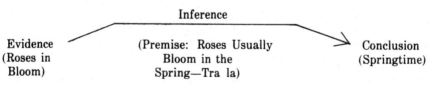

Inference

Evidence	(Premise: Roses Usually	Conclusion
(Roses in	Bloom in the	(Springtime)
Bloom)	Spring—Tra la)	

[D547]

Thus, an inference piggybacks from an item of evidence to a conclusion on the strength of a premise.

In lawsuits, then, one uses a premise to link a specific item of evidence with an element sought to be proved. Indeed, because premises are necessary to link evidence with elements, individual items of evidence, absent the adoption of a premise, prove nothing. Consider this example.

Assume Cameron is being prosecuted for armed robbery of a 7–11 store. At trial, the clerk who identifies Cameron as the culprit testifies that during the robbery Cameron brandished a gun.

In closing argument, the prosecutor and defense counsel can each use this item of evidence—i.e., the brandishing of the gun—to draw opposite conclusions about the accuracy of the clerk's identification. They can do so because each can use a different premise to link the circumstantial evidence with the fact to be proved. Thus, the prosecutor can adopt the premise that, "People whose lives are threatened with a gun usually pay close attention to the person who threatens them." From this premise, the prosecutor can draw the conclusion that the presence of the gun enhanced the likelihood that the clerk's identification was accurate.

The defense lawyer, on the other hand, can adopt the premise that, "People who are on the business end of a gun are usually nervous." From this premise the defense lawyer can draw the conclusion that the clerk was too nervous to make an accurate identification.

Both the prosecution and the defense can rely on the same piece of evidence to reach opposite conclusions because the evidence itself proves nothing. Any conclusion drawn from circumstantial evidence comes from the premise one uses to link the evidence with the inferred conclusion.

Sometimes a premise which is used as the basis of an inference is a proposition which is nearly indisputable. For example, assume a litigant with the words "rinse cycle" impressed in her head introduces evidence that a washing machine was pushed out of a window. The premise which may support an inference that the washing machine fell toward the ground is something like, "Objects pushed into the air are affected by gravity."

Sometimes the premise is one which is almost always true. From evidence that Hack Kneed is a person, one may infer that Hack has two legs. The premise which supports this inference is, "People have two legs." While this premise is perhaps not as true as the premise based on gravity, it is certainly usually true.

However, a premise may be used even if it is only occasionally true. If one introduces evidence that Noah Kantwin was driving while late to an appointment, one may infer that Noah was speeding.

The premise on which this inference is based is, "People who are late to an appointment sometimes drive faster than the speed limit." This premise is far from universally true; all of us have been late to appointments, yet have driven safely to get to them. But as long as the premise is occasionally true, it may be used as the basis of an inference. Under the law of evidence, evidence is relevant as long as it has "*any tendency* to make the existence of any fact that is of consequence . . . more probable or less probable than it would be without the evidence." [9] The tendency of evidence to prove a particular point depends on the validity of the premise used to link the evidence with the sought conclusion. If the premise is at least occasionally true, then the evidence has a tendency to prove the conclusion. Hence, where evidence is supported by a premise that is occasionally true, the evidence is relevant.

If inferences come from premises, then where do premises come from? When they are nearly indisputably true, premises are derived from universal principles of physical science. Recall the example of a falling washing machine: the premise that objects in the air are subject to gravity is based on the principle of gravity. In such instances, the principle may be so obvious that it need not be a candidate either for investigation or proof. At trial, such principles can be judicially noticed. [10]

What, however, is the basis of premises that are not supported by universal principles of physical science? Whenever one makes an inference based on a premise that is less than universally correct, one relies on a generalization. [11] A generalization is a proposition asserting that something is likely to be true about a given class or group, although it is not always true. The class or group may involve people or inanimate objects such as boats, cars and computers. When one uses a generalization, one says in essence, "All right, person (or object). I do not know enough about you—your personality, your past behavior, your intelligence, your uniqueness—to infer how you probably behaved on the occasion under investigation. But I know something about people (or objects) in general, and I assert that you probably behaved the way people (or objects) in that situation would typically behave." [12]

9. Fed.Rules of Evidence Rule 401 (emphasis added).

10. Fed.Rules of Evidence Rule 201.

11. C. Wright and K. Graham, note 7 supra, § 5165, at 56.

12. Note, however that frequently people do not articulate the generalization on which they rely. This may be because in making judgments people utilize "a variety of knowledge structures normally not expressed in propositional terms and possibly not stored in a form even analogous to propositional statements." R. Nisbett and L. Ross, *Human Inference: Strategies and Shortcomings of Social Judgment* (1980), p. 32. Nisbett and Ross describe these cognitive structures as "schema."

From this perspective, consider an example. Allie Katz has been shot to death, and Anne Athema is charged with his killing. The prosecutor introduces evidence that Allie and Anne were former lovers who had a violent quarrel an hour before Anne allegedly shot Allie. From evidence that the two lovers had a violent quarrel, one might infer that Anne was angry with Allie, from there infer further that Anne desired to kill Allie, and from there finally infer that Anne acted in accordance with her desires and killed Allie. Even though one is not compelled to draw these inferences from the evidence that Anne and Allie had a violent quarrel, one is *permitted* to do so. One may do so even though one knows nothing about Anne personally. Anne is a person in a romantic situation, and one may draw inferences based on how people in such situations may behave. Since lovers who engage in violent quarrels with each other occasionally kill each other, one might infer that Anne behaved the way people in romantic situations occasionally behave.

A generalization is, then, a premise which rests on the general behavior of people or objects. How does one formulate generalizations? Usually, one adopts conventional wisdom about how people and objects function in everyday life. All of us, through our own personal experiences, through hearing about the personal experiences of others, and through knowledge gained from books, movies, newspapers and television, have accumulated vast storehouses of commonly-held notions about how people and objects generally behave in our society. From this storehouse one formulates a generalization about typical behavior. The generalization, in turn, becomes the premise which enables one to link specific evidence with an element one hopes to prove.[13]

The case of the hypothetical murder of Allie Katz illustrates that it is simply one's knowledge gained through living which enables one to formulate generalizations. The conclusion that Anne shot Allie was based on the premise that, "Lovers who engage in violent quarrels sometimes kill the people with whom they quarrel." One need not be a sociologist, a psychologist, or even a violent lover to formulate this generalization. It is enough that one has lived in society and absorbed a knowledge of common community life.

13. When people engage in this type of reasoning, although their reasoning is often sound, they can make a variety of what social scientists call inferential errors. For example, people tend to attribute behavior to the dispositions of the actor rather than to the particular characteristics of the situation to which the actor responds. See R. Nisbett and L. Ross, note 12 supra, at 31. Thus if people characterize a certain person as an "angry man", they may assume that in any given situation he will act in a way typical of angry persons, without taking into account "those situational stimuli pertinent to the individual at the moment of action." Nisbett and Ross at 32. In short, conventional wisdom may in any given situation be erroneous.

One's awareness of how the world generally operates comes from a variety of sources. Sometimes, one formulates a generalization based on one's own personal experiences. For example, if one has spent a lifetime mistakenly waving at strangers in passing cars, one is likely in a "mistaken identity" case to formulate a generalization that, "People often walk down the street and mistakenly think they recognize someone."

However, one need not have actual experience to formulate generalizations. Many of us have had no personal experience with war. Yet if asked to decide whether a soldier who was about to go on a combat mission was tense, most of us would conclude he or she was by adopting a generalization such as, "Soldiers are usually very tense before entering combat." Even if one has not been in a war, one has probably been in some other situation where there existed more than the usual risk of physical harm. If one was tense in such analogous situations, then one is likely to believe the soldier too would be tense. Or, even if one's personal life has been stress-free, one has been to war vicariously. In books and films, one reads the words and sees the faces of soldiers about to experience combat. Most of us have seen John Wayne tell the fuzzy-cheeked green recruit just off the farm, "It's all right, son. We're all afraid." Because one has experienced war vicariously, one is likely to reach the conclusion that the soldier was tense by formulating the generalization about the strain on soldiers going into combat.

In sum, generalizations used as premises to link specific evidence with elements are usually drawn from our everyday personal and vicarious experiences. These experiences, be they identical with or merely analogous to the situation being investigated, give one the basis for constructing the generalized premise which links the item of evidence to the sought conclusion.

It may be useful to step back for a moment and reflect on what the use of generalizations tells us about our legal system. After all, one grows up with the belief that trials are searches for truth. Yet, if the bulk of the evidence in trials is circumstantial, and if the validity of circumstantial evidence rests on generalizations which all would concede may be inaccurate, our system of trial seemingly invites errant verdicts. One might well ask whether reliance on generalizations perverts the search for truth.

However, implicit in the way lawyers use generalizations is the difference between a physical science laboratory and a courtroom.[14] A physical science laboratory exists as a place where one can search for objective, immutable truth. In such a laboratory, one may ob-

14. C. Wright and K. Graham, note 7 supra, § 5165, at 53–54.

serve and record an event while it is happening, under conditions in which variables may be limited and controlled. In a courtroom, one is limited to largely verbal accounts of past events from witnesses with frail powers of observation and memory. Moreover, many issues important in a courtroom are not capable of reduction to mathematical truth either in a courtroom or in a laboratory. For example, it is impossible to prove with certainty that a person had specific intent, or that a child's "best interest" lays with one parent rather than another. A final difference between a courtroom and a laboratory is that courtrooms generally have more flags.

By allowing inferences to be drawn from evidence even when premises are only occasionally true, the legal system deals with circumstantial evidence no differently than it deals with other aspects of proof. Relativistic truth is in fact a notion which pervades trial. Criminal law, which imposes the severest burden of proof, demands proof only beyond a reasonable doubt. When the rules of evidence allow the admission of some forms of hearsay, e.g., dying declarations, they do so on the basis that not all hearsay is untrustworthy. Thus, when one asks a factfinder to draw inferences based on premises which are perhaps true, one asks no more of the factfinder than does the rest of the system of justice.

In a courtroom one must be content with a search for a pragmatic truth.[15] Courtroom truth hopefully is accurate enough, reliable enough and expedient enough to encourage litigants to bring their disputes to court. Undoubtedly, the legal system will never attain perfect accuracy and expediency, but probably it would fall far shorter if mathematical certainty were insisted upon.

When one makes a generalization based on an item of circumstantial evidence, one in essence formulates a rule of evidence for a specific piece of evidence in a specific case. In a few limited areas, courts and legislatures have already formulated rules governing generalizations to be applied to specific kinds of circumstantial evidence. For example, the long-established evidentiary rule that a witness' bias is a factor that a factfinder may take into account when determining a witness' credibility is merely a codified generalization governing evidence of bias. While not all biased witnesses have forked tongues, enough do to support the generalization used in jury instructions [16] that biased witnesses may be less trustworthy than neutral ones.

---

15. As our colleague Ken Graham has noted, courtroom truth may be more accurately labeled "political truth," in the sense that the facts courts find are accepted by the community as capable of proof. For example, society believes that a court can determine whether a person is sane, and which parent is more capable. Undoubtedly, in prior days even judges who did not believe in witches had to find some women guilty of witchcraft, because the society of that day accepted this as a fact that could be proven.

16. California Jury Instructions Criminal § 2.20 (West 1979).

Thus, in a case in which a witness who testifies that a driver was not speeding admits to being the driver's mother, one has available the codified generalization which supports an argument that the mother is not trustworthy.

But most of the time, there will not be a pre-existing rule incorporating the generalizations to be applied to specific evidence. The universe of potential generalizations is vast. Not only is there an unlimited amount of potential circumstantial evidence, but also any piece of evidence may be the subject of a large number of premises, depending on the inference one wants to draw.

For example, assume an item of circumstantial evidence is, "The child is four years old." From this evidence, one might infer that the child could not yet read, that the child was less than four feet tall, or that the child was afraid of imaginary monsters. Or one might infer a multitude of other things. Moreover, by merely changing the evidence slightly ("The child is three years old"), one may adopt another whole group of inferences. Thus, it is very unlikely either that any given item of circumstantial evidence will be the subject of an evidentiary rule governing inferences, or that any such rule that does exist would incorporate a generalization applicable to the specific evidence in a particular case. The number of possible items of evidence and the number of inferences to be drawn from each is infinite; the concept of a rule for each boggles the mind.[17]

But if a rule incorporating a generalization applicable to circumstantial evidence is unlikely to be found, the reasoning process by which one formulates generalizations is already in place. One draws upon one's common experience.

The use of generalizations to reach decisions is not unique to the factfinding process. When a legislator makes a decision about whether to adopt a particular rule of law, she or he commonly determines whether the proposed law makes sense on the basis of its potential positive and/or negative effects. Thus, a decision about whether to have a newsperson's privilege will be made (one hopes) on an analysis of whether on balance the positive effects of such a rule would outweigh the negative.

In turn, to determine what effects a rule may produce, the legislator employs generalizations to reach a decision. For example, in looking at the potential effects of the absence of a newsperson's privilege, one might infer that one potential effect would be that important information would not reach the press. If one draws this inference, one implicitly adopts a generalization such as, "People often

17. For discussion of this point, see C. Wright and K. Graham, note 7 supra, § 5162.

will not reveal important information to the press unless they are assured of anonymity."

Moreover, just as lawyers, legislators and factfinders use generalizations, law reviews, law students, and even law professors use them when analyzing the soundness of decisions reached by legislators and judges.   Here is typical classroom dialogue:

> Q: "Student Grind, do you think Justice Crony was correct in holding that a newsperson's privilege was essential if the press was to be able to fully report the news?"
>
> A: "What?   Pass.   Er, no, Professor Hearst; people who talk with the press don't even think about confidentiality when they talk to a reporter."

Whatever one may think about the accuracy of the student's response, one must see the generalization or the authors have written in vain.

3. ANALYZING THE PROBATIVE VALUE OF EXISTING AFFIRMATIVE EVIDENCE

a. Introduction

Thus far, we have suggested that the proof of facts through circumstantial evidence depends on at least the minimal truth of a generalization which makes the evidence relevant.   But in analyzing evidence on hand, one needs to know more than whether it has "any" tendency to prove the sought conclusion.   The judicial slot machine does not usually pay much when plums which are nothing more than barely relevant line up across the windows.   Jackpots are hit with persuasive plums.   Hence, when one analyzes existing affirmative evidence, one wants to determine its probative value.   Without such analysis, one may go to trial with evidence that is only "the pits."

An example of what is meant by probative value may be helpful. Assume one represents a pedestrian who was struck by a motorcyclist, and who has sued the motorcyclist for negligence on the theory the cyclist was under the influence of alcohol.   Through discovery, one learns that one hour before striking the pedestrian, the motorcyclist had been in a bar and had consumed two beers.   This evidence is relevant circumstantial evidence from which one might infer that the cyclist may have been under the influence.   But how strong is the inference?   How persuasive is the evidence of two beers?

During investigation one addresses these sorts of questions.   One wants to analyze the probative value of circumstantial evidence on hand as early as possible.   The analysis is a prelude to identifying potential affirmative and rebuttal evidence.   If analysis discloses that one's existing affirmative evidence is weak, one has time to gather additional evidence, or to consider a different career. For instance, if one concludes that consumption of two beers one hour earlier is not persuasive proof that the cyclist was drunk, one has time to gather further evidence to prove intoxication.

Similarly, the analysis is a guide to identification of potential rebuttal. If one is aware of an adversary's circumstantial evidence, and can formulate generalizations that the adversary will probably rely upon when presenting that evidence, the analysis can aid one in identifying potential rebuttal. One can do this, for example, by thinking of potential exceptions to the adversary's generalizations. Recall the earlier generalization that, "People who are late to an appointment may exceed the speed limit in order to get there." If one represents the alleged speeder, one may take the generalization on which the adversary will probably rely, add "except when" and thereby identify potential rebuttal. Thus, the generalization may be true, "except when the person has phoned to say she would be late," or "except when the person is on his way to the dentist and is in no hurry to arrive." The exceptions become the potential rebuttal evidence one might seek.

We suggest that one examine the probative value of each item of circumstantial evidence separately. We do this in full recognition of the fact that circumstantial evidence has a cumulative effect. That is, four items of circumstantial evidence, each considered in isolation, may not sustain one's burden of proving an element. Considered together, however, they may prove the element beyond even a reasonable doubt.

Nevertheless, one analyzes circumstantial evidence on an item by item basis at the investigatory stage for at least two reasons. First, one needs to know what element or elements an item of evidence actually proves. Particularly when a piece of circumstantial evidence is linked to an element only through an evidentiary chain, one may have a generalized sense that it is relevant without knowing precisely what element the evidence tends to prove. Since, as we have seen, to sustain a burden of proof one must prove each element of one's legal theory, one must have a clear sense of what elements a given item of circumstantial evidence tends to prove. An item by item analysis may reveal that while some elements are supported by substantial evidence, others are not.

An example may be helpful. Assume that a State Attorney General has charged Steer's Department Store with using "bait-and-switch" tactics in the sale of electric corkscrews. An element of the State's case is that Steer's advertised corkscrews with the intent not to sell them as advertised. Through discovery, the prosecutor learns that the sales manager in charge of advertising had been fired by Steer's following the running of the ads. This evidence seems relevant, yet is it readily apparent what element it tends to prove? In actuality, the evidence may be relevant as part of an inferential chain. From the fact that the manager was fired, one may infer that the manager did not perform duties properly; from that, one might infer that the manager placed misleading ads. Thus, the evidence may be relevant to the element that the advertisement was false. The evidence is by no means sufficient to establish that element, but if one is aware of the element it tends to prove, one will recognize the need for additional affirmative proof of this and other elements.

A second reason that one analyzes each item of circumstantial evidence separately is that the analysis enables one to evaluate the overall strength of evidence. Although circumstantial evidence has a cumulative effect, the combined strength of highly probative evidence is certainly greater than the combined strength of weak evidence. By analogy, two mountain climbers may have ropes that are a half-inch thick. But if one has a rope made of cotton fibers, and the other has one made of nylon fibers, the latter climber has a far better chance of coming down the mountain slowly. Similarly, the probative force of circumstantial evidence depends on the quality of the individual items of evidence, not merely on their quantity. Therefore, to assess the evidence on hand, one should analyze each item of circumstantial evidence individually.

When analyzing the probative value of evidence, one looks to the same sources of information one uses when formulating generalizations: personal, analogous and vicarious experience. That common experience plays a pervasive role in both the formulation and the evaluation of generalizations should come as no surprise. One uses common experience to test practically everything that is said. A friend asks one to agree that, "Mexican food is spicy." To reach a decision, one will perhaps test this assertion primarily according to Mexican food one has personally eaten. But one may also compare it to other types of food, as well as consider what one has read or seen about Mexican food. One simply cannot escape the use of common experience: it is an integral and central part of rational thought.

When using common experience to evaluate probative value, one must be careful not to become a prisoner of one's own experience.[18] At trial, it is the factfinder's common experience, not the litigator's, which determines the persuasiveness of evidence. Hence, while one cannot escape using one's own perspective of common experience to formulate and to begin to evaluate generalizations, one must be careful to consider whether the factfinder's perspective of common experience might be different.

18. See C. Wright and K. Graham, note 7 supra, § 5165 at 59.

Although people may live in the same vicinity all their lives, their common experience, and hence the generalizations they draw from such experience, may be very different. People who grow up in different parts of a single community commonly are exposed, whether personally or vicariously, to very different experiences and conventions. As a consequence, their views of how the world normally operates will often be quite divergent. Return to the evidence of the person late for an appointment. For people whose acquaintances strive to be precisely on time, this evidence will provide a fairly strong inference that the person was speeding. However, for people whose acquaintances own clocks which have "ish" after each numeral, the evidence will be less persuasive. Is it this diversity of experience which accounts in large part for the right to trial by jury, and for litigants' desires to be tried by their peers?

These potential differences in common experience should not be taken to suggest it is useless to analyze the probative value of evidence. As suggested above, one should not expect the accuracy of the physical scientist. Rather, the potential differences should serve to remind one to evaluate evidence with regard to the likely reaction of a potential judge or juror. Thus, the proper question is not, "What inference can I draw from the evidence that Noah was late?" It is, "What inference do I think the factfinder will draw from that evidence?"

One may often be unable to answer such a question. Many lawyers, especially new lawyers, lack the experience to evaluate how a factfinder will probably react to specific items of evidence. If one lacks such experience, one may use that familiar type of legal research: ask someone. That person may be an experienced trial lawyer or a friend who might have different experiences.

With the importance of the analysis of circumstantial evidence in mind, we turn to the manner in which the analysis may be carried out.

b. Articulate Generalizations

Detective Fenton Tracem rushes breathlessly into the office of the local prosecutor, Les Gettem, eager to persuade Les to issue an indictment. Fenton describes the evidence he has uncovered:

"Les, we've got a good case for bank robbery against Clyde. The gun the robber used and dropped at the door was originally purchased by Clyde. The owner of A–1 Guns can definitely identify Clyde as the purchaser and the teller can identify the gun. Moreover, the day after the $10,000 was taken, Clyde deposits $7,000 cash in a bank account using the fictitious name of Dillinger. A teller at the bank can definitely identify

Clyde. Then later that day, Clyde buys a $1,500 gold watch and pays for it in cash. The owner of A–2 Jewelry can also identify him. Finally, the next day—two days after the robbery—Clyde moves out without giving Ness, his landlord, his two neighbors, Capone and Siegel, or the post office his new address. Ness, Capone, Siegel and the post office clerk are all willing to testify. Les, we're rock-solid on this one."

The detective has disgorged a mass of circumstantial evidence which appears in the aggregate to be quite convincing. The prosecutor cannot, however, be content to rely on this presentation. In order to analyze the probative value of the evidence, Gettem must first expressly articulate the generalization which links each item of evidence to an element. As you will see in the next subsection, expressly articulating generalizations is the key to determining just how strong a piece of evidence is.

Consider, therefore, the generalization the prosecutor might articulate for the first piece of evidence, that the gun used and dropped by the robber was originally purchased by Clyde. The generalization might be something like, "People who have purchased a gun subsequently used in a robbery are more likely to have participated in the robbery than people who have not." [19]

Note how this generalization expressly links the evidence with an element. First, the generalization takes the critical evidence about the person in question—i.e. purchasing the gun subsequently used in the robbery—and attributes it to a group having the characteristics described by the evidence. This the generalization does through the phrase, "People who have purchased a gun subsequently used in a robbery." Then through the phrase, ". . . are more likely to have participated in the robbery than people who have not," the generalization asserts the link between the group characteristic and the element to be proved. Of course, as already mentioned, if the assertion does not comport with common experience, the assertion will be rejected and the evidence deemed irrelevant. In Clyde's case, the assertion seems valid enough to make the evidence relevant.

In the beginning years of practice, one must force oneself to articulate explicitly the generalizations on which one relies, for it is not a skill practiced in everyday life. In fact, there is a word for people who state the generalizations underlying all inferences they make: bores. But in the privacy of one's office, one should expressly identify the premises on which one relies.

19. This phrasing of the generalization asks whether the existence of the evidence makes it more probable that the material fact is true than if the evidence did not exist. As such, the generalization tests whether the evidence meets the definition of relevance. See Fed.Rules of Evidence Rule 401 and G. James, "Relevancy, Probability and the Law," 29 Cal. L.Rev. 687, 699 (1940–41).

c. *Analyze the Probative Value of Evidence In Terms of the Strength of the Generalization*

At this point, assume that one has articulated a premise which demonstrates that a specific item of evidence has at least some minimal tendency to prove an element. One then needs to ascertain whether one has a minimally relevant plum, a highly persuasive plum, or something in between.

As a general rule, the more uniformly that a factfinder perceives common experience to support a generalization, the more persuasive the generalization is likely to be. The generalization that, "People often walk down a street and think they recognize a friend, only to find out later they were mistaken," is likely to be highly persuasive, because almost everyone has experienced that mistake both personally and vicariously. It is the need to assess this relationship between common experience and probative value which demands that one usually articulate the generalization on which an inference is based. Only with the generalization expressly articulated is one in a position to consciously analyze how strongly it is supported by common experience.[20]

From this perspective, please return to the story related by Fenton Tracem to Les Gettem. The first bit of evidence was that the gun used during the robbery was purchased by Clyde. We may safely assume the relevance of this evidence; nearly everyone would accept the generalization that, "People who have purchased a gun subsequently used in a robbery are more likely to be the robber than people who have not."

But how probative is this evidence? The answer to that question depends on how uniformly common experience supports the generalization. If one believes that people who use guns in robberies almost always purchase them, then this evidence will be highly persuasive. But if one believes that a robber who uses a gun in a robbery may acquire it in a large variety of ways, one will find the evidence less persuasive. In either case, the point to remember is that by articulating the underlying generalization one can consciously consider the question of how strongly it is supported by common experience.

This point may be seen more clearly if one is asked to evaluate another of Det. Tracem's pieces of evidence without the aid of an expressed generalization. "The day after the $10,000 was taken, Clyde deposits $7,000 cash in a bank account using the fictitious name of Dillinger." As D.A. Les Gettem, one is asked how strongly suggestive of Clyde's guilt this piece of evidence is. Undoubtedly, one can

---

20. For a discussion of why articulation of the premise is also a prerequisite to a meaningful analysis of relevance, see G. James, note 19 supra, at note 14, p. 698–99.

have a knee-jerk reaction as to the probative value of evidence. Take a moment, and see if you have such a reaction. Do not keep reading—take a moment! Please write down your conclusion as to how probative of Clyde's guilt you find the evidence.

Now examine your answer. If it reads something like, "The only major leaguer to pitch two no-hitters in a row was Johnny Vandermeer," you have inadvertently answered the wrong question. If your answer is something like, "The evidence is strongly indicative of guilt" (or "isn't too probative of guilt"), you have had a knee-jerk reaction to the evidence. Undoubtedly some accumulation of common experience was implicit in whatever conclusion you reached. But unless the common experience is crystallized in an explicitly stated generalization, one has no focal point for considering how uniformly common experience supports the generalization.

If your conclusion did include a generalization, it may have been something like, "People who deposit $7,000 in a bank account under a fictitious name are likely to have gotten the money illegally." With this generalization explicitly stated, one has a basis for gauging with some degree of accuracy the probative value of the fictitious bank account evidence. One has an explicit premise which can be tested according to one's own and a factfinder's probable views as to how the world operates. One then has a basis for thinking about how uniformly the generalization is supported by experience.[21]

There are other reasons for articulating generalizations. Their articulation may bring to mind potential exceptions. The more exceptions there are to a generalization supporting an item of affirmative evidence, the less persuasive it tends to be. Hence, one method of testing the degree to which common experience uniformly supports a generalization is to add "except when" to a generalization, and see how many reasonable exceptions one can identify.

Tested in this manner, the generalization that, "People often walk down a street and think they recognized a friend, only to find out later they were mistaken," remains persuasive. Add "except when" to the generalization, and few exceptions are readily apparent. The generalization probably remains accurate, even if one were to add the "ultimate" exception: "except when the friend is their mother."

Compare, however, a generalization that one might make in Clyde's case: "People who move without leaving a forwarding address are usually trying to avoid detection." By adding "except when," one sees that this generalization is subject to many exceptions and is therefore less likely to be persuasive. People may be trying to avoid detection, except when they simply forget to leave a forwarding

21. Cf. G. James, note 19 supra, at 696.

address, or except when they do not yet know the permanent address to which they will be moving, or except when they will be moving around for a time and will not have a permanent address. One may be able to come up with other reasonable exceptions. Again, it is a good idea to test one's generalizations on one's friends and colleagues before testing them on a factfinder. The more reasonable exceptions that are found, the less persuasive one's evidence will be.

As may be apparent, by identifying the generalizations which support an adversary's affirmative evidence, one identifies *potential* rebuttal to that evidence. That is, the exceptions identify potential evidence which might undermine the adversary's affirmative evidence. That is why, in Chapter 10, we suggest that when identifying potential rebuttal evidence one also articulate the premises underlying the adversary's affirmative evidence.

If the "except when" analysis reveals weaknesses in one's affirmative evidence, one typically attempts to identify additional evidence to overcome those weaknesses. If evidence lacks probative force because there are a number of exceptions to the underlying premise, one may be generalizing about too large a group. If that group can be narrowed, however, the exceptions may diminish and the evidence become more persuasive. To identify evidence that might narrow a group, one articulates the underlying generalization and, instead of adding "except when," adds "especially when." Then, experience may suggest additional evidence that strengthens a generalization.

For example, the generalization, "People have two legs," is subject to a number of exceptions. If one wanted to identify additional evidence to strengthen it, one may add "especially when." "People have two legs, especially when they are dancers or professional athletes." The "especially when" device identifies potential evidence which narrows the initial group, and thereby curtails exceptions.

Taken all together, these comments illustrate that relying on reflex reactions to circumstantial evidence rather than on expressly articulated generalizations tends to produce error in the evaluation of probative value. Because one does not with a reflex reaction isolate the specific part of the world of experience applicable to a particular piece of evidence, one's reflex may be off. Moreover, it is likely to be off in the "high" direction—one tends in a reflex response to give circumstantial evidence more weight than it is otherwise entitled to. For example, as you read Fenton Tracem's litany of circumstantial evidence, did it appear more persuasive than it does now?

After using common experience to formulate a generalization and to evaluate it with regard to its potential exceptions, one may attempt a loose approximation of the potential probative value of an item of evidence. There is no way we know of to measure the precise degree of accuracy of any generalization. Fortunately, litigation focuses on probability, not precision. If one cannot say that, "This generalization is 79.8% accurate," one may at least be able to assess more generally its probative worth.

One may typically place a generalization into one of four broad categories. A generalization may be true:

(1) almost always.

(2) usually (more often than not).

(3) sometimes (less often than 50%).

(4) rarely (be ready to duck!).

(At least, a generalization will fall into one of these categories 92% of the time!) For example, one may state that, "People who purchase guns subsequently used in a robbery:

(1) almost always are the robber."

(2) usually are the robber."

(3) sometimes are the robber."

(4) rarely are the robber."

Even if, as is typically the case, one can do no more than choose between "usually" and "sometimes," one has some guide to the factfinder's probable evaluation of a generalization.

d. Getting Experience

The admonition to "use one's experience" may be reminiscent of those "help wanted" signs that so frequently frustrate teenagers—those that stipulate, "experience needed." If one always needs experience, where does one go when one does not have it?

Since the type of experience one needs in lawsuits is primarily the kind one acquires by living and observing, litigators are not frustrated to the same degree as teenagers. However, litigators too can run short on experience, especially since lawsuits can involve every factual matter under the sun. (Although given lawyer creativity and the space program, even this limitation may have run its course.)

Lack of experience may manifest itself in a number of ways. One may have a highly probative piece of circumstantial evidence on hand which is unrecognized because of one's inexperience. For example, assume that in a suit for negligent paving of a road, one of the asphalt company employees states that when the asphalt was laid down, the thermometer measuring the asphalt's temperature registered 120 degrees. Unless one's career has been blessed with a number of asphalt paving cases, one may not have the experience to understand that the temperature of the asphalt is a critical fact.

Lack of experience may arise in a related context. If one lacks experience in a given subject matter area, one may be unable to understand what facts are *potentially* significant, and worthy of pursuit during investigation. In the asphalt paving case, again, if one knew nothing about such cases, would one automatically think to inquire about the temperature of the asphalt?

This example also demonstrates a third way in which a lack of experience may be manifested. Even if one is the leading legal light where asphalt paving cases are concerned, a case may be tried before a factfinder who does not know the difference between asphalt and a hole in the ground. Because of the ethical rules forbidding attorneys to testify in cases in which they are counsel of record, one's experience cannot be put directly before the factfinder.

Regardless of the situation in which lack of experience arises, the solution is the same: involve someone who has the necessary experience. The experienced person may, for convenience, be termed an "expert."

The role of an expert is to supply experience to lawyers as investigators and to judges and jurors as factfinders. From this perspective, the universe of experts is not limited to people who carry stethoscopes or perform experiments. (Lawyers may not be physical scientists, but we admittedly love to hire them.) Whenever one is involved in factual situations with which one has little or no experience, one may be greatly aided by reviewing the evidence with a person who has such experience. During investigation, the "expert" may use experience to suggest potential evidence and to point out the significance of evidence already on hand. During trial, the expert may communicate that experience to the factfinder so it has the basis (the experience) to draw inferences from evidence in the record.[22] We will return to the role of an expert in later chapters. Here, it is enough that one understand that an expert's principal role is simply to supply both lawyers and factfinders with the experience from which inferences can be drawn from evidence.

4. OUTLINING EXISTING AFFIRMATIVE EVIDENCE

a. *Additional Data re Phillips v. Landview*

This section focuses on the analysis of circumstantial evidence in conjunction with the preparation of outlines of existing affirmative evidence. We first provide you with additional data in the form of excerpts from the deposition of Liv Urwurst, who, around the time

---

22. For more discussion of when experts will be permitted to convey their experience to factfinders, see Levin & Levy, "Persuading the Jury With Facts Not in Evidence: the Fiction-Science Spectrum," 105 U.Pa.L.Rev. 139, 173 (1965). See also Fed.Rules of Evidence Rule 702.

the Phillipses' purchased the lots, was Landview's on-site office manager in Campion Hills.

Deposition of Liv Urwurst

Taken by Jerry Mason, Counsel for the Phillipses

. . .

Q: And were you employed by Landview as its on-site office manager during the months of February through December of the year the Phillipses purchased their lots?

A: I was.

Q: Could you briefly describe your duties as office manager during that period?

A: I would be happy to. I was in charge of the secretarial staff. During that period we normally had three secretaries: Bob Farrell, Hilda Trek and Lance Boyle. I also supervised the sales staff along with Paul Lade. I conducted sales meetings for the sales staff, filled out lot purchase agreements, did basic accounting, and acted as liaison between lot owners and Landview.

. . .

Q: Now, earlier you mentioned an artist's rendition of the proposed recreation center. Do you recall that?

A: I do.

Q: I show you what appears to be a picture of a building which is marked in the upper right hand corner as Plaintiffs' 6. Do you recognize this picture?

A: Yes. That is an artist's drawing of what the recreation center was supposed to look like. It was hanging in the sales office for prospective purchasers to see during all the time I was the office manager.

Q: All right. I also have a document, which I will unroll and mark as Plaintiffs' 7 in the upper right corner. Ms. Darrow, can you see this all right?

Ms. Darrow: Yes, fine, thank you.

Q: Ms. Urwurst, could you describe Plaintiffs' 7 please?

A: Yes. These are the plans for the recreation center that were drawn up by an architect, Blanche Almon.

Q: When were the plans drawn up?

A: I'm not exactly sure, but I know they had been drawn up sometime before I started working for Landview in February of the year the Phillipses purchased their lots.

Q: Were the plans ever sent out for bid?

A: Yes. They were sent out just before I started with Landview. I remember we were just starting to get some bids in during February and March.

Q: Do you recall how many bids were received?

A: To my best recollection, around five.

. . .

Q: Now, you mentioned earlier that Landview had applied to Wastrel Bank to obtain a loan to finance the construction of the recreation center. Do you recall that?

A: I do.

Q: What happened with respect to that loan application?

A: We were turned down. According to my file, I got a phone call from Kein Geld, Wastrel's branch manager. He told me that the loan committee had decided they would approve the loan if we changed the plans to include ceiling sprinklers. I talked with Mr. Lade about the call. He said that since the building code didn't require sprinklers, we should go elsewhere for a loan.

Q: What, if anything, did you do after you had this conversation with Lade?

A: I did two things. I called Geld and told him of Lade's decision, and at our weekly sales meeting I handed out a memo to the sales staff— Lotz, Firma, Hill and Dale—informing them that the loan had not been approved. I told them as well that Landview would probably apply for a loan elsewhere.

Q: I hand you a memo marked Plaintiffs' 10, of the year of the Phillipses' purchase. Is this the memo to which you have just testified?

A: It is.

Q: By the way, did Landview actually reapply for a loan?

A: Yes, we applied to the Haypenny Bank for a loan in late September. We had not received an answer by the time I left Landview in December.

. . .

Q: Let's focus on the sales staff for a few minutes. How were they paid?

A: All of them were on salary plus commission.

Q: Was Mr. Lotz paid on this basis?

A: Yes, during the time I was there, his salary was $300 per week; his commission factor was 2% of gross.

Q: During the approximately six months between the time you started with Landview and the date the Phillipses purchased lots 70 and 71, how much money had Lotz earned in commissions?

A: I'd have to check my records to give you an accurate figure, about $8,000.

. . .

Q: Was Mr. Lade involved in the sale of lots?

A: No, he had no direct sales responsibility.

Q: With respect to Mr. Lade, did he ever discuss with you his past business dealings?

A: Yes, I recall that.

Q: And did he mention to you the name of Joad?

A: Yes. This was sometime in June. He told me that I should make sure that all the sales staff were totally honest and above-board. He said that three years earlier he had been sued for inducing Don Joad to buy a supposedly worthless piece of desert property because he had told Joad a major shopping center was going to be built right across the street. When the center was not built, the court awarded Joad a judgment for $75,000, and Lade almost lost his license.

. . .

Q: Did Mr. Lade know Mr. Lotz well?

A: Yes. Mr. Lotz worked with Mr. Lade, when Lade was selling desert property.

. . .

Q: Were any salespeople ever fired during your tenure with Landview?

A: Yes, in July I fired Terry Firma. I found out that Terry had written a letter to a prospective purchaser stating that the center would be definitely completed within 18 months.

. . .

Q: Were you ever aware that Mr. Lotz told prospective buyers that the recreation center would be built?

A: Yes, on two occasions in early August, I heard him tell two different prospects that the recreation center would be built. On each occasion, he pointed to an area about 100 yards from the sales office, which had been graded and staked, and indicated that that was where the center was going to be built.

Q: Was the grading being done specifically for the recreation center?

A: Yes, but it hadn't been finished.

Q: Why not?

A: Lade and the grading contractor got into an argument when Lade wanted the contractor to wait an extra four weeks for a progress payment. The contractor quit.

Q: Did you talk to Mr. Lotz concerning his telling people the center would be built?

A: Yes, after the second occasion I told him that Landview could not be certain that the recreation center would be built and that we could not make promises that it would be. Lotz promised me that he would make no further definite statements about the recreation center. He also promised to call the people in question and correct any misimpression he had given.

Q: Do you know whether he kept that promise?

A: Well, I know that at least on two occasions, one in the middle of August, and one after Labor Day, he told prospects that while Landview hoped to build the recreation center, nothing was definite at that time.

Q: When was the August occasion, with respect to August 31, the date the Phillipses signed the sales agreement?

A: I remember seeing the Phillipses in the sales office. I did not hear what Lotz may have said to them about the recreation center, but I know that a day or two before, or a day or two after he met with the Phillipses, he told an elderly couple that there was nothing definite about the building of the center.

· · ·

Q: Did you ever hear the Phillipses make any remarks concerning the recreation center?

A: Yes, one day around the middle of October I was in the outer office talking to Bob Farrell. The Phillipses were there with another couple, apparently taking them around the development. Mr. Phillips pointed to the picture on the wall and said it was the recreation center that he hoped would someday be built.

Q: Do you remember his exact words?

A: No.

Q: Now, turning your attention to the giant toad that one afternoon entered your office . . . .

b. Initial Preparation of Outline of Existing Affirmative Evidence

This subsection suggests how one might marshal circumstantial evidence in an outline of existing affirmative evidence. Of course, one marshals evidence, direct or circumstantial, under each element of a theory of relief which the evidence tends to prove. When evidence is circumstantial, we suggest that one often include not only the item of evidence, but also the generalization which supports the probative value of the evidence.

From the deposition excerpts above, we have selected two items of circumstantial evidence—one which supports the Phillipses' theory that Landview fraudulently represented that a recreation center would be built, and one which supports Landview's position that no such representation was made. The evidence is placed in the outlines that Mason would prepare for each party's affirmative evidence. Remember that in practice, Mason would prepare an outline of both the Phillipses' and Landview's existing affirmative evidence, and Darrow would do likewise.

For purposes of clarity, in the first outline we list all of the elements in factual terms which Mason must prove to sustain one theory of relief, and then we insert one item of existing affirmative evidence for one element in that outline. For the second outline, that which

Mason will prepare of Landview's affirmative evidence, we include only the one element to which the piece of evidence we have selected pertains. Following the two illustrations is a brief exploration of our suggested outline format.

A. Mason's Outline of Phillipses' Existing Affirmative Evidence

(Theory of Relief—Fraud: Intentional Misrepresentation of a Material Fact)

1. Prior to selling lots 70 and 71 to the Phillipses, Landview represented that a recreation center would be built in Campion Hills within 18 months.

2. Prior to selling lots 70 and 71 to the Phillipses, Landview had no definite plans to build a recreation center in Campion Hills within 18 months.

3. Prior to selling lots 70 and 71 to the Phillipses, Landview knew that the representation that a recreation center would be built within 18 months was false.

4. Landview represented to the Phillipses that the recreation center would be built within 18 months in order to induce them to purchase.

5. Had the Phillipses known that a recreation center would not be built within 18 months in Campion Hills, they would not have purchased lots 70 and 71.

6. The Phillipses have suffered damages of at least _____ because without a recreation center each lot was worth only

_____.

Element 1. Prior to selling lots 70 and 71 to the Phillipses, Landview represented that a recreation center would be built in Campion Hills within 18 months.

Phillipses' Existing Evidence	Landview's Rebuttal
1. Prior to the Phillipses' purchase a sketch of the recreation center was hanging in Landview's sales office where Lotz worked (Depo of Liv Urwurst p. ——) (Gen: Land salespeople who work in a sales office in which a picture of a recreation center is hanging usually tell prospective customers that the center will be built. Land salespeople who tell prospective customers that a recreation	

Phillipses' Existing Evidence	Landview's Rebuttal
center will be built sometimes state that it will be built within an ascertainable time period. Land salespeople who state that a recreation center will be built within an ascertainable time period sometimes state that it will be built within 18 months.)	

B. Mason's Outline of Landview's Existing Affirmative Evidence

(Theory: No Intentional Misrepresentation)

Element 1.   Landview did not represent that a recreation center would be built within 18 months.

Landview's Existing Evidence	Phillipses' Rebuttal
1. Mr. Phillips stated in October that he hoped the recreation center would someday be built. (Depo of Urwurst, p. ——) (Gen: People who have purchased property in a development and later state they hope a recreation center may someday be built there usually have not been told by the developer that it will be built within 18 months.)	

With respect to the format, please consider several points. Under each element is a column for existing affirmative evidence and for rebuttal evidence. If and when one learns rebuttal evidence, one simply inserts it (perhaps accompanied by a supporting generalization) opposite the affirmative evidence which it tends to rebut.

Also, the source of evidence in one's file is listed under each item of evidence. This enables one to locate the source quickly. Moreover, reference to the source makes it unnecessary to include in an outline all of the details surrounding the important fact, such as precisely where and to whom a statement was made, who else was present, and so forth. One may refer back to the file for such details.

Specifically with regard to the generalizations, they might be inserted into outlines beneath the circumstantial evidence to which they apply for several reasons. First, their inclusion ensures that one has thought through just what it is a piece of circumstantial evidence tends to prove. In this respect, one can determine whether a single inference (outline B) or an inferential chain (outline A) is needed to link an item of circumstantial evidence to an element.

Moreover, listing a generalization enables one to remember, as the months and other cases with other factual situations go by, just what one was thinking when one analyzed the evidence's probative value. Additionally, including generalizations for the adversary's affirmative evidence enables one to identify potential rebuttal more readily. Finally, including the generalization will be helpful to a colleague who picks up a file a day or so prior to a deposition or a court appearance, and who has to learn quickly what a case is about.

In setting forth the generalizations, we worded them so that one could consciously consider just how probative the evidence is. By way of example, one generalization was:

> People who have purchased property in a development and later state they hope a recreation center may someday be built there *usually* have not been told by the developer that it will definitely be built.

In place of "usually" one might have inserted "almost always," or "rarely," depending upon one's assessment of how uniformly common experience supports the generalization.

These reasons aside, we would be disingenuous were we to insist that one automatically list generalizations beneath *all* items of circumstantial evidence in one's outlines. The time and space their inclusion might require would often outweigh the benefits. In the final analysis, one's judgment must determine how often generalizations are listed. At least when evidence is critical, or its probative value is somewhat obscure, or one or more colleagues are to work on a file, one may tend to list generalizations.

5. EMOTIONAL EVIDENCE

Throughout, this text approaches litigation primarily as an exercise in rationality. Factfinders separate theories into component elements; they marshal evidence pursuant to each element; and they draw logical inferences from circumstantial evidence according to their perspectives of how the world operates.

If this rational image of litigation is not a distortion, neither is it completely accurate. There is a reason that trials have, but works on mathematical logic have not, been turned into colorful tales and juicy plays, movies and television series: Emotion. No less than pure logic, emotion is a real and vital part of human reasoning.

Trials produce colorful characters like Clarence Darrow; angry exchanges between witnesses and cross-examiners; emotional details which are the stuff of soap operas—greed, love, hate; elated winners and anguished losers. Undoubtedly these factors have been overplayed by dramatists. But none who try cases would deny their existence or their lure.

Evidentiary rules may filter out some emotional evidence. But they cannot eliminate it, for so often the emotion is inextricably bound up with the critical elements.[23] And even if a story is an emotional void, a factfinder may respond emotionally to a witness' background.[24]

People are emotional beings. When they act, they act in part for emotional reasons. And when they judge, they are influenced by emotional factors. These are among the most ancient of truths. It was Aristotle who noted:

> "When they feel friendly to the man who comes before them for judgment, they regard him as having done little wrong, if any; when they feel hostile they take the opposite view.[25]

We do not suggest that one specifically outline emotional evidence in a separate category. Nor need one understand fully how it is that emotions influence a factfinder. For example, does a factfinder find that a fact is true, and then disregard that fact because of feelings of sympathy for the person harmed by the fact? Or does emotion influence which facts a factfinder finds to be true? Or does emotion simply alter the burden of proof? However it works, it probably works on a subliminal level,[26] and perhaps only when the "rational" evidence is closely balanced.[27]

However, as one investigates a case, one typically comes across evidence that has emotional overtones. As just noted, the evidence is that which is likely to engender in the factfinder feelings either of sympathy or hostility. When one comes across such evidence one might at least note it mentally, or perhaps through a small notation on an outline.

One should take special note when emotional evidence begins to fall into a pattern. When one does find a pattern, one perhaps can take advantage of emotion to portray one's entire case. For example, in an automobile accident case one may learn that after a collision, one driver made statements showing lack of concern about his driving and about injuries to the other driver. One may think of portraying the case as one in which, "An innocent victim has suffered injuries at the hands of a cruel, callous driver," and then during investigation consciously pursue emotional evidence demonstrating or

---

23. For example, in criminal cases, the prosecution may need to prove a defendant's intent, and may often show a motive such as greed. In civil cases, emotional factors are inherent in a claim for punitive damages. These are but a few examples. For further discussion of this point, see p. 108 infra and Chapter 9.

24. For a case holding that background data is permissible, see Cushing

v. Jolles, 292 Mass. 72, 197 N.E. 466 (1935).

25. Aristotle, *Rhetoria* Book II.1.

26. H. Kalven and H. Zeisel, *The American Jury* 165, 218, 495 (1966).

27. For more discussion of this proposition, see the discussion in Chapter 9 regarding explanatory hypotheses.

accounting for the driver's callous actions. The emotional evidence may be stressed during opening statement, witness testimony, and closing argument. By so doing, one tries to build an overall theme to persuade the factfinder to respond emotionally as well as rationally.

For investigative purposes, emotional evidence may be seen as falling into two broad categories: transactional facts and personal facts. The "transactional" category suggests areas for exploration when inquiring about what occurred. The "personal" category suggests areas for exploration when investigating the people involved. In each category, one should be alert for evidence indicating either sympathy or hostility.

In the transactional category, one considers the historical facts. From the point of view of hostility, did one party's conduct show a high degree of disregard for others,[28] a high degree of greed, or socially inappropriate conduct collateral to the principal activity? Did one party's conduct cause substantial injury to others? [29] From the point of view of sympathy, transactional facts may consist of acting for a noble purpose, suffering great injury,[30] or aiding others who are injured.

The personal category consists of evidence relating to the actors, and may have nothing to do with the historical facts. This category typically includes observable characteristics such as physical attributes and dress; personality; attitude, in particular attitudes toward the proceedings and the case; and personal background, including economic status, educational status, job status, family status, residence, and previous similar involvements.

In any given case, however, it is difficult to categorize generally the emotional response that transactional or personal facts may generate in a factfinder. For example, one factfinder may respect the testimony of a wealthy individual, while another is hostile toward that testimony. One factfinder may sympathize with a person confined to a wheelchair, while another may hostilely view the wheelchair as a ploy. Thus, when assessing the likelihood that sympathy or hostility will arise from given evidence, one must always keep in mind the variable effect of any such fact and appraise a case in light

28. In criminal cases disregard of the victim can result in conviction for a greater crime even though the treatment of the victim is not an element of the offense. See H. Kalven and H. Zeisel, note 26 supra, at 399–400. In personal injury cases, gross negligence can increase an award of damages even when the law does not provide punitive damages for gross negligence.

29. The jury might, for example, find the defendant guilty of a higher homicide offense if prior to the killing, the defendant and victim engaged in a drunken perverted orgy. H. Kalven and H. Zeisel, note 26 supra, at 381–382.

30. For example, juries are sometimes lenient to drunken drivers if they receive severe injuries in the accident. See H. Kalven and H. Zeisel, note 26 supra, at 301, 399–400.

of the specifics of the case, current community standards, and the personality and background of the potential factfinder.

To this point, our assumption has been that emotional evidence will invariably enter the fray. Is this assumption correct? Probably so. Personal characteristics seem almost impossible to eliminate. Even in criminal cases in which a defendant does not take the stand, much will be learned from simply observing the defendant in the courtroom. For instance, the defendant's demeanor at the counsel table may seem to reveal the defendant's attitude toward what has occurred.[31] Moreover, when a party desires to introduce sympathetic evidence, the introduction can often easily be accomplished under the rubric of "the witness' background" or "the credibility of the witness." [32]

Transactional emotional facts also frequently reach a factfinder. Typically, transactional evidence closely adheres to or constitutes an inherent part of the historical facts. Consider the following testimony in an automobile accident case.

Q: After Ms. Jones got out of her car, what happened?

A: She went over to the other car.

Q: What did she do then?

A: She said to the other driver something like, "Hey you 'fuckin' asshole,' where did you come from?"

Q: What was her tone of voice?

A: She was yelling.

Q: Where was the other driver when Ms. Jones called her a "fuckin' asshole"?

A: She was still inside her car.

Q: What did the other driver say?

A: She didn't say much except for saying, "I'm hurt;" her face was all bloody.[33]

Creative lawyering will almost always find a legal window through which to insert emotional evidence.

However, at least some mitigation of the effects of emotional evidence may be possible. Careful voir dire, or effective judge shop-

---

31. H. Kalven and H. Zeisel, note 26 supra, at 382.

32. See Cushing v. Jolles, 292 Mass. 72, 197 N.E. 466 (1935). As Kalven and Zeisel note, it is perhaps heroic to attempt to draw distinctions between characteristics which affect credibility and those which arouse sympathy and hostility. H. Kalven and H. Zeisel, note 26 supra, at 193–194, 381–383.

33. Perhaps, the jury reacts to both the callousness of the defendant and the helplessness of the victim. "The defendant has conspicuously failed to come to the aid of the victim, and it is this gross act of neglect which arouses the jury." In a sense, the defendant is convicted for not having been a Good Samaritan. H. Kalven and H. Zeisel, note 26 supra, at 399.

ping, may produce a factfinder whose emotional reactions are likely to be favorable. Additionally, making the factfinder conscious of the potential influence may immunize the factfinder against being swayed. Many lawyers believe, perhaps correctly so, that if the potential distorting influence of emotional evidence can be brought to the attention of the factfinder, the factfinder will tend to disregard it.[34]

Also, often there is the possibility of introducing antidotes. For example, if hostility may arise because of a criminal defendant's excessive mistreatment of the victim, perhaps some countervailing sympathy can be introduced by shedding light on the defendant's pathetic family situation.[35]

Undoubtedly, other methods of counteracting emotional evidence exist. However, this is a tactical subject more properly considered in a work on trial advocacy. For now, remember that this evidence often will reach a factfinder, and one's investigation therefore must include an effort to learn of its existence.

Finally, note that emotional evidence is not the only factor which may cause a factfinder to take less than an objective view of evidence. Other phenomena—such as the factfinder's sentiment toward the law, the factfinder's concern about the popularity of its decision, and the factfinder's concern over the societal implications of its decision—can also distort its view of the "objective" evidence.

6. EXISTING AFFIRMATIVE EVIDENCE OUTLINE EXERCISE

A. The substantive structure of the Phillipses' theory that Landview made fraudulent misrepresentations concerning the recreation center is on p. 103. Copy this structure, one element per page. Then, prepare a substantive structure, from Darrow's perspective, for Landview's theory that no misrepresentations were made. Use a separate page for each element.

B. Based on the deposition of Liv Urwurst, insert into each of these outlines at least three items of circumstantial evidence, including for each item of evidence the most persuasive generalization(s) that appear to link the evidence to the element.

C. List any emotional evidence contained in the Urwurst deposition. Does such evidence belong someplace in an outline? If so, where?

D. For go-getters, update the story outline in Chapter 4 based on the information learned in the Urwurst deposition.

---

34. See I. Goldstein, *Trial Techniques* 167–168 (1935); Ginger, Ed. *Minimizing Racism in Jury Trials* 199–204 (1969).

35. H. Kalven and H. Zeisel, note 26 supra, at 205.

Chapter 7

ANALYSIS OF REBUTTAL EVIDENCE

1. INTRODUCTION

In some respects, a trial resembles the balancing of a scale of justice. Each party's evidence is figuratively placed on opposite sides of the scale, and the evidence that is the heaviest—that is, the most probative—prevails (assuming it outweighs the adversary's evidence by a margin wide enough to satisfy the party's burden of proof). If this analogy is carried a step further, one sees that the scales can be tipped not only by adding evidence to one's own case, but also by subtracting evidence from that of the adversary. Hence, one's analysis of evidence is not complete without a review of evidence which detracts from affirmative evidence. As you recall, our term for evidence which detracts from affirmative evidence is "rebuttal."

An example may illustrate the function of rebuttal evidence. Assume that Crashem and Avoidum are involved in a lawsuit growing out of an intersection collision; each claims that the traffic light in his direction was green, and that the other driver's carelessness caused the accident. Assume further that Crashem produces a witness, Drunkum, who states that she saw the collision, and that Crashem's car entered the intersection on the green light. Evidence by a witness for Avoidum, Sawum, that Drunkum was intoxicated at the time she saw the accident would be rebuttal evidence for Avoidum. It would not be affirmative evidence for Avoidum: evidence that Crashem's witness, Drunkum, was intoxicated does not tend to prove that the light for Avoidum was green. But it does detract from Crashem's affirmative evidence, and is classic rebuttal.

At first blush one may be inclined to the view that rebuttal evidence defies analysis. After all, there are undoubtedly innumerable specific items of evidence which can be used to rebut affirmative evidence. For example, Drunkum's testimony about the color of the light might also have been rebutted by evidence that Drunkum is a close friend of Crashem; that Drunkum needs glasses but was not wearing them; that Drunkum was 200 feet away from the intersection; that Drunkum is colorblind; that there is no traffic light on the specific corner where Drunkum allegedly saw the light; or by a variety of other pieces of evidence.

Given the potential array of rebuttal evidence, it is perhaps surprising then that all rebuttal evidence actually falls into one of two separate categories. One rebuts either by denying the existence of the adversary's affirmative evidence; or one rebuts by admitting the adversary's affirmative evidence and then offering evidence explaining away its import. In short, to rebut, one either (1) denies, or (2) admits and explains.[1]

Before exploring these categories, consider first why it is important during investigation to have these two separate categories of rebuttal in mind.

2.　CATEGORIES OF REBUTTAL AS AN AID TO INVESTIGATION

The primary reason we identify the two categories of rebuttal ("denial" and "explanation") is a simple and a practical one—they are an aid to effective and efficient investigation. When one analyzes an *adversary's affirmative* evidence, understanding that there are two potential categories of rebuttal alerts one to the opportunity to counter that evidence in two different ways. And depending on which category an *adversary's rebuttal* of one's affirmative evidence falls into, one may look to entirely different evidence and sources of information to overcome that rebuttal.

a.　*Rebuttal to Adversary's Affirmative Evidence*

The Crashem-Avoidum collision case may be used to illustrate how the categories create two opportunities to rebut an adversary's affirmative evidence. Assume that plaintiff Crashem, attempting to prove that Avoidum was driving carelessly, unearths witness Heardem. Heardem states that just before Avoidum left the office in his car on the journey that ended with the collision, Avoidum had gotten a telephone call in which Avoidum was ordered to be across town

---

1. Wigmore suggested that there are three categories of rebuttal evidence: deny; admit and explain; and advance a rival fact. Wigmore's third category is, in effect, our category of affirmative evidence. For example, Wigmore believed that if a defense to a criminal charge was an alibi, that defense was rebuttal by advancement of a rival fact. We prefer to think of this defense not as rebuttal, but as affirmative evidence by the defendant. As we pointed out in Chapter 2, we believe our organization is more descriptive of what happens at trial. Logically, however, there seems to be no real differences between Wigmore's categories and our own. See J. Wigmore, *The Science of Judicial Proof* 29–30 (3rd Ed.1937).

for an important meeting in fifteen minutes. From this evidence, one might infer that Avoidum was thinking about the impending meeting and therefore not paying attention to the road and in addition, speeding in order to be on time. Thus, Heardem's story about the phone call provides affirmative evidence for Crashem.

Rebuttal by way of denial would consist of evidence that no such phone call was made, or that Avoidum did not receive the call. Rebuttal by way of "admit and explain" would not challenge the evidence that a phone call was made and received. Rather, it would attack the inferences that Avoidum was in deep thought and in a hurry, perhaps by offering evidence that the meeting was not an important one. In short, Avoidum's counsel will not have to instruct Avoidum on the proper spelling of Crashem's name on a check if Avoidum says, "Yes, I got that call."

One might be tempted to respond that these categories are analytically interesting, but of little practical significance, with a response such as:

> Why bother to categorize rebuttal? I've got a witness sitting there—I'll just ask for the witness' response to the adversary's evidence. For example, if I were Avoidum's attorney in this case, I would just ask Avoidum if he has any response to evidence that he got a phone call ordering him to an important meeting in 15 minutes. Anyway, if I were to do more, I might be putting evidence in a witness' mouth, and that seems unethical and unsanitary.

Such a response may in fact be adequate in some cases, and with some informants. The question, "How do you respond to that?" may result in a story providing evidence which constitutes a denial or admission and explanation. Or, it may produce a response which leaves one satisfied that a witness is unable to supply rebuttal. But at least as often as this type of question provides a definitive response from a witness, it produces responses such as the following by Avoidum:

(a) Silence.

(b) "I don't know."

(c) "It all happened so long ago; I can't remember."

(d) "Whose side are you on anyway?"

(e) "I have a rare allergy to speeds in excess of 35 m.p.h." (an explanation which is implausible).

(f) "I can get at least a half a dozen people who'll tell you I never exceed the speed limit." (an explanation which in counsel's opinion may not be acceptable to the factfinder).

Such responses may indicate that Avoidum cannot produce rebuttal evidence. But they may also be attributed to the fact that a question such as "How do you respond to that?" does little to stimulate recall.

After all, clients and witnesses normally are not legally trained. Without specific prodding, they may be unable to link up evidence known to them with evidence it tends to rebut. Considering both categories of rebuttal enhances one's ability to identify evidentiary possibilities to prod a witness' memory.

In the above example, perhaps Avoidum's only fault was inability to think of everything that might be helpful. But sometimes people are worse off than unhelpful—they are deceased. If in this case one were representing Avoidum's estate, one could not merely turn to Avoidum for potential rebuttal evidence (unless one practices in the Twilight Zone.) Instead, one would have to probe for information from witnesses on the periphery of the critical events. Because such witnesses are especially unlikely to be able to connect specific items of rebuttal evidence with the issues, one often needs to identify potential rebuttal before a witness is able to recall it.

Finally, note that the dual categories are helpful in many cases in which witnesses are both helpful and alive. In many disputes, an issue is whether an organization did or did not engage in certain activity. A major accomplishment of large, bureaucratic structures is to ensure that no one individual is responsible for all aspects of anything. Information about bureaucratic activities is often spread among a number of people. Just as in the situation in which the person who knows most of the story is deceased, there is not "a" person to whom one can turn and ask, "How can we rebut this piece of evidence?" Since no one knows the entire story, one will usually have to ask specific, probing questions to attempt to fit the bureaucratic response together.

In the following conversation between Avoidum and his attorney, Defendum, note how Defendum uses the dual rebuttal categories to identify potential rebuttal:

Defendum: Avoidum, as I told you last week, Crashem has a witness who will testify that just before you left your office, you got a phone call to be at an important meeting across town in 15 minutes. Crashem's attorney, Suem, told me that that evidence supports an inference that you were probably in a hurry and therefore were speeding at the time of the collision. Any ideas on how we should respond to that evidence?

Avoidum: As you know, I feel strongly that I wasn't speeding. Darned if I can remember anything about a phone call, though. It's been three "bleeping" years.

Defendum: Well, do you keep records of all calls you make and receive?

Avoidum: No, isn't that a bit compulsive?

Defendum: What? I'm sorry, I was just recording the fact that someone just touched my Porsche. OK, so you really can't recall anything about a phone call?

Avoidum: No, not right off.

Defendum: The day of the accident you were in your office, I believe you told me. Were you having any trouble with your telephones that day?

Avoidum: I don't think so.

Defendum: Is it possible that someone else in your office got the call and only told you about the meeting, but said nothing about the 15 minutes?

Avoidum: I guess you could check with Chris, my secretary, but I don't remember that.

Defendum: OK, we may not be able to deny that you received the phone call, but according to this book on fact investigation I just read, there's another possibility. Do you have a car phone?

Avoidum: Of course.

Defendum: Is it possible you got a second call on the car phone, cancelling the meeting, delaying it, anything like that?

Avoidum: Again, I don't remember that.

Defendum: Well, think back, is it possible you were driving slowly despite the meeting, in order to have time to collect your thoughts?

Avoidum: That's possible. I'll see if I can find any notes relating to the meeting—maybe those will help.

Defendum: Another thing. Is there anything about the nature of that meeting which would have made it unimportant for you to be there at the beginning?

Avoidum: Well, I'm not sure. I'd have to check my notes to see what the meeting was about.

Defendum: As we've been talking, have you thought of anything else in connection with that telephone call?

Avoidum: No, I haven't.

Defendum: One last point. Wait a minute . . . someone else just touched my Porsche. I must record that . . .

With regard to the categories of "deny" and "admit and explain," can you think of other specific questions Defendum could have asked?

The suggested categories are not magic keys which unlock the doors to all rebuttal evidence. One's common sense, legal knowledge, experience and imagination are still needed to translate each category into specific questions. However, recognizing that rebuttal consists of both categories makes it more likely that one will identify potential rebuttal.

Still less are the categories a guarantee that the potential evidence one identifies will become admissible evidence. In the example above, Defendum uncovered a couple of rebuttal possibilities, but no more than that. The categories guarantee not success, but the exercise of professional responsibilities on behalf of a client.

Finally, what response to the remark that the suggestion of possible evidence, albeit in the form of questions, raises ethical concerns?

In part, an affirmation: ethical problems do arise when informational suggestions originate with an attorney rather than with a witness. Certainly it is unethical for one to suggest certain answers. But just as certainly, one cannot abandon a topic as soon as a witness is unable to remember what occurred. Surely competence requires some probing of memory. In the gulf between these extremes is a variety of permitted and forbidden behavior. We examine that gulf in more detail in Chapter 15. Here, suffice it to say that ethical rules often permit, and principles of professional responsibility demand, that one probe a witness' memory by inquiring whether specific items of helpful evidence exist.

b. Adversary's Rebuttal to Client's Affirmative Evidence

Just as an investigation focuses on rebuttal to an adversary's affirmative evidence, so too must it focus on learning how the adversary might rebut one's own affirmative evidence. The latter effort is not mere nosiness, but rather a necessary part of investigation. The investigation one pursues in an effort to overcome an adversary's rebuttal will vary, depending upon whether an adversary's rebuttal constitutes a denial, or an explanation.

If an adversary admits one's affirmative evidence, and offers other evidence to explain it away, one need not worry about corroborating the affirmative evidence. Instead, one can concentrate investigation on evidence and witnesses that might rebut the explanation. On the other hand, if an adversary's rebuttal constitutes a denial, then one must indeed consider corroboration. To do so, one may pursue one or both of two investigatory options. One might seek evidence which rebuts the denial evidence. In addition one might seek evidence which corroborates one's own affirmative evidence. In either event, the evidence one identifies when an adversary rebuts by denial is very different from that one turns to when facing an explanation.

These principles may be illustrated in the now familiar context of Crashem v. Avoidum. Assume now that one represents Crashem, and that one has triumphantly produced Heardem, who has described the "meeting in fifteen minutes" phone call. Since Heardem's information is important, one may predict that Avoidum's attorney will seek in some way to rebut it. If one learns what that rebuttal is, one may then attempt to overcome Avoidum's rebuttal.

Assume first that Avoidum's rebuttal is a denial. "Counsel, I've talked to my client, Avoidum, and his office staff. It turns out it was Avoidum's secretary, Chris, who got the phone call. Avoidum never got that call, and totally denies what Heardem says." On Crashem's behalf, an option one now has is to search for evidence that corroborates Heardem's story. One may identify evidence such as the following:

(1) Another witness who heard Avoidum's telephone conversation.

(2) Avoidum made previous statements admitting he received the telephone call.

(3) Avoidum left the office immediately after the call was made.

Since Avoidum's rebuttal is a denial, one has a second investigatory option. One may also seek to rebut the denial evidence itself. Thus, one may identify evidence which might rebut Chris' evidence. Perhaps Chris was out of the office at the time of the phone call; biased in favor of Avoidum; or in the habit of immediately relaying information concerning all telephone calls to Avoidum.

Note that when an adversary rebuts by denial, one may pursue both of the above options: one may corroborate one's affirmative evidence, and also rebut the adversary's rebuttal. In the situation above, one might identify items of evidence which corroborate Heardem's testimony, and other items which rebut Chris' story. However, whatever one's response, the focus of investigation is the telephone call itself. The adversary has denied that the phone call was made or received, and to overcome that denial one's attention must be centered on that call.

By contrast, evidence bolstering Heardem's story is totally irrelevant if Avoidum's rebuttal is of the "admit and explain" variety. Then, the issue becomes not the phone call, but the explanation. Thus, whether Avoidum's rebuttal to Heardem's story is that he received a second call on a car phone cancelling or delaying the meeting; that he drove slowly in order to collect his thoughts; or that it was unimportant for him to be there at the beginning of the meeting, *none of these responses requires evidence which corroborates Heardem or rebuts Chris.* Instead, one attempts to identify evidence which might rebut Avoidum's explanation. The evidence one identifies depends, of course, entirely on the explanation. However, the important point to remember is that the evidence one attempts to identify is vastly different, depending on whether an adversary's rebuttal consists of denial or of an explanation.

3. REBUTTAL BY EXPLANATION

Now that the usefulness of categorizing rebuttal evidence has been explored, let us expand a bit more on what is meant by each category.

Rebuttal by way of "admit and explain" is a method of overcoming an adversary's evidence without directly contesting it. At trial it is a powerful weapon, because it permits a factfinder to resolve a case in one's favor without having to disbelieve the adversary's evidence.[2] When one "admits and explains," one in effect tells the factfinder, "We do not question the veracity of the particular item of evidence offered by our opponent. But in reality, our opponent's evidence is incomplete. With our evidence also before you, you will see that the adversary's evidence lacks probative value."

An example illustrates how rebuttal by "admit and explain" contests an adversary's evidence without directly confronting it. Assume that the unfortunate Avoidum, already knee deep in the litigation started by Crashem, is also charged criminally with drunk driving. To support its charge, the prosecution produces witness Smeldum, who states that she saw Avoidum in a bar about an hour before the accident where Avoidum drank three boilermakers. To deny this evidence, Avoidum's counsel would have to "take on" Smeldum directly. But if Avoidum's counsel admits and explains, no direct contest is necessary.

Assume that Avoidum offers evidence from his doctor, Dr. Stickum, that Avoidum is on special medication, the effect of which is to render Avoidum impervious to the effects of alcohol. This evidence rebuts Smeldum's testimony about the boilermakers without directly controverting it. Avoidum does not in any way dispute Smeldum's testimony, or Smeldum's personal credibility. Instead, Avoidum makes an end run around Smeldum's evidence, offering an explanation which eliminates its probative value.

It is the inferential nature of circumstantial evidence which permits one to rebut evidence without directly controverting it. Remember, circumstantial evidence proves an element only through the aid of an underlying premise. In the case of Smeldum's testimony, the premise the prosecutor might draw is, "People who drink three boilermakers are usually (almost always?) under the influence of alcohol one hour later." It is the inference which lends probative value to Smeldum's testimony. When one admits and explains, one attacks only the inference and leaves untouched the evidence on which the premise was based.

In the above example, the prosecutor's premise was based on common knowledge of how alcohol affects people. The evidence of Dr. Stickum, however, demonstrates that Avoidum has a unique personal characteristic. That unique characteristic takes Avoidum outside the

2. Factfinders, be they judges or jurors, are loathe to find that one side has lied, or even that one side has grossly distorted evidence. Instead, factfinders tend to look for a "neutral" story which can bring the otherwise conflicting stories into harmony. See R. Keeton, *Trial Tactics and Methods* § 7.19 (2d Ed.1973), observing that, ". . . jurors are inclined to decide cases on a basis that does not imply a finding of misconduct, if by doing so they can reach (or think they can reach) the result they desire."

ambit of the prosecutor's broad generalization, and thereby negates the inference which the factfinder might otherwise draw from Smeldum's evidence. The evidence is no longer that Avoidum had three boilermakers. Rather, the evidence is that Avoidum, who was taking the magic medicine, had three boilermakers. Accordingly, in the absence of experience that people with this combination are usually under the influence, an inference that Avoidum was under the influence will not be possible.[3]

As is true with many aspects of litigation, the "admit and explain" tactic is not unique to legal factfinding. In fact, it is a tactic in which pre-adolescents excel. Imagine a small playground filled with young children. One child is crying, and another is scurrying towards a teacher, sporting a somewhat worried look. Even before the teacher says anything, the child will typically offer an explanation. "He hit me first." "She pushed me into her." "There was a sudden, though temporary, localized shift in the earth's gravitational field." Because the "admit and explain" device is so familiar to us, it is effective in litigation.

Explanation is essentially a rebuttal tactic, as it counters inferences which might otherwise be drawn from circumstantial evidence. Often, however, an explanation constitutes both affirmative and rebuttal evidence. In the example in which Avoidum is charged with drunk driving, Avoidum's story might be that he was not under the influence of alcohol. If so, Dr. Stickum's evidence rebuts that of Smeldum, and it also lends affirmative support to Avoidum's story that he was not drunk.

That an explanation may constitute both affirmative and rebuttal evidence serves to emphasize the point that the categories in and of themselves have little intrinsic value. The value of the categories is to alert one to various investigatory possibilities so one may pursue each consciously.

4. REBUTTAL BY DENIAL

Consider now rebuttal by denial. Denial is not as subtle or refined as explanation, for one can not take the position that the adversary witness, well-intentioned and honest though she or he be, is simply incompletely informed. Instead, denial pits one item of evidence directly against another: the war is on!

Denial is a war that can be fought on two fronts. One may deny by producing evidence which *contradicts the evidence of* an adverse

3. Of course, the factfinder is free to disbelieve Dr. Stickum's testimony. Our point is simply that the doctor's testimony, if believed, prevents the factfinder from drawing any adverse inference from Smeldum's testimony, even though it in no way disbelieves that testimony.

witness or by producing evidence that *attacks the credibility* of an adverse witness. As for the first front, denial by contradicting the evidence of an adversary witness, please return to the testimony of Smeldum that Smeldum saw Avoidum drink three boilermakers. Each of the following constitutes rebuttal by contradictory evidence:

(1) Avoidum's testimony that the glasses were filled with apple juice.

(2) The story of Chris, Avoidum's secretary, that Avoidum was in the office all day up until the time he left for the meeting.

(3) The bartender's story that since she flunked "Boilermaker" in bartending school, she does not serve them.

The other denial front consists of an attack on the *source* of the adverse evidence: an attack on the adverse witness' credibility. Credibility is explored in detail in Chapter 8. However, the term is a familiar one, and each of the following is an illustration of denial by attack on credibility of the source:

(1) Evidence by the bartender that at the time Smeldum and Avoidum were together in the bar, Smeldum was stewed to the gills.

(2) Evidence from Chris that one year before the collision, Avoidum fired Smeldum, and as Smeldum left the office for the last time, she muttered darkly to Avoidum, "I will pay you back if it's the last thing I do." (This attack works well on factfinders who enjoy melodrama.)

Whether the rebuttal by denial war is waged on one or both fronts, the result is that the factfinder is asked to find that an adversary's affirmative evidence is not true. When one produces evidence that contradicts the evidence of an adverse witness, one directly denies the existence of that adverse evidence. When one produces evidence which attacks the credibility of the source of the evidence, the existence of the adverse facts is indirectly denied. The reasoning process the factfinder is asked to accept is that because a witness is not credible, the information supplied by the witness is unworthy of belief.

The distinction between these two forms of denial carries over into the affirmative evidence-rebuttal evidence dichotomy. Denial by attack on credibility is almost by definition strictly rebuttal evidence. Evidence that an adverse witness is for some reason not credible rebuts the testimony of that witness, but typically it does not add to one's affirmative story. Review again the first potential attack on Smeldum's credibility listed above—that Smeldum was herself drunk. That evidence is not part of Avoidum's affirmative story that he was as sober as a judge . . . , well, as authors . . . well, that he was sober.

On the other hand, denial by direct attack on adverse evidence may sometimes constitute both affirmative and rebuttal evidence. In the earlier examples of rebuttal by denial of evidence, numbers one and two may most accurately be considered both affirmative and rebuttal evidence. Avoidum's evidence that he was drinking apple juice and Chris' evidence that Avoidum never left the office until leaving for the meeting rebut Smeldum and also provide affirmative evidence that Avoidum was not drunk. However, evidence that the bartender does not know how to make a boilermaker does not prove affirmatively that Avoidum was not drunk. Just as was the case with explanation, however, remember that categorical purity is not an end in itself. The categories are an investigative tool for identifying and pursuing evidence.

5. REBUTTAL BY ARGUMENT

To the extent that investigation does not uncover evidence which rebuts an item of an adversary's affirmative evidence, must that item go unrebutted? Perhaps surprisingly, the answer is often, "No." One may sometimes rebut exclusively through closing argument, though care must be taken when phrasing the argument.

a. *Adopting a Different Premise*

One form of rebuttal by argument is particularly interesting, since it is not available during the evidentiary phase of trial. Moreover, it typically presents few legal difficulties. During argument, one may simply attach a favorable premise to an item of an adversary's evidence, and based on that premise urge a conclusion on a factfinder which is helpful to one's client. Because the argument depends upon drawing inferences, it is of course available only to rebut an item of circumstantial evidence.

A simple example demonstrates this form of rebuttal by argument. Assume evidence that a defense witness is the defendant's father. Based on this evidence, plaintiff may argue that the father's testimony should be discredited, because of the father's bias. In making this argument, the plaintiff's premise is something like, "Parents often slant information in favor of their children." But the defense can attempt to rebut this inference merely by attaching a different premise to the evidence of fatherhood: "Parents do not usually commit perjury, even to help their children." Which premise the factfinder accepts, of course, will depend on its view of which is more consistent with common experience and other evidence in the case. However, the point is simply that because one can adopt a different premise to draw a different inference, one can rebut by argument alone. The argument need not be supported by evidence of the father's lack of bias.

b. Arguing the Premise's Weakness

The other forms of rebuttal by argument use the concepts of "denial" or "admit and explain." In each form of rebuttal argument, one suggests to a factfinder factual possibilities that lessen the probative force of an item of the adversary's affirmative evidence. One does so because the very nature of circumstantial evidence practically invites one to suggest such factual possibilities. Remember, inferences are based on generalizations which are by definition less than completely accurate. When one suggests factual possibilities that may weaken the inference, one does no more than suggest the possible limitations of those generalizations. On the other hand, one must be careful not to suggest that these factual possibilities are actually supported by evidence in the record. Such a suggestion would amount to improper argument based on "facts outside the record." [4] Since potential consequences for arguing "facts outside the record" include apoplexy by opposing counsel, and a declaration of a mistrial by the court, the subtle distinction between proper and improper suggestions is worthy of consideration.

Consider a case in which a witness purports to identify one's client as the person who was seen at a glance running away from the scene of a murder at high speed. The witness estimates her distance from the scene as 50 feet. As defense counsel, one is after the award for "Best Rebuttal Arguer of the Year," and so introduces no evidence to rebut the witness' testimony. What can one properly argue?

First, one can simply draw a contrary inference. One might argue that an identification based on a short glimpse at a distance of 50 feet is not reliable.

Second, one may with some care use a "denial" or "admit and explain" approach, as follows:

(i) Denial Through Attack on Credibility

"What do we really know about the witness—her ability to perceive, her memory, her condition at that time? Is she a reliable source of information? Might she have any biases?"

This type of argument attempts to deny by raising questions about the credibility of the witness. The argument does not assert that there is evidence that the witness is unreliable. By carefully limiting the argument to possibilities that might make the witness

---

4. See A. Levin and R. Levy, "Persuading the Jury With Facts Not in Evidence: The Fiction-Science Spectrum," 105 U.Pa.L.Rev. 139, 173 (1965); R. Keeton, note 2, supra, at 274.

less than reliable, one argues that the evidence at hand does not conclusively establish credibility.

(ii) Explanation

"What do we really know about why my client was in the area of the crime? Perhaps he ran because he was afraid of becoming the next victim, or because he was jogging."

This argument as well attempts to show that the evidence is of limited probative value. It does so by pointing out that other explanations, consistent with innocence, might account for the defendant's presence at the scene.

(iii) Denial by Contradictory Evidence

Even under the most malleable concept of proper argument, this form of denial is available during argument only if supported by facts in the record. In the context of the same example, consider this potential denial argument:

"Now, the witness has stated that she observed my client from a distance of 50 feet. But can we really be sure my client was there? Maybe he was in Church, or maybe he was on a safari at the time."

This argument does more than simply cast doubt on the probative force of the adversary's evidence. It suggests new and different facts which have no evidentiary basis whatsoever. It is one thing to point out the limited probative worth of an adversary's evidence. But it is quite another to suggest altogether new facts. This last form of rebuttal argument, even though it was phrased in the language of possibilities, is generally regarded as improper.

Thus, in two out of the three rebuttal categories, one may suggest possible reasons that cast doubt on the adversary's evidence, as long as one does not portray those possibilities as existing evidence. Beware, however, that the line between proper and improper suggestion is a thin one, and it may be drawn at different places by different judges at different times. Or even by the same judge at different places at different times, perhaps during the same trial.

c. Weakness of Rebuttal by Argument

Finally, beware too that rebuttal by argument (other than that which adopts a different premise) has one glaring weakness: one's adversary can emphasize that one's suggestions are entirely devoid of evidentiary support. So be it. One prefers to have uncovered rebuttal evidence during investigation. But if one has not done so, rebuttal through argument is at least possible.

One might legitimately wonder how rebuttal by argument relates to investigation. After all, this form of rebuttal is produced by a lack of evidence. Consider, however, whether thinking about rebuttal arguments might be useful when analyzing affirmative evidence and identifying potential rebuttal. For example, when one thought of the rebuttal argument suggesting possible explanations for the defendant's presence in the area of a crime, one identified potential items of rebuttal evidence. Hence, in part because the proper boundaries of rebuttal by argument are often tenuous, we describe it primarily for its utility as a method of identifying potential rebuttal evidence.

6. DIAGRAM SUMMARY

It may be useful to summarize the foregoing principles in a simple diagram:

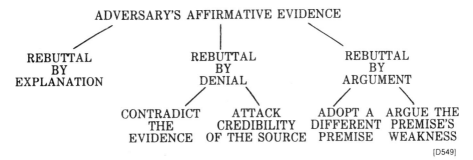

[D549]

7. LEARNING AN ADVERSARY'S REBUTTAL: A MANDATE FOR DISCLOSURE OF EVIDENCE?

Formal discovery methods were established in part to overcome attorneys' unwillingness to disclose information voluntarily to an adversary.[5] Nonetheless, many attorneys guard information they have gathered through investigation with the same suspicious eyes with which they protected their favorite toys when they were three years old. They keep the information to themselves for as long as possible. Indeed, given the culture of the adversary system, it is not surprising that some attorneys view the keeping of information from an adversary, despite the adversary's resort to formal discovery, as an important pretrial goal.[6]

5. W. Brazil, "The Adversary Character of Civil Discovery: A Critique and Proposals for Change," 31 Vanderbilt L.Rev. 1295, (Nov. 1978); D. Shapiro, "Some Problems of Discovery in an Adversary System," 63 Minnesota L.Rev. 1055 (July 1979); A. Holtzoff, "The Elimination of Surprise in Federal Practice," 7 Vanderbilt L.Rev. 576 (June 1954); Greyhound Corp. v. Superior Court, 56 Cal.2d 355, 15 Cal.Rptr. 90, 364 P.2d 266 (1961).

6. W. Brazil, supra; D. Shapiro, supra; W. Simon, "The Ideology of Advocacy: Procedural Justice and Professional Ethics," Vol. 1978, Wisconsin L.Rev. 29 (1978).

Ironically, in some instances secreting information from an adversary may be the legal equivalent of cutting off one's nose to spite one's face. Remember, one purpose of investigation is to learn the rebuttal evidence with which an opponent might counter one's affirmative evidence. Depending on whether that rebuttal consists of denial or explanation, one looks to different evidence to overcome the adversary's rebuttal. Yet, unless one intentionally discloses items of one's affirmative evidence to an opponent, one might not be able to learn how the opponent intends to rebut such evidence! Concealment, then, may have a price: the inability to prepare a response to that rebuttal. Thus, one who continues one's behavior as a three-year-old during case investigation may, in reality, frustrate a primary investigative goal.

When one is bent both on concealment of affirmative evidence and discovery of an adversary's rebuttal, the following type of pretrial conversation may result:

Lawyer 1: By the way, I'm interested in any rebuttal evidence you might have.

Lawyer B: Rebuttal to what?

Lawyer 1: Well, that doesn't matter. Just anything that might be rebuttal.

Lawyer B: I can't tell you that, unless I know what evidence you want me to rebut.

Lawyer 1: Well, then just tell me everything you know about the case.

Lawyer B: I'm sorry. I just can't respond to such a broad request for information.

And so forth. At some point, Lawyer 1 is going to have to disclose affirmative evidence, or Lawyer 1 probably will not learn B's rebuttal, if any.

An example illustrates the point further. One represents Ted Deebare, who is charged with first degree murder. Through diligent investigation, one locates a witness, Winnie Derpu, whose story is that one-half hour before the commission of the crime, Deebare was in a bar and got very drunk. Assume that Deebare's drunkenness under applicable substantive law would establish a defense that Deebare did not have the requisite mental intent to be guilty of first degree murder. Obviously, one cannot fully counsel Deebare unless one evaluates the probative worth of Derpu's testimony. Whether Deebare is likely to be convicted of first-degree murder, or perhaps only manslaughter, may very well depend on whether Derpu's evidence is believed. And to evaluate Derpu's evidence, one must ideally take into account any evidence the prosecution might have to rebut that evidence.

In this situation, probably the prosecution has no formal method of compelling one to disclose Derpu's evidence. And, one's instinct may be to conceal Derpu's evidence during any informal discussions with the prosecutor. But—is that instinct the product of sound tactical thought, or is it a remnant of behavior as a three-year-old?

First, recognize that unless one reveals Derpu and his evidence to the prosecutor, one will probably not learn what rebuttal the prosecutor might have. The plea of "Not Guilty" does not inform the prosecutor even that Deebare will offer affirmative evidence. The plea of "Diminished Capacity," if such a plea is required in a jurisdiction, does indicate that some affirmative defense evidence will be offered. But unless one tells the prosecutor at least some of the evidence on which the defense of "diminished capacity" is based, one will probably be unable to uncover evidence known to the prosecution that might rebut Derpu's evidence. Test this yourself: Imagine you are informally discussing Deebare's case with the prosecution. Can you think of any way of learning about the prosecution's rebuttal to Derpu's evidence without first revealing some of the evidence on which the diminished capacity defense is based? Aside from a "fishing expedition" request for everything the prosecutor knows, a type of request which is frequently rejected, we cannot think of any. Unless you tell the prosecutor that a witness will testify that Deebare was stewed to the gills shortly before the incident, you will probably not learn the prosecution's rebuttal. Therefore, you should at least consider revealing the information to the prosecutor, and regard it as the price of learning rebuttal.

One may respond to this suggestion by saying, "I am not at all convinced that I should reveal Derpu's evidence. Then the prosecution will have time to gather rebuttal. Better to spring Derpu at trial, when the prosecution will not have time to gather rebuttal evidence."

There is some force to such a response. For that reason, one should not automatically reveal information any more than one should automatically conceal it. However, one should recognize that a tactical choice must be made. The choice to spring Derpu on an unknowing prosecutor at trial is not necessarily the correct one. First, the decision assumes that by the time of trial, the prosecutor will be unable to develop rebuttal. That assumption may dangerously underestimate the prosecutor. The prosecutor may rebut Derpu through cross-examination. Moreover, with the police investigative resources that might be available, the prosecutor may gather rebuttal evidence very quickly. Or, the prosecutor may even be granted a short continuance in order to meet the surprise evidence. Finally,

Derpu's evidence may not even be a surprise. Perhaps the prosecution knew about Derpu all the time, but never said anything. After all, the prosecutor was once three years old too.

In all of these situations, it may be Deebare's attorney who is ill-prepared to meet whatever rebuttal to Derpu's evidence the prosecution offers. Recall that Deebare's response to that rebuttal will probably be very different depending on whether the prosecutor's rebuttal is (1) denial by attack on credibility ("Derpu has been convicted of perjury"); (2) denial by attack on the evidence ("The bar where *Deebare* was allegedly drinking was closed."); or (3) explanation ("Dr. Stickum says that no amount of alcohol will overcome someone's intent.") If Deebare's counsel is therefore at a disadvantage at trial, counsel is at that same disadvantage prior to trial, when decisions may be made as to whether or not Deebare should plead guilty to a reduced murder charge. At the least, if Deebare's attorney never even considered telling the prosecutor about Derpu's evidence, then Deebare certainly got less than thoroughly competent legal assistance.

8.   OUTLINING EXISTING REBUTTAL EVIDENCE

Existing rebuttal evidence is included in a story outline, in an outline of one's existing affirmative evidence, and in an outline of the adversary's existing affirmative evidence.

In a story outline, events in the stories of both parties are listed in chronological order. Therefore, in the story outline there may well be a wide gap between one item of evidence, and another item which rebuts it. For example, if Item A happens at Time 3 in the story, and Item L happens at time 19, physically the two items will be separated by a variety of other events and details. As a result, if Item L tends to rebut Item A (or vice versa), the rebuttal will not be readily apparent from the story outline.

However, the relationship of Items A and L is clarified in the outlines of existing affirmative evidence. In the outline of one's own existing affirmative evidence, one lists the opponent's rebuttal opposite the item of affirmative evidence which it tends to rebut. Similarly, in the outline of the adversary's existing affirmative evidence, one's own rebuttal is listed opposite the affirmative evidence which it tends to rebut.

a.   Additional Data re Phillips v. Landview

Below is additional information in *Phillips v. Landview*. It consists of a summary of a deposition of Paul Lade, Landview's Vice-President; one witness statement; and a report from an investigator employed by defense counsel Darrow.

After providing this information, we list portions of that information which constitute affirmative evidence for Landview in Darrow's outline of Existing Affirmative Evidence for Landview, as well as other portions of the information which rebut that affirmative evidence. You are then asked to identify and list in the outline additional items of rebuttal evidence, based on the same information. As you read through this information, please focus on the Phillipses' theory of relief that Landview fraudulently represented that the two lots bought by the Phillipses were suitable for building without the need for further improvement of the lots.

(i) Lade Deposition Summary—Representations about Suitability of Lots for Building

a. Lade is Vice-President of Landview (p. 8, lines 11–13)

b. Lade instructs all salespeople when they are hired to tell prospective purchasers that all lots are sold on an "as is" basis and that Landview will make no land improvements beyond the original subdivision grading. (p. 25, lines 7–17)

c. Lade is certain that he had given the foregoing instructions to Lotz at least two times in the six months preceding the Phillipses' purchase. (p. 25, line 22; p. 26, line 7)

d. Two months after the Phillipses purchased their lots, James Phillips wrote Lade a letter stating, "Lotz told us before we closed the deal that Landview would not make further improvements to the lots." (p. 27, lines 4–8)

e. At the time of the Phillipses' purchase, Lotz was 40% above the sales figures that had been projected for him at the start of the year. (p. 28, lines 24–28)

f. In the six months preceding the Phillipses' purchase, Lotz and Lade had discussed the fact that lots 20 and 84, in the south section, were having caissons installed on them prior to the erection of homes. (p. 33, lines 3–11)

g. Landview's brochures about "Campion Hills" expressly state that "Landview makes no representations or warranties concerning the suitability of any lot in Campion Hills as a building site." (p. 33, lines 12–20)

h. Liv Urwurst, Landview's on-site office manager, was told by Mr. Phillips sometime in early October that, "As Lotz suggested, I'm going to contact a soil engineer. We may need to drill core samples." (p. 34, lines 9–35; line 15)

i. Landview gave to all prospective purchasers basic architectural drawings for three potential house plans. Stamped on each drawing was a notation that "Revisions may be required because of the conditions of particular lots."

(ii) Statement of Lou Purvisor

I am in charge of the maintenance of the public areas in Campion Hills and have been employed by Landview for six years. I'm told this couple, the Phillipses, bought lots 70 and 71 in the north section sometime in August or September. I remember talking to them once—must have been in late July. They were looking at the lots, and I told them I thought the lots were two of the nicest ones. I remember Mrs. Phillips said, "They are nice, but it's such a shame that you can't just buy a lot and build a house right away without checking out the lot." I asked if they were going to live here themselves. She said no—that they wanted to build houses and sell them. I didn't care for that too much—maybe I'm old fashioned, but the idea of all these speculators just trying to get rich in a hurry really annoys me. I don't remember if Mr. Phillips was around when Mrs. Phillips told me this.

A few weeks later, sometime in late August or early September, I remember seeing Guy Lotz. I asked him how things were going. He said, "Not so good, Lou. I've sold lots of lots, but those child support payments are just killing me."

Around the middle of October, I saw a pickup truck parked in front of lot 71, one of the lots owned by the Phillipses. On the door of the truck was a sign that said, "Acme Soil Engineers," with an address and phone number. A woman got out of the truck and walked over lot 71 from the street to the slope at the rear of the lot. I should explain that the Campion Hills lots were cut out from gently sloping hills, in terrace fashion. Typically, a lot consists of a flat, graded portion and a slope, with additional lots either above or below it. This woman stood for a while on the slope at the rear of lot 71, looked up and down the slope for a while, picked up some soil, and left.

(iii) Investigative Report of Mike Hidden to Florence Darrow

As you requested, I've done some checking into the Phillips-Landview matter. Here's what I've come up with so far.

a. I've talked to a couple of Landview salespeople. Terry Firma doesn't remember whether Lade ever said that all lots are sold "as is" and that Landview makes no improvements beyond the initial subdivision grading. On the other hand, another salesman, Chip N. Dale, is quite positive that Lade never made such a statement to him. Dale and Firma have been working for Landview since about a year before the Phillipses' lot purchases.

b. I went over to Acme Soil Engineering, and talked to the soil engineer who Purvisor saw on lot 71. Her name is Lotta Samples, and she's a licensed soil engineer. She told me that she had been hired by the Joneses, who owned lot 72, to make a boundary survey of their property. She was out there making some preliminary boundary determinations when Purvisor apparently saw her.

c. I checked on those Campion Hills brochures for you. They were printed in late September; they were a few months late, and apparently were available to prospective purchasers on October 1.

d. I attach the letter that Lade gave me from his files that he got from James Phillips, the letter which stated that Lotz had told them that Landview would make no further improvements to the lots. As you can see, the full text of the letter is:

"My wife and I would very much appreciate it if you people could do some tree and shrub removal, particularly on lot 70. I know that Lotz told us before we closed the deal that Landview would not make further improvements to the lots. But those weedy shrubs have become denser than the molecules in a Black Hole (sorry, my astronomy background), and perhaps you could take care of it. Anyway, as Judge Magruder ruled (sorry, my law school background), 'There's no harm in the asking.' "

e. According to the tract map of Campion Hills, lots 20 and 84, the ones with the caissons, are both in the south section, a good mile from the Phillipses' lots.

f. When I was looking through Lade's file, I found the attached letter from Mr. Phillips to Lade. As you can see, it is dated October 5 and has a notation, "cc: Liv Urwurst," and states, "Sorry I was too self-oriented during the week before I left for London to call you (my psychologist background, I guess), but I really wanted to tell you how unhappy I was about Liv Urwurst. As you know, there were a lot of small details that had to be cleared up when we were signing the papers, and she was never around. I'd suggest you fire her, and by copy of this letter I'm making sure she knows how I feel."

After I saw this letter, I found out that the Phillipses travel often and always use Arrivederci Travel Service to make travel arrangements. I checked with them. According to their records, the Phillipses were in London for the first two weeks of October.

g. I also did some checking into the financial background of the Phillipses' company, Best Plumbing Supply Co. Your hunch was right—the company suffered a severe business reversal in late November, and the company has filed bankruptcy proceedings under Chapter 11.

b. Initial Preparation of Landview's Outline of Existing Affirmative Evidence, Including Phillipses' Rebuttal

Based on the information above, below is a portion of Darrow's outline of Landview's existing affirmative evidence, together with evidence which tends to rebut it. In the next section, you are asked to complete the outline.

Darrow's Outline of Landview's Existing Affirmative Evidence

Theory. Landview Did Not Represent that Lots 70 and 71 Were Suitable for Building Without Additional Improvements.

Element 1. Prior to selling the lots to the Phillipses in late August, Lotz did not tell the Phillipses that lots 70 and 71 were suitable for building without additional improvements.

Landview's Affirmative Evidence	Phillipses' Rebuttal
1. Lade instructed all salespeople when hired to tell prospective purchasers that lots are sold "as is" and that Landview makes no land improvements beyond initial subdivision grading. (Lade Depo., p. 25) [Gen: "Salespeople who are told by company vice-presidents to tell prospective purchasers that lots are sold 'as is' and that no lot improvements beyond initial grading will be made usually do not tell prospective purchasers that lots are suitable for building without additional improvements."]	
2. Lade had on two occasions within six months of the Phillipses' purchase given Lotz the instructions in # 1. (Lade Depo., pp. 25–26) [Gen: Same as # 1]	
3. Phillips wrote letter stating that Lotz had told him and wife that Landview would make no further improvements to the lots (Lade Depo., p. 27)	
4. At the time of the Phillipses' purchase, Lotz was 40% ahead of his projected sales figures. (Lade Depo., p. 28) [Gen: Salespeople who are well ahead of their projected sales figures usually are under little pressure to make additional sales. People under little pressure to make additional sales usually will not make unauthorized statements.]	(a) Lotz told Lou Purvisor around time of Phillipses' purchase that child support payments were killing him. (Statement of Purvisor) (b) Possible rebuttal by argument? Lotz was possibly ahead of projections because he was misleading other customers. (Proper argument?)

Landview's Affirmative Evidence	Phillipses' Rebuttal
5. During the six months preceding the Phillipses' purchase, Lade and Lotz had discussed the fact that lots 20 and 84 were having caissons installed. (Lade Depo., p. 33) [Gen: Salespeople who are aware that caissons are being installed on two lots in a tract usually will not state to a prospective purchaser that no land improvements will be needed on other lots.]	
6. Landview's Campion Hills brochures state that Landview makes no representations concerning the suitability of any lot as a building site. (Lade Depo., p. 33)	
7. Mrs. Phillips told Lou Purvisor that it was a shame not to be able to buy a lot and build a house right away without checking out the lot. (Purvisor statement)	(a) Purvisor cannot remember if Mr. Phillips was present at time statement was made. (Statement of Purvisor) [Gen: People who cannot remember who was present when a statement was made often cannot remember . . .]

Even though the outline is only partially completed, its advantages should be plain. The outline marshals existing evidence according to a particular theory of relief, and enables one to evaluate the probative worth of the evidence in at least two ways. First, one may include the generalization which supports the probative value of evidence. Second, one lists opposite each item of affirmative evidence any rebuttal which tends to detract from probative value.

Opposite Affirmative Evidence Item # 4, Darrow recognized a potential rebuttal argument that the Phillipses might make. This is in a strict sense not necessary. Such notations, however, can be included in the outline as important reminders of the potential weaknesses of one's evidence.

Finally, remember that this is one of two outlines of affirmative and rebuttal evidence that Darrow will make. In this outline, Darrow marshals Landview's affirmative evidence, and lists the Phillipses' rebuttal to aid evaluation of the probative worth of Landview's evidence. In a separate outline, Darrow will marshal the Phillipses' affirmative evidence according to the Phillipses' theories of relief, and list Landview's rebuttal to that evidence. By preparing both outlines, Darrow gets a balanced view of each side's strengths and weaknesses.

c. *Affirmative Evidence-Rebuttal Exercises*

The outline in subsection "B" is incomplete in various ways. There are no generalizations for some of the listed items of affirmative evidence, and there is no rebuttal for other items. Also, there is both affirmative and rebuttal evidence in the information provided that has not been listed in the outline at all. Thus, you should do the following:

1. For the items of affirmative evidence listed in Darrow's outline above include generalizations where you think they are needed.

2. Complete the "Affirmative" portion of Darrow's outline by listing the additional items of affirmative evidence and their sources that support Landview's theory that no misrepresentation was made by Landview.

3. For each additional item of affirmative evidence, form a generalization(s) supporting its probative value. Consider listing the generalization(s) in the outline.

4. Take a break and relax—you deserve it.

5. List rebuttal evidence and its source, opposite any item of affirmative evidence which it rebuts.

6. For eager beavers, insert the items of affirmative and rebuttal evidence into the story outline.

Chapter 8

CREDIBILITY

1. INTRODUCTION

Our discussion of affirmative and rebuttal evidence has thus far emphasized the relationship between evidence and various theories, legal and factual, which a party seeks to prove or disprove. Recall, however, that in Chapter 2 we pointed out that affirmative and rebuttal evidence includes evidence relating to a witness' credibility. Thereafter, we have from time to time alluded to certain familiar aspects of credibility, such as bias, inability to observe, and making inconsistent statements. This chapter focuses specifically on those features of stories and witnesses which enhance or detract from credibility.

Although at trial credibility evidence is incorporated into witnesses' stories, during investigation one should separately think about existing and potential credibility evidence. Credibility is central to the outcome of most trials. No matter how much substantive affirmative or rebuttal evidence one produces, unless that evidence is credible it will carry little sway with a trier of fact. Thus, if a witness who supplies an alibi for a defendant in a criminal case is not believable, the alibi defense will fail. And that defense will not be aided by the testimony of five additional alibi witnesses who are no more credible than the first. As a mathematician might view it, six times zero is still zero. Hence, one needs to search not only for the affirmative and rebuttal evidence that supports the parties' theories, but also for evidence that affects the credibility of that evidence.

Moreover, credibility evidence is more than a determinant of a case's outcome at trial. Recall that most lawsuits grow out of disputed versions of historical fact. As a litigator, one is constantly in the position of attempting to persuade someone—opposing counsel, even an appellate court on occasion—that one's own version of historical facts is more believable than the adversary's.

Finally, an oft-expressed attitude of appellate courts further demonstrates the centrality of credibility evidence. A familiar ruling on appeal is that an appellate court is extremely reluctant to overturn facts found to be true during a trial.[1] Indeed, an appellate court will often assume that the trier of fact found to be true those facts supporting its decision.[2] Why such a strong reluctance to reassess evidence? After all, an appellate court usually is supplied with a transcript of all testimony, as well as with any exhibits lodged with the trial court. But this, as one is always reminded, is a "cold record." Appellate courts can neither see nor hear witnesses. As a consequence, they are deprived of fully evaluating credibility, and therefore have strong reason to give great deference to facts found to be true during trial.[3]

Perhaps surprisingly, despite the centrality of credibility evidence, the concept of credibility remains a nebulous one. Many times, it is impossible to distinguish that part of a story which is affirmative or rebuttal evidence from evidence which merely "goes to credibility." For example, assume that in an armed robbery case a store clerk who was held up at gunpoint testifies that the defendant (who has a scar) is the robber and also testifies, "The robber had a scar on his left cheek." From one perspective, the evidence of the scar "goes to credibility"—the testimony suggests the clerk's ability to observe detail and thus enhances the believability of the clerk's identification. But from another perspective, the scar testimony is part of the prosecution's affirmative evidence—it is evidence tending to identify the defendant as the robber.

Moreover, sometimes the term "credibility" refers to a story itself, and sometimes to a witness who tells a story. As to the former, consider a story containing this information: "I saw that it was raining hard outside, so I decided to leave my raincoat and umbrella at home." Even if one knows nothing about the teller of the story, one is unlikely to place much faith in the story. The story recites actions and observations which in common experience are inconsistent.

On the other hand, the focus of credibility may be the teller, not the story. This time, assume the story is that, "I was upset and really depressed because my cat died." This story, in and of itself, seems very believable. But if it is told to us by a person wearing a big smile and a red rubber nose, the story becomes less believable. Our

---

1. See 5A *Moore's Federal Practice,* § 52.03[1].

2. Cf. 5A *Moore's Federal Practice,* § 49.03[4]; West's Ann.Cal.Evid.Code § 402.

3. There are of course other reasons why appellate courts are reluctant to overturn determinations of fact made by trial courts. See, e.g., 5A *Moore's Federal Practice,* note 1 supra.

disbelief in this situation is caused by features of the person who tells the story, not by the story itself.

Although credibility evidence takes a variety of forms, its effect is the same: it is evidence which produces for a trier of fact some degree of belief or disbelief in the trustworthiness of a story. Whether the belief or disbelief grows out of the story itself, or out of the person who tells the story, ultimately it is the believability of the story which is affected. Hence, one should keep in mind that even when one considers the impact of evidence affecting the personal credibility of a witness, it is the credibility of the witness' story which is really the focus.

Interestingly (to us, anyway), the need to search for credibility evidence seems apparent to new lawyers when a witness supplies information harmful to one's client. Yet that need is often overlooked when a witness provides helpful information. Assume a witness states, "There was a yellow ribbon tied round the old oak tree." If this information is harmful to one's case, then almost instinctively one looks to ways that the credibility of that information can be attacked. The thought process is something like, "Yellow ribbon? I'll cut this witness to ribbons! The witness is probably biased. And how far from the oak was the witness, anyway?"

But if the information is helpful to one's case, one may overlook the importance of credibility. In this situation, the thought process all too often is, "Good. This witness takes care of the missing yellow ribbon. Now I can go on to some other area."

It is important that one probe the credibility of a story without regard to whether the story is helpful or harmful. Unless one does so, one cannot be sure either that one's own case is presented in the strongest light, or that one has fully considered an adversary's potential response to one's evidence.

When thinking about the credibility factors enumerated in this chapter, please keep three general thoughts in mind. First, evidence touching on credibility is circumstantial in nature. The factfinder is asked *to infer* that because a story or a witness has a particular characteristic that affects credibility, that the story is more or less believable. As with all other circumstantial evidence, the inference will rest on a generalization. It follows, then, that not all triers of fact will accept the same generalization. For example, from evidence that a witness made a prior inconsistent statement, one trier of fact may infer that the witness is uncertain and thus not credible, while another may infer that the witness is thoughtful and flexible, and therefore more credible.

Second, even assuming that a factfinder accepts an inference that a witness is more or less credible because a certain credibility factor exists, it is often impossible to determine the "spill-over" effect of the evidence. For example, simply because a factfinder finds one portion of a witness' story implausible, or impeached by a prior inconsistent statement, does not mean that the factfinder will automatically reject the remainder of the story.

Finally, do not regard the factors enumerated in this chapter as a comprehensive list. The factors touched on here are necessarily incomplete. One should feel quite free in any individual case to draw upon one's own experience to supplement our list. Undoubtedly such experience can substantially enlarge the list of factors we describe.

Though the ultimate result of all of the listed factors is to affect the factfinder's evaluation of witnesses' stories, for analytical purposes we group the factors into the two categories mentioned above. We first discuss those factors which primarily affect the *believability of a story* told by a witness, and then those factors which primarily affect the personal *believability of witnesses.*

2. FACTORS AFFECTING THE CREDIBILITY OF A STORY

This section focuses on those aspects of stories which typically affect believability. Remember that even if one knows nothing of a person who tells a story, certain features of a story itself may cause one to place either little or great faith in it. Consider the more common features.

a. Story Plausibility in General

Chapter 6 described the vital role of common experience in the development and the evaluation of circumstantial evidence. Thus, it should not be surprising that factfinders use common experience to assess the credibility of stories. Consider these examples:

Story 1. I was in the back part of the corner grocery store about 9 p.m.—they were getting ready to close. I was trying to decide what flavor yoghurt to buy when I heard a voice up front say, "Stay calm and I won't shoot. Just give me all your cash." I thought there was a robbery; I got very scared, and didn't move at first. Then I tried to lower myself down behind the grocery shelves that were next to the dairy case. I heard the clerk and this robber talking, but I was too scared to pay much attention. I remember, "Hurry up" a few times. That's about it. Then suddenly the robber ran right by me, through the storage area in the back of the store and out the back door. I guess he didn't see me, because I was crouching down. I did see his face directly as he approached me and ran by, and I think I'd recognize him if I saw him again.

Story 2. I was in the back part of the corner grocery store about 9 p.m.—they were getting ready to close. I was trying to decide what flavor yoghurt to buy when I heard a voice up front say, "Stay calm and I won't shoot. Just give me all your cash." I thought there was a robbery; I got very scared, but I decided it might be very important if I could identify the robber. I walked quietly towards the front of the store, next to one of the grocery shelves. As I walked, I got out a pencil and a piece of paper and wrote down what the robber and the clerk said, but later I lost the piece of paper. I can remember it anyway, just about word for word. Within about thirty seconds I was five feet from the robber, to his side and a little behind him. By looking out from in back of the shelf, I got a good look at his profile. I just stared at him the whole time he was there. Just before he left the cash register area, he fired a shot. I couldn't tell if it hit the clerk. Then the robber ran toward the back of the store, on the other side of the shelves I was standing behind. I immediately chased him and yelled at him to stop, but he kept running and I didn't see which way he went after he got out the back door. I know I'd recognize him if I saw him again.

Even if one has never been in the immediate vicinity of an armed robbery, one is likely to find the first story more credible. Or even if one has never even been in an analogous life-threatening situation, one has a wealth of experience with which one can evaluate the respective stories. Recall, experience includes what we have read, seen and heard. The first story probably meshes with the way one believes most people in the storyteller's predicament would react. The person was in a frightening situation; acknowledges fear; and behaves as a fearful person probably would. In the second story, the witness flaunts death; takes inappropriate notes, then loses them, and yet claims to have perfect memory anyway. Even though both witnesses believe they can identify the robber, and indeed even though the second story results in apparently greater opportunity to perceive, the first story is probably more credible. It is more consistent with our assessment of how people in general would behave in such a situation.

Nevertheless, the second story is not palpably impossible. Greater plausibility may result if we learned enough about the second witness to take the witness out of the category of "people in general." The witness might be James Bond, or the winner of 10 Samaritan of the Year awards, or a person trained in self-defense. Similarly, greater credibility may be derived by adding elements to the story. For example, perhaps it was very dark in the part of the store where the witness was. Any such additional factors, among others, add to the credibility of the story by changing the types of experiences to which one compares the witness' story.

From the standpoint of investigation, then, one must listen to stories with an eye to their plausibility. When stories do not comport with common experience, one may need to explore the implausibility. We discuss how and when one may do this in Chapter 15.

b. Story Consistency

The major factor affecting the general plausibility of a story is the extent to which portions of it are consistent. If a story meshes, one views it as "hanging together," and therefore more credible.

There are at least three types of story inconsistencies which detract from plausibility. The first type is an "internal" inconsistency: considered as a whole, and without reference to other stories in a case, the parts of a story do not jibe. Consider the previous stories. In Story # 2, the witness admits to being "scared," but then takes actions which, in the light of common experience, seem inconsistent with fright. Similarly, based on common experience, it seems unlikely that the witness would take no action to stop the robber before the shot was fired, and then decide suddenly to pursue him after the shot was fired. By contrast, in Story # 1, the witness' actions are consistent with the witness' predicament. Again, one is likely to find Story # 1 more credible.

Whether or not "consistency is the hobgoblin of small minds," it is nevertheless an element of a believable story. Based on common experience, most of us believe that events proceed in recognizable patterns and that people's emotional states and actions remain relatively consistent from one moment to the next. Therefore, when the different parts of a story are in harmony, we tend to trust the story.

The second and third types of story inconsistencies affecting plausibility rely on factors "external" to the story itself. One such external inconsistency concerns the consistency of a story with "established facts." In any case, there are likely to be certain facts which a trier of fact will accept as unimpeachably accurate. To the extent a story is consistent with such facts, one will regard it as credible. If a story is inconsistent with such facts, its credibility will suffer.

Facts likely to be accepted as unimpeachably accurate are those which all parties accept as true, or which come from a source whose personal credibility is beyond attack. If a wino's story is that a person was wearing glasses, and every member of the "Sisters of Truth" says the person was not wearing glasses, we know which story will be believed. The factfinder will take as an established fact that the person was "glassless." If the story of another witness then includes testimony that the person wore glasses, it may be less credible because it clashes with an "established fact."

This same principle may be illustrated in the context of the robbery Story # 1. Assume that a police officer testifies that the officer saw the robber running out of the market wearing tennis shoes. The officer's testimony on this point is likely to be regarded as an established fact. If another witness' story is that the robber was wearing penny loafers, that story may well be regarded as less credible.

A second "external" inconsistency concerns the familiar "prior inconsistent statement." When a witness tells one story one time, and another story at a different time, one may doubt one or both of the stories. Each story may be credible in and of itself, but their coexistence may render each unbelievable. For example, assume that at trial, on direct examination a witness testifies to Story # 1. On cross-examination, opposing counsel elicits testimony that shortly after the robbery, the witness had told the police that the witness was in the front of the store crouched down, and saw the robber as he escaped through the front door.

After this cross-examination, one is likely to distrust the story told on direct. Conventional wisdom tells us that if a witness' perceptions and memory of an event are accurate, the witness' telling of the event should remain consistent over time. By showing that a story has changed, therefore, the cross-examiner causes one to doubt the story's accuracy. Note that in this situation, the "external" inconsistency affects the credibility of Story # 1 even though the two stories are in and of themselves equally plausible and equally damaging to the defendant. That is, no matter which version of the robbery is the accurate one (assuming one version *is* accurate), the witness had a golden opportunity to see the robber. But it is the *fact* that the story has changed that affects its credibility, quite apart from *how* it has changed. Of course, if the "external" story were itself more favorable (witness told the police, "I had fallen into the yoghurt and never saw a thing"), the cross-examiner will want not only to elicit the inconsistent evidence, but also to persuade the factfinder that the "external" version is more accurate.

The extent to which a prior inconsistent statement affects a story's credibility varies according to a variety of factors:

(1) How important to the outcome of a case is an inconsistency? If in the robbery example above the defense is an alibi, an inconsistency concerning the witness' visual perception of the robber is important. On the other hand, an inconsistency as to whether prior to the robbery the witness had been looking for banana nut or cherry-apple yoghurt will probably have a lesser effect on credibility.

(2) The number of inconsistencies.

(3) A witness' explanation, if any, for an inconsistency. An explanation which according to one's experience may be believable ("I told the police I was in the front of the store because I always come in through the alley, and I just think of the back as the front of the store") may alleviate or even eliminate any adverse effect on credibility. But an explanation which according to experience is itself implausible ("I told the police I didn't see anything because I was really hungry and just wanted to get a yoghurt") usually only adds to a story's lack of credibility.

(4) The regard of the factfinder for the Latin saying, "Falso in uno, falso in unum." Loosely translated, this means, "A witness who can't be trusted in one part of the witness' testimony can't be trusted in others." In other words, if one part of a witness' story is inconsistent, will the consequent loss of credibility spread to the rest of the testimony? This probably depends on an individual factfinder, and on the first three factors.

This analysis, which examines the "spill-over" effect of an inconsistency, is of course also applicable to other aspects of story credibility. A trier of fact may find one part of a witness' story implausible, yet believe other parts of it. For example, a trier of fact may disbelieve that part of a witness' story which states that a hamburger at a fast food chain store was served "piping hot," yet still believe the other part of the story that there was a piece of glass in the hamburger. Similarly, a trier of fact may find that part of a witness' story is inconsistent with established facts, yet believe other parts of the story.

c. *Explanation*

When a story contains evidence which explains not only *what* happened, but also *why* substantively critical events happened as one contends, credibility of the story is typically enhanced. Rarely does substantive law require one to prove why certain events took place. That is, one need not often prove why two parties entered into a contract or why a person was driving negligently. Occasionally, some degree of explanation may be required. For example, in a civil rights case, a plaintiff may need to prove that defendant discriminated because the plaintiff is a member of a minority group. Even in such instances, however, the required explanation is quite limited. One would not be required to prove why the defendant might have discriminated against a minority group person.

Hence, when one includes explanatory evidence in a story, one does so almost entirely for reasons of credibility. Because the notion of cause-and-effect is so engrained in our reasoning processes, stories tend to have added credibility when they include events explaining why disputed events occurred as one contends. Thus, if defendant denies entering into an oral contract for the sale of a 1932 Packard to plaintiff, plaintiff's descriptive tale of a series of negotiations culminating in an agreement may be difficult for a factfinder to evaluate. However, add to that tale explanatory evidence such as plaintiff's collection of vintage Packards, or defendant's need for money, and the tale becomes more believable.

The value of explanatory evidence may be somewhat different, depending on whether the party offering the explanation is plaintiff or defendant. Plaintiffs, aside from typically having the burden of proving specific legal elements, have to persuade a factfinder, in a broad sense, to penalize an individual or an entity. This is an added burden, for it requires a trier of fact to find in some sense that a defendant is morally culpable. Explanatory evidence often helps to show why behavior is deserving of punishment.

From defendants' perspectives, their frequent dilemma is that plaintiffs are a class of people who have suffered some injury or damage. Defendants may argue that they are not responsible for the wrong done. Yet, factfinders may feel emotional tugs on plaintiffs' behalfs, since plaintiffs have generally suffered some ill. Again, explanatory evidence may help to overcome the emotional leaning by demonstrating why, as one contends, someone other than the defendant is responsible for the plaintiff's injury.

d. *Adequacy of Detail*

As you know, details are an essential part of a story. To build credible stories, one must distinguish conclusions from the factual details which often lend credibility to those conclusions. The following example shows how details may add to credibility. Assume that in a civil action for damages for assault and battery, the plaintiff tells this story. On March 12, the plaintiff drove into a gas station to get gas. He was in a hurry, and he and the station attendant (defendant) began yelling at each other when the attendant could not help him immediately. The plaintiff then began serving himself from the gas pump in violation of a posted station rule, and the station attendant then struck plaintiff on the head with a broom the attendant was carrying. The plaintiff began bleeding from the head and had to be taken to a hospital.

As it stands, this story does contain some details. It states, for example, that the station rule regarding self-service was posted. But would the story be more credible if it were much richer in detail? What words were spoken by the combatants? In what tone of voice?

At what distance? What did the broom look like? How was it held? How was it swung? What movements, if any, did the plaintiff make? Aren't these the sort of details that would add credibility to the conclusion that the defendant committed battery? Would not the details paint a more precise picture, thereby removing the uncertainty of the earlier more general and vague description?

When gathering evidence one must always take care to distinguish details from conclusions. When a witness gives a summary opinion of an event, that opinion may be something like, "She was drunk," or "I got a good look at him." Unless the witness can amplify the conclusion with details which would allow the trier of fact to draw the same conclusion, the story will often lack credibility. It may even lack admissibility.

When a conclusion is a summary opinion of a series of events, "weasel words" such as "always" or "usually" are typically found in the story. A witness states, for example, that another person was "always staying out late at night," or that he "usually spent a lot of time at work on the phone." Such summary opinions, devoid of underlying details, typically are of doubtful credibility.

Details not only add credibility to conclusions; they also help to convince a factfinder that a person was a percipient witness with a good memory. Based on common experience, factfinders tend to adopt the premise that if a witness did see an event and can remember it accurately, the witness will be able to provide a number of details pertaining to the event.[4]

On the other hand, stories which overwhelm a factfinder with details are likely not to be credible either. Given the well-documented failings of human perceptual abilities, all recognize that the ability to observe and recollect detail is limited. We may not all place the limit line at the same place, but limits there are. Thus, a story which includes the combination of each of the thirty-two combination locks a witness has owned since childhood will probably not be believable.

As usual, there are no obvious boundaries which separate "too much detail" and "not enough detail" from "just the right amount of detail." Factors which affect credibility in a particular case probably include the apparent perceptual and memory abilities of a witness; the nature of the details (e.g., are they particularly exciting?); the number of details; and the consistency of details with other parts of a story.

4. But recall that eyewitness testimony may be suspect. See Chapter 2, note 8.

e. Emotional Content

Emotional evidence, which typically engenders feelings either of sympathy or hostility, may operate by affecting a factfinder's appraisal of a story's credibility. A story which makes a trier of fact sympathetic to a witness, or which supports a party to whom the factfinder is already sympathetic, may be more credible than one which does not have such features.

Just how emotional evidence operates on a factfinder's perception of credibility is not clear. Perhaps, its primary impact is on the factfinder's subconscious, and it only comes into play in cases in which evidence is closely balanced.[5] By contrast, the previously-discussed credibility factors are likely to be consciously related to credibility. A factfinder's reasoning may go as follows: "That story isn't credible—

(a) there are not enough details" or

(b) too much of it is implausible" or

(c) the witness said different things at different times."

But, a factfinder is unlikely to reason consciously, "I believe this story—it is really a sympathetic one," or, "I do not believe that story—it supports a party who is evil."

Consider how emotional evidence might affect the appraisal of credibility in the following example. Assume a suit has been brought by a handicapped widower with twenty children against Gigantic Monolith, Inc. The complaint alleges that the widower's spouse was killed when a Gigantic truck driver who in her regular course of business was on her way to dump toxic nuclear waste materials into the municipal water supply, negligently slammed into the spouse. At the time of the collision, the victim was aiding a group of orphaned grandmothers across a street.

Perhaps a more sympathetic plaintiff could not possibly be paired with a more reprehensible defendant. Because of the emotional overtones, the trier of fact may strain to resolve the case in favor of the plaintiff by finding the plaintiff's version of the events more credible than the defendant's. However, it is not at all clear that even if the emotional evidence does affect the factfinder's appraisal of credibility, the factfinder will *consciously* alter its appraisal.[6]

f. Socio-Political Content of Story

Just as we bring to a courtroom bundles of past experiences, so too do we bring innumerable varieties of socio-political attitudes and opinions shaped by those experiences. For example, all of us have

---

5. See H. Kalven and H. Zeisel, *The American Jury* 164–165 (1966).

6. Ibid. at 193–4; 217–18.

some personal beliefs concerning the causes of economic problems, public school deficiencies, and proper sexual roles. When a party's story at trial touches upon an issue on which a trier of fact has some pre-formed opinions, the trier may evaluate the credibility of a story in the light of those attitudes and opinions. Like emotional evidence, the influence of socio-political attitudes is unclear; they may operate largely on the subconscious. But this influence is nonetheless real for all of that.

In some factual contexts, the possibility of a determination of credibility based on socio-political outlook is apparent. A member of a minority group brings a suit based on "police harrassment and abuse" against a local police force. The trier of fact decides that the stories of the plaintiff's witnesses are not credible. That decision might be based on story inconsistencies or variances from common experience. But the decision might, at least in part, be based on the factfinder's negative attitude towards such lawsuits. The factfinder may believe that the local police force is an excellent one or that any problems are best handled by the police internally. With either belief, the factfinder may have a bias against police suits, and this bias may result in a finding that the stories of the plaintiff's witnesses are not credible. Similarly, if the factfinder's attitude is that minority groups have suffered at the hands of police forces, the factfinder may find the plaintiff's witnesses more credible than the police officer witnesses. In all events, when a case is resolved on such a basis, there is little an appellate court can do. An appellate court can review a perceptible legally impermissible basis of decision. But when that impermissible basis masquerades as a finding of lack of credibility, appellate reversal is far less likely.[7]

The influence of socio-political attitudes is not, however, limited to cases with obvious political overtones. Assume a standard medical malpractice case, with the plaintiff seeking damages for an operation negligently performed. If the trier of fact's attitude is that doctors are often unfairly subjected to malpractice suits, the trier may translate this belief into a finding that the defense story is more credible than that of the plaintiff. Thus, in any type of case there is the possibility of factfinding based on socio-political factors.

One is not totally at the mercy of this kind of factfinding. One may, of course, investigate available factfinders, in order to secure a sympathetic ear at trial. Or, if one is aware of this method of reasoning, one may probe for evidence that will circumvent it. One may attempt to construct a story that does not attack an attitude, but rather is outside the scope of the attitude. For example, in the police

---

7. Recall that appellate courts do not typically overturn factual decisions of lower courts, because of the appellate courts' relative inability to evaluate credibility. See 5A *Moore's Federal Practice,* note 1 supra.

abuse case, if the factfinder is likely to have a bias against such suits, one may pursue evidence showing that the suit is aimed at a couple of "bad apples," not an entire police force. On this basis, a factfinder may find the story of police abuse credible, while maintaining a belief that the department as a whole is excellent. A similar effort might be made in the medical malpractice situation. From an investigatory standpoint, what is important to recognize is that socio-political factors may affect a factfinder's views about a story's credibility. From this recognition, one has a chance during investigation to consider ways of overcoming those views.

3. CREDIBILITY OF THE SOURCE

A factfinder's evaluation of credibility is not confined to the storyteller's message. In trials, as in all aspects of life, we evaluate the credibility of a message in part by what we know of the speaker. The assertion that "Artichokes reduce stress" may be evaluated in one way if the speaker is a doctor, and in another if the speaker is the Director of the Artichoke Growers Association. This section explores the principal factors which are likely to affect the personal credibility of a storyteller. By way of introduction, we illustrate some of the factors in the context of the "artichoke" example:

(1) How much does the witness know about the medical effect of artichoke eating? Where does that knowledge come from? The more training and experience a witness has that relates to the specific subject matter of an assertion, the more likely we are to believe it. This factor is "expertise."

(2) Does the witness have a personal commitment to any of the parties or the issues? Is the witness better off if citizens start consuming artichokes in unprecedented numbers? If the commitment is purely emotional, this factor is generally called "bias." When the emotional commitment is added to or replaced by a financial one, the factor is generally called "interest." The factors may be grouped under the single heading, "motive."

(3) What are the facial, vocal and body language characteristics of the speaker? Does the speaker's manner convey a sense of confidence? Does the speaker appear to speak from the "heart?" This factor is called "demeanor."

Against this background, we turn to a discussion of the principal factors that affect personal credibility of a storyteller.

a. Expertise

One of Will Rogers' most accurate quotes is to the effect that, "All of us are dumb, except in different areas." Lawyers intuit, again based on their own personal and vicarious experiences, that persons who are familiar with a certain subject are more likely to speak knowingly and accurately about the subject. All of us welcome the opinions and observations of someone in the know. Such a person will generally enjoy greater credibility.

To most readers' minds, mention of the word expert probably conjures up immediate visions of someone in a white jacket with a stethoscope hanging out of a pocket. To other readers, the image of a doctor will immediately appear. But the field of expertise is far wider than that. A cocktail waitress may not ordinarily testify at a trial as a witness imbued with high credibility. But on the issue of whether or not an individual was drunk, she may well qualify as an expert. A shoe salesman is certainly not automatically vested with expertise. But if identification rests in part on the shoes worn by an alleged suspect, the testimony of a shoe salesman may take on added significance.

In other words, the world is not divided into experts and non-experts. Any witness may have in her background certain experiences or training of particular relevance to the case.[8]

Experience and training is one method by which a person gains special familiarity with a subject matter and thereby demonstrates expertise. One may also gain special familiarity by having a particular ability to perceive an event. For example, other factors being equal, consider the relative credibility of two witnesses to an auto collision. One witness was at the intersection where the collision occurred; the other was a block away. In another case, two witnesses testify to overhearing a conversation. One witness had the duty to later prepare a summary of the conversation; the other witness was doing some repair work in the office at the time the conversation took place. In each case, a witness' credibility will be affected by perceptual hurdles at the scene. The fewer the hurdles, or the more a witness' training and experience enables the witness to overcome the hurdles, the greater a witness' expertise and, therefore, credibility.[9]

b. Motive

A witness' credibility may be affected by any bias, interest or other motive of the witness concerning the subject matter of his or her testimony. Thus, litigators are quick to point out when favorable evidence is provided by "neutral" witnesses. Typically, neutral witnesses are people who did not know either of the parties prior to the incidents giving rise to the lawsuit, who since those incidents have not become affiliated in some way with one of the parties, and who have no financial or emotional stake in the outcome of the lawsuit.

In view of these characteristics of a neutral witness, one may wonder whether at trial neutrality of a witness is prized for its effect

8. P. Bergman, *Trial Advocacy in a Nutshell* 32–33 (West, 1979).

9. In Chapter 15, we discuss in more detail a variety of perceptual hurdles that may affect a witness' ability to perceive.

on credibility, or just for its rarity. Although specific data is unattainable, it is clear that many witnesses who testify in court have some attachment with one party, or some emotional or financial stake in the outcome of a case. After all, most of us spend the bulk of our lives in the company of people with whom we have a personal or an employment-related relationship. When a dispute concerning something that has happened reaches the courts, therefore, the people who are aware of it, and who therefore are potential witnesses, are generally people with whom the parties have some prior relationship.

Consider the following examples. Two cars collide in an intersection; there was a driver and a passenger or two in each car. The two drivers are injured; they are medically treated for their injuries; and they file suit against each other for damages caused by their injuries. Who are the most likely witnesses? The drivers, passengers and doctors. Each of these witnesses is vulnerable to a claim that his or her testimony may be influenced by motive. Clearly this is so for the two drivers. They are the parties, and stand to win or lose money depending on the outcome of the case. And it is probably true for the passengers as well. Most passengers in cars are friends, relatives or co-workers of the drivers. Thus, each adversary could claim that the opposing passengers' testimony is less credible because it is motivated by friendship. As for the doctors, even if they have already been paid, they need to justify both their fee, and perhaps their continued employment as expert witnesses in future cases.

Expanding the net of possible witnesses, other witnesses may testify to the extent to which injuries have affected a driver's lifestyle, or job attendance and performance, or future. All of such witnesses are likely to be either personal acquaintances of a party, people who have provided services to a party, or experts who have been paid for testifying. "It goes without saying" that most of these people would have some degree of personal stake in the outcome of the case, and are subject to potential claims of "motive."

Finally, even the neutrality of the occasional passerby is probably something of a myth. What one sees (or thinks one sees) is likely to be colored by one's past experiences and current attitudes. These experiences and attitudes give one an "expectancy"—a mind set that an event which is occurring will happen as past experience suggests or as one's attitude suggests it will occur. For example, if one's past experience suggests that sports car drivers are likely to speed, and one observes a sports car involved in a collision, one may conclude from one's prior experience rather than from one's actual observations that the sports car was speeding just prior to the collision. Similarly, consider the following picture.[10]

10. The following pictures and experimental results are taken from R. Buckhout, "Eyewitness Testimony," Vol. 231, No. 6 *Scientific American* 23 (Dec. 1974).

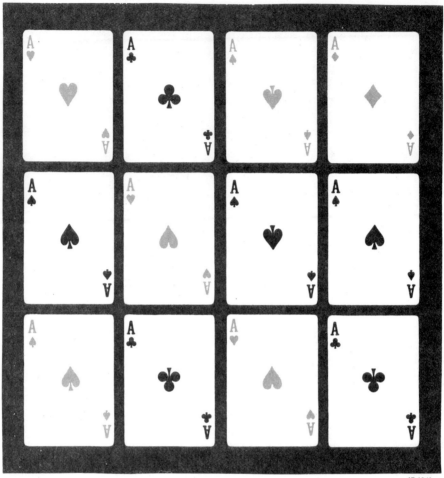

[D494]

The picture consists of cards arranged in three rows. Subjects are asked to look at the picture, and then to state how many aces of spades they see. If one looks at the picture carefully, one sees that five of the cards are the ace of spades. Because people expect an ace of spades to be black, not red, (grey) they typically report that there are but three aces of spades among the cards.

"Expectancy" is not the only psychological factor which detracts from the myth of the neutrality. Witnesses with no particular expectancy often "fill in" the details of what they observe. Consider the following experiment, illustrated on p. 149.

Observers are shown a figure roughly the equivalent of figure "a." When they are asked to reproduce the figure immediately afterward, the observers draw a fairly accurate reproduction. A month later, the observers are again asked to reproduce the figure. The

a  b 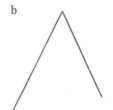 c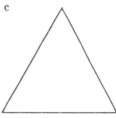

[D548]

second set of drawings is shown in (b)—they have become more regular. Finally, when after three months the observers are asked to make a third reproduction of the figure, they draw complete, symmetrical figures (figure "c"). The observers have literally filled in, so that the new figure reflects their beliefs as to what they saw.

In short, because of our "expectancies," "mind sets," and tendencies to fill, most of us rarely are objective observers—we all look through glasses that are colored by attitudes and experiences.

In addition, neutrality may be a myth for other reasons. In nearly every instance, a witness discusses potential testimony with attorneys. Through that discussion, a witness may unconsciously develop a view of events that favors one party over the other.[11]

Moreover, a witness often builds up an emotional commitment to himself or herself. Once a witness tells a story of an event, the story becomes the reality. A witness becomes committed not so much to the actual event, as to the story. Since all witnesses have told their stories before trial to friends, reporters or attorneys, by the time of trial there may be no neutral witnesses.

One should not conclude from all this that since true neutrality is impossible, the credibility of all witnesses is dubious. Instead, view it from the opposite perspective. Because all witnesses are in some way subject to a charge of bias, a factfinder probably will not discount credibility unless in a particular instance the biasing factor is especially strong.

To conclude this subsection, please consider the following short factual situations. In each situation, who are the witnesses who might testify for either party? To what claims of "motive" might these witnesses be subject?

1. *Criminal prosecution for sale of cocaine.* A police informant testifies that he arranged to purchase cocaine from defendant at a motel, in the perception of officers concealed in a different room.

2. *Civil contract case.* Two company Vice-Presidents negotiated the sale and purchase of a large piece of industrial machin-

11. For further discussion of this phenomenon, see G. Bellow and B. Moulton, *The Lawyering Process—Materials For* *Clinical Instruction in Advocacy* 364–392 (1978).

ery. There is a dispute over whether the seller or the buyer was to pay for installation of the machine in the buyer's plant, and over whether training in the use of the machine would be offered to the buyer's employees.

c. Status

Status is a familiar concept. Certain walks of life produce a sense of respect. One's instinct is to give deference to people in such walks of life, and therefore to regard their assertions as more believable. Even though the background which produces the high status has nothing to do with the facts of a lawsuit (if it did, the background might more accurately be viewed as "expertise"), factfinders sometimes regard a witness with high status as more credible than other witnesses.[12]

The symbiotic relationship between status and credibility was experienced by most of us during childhood. If one thinks back to life as a 10-year-old, one can usually recall one or two other children who were the "most popular." A dispute may have arisen, with the most popular child's version of events pitted against another child's. The other child may have been your standard non-athletic skinny kid (author # 1) or your athletic-but-stout kid (author # 2). Typically, most believed the popular child's story. Perhaps siding with the popular child made us feel more popular, or made us feel that the popular child would look with favor on us.[13] Whatever the reason, each of us has probably observed a connection between status and credibility.

Among adults, a variety of factors enhance one's status. One may acquire high status because one is in the public eye as royalty (Lady Penelope Pettifogg), as a sports-entertainment celebrity, or perhaps even as a notorious but self-confessed criminal. One may have a career regarded as demanding training and responsibility. Or, one may have made a noteworthy achievement of some kind—lived to a very old age, climbed Mt. Everest, or never watched a soap opera on television. These are the sorts of factors that may enhance status, and therefore credibility.

To some extent, this credibility factor borders on the irrational. If two people view an automobile collision, and all other factors are equal, is an accountant's story of what occurred really entitled to greater weight than that of a dishwasher? What of the accountant who worked her way through school by washing dishes—were her

12. G. Lindzey and E. Aronson, (Eds.) III Handbook of Social Psychology 182 (2d ed. 1969); W. Minnick, *The Art of Persuasion* 162–164 (2d ed. 1968); J. Freedman, J. Carlsmith, D. Sears, *Social Psychology* 53 (2d ed. 1974).

13. B. Collins, *Social Psychology* 23–26, 32, cf. 118–119 (1970); cf. J. Freedman, et al. *Social Psychology* note 12 supra, at 192, 226.

perceptual abilities suddenly advanced when she received her degree? Such questions suggest that there may be little in the way of objective data that might support the connection between status and credibility. But since a factfinder may make that connection, one must be prepared either to realize its advantages, or to rebut it.

d. *Similarity*

Often a witness will be similar in some way to a factfinder. The similarity may consist of physical appearance, personal background, or even attitudes and opinions. For example, one may hear a political speaker whose position on an issue matches one's own. In such a case, one tends to believe that the speaker is knowledgeable and trustworthy, and that any statistics cited by the speaker are accurate.

A trial, of course, is not generally an arena for political dogma. However, the factfinder can observe the physical appearance of those who testify; and something of a witness' personal background usually emerges through testimony. Moreover, there are often opportunities during trials for witnesses to express attitudes and opinions in addition to "the facts." In a child custody dispute, for instance, a witness may testify that, "I always noticed how Mrs. Crawford disciplined her children, because I believe that discipline is very important." In a prosecution for drunk driving, a defense witness may testify, "Sure he had had a few beers and a couple of martinis, but he wasn't drunk." Or in an automobile accident case, a witness may testify, "He was going 50, maybe 55 m.p.h.—not really speeding." Thus, both through testimony and simple observation, a factfinder will often be able to determine how "similar" a witness is to himself or herself.

When a witness is in some way similar to a factfinder, a witness' credibility may increase. And when the witness is dissimilar, credibility may well decrease.[14]

There is another way in which similarity may add to a witness' credibility, one which in effect gives a "double bump" to a witness. A trier of fact is not supposed to begin determining facts until after all parties have completed their presentation of evidence and the case has been submitted to it. If there is a jury, the jury is normally informed of this principle. However, this rule flies in the face of the "primacy" principle. According to this principle, all of us tend to make determinations as soon as information becomes available. Thus, in a trial context, if an initial presentation of evidence impresses a trier of fact, the trier may tend towards resolution of a case in accordance with its early impression. This does not mean that the

14. B. Collins, *Social Psychology,* 119–125 (1970).

impression cannot be reversed. It does mean that a party may have to produce evidence to overcome both the adversary's evidence and the initial impression created by that evidence.[15]

How does "primacy" give a double bump to credibility? If a trier of fact, based on early evidence, has begun to form a favorable impression of one of the parties, then the trier may tend to accord greater credibility to other witnesses who support the same party. The party thus gains a double advantage: the early evidence establishes an impression favorable to that party. In turn, that impression casts a favorable glow on the credibility of witnesses who later testify for that party. The similarity between the later witnesses and the factfinder's impression is the credibility catalyst.[16]

e. Physical Appearance; Demeanor

A group of factors relating to a witness' appearance, style and personality also affects a witness' credibility. Many of these factors are neither tangible nor unique to trials. Why are some sports figures regarded as superstars, while others with equal or even greater credentials get scant attention? Why is it that of the many movies and television personalities, some are so much more successful than others in selling products or political ideas? On what bases do most of us form "first impressions" of those we meet? Definitive answers to such questions are no doubt impossible. In part, answers probably consist of the credibility factors discussed above. A movie star who is regarded as having "expertise" and no bias in a certain field may be a more credible salesperson than a biased star without such expertise. And in part, answers probably lie in a variety of elements which combine to form a person's unique style: physical attractiveness; tone of voice; eye contact; hesitancy; apparent sincerity; physical gestures and body language; naturalness; sense of humor. If this list is not exhaustive, it is at least suggestive of the elements of style and demeanor which may make one person appear more credible than another.[17]

However, even with respect to this list, few universal assumptions are possible. A person's hesitancy in responding to questions may be taken as a sign of nervousness and uncertainty, or deep thought and

---

15. For a somewhat more detailed discussion of primacy, see Lawson, "Order of Presentation as a Factor In Jury Persuasion," 56 Ken.L.J. 523 (Spring 1968).

16. On the other hand, similarity may breed contempt. See III Handbook of Social Psychology, note 12 supra, at 189–191.

17. Other factors, for example, can be found under rules relating to character

evidence. For instance, a witness' credibility may be affected by evidence that the witness has a poor reputation for telling the truth, or that in another witness' opinion the witness is not a truth teller. Personal credibility may similarly be attacked by evidence that the witness has been convicted of a felony relating to honesty. See Federal Rules of Evidence, Rule 609.

consideration. Physical gestures may be dramatic underlines to testimony, or theatrical excesses which overwhelm testimony. What seems natural to one factfinder may appear glib to another. Perhaps the only assertion that is universally true is that a witness' overall style is lesser than or greater than, but rarely equal to, the sum of the individual stylistic and demeanor elements.

At times, one's choices with respect to the physical appearances of witnesses are limited. After all, if the only witness to an automobile accident has the personal style of a patient on his way to have teeth pulled by a dentist, one may have no choice other than to call that witness. In such cases, one may at least be aware of those elements which detract from the witness' appearance, and then consider before trial which of those elements, if any, are amenable to change.

At other times, one may be able to make choices depending on witnesses' relative personal appearances. One may be able to choose between lay, percipient witnesses. And, if an expert witness will testify, one may select an expert based on physical appearance as well as credentials.

Finally, from a positive standpoint, one must be alert to aspects of a witness' appearance which enhance credibility. A witness may use certain words or colorful phrases which carry the stamp of credibility. A witness' manner may be inextricably bound up with the witness' employment or geographical origin. Stereotypes definitely exist, and in trials they may be quite useful. A Maine lobster fisherperson will probably be more credible if he fits everyone's stereotype, even if a case is tried in Arizona. Where such positive elements exist, one's need is to recognize them during investigation and then to preserve them at trial.[18]

4. LACK OF CREDIBILITY: MISTAKE OR FABRICATION?

After reading this far, one's eyes and ears should be alert to features in stories or witnesses which tend to affect credibility. However, identifying a lack of credibility may be like hooking an octopus while fishing: it is easy to identify it, but it is hard to know what to do with it.

If a factor such as bias suggests that a witness lacks credibility, what is the bottom line? What inference is to be drawn? Is the story a fabrication? Or is the story simply inaccurate? These are two very different bottom lines. It is one thing to suggest to a trier of

18. For more in-depth discussion of language and its effects on credibility, see W. O'Barr, *Linguistic Evidence: Language, Power, and Strategy in the* *Courtroom* (1982); W. O'Barr, "Subtleties in Courtroom Style," Vol. 3, No. 1 California Lawyer 30 (Jan. 1983).

fact that a witness is mistaken. It is quite another to suggest that a witness is a liar.

Which bottom line one chooses will, of course, vary from case to case. In general, however, the experience of litigators is that triers of fact are not easily convinced that a witness is a liar. Various reasons may account for this. For one thing, people may be reluctant to believe that a witness who has sat a few feet away and who has sworn to tell the truth has consciously lied. For another, common experience suggests it is very easy for a witness to be mistaken. Recall for example the errors that "expectancy" can cause. For whatever reason, however, a factfinder will not, in the absence of highly probative evidence, readily equate lack of credibility with fabrication.

Accordingly, when one comes upon evidence which may detract from credibility, one normally has a choice of applicable premises. For example, if there is evidence that a witness is biased, one can adopt generalizations suggesting mistake. One such generalization might be, "People who are emotionally committed to another person often fail to notice facts that are adverse to that person." Phrased slightly differently, this generalization might be put, "People who are emotionally committed to another person often unconsciously interpret events in a way that favors that person."

Contrast those generalizations with this premise: "People who are emotionally committed to another person often fabricate (slant) their testimony in order to aid that person." The latter generalization, with its implied charge of perjury, should be selected only after carefully considering whether there is sufficient evidence to make it acceptable to the factfinder. At the very least, if one is considering the use of a "fabrication" premise, one should subject it to the "exceptions" test suggested in Chapter 6.

5. OUTLINING CREDIBILITY EVIDENCE

a. *Introduction*

Though this chapter isolates a variety of credibility factors, its focus should not obscure the fact that at trial, credibility evidence is woven into witnesses' stories. For example, assume that in a prosecution for assault with a deadly weapon, the testimony, "I saw Puckett from a distance of 3 feet," is affirmative evidence. Analytically, perhaps one could divide the testimony into affirmative evidence ("I saw Puckett") and credibility evidence demonstrating expertise ("I was 3 feet away"). But there seems little reason to divide the testimony in this way, since at trial the testimony will blend together in the story. One's outlines should reflect this reality, and simply interweave credibility evidence with the affirmative or rebuttal evidence to which it relates. Separate credibility outlines are not necessary.

Within the evidence-marshalling outlines, however, one may need to decide just where to locate credibility evidence. When a credibility factor affects the *source* of the testimony, the credibility evidence may affect a witness' story as a whole, rather than a specific portion of it. By way of illustration, assume that in previous testimony, "I saw Puckett from a distance of 3 feet," the testifying witness is a prosecution witness who is a member of a street gang that is a rival of the gang to which Puckett belongs. Does evidence of the gang rivalry affect the witness' credibility? Sure—it indicates a potential motive to get Puckett in trouble. What kind of evidence is it? Rebuttal—it detracts from the prosecution's evidence, yet does not provide affirmative evidence of innocence. Listing the rebuttal in the outline of defendant's rebuttal poses no problem. But where should it be located in the "rebuttal" column of the parties' outlines of the prosecution's affirmative evidence? After all, it does not rebut any specific piece of evidence.[19]

In such situations, one must list the credibility evidence in whatever way is most meaningful. In theory, one could repeat the credibility evidence every time a piece of evidence from the witness whose credibility is affected is listed in an outline. That seems a bit much, however. Perhaps it is necessary only to include the credibility evidence once in an outline, at the first listing of evidence from the particular witness. Whatever method best suits one's needs in a given case should be chosen.

Of course, there will be other situations in which a credibility factor affects only individual parts of a story. For example, assume that the witness' story is that at the time he saw Puckett from a distance of 3 feet, he (the witness) was on his way home from church. Earlier, however, the witness had told a defense investigator that he (the witness) was on his way home from a poker game. Although there may be a "spill-over" effect, the witness' inconsistent statement affects primarily one portion of his story. In the evidence-marshalling outlines, therefore, one would probably list the prior statement opposite the statement it rebuts.

The question of how to list credibility evidence may also arise with the story outline. The credibility evidence may not constitute an "event" that occurred during the time of the disputed historical facts. When this is so, there is no neat place to locate the evidence in a story outline. In the Puckett case, for example, evidence that the witness is a biased gang rival is not an event that can be neatly inserted into the chronological story. One may choose to omit such

19. Note that the same issue may arise when the source credibility factor is part of one's *affirmative* evidence. If the factor supports the witness' credibility as a whole (e.g., evidence demonstrates the witness' neutrality), there is the same issue of where to locate the evidence.

evidence from the story outline. More likely one will include the evidence, and locate it at a sensible spot.[20]

b. Additional Data Re Phillips v. Landview

Below is a report from an investigator hired by plaintiff's attorney, Jerry Mason. Note that the report is limited almost entirely to evidence which affects the credibility of Paul Lade and Lou Purvisor, two potential defense witnesses whose partial stories were set out at the end of Chapter 7. In practice, one of course would expect to receive substantive evidence and credibility evidence more or less simultaneously. Thus, before reading the investigative credibility report, please reread the stories of Lade and Purvisor and the report of Mike Hidden in Chapter 7, noting particularly any credibility evidence in those stories. Then, as you read the additional data pertaining to credibility below, please consider (1) whether you would classify the credibility evidence as affirmative or rebuttal evidence; and (2) where in the appropriate outline you might list the credibility evidence.

Following the report, we illustrate how credibility evidence might be included in the affirmative and rebuttal sections of outlines. You are then asked to outline the remaining pieces of credibility evidence.

Investigative Report

From: Freddy Billity
To: Jerry Mason

I've learned some new information both about Lade and Lou Purvisor. I'll summarize the information here. If my summary indicates a source of information, then that source is a written witness statement or other document which is attached to the summary.

A. With Respect to Lade:

1. Lade is 5'3" tall, and weighs about 230 pounds.

2. Two weeks before the Phillipses bought their lots, Lade sent a memo to Lotz informing him that he was 20% behind his projected sales figures. (Memo attached, dated August 15).

3. The second time Lade told Lotz to make sure that all prospective purchasers are told that all lots are sold on an "as is" basis and that Landview will make no further land improvements, he remembers staying extra late at the office and missing his son's first birthday party in order to tell that to Lotz. (Lade Depo., p. 1072, lines 1–3).

4. Get this—Lotz is Lade's son-in-law! (Statement of Liv Urwurst).

5. About a year ago, Lade wrote a chapter in a book, *Subdivisions in a Nutshell,* entitled "The Illicit Destruction of Caveat Emptor: Is Civilization As We Know It About To End?"

---

20. For a related discussion of this issue, see Chapter 4, pages 52–54.

6. Lade has no training or experience in soil engineering (Lade Depo., p. 108, lines 15–17).

B. With Regard to Purvisor:

1. Mrs. Phillips remembers talking to Purvisor, sometime in late July, when she and her husband were looking at the two lots they eventually bought. Purvisor said something to them, but she could not understand what he said. According to her, he was really drunk, his speech was thick and slurred, and he smelled heavily of alcohol. She noticed these things when she walked closer to him, trying to figure out what he had said. When she noticed his condition, she walked away without replying to whatever it was he said. (Statement of Mrs. Phillips).

2. Purvisor was convicted of perjury about a year ago. (Judgment of conviction attached).

3. I was able to speak to one Landview salesman, Chip N. Dale. He told me that he is positive that Lade never told him to tell prospective purchasers that all lots were sold on an "as is" basis. Dale is very conscientious apparently, and he records all specific instructions he's given in a small sales diary. He's checked the diary for the entire year before the Phillipses' purchase. There are a number of entries for Lade's instructions, but nothing at all about soil conditions. (Personal interview).

4. Purvisor had some difficulties on the job and was placed on probationary status by Lade at the end of last year. (Landview records).

5. According to Purvisor, before Lotz spoke to him about being behind in child support payments, Purvisor had never spoken to Lotz. Lotz was asking Purvisor's advice as to whether Lotz should try to modify the child support payments. Purvisor could give him little advice since he has no children and had never been in Lotz's situation. (Phone conversation with Purvisor).

6. Purvisor told me that when he saw the woman from Acme Soil Engineers, she was actually on Lot 70. (Phone conversation with Purvisor).

c. Making the Outlines

As one will typically include credibility evidence in the affirmative and rebuttal sections of outlines, we illustrate its use with two pieces of evidence relating to the credibility of Lade and Purvisor.

Item of Evidence # 1. Purvisor on probationary status on the job.

This evidence affects the credibility of Purvisor, a witness who ostensibly provides affirmative evidence for Landview. From this evidence, the factfinder may infer, among other things, that Purvisor has a motive to testify in Landview's favor: to save his job. Therefore, this item of credibility evidence is rebuttal evidence for the Phillipses.

In the Outline of Landview's Existing Affirmative Evidence begun in Chapter 7, regarding the suitability of lots 70 and 71 for building, the first piece of affirmative evidence from Purvisor appears as Item

7. With the addition of this new piece of credibility evidence, that portion of that same outline would be as follows:

Landview's Affirmative Evidence	Phillipses' Rebuttal
7. Mrs. Phillips told Lou Purvisor that it was a shame not to be able to buy a lot and build a house right away without checking out the lot. (Purvisor statement)	(a) Purvisor cannot remember if Mr. Phillips was present at time statement was made. (Statement of Purvisor) (b) Because of job difficulties, Purvisor was placed on probationary status by Lade around the end of the year. (Landview's records)

In this outline excerpt, note that no special notice is taken that the new item of rebuttal is strictly credibility evidence. Nor does the outline refer to the particular credibility factor affected by the evidence. Though one might imagine situations in which one might want to include such details, in the typical case that should not be necessary. Moreover, we have not included the generalizations which support the link between the rebuttal evidence and its effect on credibility; in an actual case, one may want to include those generalizations.

This particular piece of evidence is of course a *source* credibility factor. One may then have to decide when and how often to list this same piece of evidence. For example, assume that in the outline of Landview's affirmative evidence, items 7, 14 and 21 are supplied by Purvisor. Should one include this same piece of rebuttal each time? Is it sufficient to list it once, perhaps when evidence from Purvisor is first listed? Or should one just list it once, and then cross reference to it in other places? We suggest no answers, but simply remind you that the outline system is flexible and may be adjusted to the demands of specific cases.

Item of Evidence # 2. Two weeks before the Phillipses purchased their lots, Lade sent a memo to Lotz stating that Lotz was 20% behind his projected sales figures.

This is an interesting piece of evidence. On the one hand, the evidence is inconsistent with Lade's deposition testimony that around the time of the Phillipses' purchase, Lotz was 40% ahead of sales projections. Thus, with reference again to the outline of Landview's existing affirmative evidence, this piece of evidence could be listed as rebuttal to Item # 4 in that outline.

At the same time, the evidence is affirmative evidence for the Phillipses. From evidence that Lotz had been told that he was 20% behind his sales projections, one may infer that he had a motive to induce the Phillipses' purchase. This same piece of evidence could also therefore be listed as affirmative evidence in the outline of the Phillipses' existing evidence.

The outline portions below illustrate both of these possibilities:

(i) Outline of Landview's Existing Evidence

Landview's Affirmative Evidence	Phillipses' Rebuttal
4. At the time of the Phillipses' purchase, Lotz was 40% ahead of his projected sales figures. (Lade Depo., p. 28) [Generalization omitted, but see Outline in Chap. 7]	(a) Lotz told Purvisor around the time of the Phillipses' purchase that child support payments were killing him. (Statement of Purvisor) (b) Lade wrote memo to Lotz around time of the Phillipses' purchase stating that Lotz was 20% behind projected sales figures. (Memo of Lade)

(ii) Outline of the Phillipses' Existing Evidence

Phillipses' Affirmative Evidence	Landview's Rebuttal
1. Around the time of the Phillipses' purchase, Lotz was 20% behind his projected sales figures. (Lade memo) [Generalization omitted]	(a) Around the time of the Phillipses' purchase, Lotz was 40% ahead of his projected sales figures. (Lade Depo, p. 28)

The possibility of listing the same piece of evidence twice in both parties' outlines exists whenever credibility evidence both rebuts the adversary and provides affirmative evidence on one's own behalf. Unless one has a good reason to do otherwise, one will normally include such evidence in both parties' outlines.

d. Credibility Evidence Exercises

1. Review the "Additional Data" portions of Chapters 7 and 8. Using the "story" and "source" factors set forth earlier in this chapter, list any credibility evidence you can identify in that data according to each category.

2.   For each item of evidence identified in response to Question # 1, please indicate whether it is affirmative or rebuttal evidence, or both, and for which party.

3.   Prepare a "mini-outline," listing each piece of credibility evidence opposite the affirmative evidence which it calls into question. If the evidence does not rebut a specific piece of evidence, but rather rebuts a witness' testimony as a whole, please so indicate.

Part III

IDENTIFYING POTENTIAL
ADDITIONAL EVIDENCE

Part II primarily described a number of ways of analyzing evidence and a system for recording it. We hope it provided some insight into one aspect of what it means to "think like a lawyer:" how to dissect stories of human behavior with an eye to identifying evidence useful in telling a persuasive legal story.

The process described in Part II was essentially static; it called upon one only to analyze evidence that was already available. Part III moves to a more dynamic phase of investigation, a phase which for many lawyers involves one of the more creative aspects of litigation. One sits back, thinks creatively, and exercises what Agatha Christie's fictional hero, Hercule Poirot, was fond of referring to as "the little gray cells."

During the phase of investigation described in Part III, one determines *potential* evidence to pursue.[1] In thinking about potential additional evidence, one asks oneself such questions as, "What are our theories as to what happened in this case?" "Can we explain to the factfinder why things happened as our story suggests they happened?" "What evidence should we look for which might support our theories?"

After identifying areas for further investigation, one then considers tactics and techniques for their pursuit. Those tactics and techniques are the subject of Part IV.

---

1. Remember that, as noted earlier, the processes of analyzing existing evidence and identifying potential evidence often go on simultaneously in the real world. We divide them primarily for purposes of analysis.

Chapter 9

IDENTIFYING LEGAL AND FACTUAL THEORIES

1. INTRODUCTION

Investigation is often all too readily thought of as merely a time to learn evidence. But remember that the evidence-gathering phase of investigation is normally preceded by analysis which ultimately dictates what evidence one pursues. This analysis concerns in part the potential legal theories and factual hypotheses that one may pursue during investigation. And, in part, it concerns the specific evidence which might prove the theories and hypotheses true. This chapter explores how one formulates legal theories and factual hypotheses. How one then adorns these hypotheses with specific items of potential evidence is the subject of Chapter 10.

Throughout the book, we have emphasized how each party tells a selective story at trial. From the universe of potentially relevant evidence, a party tries to select that evidence which tells the most persuasive story. Legal theories and factual hypotheses form the base from which one identifies the affirmative and rebuttal evidence ultimately included in a party's story; they are the principal guides to investigatory pursuits.

The consideration of potentially applicable legal theories does not end with the filing of a complaint or an answer. As more evidence is uncovered, one may need to abandon one or more initial legal theories, to adopt new ones, and to file amended pleadings which reflect the changes.

Factual hypotheses are potential stories of historical events which trigger (or are triggered by) one or more legal theories. As you know, a legal theory is useless unless it is supported by a story which activates it. Sometimes a client's story supplies the only factual hypothesis one needs to investigate. Often, however, one must formulate additional factual hypotheses. This is typically true because multiple factual hypotheses may activate a single legal theory.

A short example demonstrates the difference between legal theories and factual hypotheses. Assume a landlord seeks to evict a tenant because of the tenant's failure to pay rent. A legal theory on which the landlord will probably rely is "breach of lease." As attorney for the landlord, one may also want to consider possible legal theories other than breach of lease. For instance, lease provisions aside, did the tenant commit a nuisance on the premises or violate any zoning laws? And within the single legal theory of breach of lease, one may want to consider factual hypotheses in addition to failure to pay rent. For instance, one may consider whether the tenant breached by failing to maintain the premises in good repair or by failing to pay required taxes.

2. WHY THEORY DEVELOPMENT TYPICALLY PRECEDES FACT INVESTIGATION

It is nearly impossible to question witnesses in the absence of some legal theory, whether or not that theory is explicitly identified. Assume a grieving widow enters one's law office wishing to fasten upon someone liability for her husband's death. All the widow knows is that her husband was driving a motorboat in the middle of a misty lake, that the motorboat was found overturned, and that her husband was found on the lake bottom. In an effort to find out if anyone is legally responsible for the husband's death, please develop a short list of questions that you might ask of different potential witnesses. We pause while you write. [Time passes.]

Now, examine the questions. Some may have been broad and non-specific such as, "Please tell me all you know about what happened." Such questions are probably not asked in pursuit of a particular theory. They are perhaps more accurately thought of as part of a search for a theory.

Other questions, however, probably sought more specific information. Almost inevitably, those questions were asked with one or more theories of liability in mind, regardless of whether one consciously articulated a specific theory. For example, if one question asked another boater whether any boats were being driven dangerously on the lake that day, it would be disingenuous to suggest that one did not have a theory in mind. Similarly, if one asked the widow about the condition of the husband's boat, one probably has some theory in mind.[1]

1. Though theories are inevitably in one's mind, especially during the early phases of interviews one often seeks to learn about all pertinent events known to

For the most part, then, one cannot seek information in the absence of a theory which makes that information relevant. Since the theories will be there subconsciously anyway, one should consciously decide which theory or theories are most worthy of pursuit. At least, one's conscious choices are likely to produce better results than one's subconscious wanderings.

Lawyers are not the only professionals whose inquiries are dominated by theory. Recall that in a very real sense, litigators are historians. Litigators attempt to reconstruct past events into stories that convince factfinders that those events happened in a certain way. Interestingly, historians' explorations of the past are often as controlled by theories as are those of litigators:

> It follows that theory . . . plays a crucial role in historical reconstruction . . . . [T]heory is usually part of a historian's mental baggage before he immerses himself in a particular topic. It encourages historians to ask certain questions, and not to ask others; it tends to single out particular areas of investigation as worthy of testing, and to dismiss other areas of inquiry as either irrelevant or uninteresting. Thus anyone who ventures into the field of history—the lay reader as well as the professional researcher—needs to be aware of how . . . theory exerts its pervasive influence.[2]

Litigators, perhaps, operate in a different kind of world from historians. Historians, we assume, seek "objective" truth. Litigators, by contrast, are more overtly instrumental. They represent clients who seek, or seek to avoid, specific relief. A litigator will usually pursue a theory (or set of theories) that will most likely enable the litigator to tell a story that effectuates a client's interests. Thus, theories in litigation, like litigators, are instrumental. They are chosen in an effort to persuade a listener that one's client should win.

In recognizing that litigators select their theories with persuasive purposes in mind, we do not mean to suggest that litigators are necessarily less likely than historians to tell stories which produce "objective" truth. Rather, the recognition is made in order to ensure that all of us expressly acknowledge what litigators actually do in carrying out their role as advocates. Indeed, without such express recognition of how lawyers as advocates select theories to guide their investigations and present their clients' stories, courtroom stories are perhaps unlikely ever to produce "objective" truth.

witnesses without limiting questioning to previously-identified theories. See Chapter 14.

2. J. Davidson and M. Lytle, *After the Fact: The Art of Historical Detection*

(1982). Cf. F. Schauer, An Essay on Constitutional Language, 29 UCLA L.Rev. 797, 818 (1982).

Given that theories are a necessary prerequisite to effective fact investigation and to a client's story ultimately told, it follows that success in litigation often depends on one's ability to develop legal theories. To that development we now turn. First, we consider the theories that guide the selection of affirmative evidence.

3. BUILDING HYPOTHESES FOR AFFIRMATIVE STORIES

a. *Identify Alternative Legal Theories*

Before filing a complaint, one has typically learned something about a client's version of historical events and developed one or more legal stories which might eventually persuade a trier of fact to grant relief. A plaintiff's legal story is one which, if believed, establishes each element necessary to entitle a client to relief under an applicable legal theory. If one is representing a defendant, before filing a response the client's story often has generated legal stories on which potential affirmative defenses and cross actions can be based. Since from either a plaintiff's or a defendant's standpoint theory development typically precedes the bulk of fact investigation, it makes sense to focus first on ways of developing alternative legal theories.

Investigation would be simpler if lawyers could act like homing pigeons—if once tagged with evidence of a written contract, a tort, or some other legal theory, they could single-mindedly home in on the path suggested by that one legal theory. However, in most cases one's client is better served by identification and investigation of more than one theory. Consider why this is so.

Most importantly, multiple theories are essential to thorough investigation. As mentioned in Chapter 2, because clients and witnesses usually do not understand what substantive law may be applicable in a given situation, they do not usually report all relevant information that they know. Therefore, if one is to learn all relevant information which a client or witness knows, one must usually be aware of all potentially applicable theories. In the context of a particular substantive theory, one asks questions that would be irrelevant or would go unnoticed in the context of a different theory. By framing questions relevant to separate theories, one is more likely to bring out the relevant data a client or witness knows but does not report because its importance is not realized.

For example, assume that Mr. Varat, who is black, resides in Waco, Texas. He contacts a lawyer and complains that his employer, The Waco Republic Oil Company, is always passing him over for promotion. He states that his department supervisor has often made disparaging remarks about minorities. Mr. Varat believes he is a victim of racial discrimination and wants to know what, if anything, he can do about the situation.

Investigating this case merely from Mr. Varat's perspective, one might pursue only a theory of racial discrimination. Yet, fulfilling one's professional duty to Mr. Varat requires that other theories of relief be considered. Perhaps Mr. Varat was discriminated against for non-racial reasons—e.g., because of age, sex, religion, or union activities. Mr. Varat may not have mentioned facts suggesting that such reasons exist, but one cannot rely on laypeople to be aware of all potential legal theories of relief. If preliminary probing indicates some support for alternative theories, one should investigate those theories further.

Thus, it is not accurate to state either that theories must grow out of evidence, or that evidence must emanate from theories. In any given case, both processes may occur. Sometimes one pursues evidence to support a theory because a client's or witness' tale suggests the theory's applicability. Other times, one pursues evidence because one's knowledge of substantive theories suggests untold facts may be lurking. In either situation, successful investigation requires identification not only of substantive theories directly suggested by evidence, but also of those suggested by one's knowledge of potentially related theories.

Another reason to identify alternative theories is that one theory may provide more helpful relief than another. Punitive damages may be recoverable if intentional fraud is proved, but not if negligent misrepresentation is shown. Conviction for assault with a deadly weapon may allow for imprisonment in the "Big House up the River," whereas conviction for simple assault may result merely in county jail time. From a defense perspective, an "assumption of the risk" defense may negate a plaintiff's entire claim, whereas a "comparative negligence" defense defeats only a portion of it. In a criminal case, a defendant whose alibi defense is successful goes home, whereas one whose insanity defense is sustained perhaps goes to a mental institution. If one's outlines contain alternative theories, then one is more likely to pursue all potential relief which might satisfy a client's needs.

Finally, if one investigates multiple theories, one may have the luxury of deciding which theories to put forward at trial. When it comes time for trial, some theories often are eminently more provable than others. Perhaps a witness relevant to one theory has disappeared or a witness who supports one theory is more credible than a witness for another. Or, perhaps the political and social climate has changed since the time the case began, so that one theory may be more palatable to the factfinder than another. In sum, at trial one theory may stand a better chance of factfinder acceptance than another.

If one is to have the luxury of presenting a factfinder with alternative theories of relief or defense, then one should identify these theories at the earliest possible time.[3] The earlier a theory is identified, of course, the more time one has to pursue investigation to support it. Yet, there is typically no one stage of a case at which all potential theories are identified. Theory development is very much a cyclical process. In Chapter 3, Section 1, we noted that the process of identifying potential evidence is a continuing one. As one learns potential evidence, that evidence becomes the basis for the identification of additional potential evidence. The process of theory development is much the same. After hearing a client's initial story, one usually begins investigation with at least tentative theories in mind. As the pursuit of these theories produces evidence, that evidence may become the basis for new theories. The new theories may replace or be added to those one had at the beginning. As a result, an investigator must maintain a flexible outlook. One must pursue current theories in the knowledge that those theories may be transitory.[4]

However, how does one go about identifying alternative theories? Unfortunately for the homing pigeons among us, there is no single place to look. Obviously, the more substantive law with which one is familiar, the better able one will be to develop alternative theories. If one does not work regularly in a particular field of law, or if facts cross over into multiple fields, one may have difficulty identifying a single theory of relief or defense, let alone multiple theories. For example, assume a representative of a local homeowners' group comes into your office, states that the group has learned that a toxic waste disposal site is located nearby and asks you to do something to have the site inspected, closed and de-toxified. You are likely to have difficulty spinning out alternative substantive theories that might provide the client with this relief, though you may have no difficulty deciding to relocate your law office.

When confronted with such a predicament, the first step to overcoming it is to recognize the propriety of being unable to supply an

3. Tactics may dictate that only one theory be used at trial. In a criminal case, for example, a lawyer may urge only that a defendant is not guilty, and spurn an argument that the defendant is guilty of at most a lesser included offense. See also, R. Simmons, *Winning Before Trial: How to Prepare Cases for the Best Settlement or Trial Result* 1124–1129 (1974).

4. However, one is not necessarily free to identify new theories any time one wishes. Particularly in criminal cases, due process limitations may at trial confine a prosecutor to those offenses (including lesser-included offenses) contained in an information, indictment or complaint. In re Robert G., 31 Cal.3d 437, 182 Cal.Rptr. 644, 644 P.2d 837 (1982). In civil cases, those due process limitations become more elastic, and one may more freely amend pleadings prior to trial, or even at the conclusion of testimony to conform to proof. Early identification of theories is perhaps always desirable, in order that they may be fully investigated. In criminal cases, this desirability is transformed into a constitutional mandate.

immediate legal response. New lawyers often graduate from law school believing they ought to know almost all the law, and then feeling very inadequate when they realize they do not. By accepting one's unfamiliarity with an area of law, one is on the way to gaining familiarity.

Now that one is in the proper frame of mind, the next step is to realize that one is never quite as unfamiliar with an area of law as may first appear. At least, one usually has a sufficient basis for making preliminary judgments about substantive theories that might be researched. Return to the toxic waste disposal hypothetical. Even if one knows nothing about this area of law, one realizes from newspapers and magazines that the topic has attracted much governmental interest. It is likely, therefore, that civil or criminal statutes, at the municipal, state, or federal level, have been passed which touch on the matter. Searching for such statutes should provide one good starting point for legal research.

Second, if one is unfamiliar with a specific topic, one can normally analogize it to a topic with which one is familiar. Given the legal system's tendency to deal with similar problems in similar ways,[5] the legal theories which apply to the analogous situation are likely to apply to the unfamiliar one. Thus, a toxic waste disposal site is like a nuisance or an ultrahazardous activity. If one thinks about these perhaps more familiar topics and the way the legal system has dealt with them, then one can probably begin to develop potential theories that will apply to the unfamiliar topics.

There is an additional method of becoming knowledgeable about unfamiliar legal topics. Admittedly, it is one apparently so threatening that it has been concealed from generations of law students. The secret method is: Ask somebody who knows! After all, one reason lawyers huddle together in law firms is that help on an unfamiliar topic may be close at hand. If legal research were purely a private struggle between a lawyer and a law library, there would probably be a lot more law libraries and a lot fewer law firms. Litigators tend to be very knowledgeable in areas in which they have litigated and very uninformed in areas in which they have not. And, when they need a push to get started with an unfamiliar topic, they are more likely to consult someone who may know than to consult a descriptive word index. So, when in an unfamiliar legal area, take the advice of the telephone company: Reach out and touch someone.

A word of caution is in order here. All of these methods are designed to get one started on research, not to replace it. An ancient authority states, "All beginnings are hard." Methods such as those

5. See S. Yeazell, "Convention, Fiction and Law, XIII New Literary History 89 (1981).

suggested above enable one to make a beginning. The beginning must be followed by careful, professional research if one is to marshal evidence in order to tell viable legal stories.

At this point, one might be fearful of being advised to spin out theories the way the miller's daughter spun gold in Rumplestiltskin. After all, is there not a risk that if one identifies a large number of potentially applicable theories, one will not have the time, and clients will not have the resources, to pursue them all? If that is a risk, it is one which is greatly lessened by the distinction between identification of theories and their complete pursuit.

We do urge one, especially at the early stages of a case, before and after pleadings are filed, to consider a variety of theories, even those that seem at first blush absurd. In the days before "trover" and "assumpsit," the first pleading for specific performance may have provoked a few chuckles. There is no obligation to identify a set number of theories. (Neanderthal lawyers put the figure at three. Remember, however, their numbering system went only to four.) Today, for reasons stated above, one should at least consider whether more than one substantive theory is sufficiently viable to be included in an outline.

Even after preliminarily identifying a number of theories, one is not committed to their complete pursuit. One may discard theories because they appear fruitless, because they are too expensive to prove, or because other theories are more promising.

Still less does one need to put forward at trial all theories pursued during investigation. A strategy of pouring the maximum number of possible theories on the factfinder, in the hope that one will stick, is not often successful. Instead, the weaker theories may detract the factfinder's attention from the stronger ones. Thus, initially one should attempt to identify an array of potentially applicable substantive theories. After some preliminary investigation, one may pursue in earnest fewer theories than were first identified. At trial, the theories may be culled still further to create maximum persuasive effect.[6]

b. Identify Alternative Factual Theories

Even after identifying one or more legal theories, one is only part way on the road to starting investigation.

Each legal theory must have a factual story which activates (or, from a defense perspective, defuses) the theory. That is, a legal theory is useless unless it is supported by facts demonstrating that the theory applies. Hence, the rest of the road to starting investigation

6. See note 3, supra.

is often the development of factual theories which activate (or defuse) a particular legal theory. Sometimes the development of additional factual theories is not reasonably possible; a client's story is such that if a legal theory is to be proved or disproved, the client's story provides the only one that can be told. In other situations, one may have to develop factual theories in addition to those suggested by a client's story. Finally, in some cases one's task may be to develop factual theories largely unaided by a client's initial description. These three situations are illustrated below.

First, consider a situation in which a client's story is such that reasonably there is but one factual theory which will activate a legal theory. Assume that in a criminal case, defendant Tommy Ache is charged with petty theft. The prosecution's story is provided by a security guard at the market allegedly victimized by Ache. The guard states that he saw Ache place a jar of peanut butter, a loaf of white bread, a pound of pastrami and a bottle of bicarbonate of soda in a bag and leave the store without paying. In this example, the prosecutor may need to search for evidence that adds to the persuasiveness of his or her case. But in terms of factual theories as to how the petty theft was committed, the security guard's story provides the only factual theory reasonably possible.

In a middle range of situations, an initial story does provide a factual theory as to what may have happened but leaves room for alternative factual theories. Assume that one represents Shubin Inc., a manufacturer of aluminum sheeting, which sold large coils of the sheeting to Universal Molded, which roll-formed the aluminum into a finished product. Universal has filed suit against Shubin for breach of contract, alleging that the aluminum sheeting was badly manufactured and therefore cracked during Universal's roll-forming process. Shubin's Vice-President, Dorothy, states that the aluminum sheeting was satisfactorily made and that any problem with it must have been caused by something Universal did. Dorothy is not certain what Universal did to the sheeting but knows that if raw sheeting is subjected to undue pressure during roll-forming, it tends to crack. However, according to Dorothy, there could be other reasons why well-made sheeting cracks. As attorney for Shubin, one has one clear factual theory that defuses Universal's legal theory that there was a breach of contract: Universal caused the sheeting to crack by subjecting it to undue pressure. However, other factual theories may also defuse Universal's legal theory; according to Dorothy, Universal might have done other things to the sheeting during the manufacturing process to cause it to crack. In fact, even if Dorothy had not suggested the possibility of other reasons why the sheeting might have cracked, as Shubin's attorney one still might be responsible for developing alternative factual theories on one's own.

Finally, sometimes an initial story may suggest one or more legal theories, but no factual hypothesis as to what may have happened. Consider the case mentioned at the outset of this chapter: the boat that overturned in the middle of a misty lake. One legal theory which might provide relief to the grieving widow is products liability—the boat was defectively designed or made. But the widow herself probably has no idea as to how the accident actually occurred and unless one is very familiar with boat design (or has seen "Raise the Titantic" at least twelve times), one probably will not have a factual hypothesis that supports the legal theory of defective manufacture or design.

A lack of a factual hypothesis is a real possibility in a variety of contexts. Assume one represents an investor who bought stock in a company after reading the company's prospectus. A month after the investment, the company is bankrupt and the investor is angry. Again, the client's story may suggest a legal theory, securities fraud: the prospectus concealed important data about the company. But the client may well lack a factual theory concerning the kind of data withheld.

Thus, in many cases, one's responsibility is to identify hypotheses that might activate legal theories suggested by a client's story. This is necessary either because the client's own factual theories are limited, or because they are totally lacking. How then does one go about developing factual theories?

It may not be possible to describe exactly how one develops factual hypotheses. Perhaps all that can be safely said is that dogma such as, "In Rule 10(b)(5) securities cases, always formulate a factual hypothesis concerning the stockbroker," might be comforting, but it would be wrong.

We believe that the process of developing factual hypotheses usually goes something like this. One listens to a story, which triggers one or more potentially applicable legal theories. Contemporaneously, or subsequently, one reviews the story in light of each legal theory. If a story describes what happened in a way that completely coincides with a legal theory—that is, if the story can be termed a "legal story"—one *may* not bother to consider additional factual hypotheses. This was the situation in the Tommy Ache petty theft hypothetical. In that hypothetical, the combination of a trained eyewitness and a relatively straightforward and focused factual description may well result in the prosecutor not considering other ways in which the petty theft might have been committed.

But the comparison of a story with a legal theory may reveal that the story does not explain what happened in a way that fully activates or defuses the legal theory. Or the comparison may reveal that the story is but one of a number of reasonably possible ways that the legal story might be told. In either situation, one is likely to "conjure up" other stories about what happened that might activate the legal theory. These factual possibilities then become the bases for ensuing investigation.

When one "conjures up" factual hypotheses about what might have happened, one combines two different skills. One skill, purely a legal one, is to develop hypotheses which, if found to be accurate, produce stories that can be told with respect to particular legal theories. For example, if an initial story suggests breach of contract, developing a factual hypothesis about a party's negligence in no way activates the suggested theory.

But conjuring up legal stories requires more than legal skill. To develop factual hypotheses, one draws upon experience, common sense, and creativity to formulate stories that appear realistic and plausible. For this purpose, one looks to the type of situation, or perhaps to the industry, which appears to be involved in an initial story. One then posits one or more ways that events may have happened that satisfy a legal theory. For example, if one is told that a car plunged off a steep mountain road, one may formulate a legal theory of defective design or manufacture. This formulation is a product of legal analysis. But to develop stories that activate this legal theory, one must draw upon one's experience about what sorts of mechanical defects may cause a car to plunge off a road. For example, one may hypothesize that the plunge was caused by defective brakes, steering, or tires.

Sometimes, as in the example above, the experience and common sense upon which one bases hypotheses most likely would be shared by the populace as a whole. But in many instances, one needs more than everyday common experience to develop a complete hypothesis. Even if the average "person on the street" would be aware that defective brakes may cause a car to leave the road, the average person probably would not know what it is about a brake's manufacture or design that may render it defective. When subject matter is beyond common experience, attorneys who specialize occasionally are able to develop complete hypotheses on their own. More often than not, attorneys must turn to experts to develop complete factual hypotheses.

c. Using Experts

Since factual hypotheses grow primarily out of experience, it follows that the less experience one has in a particular walk of life or industry, the more one needs to acquire experience before one can formulate hypotheses. One way that litigators acquire experience in an area is to talk to someone who, broadly speaking, is an expert.[7] An "expert" is a person who is familiar with a given field, industry, culture, or other subject and who can provide one with experience in the form of information and conclusions about what might have happened. Based on the data supplied by an expert, one may select one or more hypotheses which might constitute legal stories on behalf of one's client, or defuse those of the adversary.

For example, return to the example of the car that plunged off the cliff while headed downhill on a steep mountain road. As we have seen, certain hypotheses about what might have happened to cause the car to go over the cliff may be drawn from common experience. From the point of view of the driver's estate, some of these may be legal stories (the driver of another car forced the car off the road) and some may be nonlegal (the driver was drunk and was trying to prove that at speeds in excess of 100 m.p.h., cars are not subject to gravity). Other factual hypotheses may call for a combination of common experience and expert advice. That is, one may know that a possible legal story is that the brakes were defectively designed or manufactured, but without an expert one may not know what sorts of design or manufacturing problems render brakes defective. Finally, still other potential hypotheses may be entirely in the realm of an expert. There might well be mechanical conditions less obvious to the average person than defective brakes which might cause a car to leave a highway. Again, the hypotheses identified by an expert may be legal or nonlegal from a client's point of view. A hypothesis by an expert that the car was modified by the driver to accommodate over-sized tires might be nonlegal, whereas one that the mishap may have been due to a faulty steering mechanism probably would be legal.

What manner of person an "expert" is varies of course with the field. In a case in which a patient in a hospital died while under anesthesia, an expert may have to be a board-certified anesthesiologist to be of any real value. On the other hand, in a case of alleged discrimination in a packaging plant, the expert might be an employee who has worked in the packaging field for a number of years. In either event, the expert serves to provide one with experience. To that experience, one adds legal skill and so produces one or more investigatory hypotheses that constitute legal stories.

These suggestions concerning the use of experts may at first blush strike one as nontraditional. One may be used to thinking of an expert as an interpreter of data already unearthed.[8] "O.K., Doc., here's everything I've been able to find out about the defendant's life

7. There are other ways of gaining experience, of course. One might, for instance, read a book about a particular walk of life or industry.

8. At trial, the data which an expert interprets is often presented through a hypothetical question. See 6 Am.Jur.

since he was three days old. What do you think—did he know right from wrong?" In reality, an expert's role is not so limited. As we conceive it, in addition to interpreting data, an expert is often needed to identify paths (factual hypotheses) that one may follow to unearth data in the first place.

d. Using Intuition

We make special mention of this method of formulating factual hypotheses not necessarily because it is so important, but because it is so neglected in lawyering literature. Intuition is a technique of arriving at plausible, yet tentative, formulations without going through a series of analytic steps. As a well-respected educational theorist has pointed out,

> Intuitive thinking, the training of hunches, is a much-neglected and essential feature of productive thinking not only in formal academic disciplines but also in everyday life. The shrewd guess, the fertile hypothesis, the courageous leap to a tentative conclusion—these are the most valuable coin of the thinker at work, whatever his [and her] line of work.[9]

We do not mean to suggest that intuition is an effective substitute for analytic thought. In fact, to intuit well one may also need to possess sound analytic skills.[10] However, intuition is a prized commodity in fields as diverse as mathematics, history and poetry;[11] and lawyers should welcome it no less warmly.

Therefore, when attempting to formulate factual hypotheses, do not be afraid to guess, to play a hunch or to make an educated guess. One may see hypotheses that might have eluded a painstaking analysis of evidence. With an intuitive hypothesis in hand, one may turn analyst to identify potential evidence to prove its correctness.

e. Defense Factual Hypotheses

Recall from Chapter 2 that defendants frequently approach cases from a dual perspective. Defendants attempt both to poke holes in plaintiffs' cases (a rebuttal story) and to tell their own stories of what happened (an affirmative story). To the extent that defendants tell their own stories of historical events, defense counsel face situations generally similar to those faced by plaintiffs' counsel.[12] Thus, sometimes a defendant's initial story will present the only possible factual hypothesis about what happened; sometimes it will present a middle

---

Proof of Facts 159–210 (1960); 5 Am.Jur Trials 678–679 (1968).

9. J. Bruner, *The Process of Education* 13–14 (1960).

10. Ibid. at 56–57.

11. Ibid. at 66–67.

12. Indeed, in seeking to prove cross actions or affirmative defenses, defense counsel are in the identical situation as plaintiff's counsel.

range situation creating a need to identify theories other than the one suggested by the initial story; and sometimes an initial story will leave one with a need to fashion hypotheses from scratch. Moreover, the skills used to develop factual hypotheses for defendants are the same as those used to identify theories on behalf of plaintiffs. And, as in developing theories for plaintiffs, one frequently needs to call upon experts in order to carry out the formulation process.

But there are at least two distinctions between how defense counsel and plaintiffs' counsel think when they identify theories about what happened. A plaintiff's lawyer typically is concerned with making sure that hypotheses result in a legal story—i.e. a story that if told in court and believed, establishes each element of a legal theory and entitles the client to some relief. By contrast, defense counsel typically seek to focus stories on one or more specific elements in order to convert plaintiffs' stories into nonlegal ones. Each element of a plaintiff's case may be thought of as a junction along a railroad track, and defense counsel consider hypotheses which might derail the plaintiff's theory at various junctions.

For example, assume that Tommy Ache was charged with grand theft, in that he allegedly stole a dried salami encased in gold leaf, worth in excess of $200, from the market. In Ache's defense, one hypothesis that might derail the prosecution at the "intent" junction would be that Ache intended to purchase the salami and only carried it with him as he left the store to get his checkbook. Similarly, a hypothesis that might derail the prosecution at the "grand theft" junction would be that the salami was not in fact worth in excess of $200. (Of course, unless the hypotheses are supported by evidence, they are nothing but a lot of baloney.) Though defense counsel theoretically could formulate a nonlegal story at each junction, typically a defense focuses on a limited number of junctions.

Another distinction between the way plaintiffs' counsel and defense counsel think about cases grows out of the reality that, apart from whether a particular defendant is legally responsible, the plaintiff usually is a person who has been in some way damaged or injured. For example, in the Tommy Ache petty theft case, somebody probably took goods from the market without paying. In the age discrimination case, plaintiff probably was not promoted. And in the "car off the cliff" case, defendant brake manufacturer will probably concede that the car did indeed go off the cliff. Because, in the abstract, plaintiffs typically have what appears to be a legitimate beef, defense counsel usually attempt to develop a factual response which not only demonstrates the defendant's lack of responsibility for any harm or injuries but which also purports to identify who is responsible for whatever harm is conceded.

The utility of a story which identifies the "real culprit" is perhaps also a creature of a thought process that places great stock in cause-and-effect. Recall that most of us believe that if something happened, its occurrence was probably caused by something else.[13] Thus, it is persuasive if a defendant shows not only that he or she was not the cause of plaintiff's harm, but also what the real cause was. For example, in the "car off the cliff" case, defendant brake manufacturer may develop one set of hypotheses about the proper design and manufacture of the brakes and another set concerning the actual cause of the mishap. This type of response is familiar to fans of the Perry Mason television show since Mason would almost always reveal the true culprit at each show's close.

To sum up then, defendants seek to respond to plaintiffs' purported legal stories by constructing hypotheses in at least the following ways:

1. Focusing on particular legal elements to poke holes in plaintiffs' stories. This is largely a "rebuttal" type of response.

2. Focusing on particular legal elements to tell affirmative stories that they are not responsible for whatever harm the plaintiffs suffered.

3. Telling stories as to who really is responsible for any harm to plaintiffs.

To translate this complicated defense view of the world into concrete terms, return to two of the hypothetical cases from this subsection. In the petty theft case, defendant Tommy Ache may offer a rebuttal story: The security guard was in a poor position to observe and was under pressure to make arrests or lose the job, and therefore cannot identify who took the goods. The defendant may also offer an affirmative story of his lack of responsibility: Tommy is innocent because at the time of the theft he was in Cucamonga. Finally, Tommy may filially reveal the actual perpetrator to be his brother, Billy Ache.

In the age discrimination case, defendant employer may rebut plaintiff's story with a story that attacks the credibility of plaintiff's witnesses. In addition, the employer may demonstrate its innocence

---

13. People's general ability to identify causal agents makes for interesting study. Faced with a plethora of contributing elements to any given occurrence, people distinguish and separate "causes" from mere conditions, and in turn ascribe responsibility to specific catalysts. See H. Hart & A. Honore, *Causation in the Law* 24–78 (1959).

While modern society can at times accept the notion that inevitably some things happen without someone being to blame, finger-pointing is by no means a byproduct only of modern life. In the case of homicide, for instance, classical Greek thought demanded the identification of the one "qua" cause, to which the "pollution" attached. See A. Adkins, *Merit and Responsibility* 102–107 (1960).

by affirmatively establishing that it has a policy against age discrimination, and that it has on various occasions promoted without respect to age. At the same time, it may indicate who is responsible, with a story that plaintiff was not promoted because of a history of tardiness and lack of ability. Note that in this example, the person responsible for plaintiff's harm would be the plaintiff.

Defense counsel will not, of course, always be able to offer proof in a rebuttal mode and both affirmative evidence modes. However, defendants typically attempt to do so. Hence, at the factual hypothesis stage of a case, one at least considers all three types of response. As a result, defendants' initial stories are inevitably incomplete, and defense counsel almost always need to conjure up a factual hypothesis or two on their own. A client may supply defense counsel with a factual hypothesis that rebuts plaintiff's story, but not with one that explains what really happened. Or vice versa. In any event, unless defense counsel considers factual hypotheses in support of all possible responses during investigation, potentially persuasive evidence on defendant's behalf may be omitted from trial.

f. Explanatory Theories

All the factual theories thus far examined, whether on behalf of plaintiffs or defendants, have been *descriptive*. By descriptive, we mean that they create narrative tales of what happened in the past. One can also develop *explanatory* factual hypotheses. As you know, an explanatory theory is one which attempts to explain *why* events happened as one contends or hypothesizes they did. Because we are usually impressed with the accuracy of a description if we are shown why events occurred, explanatory evidence often adds to a story's persuasiveness.[14]

As plaintiffs generally focus descriptive tales on affirmative stories, plaintiffs' explanatory theories often are limited to explaining why the events in their affirmative tales occurred as they contend. For example, in the "car off the cliff" hypothetical, assume that one of plaintiff's descriptive hypotheses is that a defectively manufactured tire blew up because the tire rubber was not given adequate time to cool. As plaintiff's counsel, one may identify a number of theories which might explain this affirmative story. One might hypothesize that the tire was defectively made because of employee inexperience or sabotage, or because the manufacturer was attempting to cut corners.

---

14. This is not necessarily true, however. If one offers too many explanations, a factfinder may choose to disbelieve all of them. Also, at times it may be difficult to distinguish between descriptive and explanatory hypotheses.

Defendants, by contrast, may tell three different descriptive tales at trial—an affirmative one, a rebuttal one, and a "who really did it" tale. Each type of tale may be supported by its own explanatory theory. In the Tommy Ache petty theft case, for example, Tommy's affirmative story was an alibi; he claimed to have been in Cucamonga at the time of the theft. One might include in this affirmative story an explanation of why he was in Cucamonga—say, to stomp grapes or to see a friend. Similarly, assume that Tommy's rebuttal story is that the security guard misidentified the actual thief because the guard was intoxicated. Explanatory theories supporting this rebuttal tale would attempt to identify reasons why the guard was intoxicated. Perhaps the guard is an alcoholic, or had just come from a co-worker's farewell lunch featuring spiked punch. Finally, if Tommy's "who really did it" descriptive story is that Brother Billy was the actual thief, one may posit explanatory theories as to why Billy committed the crime. Perhaps Billy is a kleptomaniac. Maybe he was out for revenge against Tommy and therefore made it appear that Tommy had committed the theft.

g. Emotional and Socio-Political Themes in Theories

Regardless of the type of factual theory identified, descriptive or explanatory, one should recognize that any given investigatory hypothesis may have an emotional cast. That is, a particular hypothesis may cause a trier of fact to be sympathetic or hostile to one of the parties. Additionally, or alternatively, one may sense that a hypothesis might trigger a socio-political response in the factfinder. One should be especially alert to emotional and socio-political hypotheses. They often may be turned into themes that may be logically persuasive because they make a factfinder *want* to decide a case for psychological reasons.

The notion that factual hypotheses may have emotional or socio-political overtones is important. Our description of the investigatory process emphasizes, as it should, rational evidentiary analysis in the context of discrete legal theories. But this emphasis should not mask a more subtle aspect of theory development. Because attorneys want to tell persuasive stories, they often attempt, to the extent permitted by rules of evidence, to structure cases so as to make use of themes that are emotional or socio-political. As one develops theories, then, one needs to be sensitive to theories which allow one to develop such themes.

By way of example, assume that one represents the individual who claims that he was not promoted because he was a victim of age discrimination. One may be able to develop a number of logical explanatory hypotheses as to why the discrimination occurred, such as the following:

(a) The immediate supervisor was biased against elderly workers;

(b) The company had a policy of not promoting older workers based on a belief that younger workers were more productive;

(c) The company did not promote the employee because it had a tacit agreement with the union to promote only younger employees.

Depending in part on who the trier of fact is, one of these hypotheses may have more emotional persuasiveness than another. For example, the theory that the employee was victimized by discrimination because of a "sweetheart deal" between company and union may arouse greater hostility toward the defendant than one based on the actions of an individual supervisor.

The defendant may similarly ferret out rational hypotheses with emotional overtones. Examine the age discrimination case from the company's point of view. The company will probably admit that it did not promote the employee, and seek at the "discrimination" junction to convert the story into a non-legal one. Consider the following hypotheses as to why the employee was not promoted:

(a) Another employee was more qualified for the position;

(b) The employee had a record of tardiness;

(c) The employee was a racist whose promotion would jeopardize future company contracts.

A similar analysis may be made with criminal cases. If one is the prosecutor in a case in which the defendant is charged with bank robbery, one may well want to hypothesize as to the reasons the defendant committed the robbery. Potential hypotheses include the defendant's need to support an expensive drug habit, participation in a gang initiation stunt, or need to pay off accumulated debts.

In each of the examples above, it is likely that depending upon who the factfinder is, one of the potential hypotheses may have more emotional or socio-political impact than the others. One need not, and indeed should not, limit investigation to those hypotheses which have such a potential impact. But when a hypothesis which includes emotional or socio-political overtones is confirmed through investigation, one has often discovered a jackpot. With such a theory confirmed by evidence, one has a theory that not only presents a complete package to the trier of fact, but also a package that appeals to a factfinder on both a rational and an emotional level.[15]

15. In articulating the reality that one often uses investigatory hypotheses to pursue evidence that can be used to present an emotionally persuasive story, we

There is a relationship between the above discussion of emotionally-based theories and earlier discussions of emotional evidence and evaluation of a story's credibility on the basis of its emotional and/or socio-political content. All the discussions of emotional and socio-political evidence—"psychological evidence"—are part of one big ball of wax, the reality that people reason with their hearts as well as their minds. Stated differently, in reality people reason with the left and right sides of their brains.

Earlier chapters pointed out that various bits and pieces of evidence introduced to support a rational inference might also activate feelings of sympathy, hostility and/or various socio-political attitudes. For example, evidence of a callous statement made by one driver to another soon after a collision not only may support an inference that the first driver was at fault but also may cause hostility toward that driver. This chapter introduces a more fundamental reality about the proof of facts through psychological means. Stories often include emotional and socio-political evidence because lawyers consciously pursue, both during investigation and at trial, legal theories and factual hypotheses which trigger emotional and/or socio-political responses.[16] In short, psychological proof often spills into the trial not as a matter of happenstance. Rather, it appears because a lawyer has consciously pursued such evidence in the course of building theories of what happened and why.

Is this proper? Should one consciously pursue investigation with the idea of developing a theory that has emotional and/or socio-political overtones? Is not our system of justice intended to be color blind?[17] That is, should not cases be decided on the basis of what happened, regardless of whether the people involved are rich or poor, nice or nasty, black or white? Though one may well answer "Yes" in the abstract to all of these questions, in the real world, "Yes" answers may impose impossible and unacceptable standards. For one thing, many disputes by their very nature involve emotionally-

do not mean to suggest that cases will have emotional or socio-economic impact only if evidence to fill such theories is introduced. Assume, for example, that one represents a plaintiff in a case in which the client fell in a market when she slipped on a banana peel. Assume further that one can produce no evidence about how or why the peel got on the floor. In such a case, even without specific evidence of the defendant's responsibility, one might be able to arouse an emotional response in the factfinder by arguing about the duty of market owners to keep their floors safe and free of debris. Indeed, such an argument might be construed as the central theme or theory of the case, although per se there is arguably no evidence around which such theme or theory is built. For discussion of this type of argument and also the notion that lawyers should build persuasive themes, see L. Smith, *Art of Advocacy* § 1.15 at 1–16 (1978).

16. By way of example, a plaintiff's lawyer may pursue a legal theory of fraud in addition to that of breach of contract, for the reason that the former theory allows greater opportunity for emotional evidence.

17. See K. Karst, "Why Equality Matters," 17 Ga.L.Rev. 245 (1983).

charged situations. For example, regardless of the parties' theories, cases involving cars that pitch over cliffs and older employees who are not promoted are, at least to some degree, inherently emotional. Moreover, regardless of the nature of a dispute, evidence which explains *why* something happened is certainly logically relevant. Yet, explanatory evidence is itself frequently emotional since it often involves human passions such as greed, revenge or envy. Thus, one could not bar emotional evidence unless one were prepared to lock courtroom doors to an array of disputes and rational proof.

Furthermore, in the middle of trials one cannot fairly expect trial judges *continuously* to make judgments as to whether the rational purpose of a given item of evidence outweighs its emotional aspect. Finally, people are emotional beings, and arguably one reason that trials are decided by people and not computers is that we want judgments based on human wisdom, concern and understanding. In the absence of emotion, those values probably would be inoperable.

Recognize, however, that one's ability to introduce emotional or socio-political evidence into trials is not without its limits. Evidentiary rules which govern character evidence [18] and which authorize judges to exclude evidence when its prejudicial effect outweighs its probative value [19] indicate that one is not permitted to inflame the passions of factfinders at will. Trials may generate heat but only with the proper fuel.

h. Selecting Among Hypotheses

Alert to the benefits of developing an array of factual hypotheses, one must consider which of the potential hypotheses to pursue. Return for a moment to the car that plunged off the mountain road. If one is approached by the driver's spouse and asked to investigate the cause of the mishap, one will find no dearth of potential factual hypotheses about what might have happened. For openers, one might posit at least the following:

(1) A passenger in the right front seat suddenly decided to pay the driver back for some epithet previously hurled, and so grabbed hold of the steering wheel and pulled the car off the road.

(2) A car being driven in the wrong lane in the uphill direction forced the driver to swerve and pitch off the road.

(3) As the car was headed downhill, the brakes failed due to (a) faulty manufacture or (b) faulty servicing, and the car gathered so much momentum that the driver could not keep it on the twisting road.

---

18. Fed.Rules of Evid., Rules 404, 405, 608 and 609.

19. Fed.Rules of Evid., Rule 403.

(4) The highway was poorly designed, creating hazardous driving conditions for downhill traffic.

Undoubtedly, one could create a good many more stories of what might have happened. However, as with legal theories the creation of factual hypotheses is not an end in itself; one receives no points for mere creativity. One develops hypotheses so investigation may produce a favorable story. Moreover, most clients do not have the time or the resources to enable one to investigate every potential hypothesis. Hence, one almost always has to select, from among potential hypotheses, those to pursue. When making that selection, one relies on common sense, experience, intuition and expert advice. In using these criteria, one must keep in mind some practical guides.

First, plaintiffs particularly are nearly always faced with identifying parties from whom they can exact the desired relief. Typically, some hypotheses will point towards defendants who can pay a judgment or otherwise be held accountable, while others will point towards defendants who are judgment-proof, absent, or otherwise useless from the plaintiffs' perspective. Ideally, then, on behalf of plaintiffs, one selects hypotheses that make responsible defendants financially liable for any harm suffered.

Second, one must often consider the parties' ongoing relationship when selecting among hypotheses. For example, even though a particular dispute has blossomed into litigation, the parties may be businesspeople who hope to continue to do business with each other in the future. The anticipated future relationship may affect the hypotheses one pursues. A hypothesis that brings the emotional wrath of a factfinder upon the head of a defendant may help to build a persuasive case, but it may ruin the future relationship.

Finally, one selects hypotheses in part for their "investigatability." As described in Chapter 10, after hypotheses have been identified, one adorns them with potential additional evidence. In going through this process, one may discover that hypotheses which seemed to be strong are very difficult to prove. One difficulty may be, for example, that a witness who might provide evidence is dead or otherwise unavailable. Hence, the ease with which a hypothesis may be investigated is an important guide to its selection.

All of the points just mentioned are perhaps "limiting" factors: their use will almost inevitably result in the pursuit of fewer hypotheses than one initially developed. Having raised these limits, we caution you against the tendency to discard hypotheses at too early a stage in an investigation. Take care not to discard out-of-hand any hypothesis which seems less than an iron-clad winner. The twists and turns that a case takes during investigation are often surprising. A case that at first blush appears to raise one set of factual issues may at the final curtain involve an entirely different set. A hypothesis which early in a case seems "silly" or unwinnable may be one's bulwark at trial. Remember, one often can talk to a witness only once. Thus, do not be too free to discard hypotheses, lest investigation reach a dead-end when hypotheses that initially seemed iron-clad prove hollow.

As is frequently true, then, selecting hypotheses for investigation pulls one in opposite directions. One guide points to the need to limit those hypotheses; the other cautions against setting those limits too early. At least if one is aware of the tension, one can exercise judgment responsibly.[20]

i. Building Hypotheses: The Joy of New Worlds

Admittedly, no one has ever accused lawyering of producing the thrill of downhill skiing or of requiring the creative genius of a Mozart. Nonetheless, thinking about possible factual theories is one of the more exciting and creative aspects of being a litigator. All of us, in our daily lives, live in a world largely shaped by the actions of others. When one has an opportunity to sit back and think of factual possibilities, one has a chance to formulate one's own stories of what the world might have looked like. The stories cannot be total fantasies. They must create a world in which factual hypotheses conform to valid legal theories and can be investigated. Yet, speculative questions such as, "How might this have happened?" and "Why might it have happened that way?" provide for litigators the freedom of thought and fascination that is usually reserved for famous fictional characters like Sam Spade and Ellery Queen.

Moreover, developing factual theories allows one to leave one's daily world in another way. As you already know, the ability to identify factual theories depends largely on one's knowledge of a subject matter or industry involved in a story. Recall the hypothetical involving alleged age discrimination in a packaging plant, in which one's ability to develop hypotheses as to how and why the discrimination may have occurred depended in part on one's knowledge of employment practices in packaging plants. Since the world involved in a story is often so different from one's own, the need to develop factual theories often plunges one into new and different aspects of society. One client's story may involve mismanagement in a rutabaga canning factory, while another's involves a claim that surgery on an elephant's maloccluded tusk was negligently performed. If one is the attorney in these cases, identifying potential factual theories will require one to learn more about canning rutabagas and operating on

20. In some instances, one may need a client's permission before abandoning a theory. See, e.g., ABA Code of Professional Responsibility, E–C 7–7.

elephants than one would have thought possible while in law school. It is this opportunity to dip into and out of the worlds of others which adds zest to litigators' lives. Indeed, if one does not find the prospect of learning about new industries and cultures challenging and interesting, one should perhaps consider a different career.

One may be tempted to reply, "But most litigators specialize—doesn't that turn the thrill of discovery into the agony of repetition?" Fortunately, that is often not the case. Even within a given specialty, cases are typically so factually dissimilar that the challenge to learn endures. The specialist in medical malpractice who works on a gall bladder surgery case one day may work on a kidney surgery the next. And even if two cases involve kidney operations, the factual issues in those cases may be quite different. Fortunately for their sanity, even specialists are frequently confronted with the need to learn about new worlds.

j. Theory of the Case

The ultimate aim of developing, selecting and adorning theories with evidence is to produce at trial what we might term a complete theory of the case. A complete theory of the case combines legal theories and descriptive and explanatory hypotheses in a story which has both rational and psychological appeal. It is a theory that describes what happened and why in a way that is persuasive both to the mind and to the heart.[21]

Obviously, a complete theory of the case is something one hopes to end up with at trial, rather than something one starts out with. Note, however, that investigation will not necessarily produce a complete theory for every case. For example, one may represent a defendant and be unable to do more than rebut portions of plaintiff's proof. In such a situation, one may have a theory about why the plaintiff's witnesses are wrong but have no "theory of the case" in the sense of describing what did happen and why.

4. BUILDING THEORIES REGARDING REBUTTAL EVIDENCE

When one turns from affirmative to rebuttal theories, one's focus becomes more limited. Instead of worrying about entire stories, one looks at specific pieces of the adversary's affirmative evidence and formulates factual hypotheses which potentially rebut them. With rebuttal, one turns from aggressive boxer to nimble counterpuncher. However, even with a different mental outlook one can still rely on

21. The term "theory of the case" can, of course, be used in other ways. For example, when one is asked, "Counsel, what's your theory of the case?" one might simply respond in legal terms: "Breach of Contract, Your Honor."

those familiar standbys, common sense, intuition and experience, to develop rebuttal hypotheses.

Certainly, in many instances one will not have to develop rebuttal theories. Just as a person's initial story may contain the only affirmative factual hypotheses one needs, so too may a client's story provide obvious rebuttal. Thus, if an auctioneer sues one's client for breach of contract, and one's client says, "Sure I held up my hand. I was grabbing for a bird", then one's rebuttal theory may already be in hand. But quite often rebuttal evidence is not in hand, but somewhere in a bush. The evidence in an adversary's affirmative story may cover spans of time when one's client was not present. Even if a client or a friendly witness was present, he or she may not be able to rebut. Hence, no less than with affirmative evidence, one must often rely on the "little gray cells" to identify potential rebuttal theories.

The unavailability of immediate rebuttal often forces one to identify and pursue contradictory rebuttal theories. In the example of the auctioneer, if one did not start out with the client's "reaching for a bird" theory, one might have to consider whether the auctioneer's evidence is erroneous (denial), as well as reasons why even though the auctioneer is accurate, the evidence lacks probative value (admit and explain). This, however, is a familiar intellectual task for lawyers. We are all familiar with the criminal defense of, "I was out of town at the time of the shooting. And even if I did shoot, it was in self-defense. Besides, I'm crazy." If one does on occasion need to investigate potentially contradictory rebuttal hypotheses, one usually winnows them out over the course of an investigation and presents a factfinder with consistent rebuttal evidence at trial.

Consider now how one formulates potential rebuttal theories. For this purpose consider a hypothetical. Assume one represents Hugh Anncry, who is charged with bank robbery. Pieces of affirmative evidence for the prosecution are supplied by Juan Thindime, who states that he saw Anncry running swiftly in a direction away from the bank shortly after the robbery; Sue Emall, who states that Anncry is her neighbor and that the day before the robbery he told her he was in desperate need of $25,000; and Jean Blue, who states that in the used cane shop where she works, Anncry paid for a cane with a marked $100 bill taken in the robbery.

First, consider rebuttal by explanation. Recall that this response accepts a witness' testimony and offers additional evidence which explains away its probative worth. To identify explanatory hypotheses one should first identify the generalization which supports the probative value of the particular item of affirmative evidence to be rebutted. Then, by adding "except when" to the generalization, one may use common sense and experience to identify situations in which the

Binder & Bergman Fact Invest. ACB—8

generalization is not accurate. These "exceptions" are the potential rebuttal explanations. For example, a generalization based on Juan Thindime's evidence might be: "People who run from a bank just after it is robbed usually have robbed the bank." By adding "except when" to the generalization, one may identify potential rebuttal theories. That is, the generalization may be true except when:

(a) the person is chasing the robber;

(b) the person is fleeing the bank in fear;

(c) the person is unaware of the robbery and is running for a different reason;

(d) the person is suddenly attempting to qualify as an Olympic sprinter. (So much for common sense.)

These, then, are potential rebuttal theories which might explain away the probative force of the evidence of "flight." Thinking through the generalizations which support the specific items of evidence provided by Sue Emall and Jean Blue, what potential rebuttal-by-explanation hypotheses can you identify?

Now focus on rebuttal by denial. Recall from Chapter 7 that one may deny with contrary evidence or with evidence attacking credibility. When one pursues denial through contrary evidence, one does not identify the adversary's underlying generalization. The denial is itself a theory. A theory of denial by evidence is simply the converse of the affirmative evidence. In Hugh Anncry's case, two denial rebuttal theories for the defendant are, "He was not running from the bank," and "He did not say he desperately needed $25,000." While these two denial theories are phrased negatively, that will not invariably be the case. If the affirmative evidence itself is phrased negatively (e.g., in a suit for fraud, affirmative evidence might be, "She never said anything about a leaky roof"), then the rebuttal theory will be phrased positively ("I did too mention the leaky roof").

Finally, when one considers rebuttal by attack on credibility, one turns to the credibility factors discussed in Chapter 8. One need not articulate generalizations underlying the credibility of witnesses and stories, because over time the experience supporting those generalizations has crystallized into those factors. For example, the familiar attack by showing a witness' motive is a result of common experience that people who have an ax to grind are usually less trustworthy than those who are axless.

Thus, one may directly use each factor as the basis of factual hypothesis. In Anncry's case, one may hypothesize that Jean Blue's story that Anncry paid for a used cane with a marked bill is implausible, in that Blue sees so many customers that Blue could not remember Anncry, and the markings on the bill were not noticeable to a layperson. Similarly, using the credibility factor of "expertise," one may develop hypotheses that Blue is not credible because Blue saw the person only for a very short time, under poor lighting conditions.

5. HYPOTHESES OF AN ADVERSARY

As an advocate, one does not expend much investigatory energy conjuring up an adversary's hypotheses. However, it is often useful to do more than simply outline an adversary's existing affirmative evidence according to legal elements. Aware of an adversary's hypotheses, one can make a more accurate appraisal of the evidence the adversary is likely to introduce at trial, and can therefore better prepare to meet that evidence and counsel the client.

One learns of an adversary's hypotheses in a variety of ways. Formally, one can send out "contention interrogatories;" these are described in Chapter 17. Informally, one can monitor the questions the adversary asks in interrogatories and in depositions and directly explore hypotheses with opposing counsel during conversations. Those who eschew methods such as the foregoing are likely to learn of an adversary's hypotheses only during the adversary's closing argument.

Keeping track of the adversary's hypotheses is generally not burdensome. If one does no more than just jot them down in the outline of the adversary's existing affirmative evidence, the investigatory purposes are served.

6. THEORY DEVELOPMENT EXERCISES

a. *The Role of Expertise*

1. As you already know, the Phillipses have sued Soil Engineers on a theory of negligence. Unless you are far more knowledgeable about soil engineering than the authors, you may have difficulty coming up with hypotheses as to how Soil Engineers was negligent. You therefore decide to seek help from an expert. What questions would you ask the expert in an effort to develop explanatory and descriptive hypotheses?

2. With respect to Landview, one theory of the Phillipses is that Landview knew the soil in Campion Hills was unstable before the Phillipses bought the lots. Why might you need an expert either to learn about other ways that Landview might have committed fraud or to learn explanatory hypotheses about why Landview might have committed fraud?

3. Assume you represent Landview, which is prepared to admit that the soil was subject to slippage, but whose position is that it relied on Soil Engineers. Under this theory, Landview's justifiable

reliance is an issue. Why might you contact an expert to identify hypotheses regarding this issue?

b. Explanatory Hypotheses

4. Your client has brought suit against Gushing Oil Co. and its president, Dry Wells, for fraud in the sale of securities. One factual descriptive hypothesis is that the defendants failed to disclose in a prospectus that an independent preliminary engineering survey indicated that the well site area was barren. Check below those statements that are explanatory hypotheses of this descriptive hypothesis.

A. ___ Attila the Hun wore pink tennis shoes.

B. ___ Dry Wells was too embarrassed to disclose the survey because his own company's engineers had previously told him the area was barren.

C. ___ Gushing Oil Co. was in need of quick capital because a large bank loan was coming due and its credit line was expiring.

D. ___ Gushing Oil Co. had been investigated some years earlier by the SEC for possible securities fraud.

E. ___ Around the time the prospectus was issued the international market price of crude oil was dropping.

F. ___ A memorandum sent by Dry Wells to others in the company states that the independent engineering survey report should not be disclosed to the public.

G. ___ An internal audit by Gushing Oil Co. revealed that the company was severely undercapitalized.

5. As attorney for the Phillipses, assume that one has identified as a descriptive factual hypotheses that Landview falsely represented that it would build a recreation center in Campion Hills. Identify as many explanatory hypotheses as you can (be reasonable—stop at seven) that explain why Landview might have made this misrepresentation. For each hypothesis you identify, be prepared to discuss the extent to which it may have emotional or socio-political overtones, as well as whether it is a hypothesis that realistically is worthy of pursuit.

6. As attorney for Landview, your position is twofold. First, Landview made no misrepresentations concerning soil conditions (an "I'm innocent" theory). Second, the Phillipses themselves are responsible for any increased building costs because despite being told by Landview to check out the soil conditions of their lots before purchasing them, they failed to do so (a "whodunnit" theory—the Phillipses themselves!). Identify as many explanatory hypotheses as you can (again, seven seems a reasonable limit) for each of these de-

scriptive hypotheses. For each explanatory hypothesis you identify, be prepared to discuss the extent to which it may have emotional or socio-political overtones, as well as whether it is a hypothesis that realistically is worthy of pursuit.

c. Additional Legal Theories

7. As attorney for the Phillipses, you have sued Soil Engineers on a theory of negligence. On what other legal theories, if any, might Soil Engineers be liable to the Phillipses? If you identify such a theory, what steps would you take, if any, to make the theory an official part of the case? If no additional legal theories immediately come to mind, in what ways might you go about identifying such theories?

d. Rebuttal Theories

8. On the issue of whether Landview represented that Lots 70 and 71 were suitable for building without any additional improvements, the following is affirmative evidence for Landview that it did not make that representation:

(a) The Phillipses wrote a letter stating that Lotz had told them prior to their purchase that Landview would make no further improvements to the lots. (Lade Depo., p. 27)

(b) During the 6 months preceding the Phillipses' purchase, Lade and Lotz had discussed the fact that lots 20 and 84 were having caissons installed. (Lade Depo., p. 33)

As attorney for the Phillipses, your task is to develop rebuttal theories of the "admit and explain" variety. Please develop a number of such theories for each piece of affirmative evidence. Do this by formulating the underlying generalizations and adding "except when."

Chapter 10

ADORNING HYPOTHESES: IDENTI-FYING POTENTIAL ADDI-TIONAL EVIDENCE

1. INTRODUCTION

Ingenious legal theories activated by heart-wrenching factual hypotheses are unavailing unless they are supported by evidence. Therefore, before questioning witnesses one needs to spend some time thinking about evidence to support affirmative and rebuttal hypotheses and recording the product of those thoughts. After all, one wants to be able to recall one's ideas as questioning proceeds. Buoyed by a sense of specific evidence that might exist if one's hypotheses are correct, one is generally prepared to pose oral and written questions.

2. A THOUGHT PROCESS: HISTORICAL RECONSTRUCTION

Recall from Chapter 9 the hypothetical case of the employee who claimed denial of a promotion because of age discrimination. One descriptive hypothesis on behalf of the employee may be that the company did not promote the employee to foreman, graveyard shift, when that position became available on September 22. This chapter describes how one may identify potential evidence to establish the accuracy of hypotheses such as this one.

Our label for a thought process one may use to identify potential evidence establishing the accuracy of an hypothesis is "historical reconstruction." Though this label may at first appear grandiose, it is quite similar to a well-known bridge ploy. In that ploy, if the success of a contract depends on a particular opponent holding a particular card, one plays the hand on the assumption that the opponent holds that card. Similarly, to use historical reconstruction, one begins with an assumption that an hypothesis is correct. Then, drawing upon one's experience, common sense, intuition and familiarity with how the world operates, one identifies events and details that one might expect to find if the hypothesis were correct. The more one is able to confirm these details and events through investigation, the more likely it is that the hypothesis itself is accurate.

As we meander through life, most of us notice that people usually behave and events usually occur in consistent patterns. If a person smiles, he or she probably is happy. If a contractor agrees to do a major building project, that contractor probably will hire various construction workers. If a person buys a car, some oral conversation with the seller probably preceded the purchase. As noted earlier, when a story consists of evidence which falls into a familiar, recognizable pattern, we tend to believe that the story is accurate. Historical reconstruction is the process of identifying evidence by thinking of events and details that are consistent with an hypothesis. In essence, one asks, "If this hypothesis is true, what else might have been true?"

Although the process of historical reconstruction is typically used to think about human behavior, one should note that it may also be used when one thinks about conditions. Many lawsuits concern conditions of inanimate objects—the condition of a house at the time of its purchase or, as in *Phillips v. Landview,* the condition of two vacant lots. One can ask the question, "If this hypothesis is true, what else might have been true?" of conditions as well as of human behavior. For example, one can ask, "If this house had a leaky roof in February, what else might have been true?"

Historical reconstruction may be likened to a magnet, which draws from an assortment of small objects all of the iron bits into a familiar and recognizable pattern. The magnet helps one gather the iron bits, and the pattern of the bits in turn establishes the presence of the magnet. Similarly, during investigation one uses a hypothesis to identify evidence which is consistent with the hypothesis; at trial, the evidence establishes the accuracy of the hypothesis.

3. BEFORE, DURING AND AFTER

As you know, in most legal disputes, for each legal element there is what might be termed a "moment (or moments) of substantive importance." At some particular point in time, if at all, a company entered into, performed or breached a contract; a newspaper published a libelous story; a thief took property by force or fear. However, events at the "moment of substantive importance" typically are neither random nor isolated. If such an event occurs, usually it is but part of a common pattern which includes a number of preceding and subsequent events. The events that happen "before" and "after" may be causally related to the substantively critical event, or they may in everyday experience simply be often intertwined with it. In either case, the chronology of events typically forms a pattern which stamps a party's version of substantively critical events as "accurate."

The notion that a substantively critical event may be caused by preceding events treads on familiar cause-and-effect turf. A verbal quarrel may "cause" a later violent dispute. A sudden rise in interest rates may "cause" a manufacturer to make misstatements in an effort to increase sales. Impending law school exams may "cause" nervous anxiety and hair to grow on one's palms.

Similarly, a substantively critical event may well "cause" later events. Even the proverbial "tree that falls in a forest with nobody around" leaves its imprint on the forest floor. Robbing a bank may "cause" the robber to flee town.

On other occasions, though "before" and "after" events may not in any sense be causally related to a substantively critical event, they are intertwined with it in a familiar pattern. A bank robber's acquisition of a gun may not "cause" the robbery, but all would recognize the purchase as part and parcel of a common robbery pattern. And while the robbery may not "cause" the robber to brag to the local bartender, evidence of those boastful statements gives one added assurance that the speaker robbed the bank.

Hence, unless one lives somewhere on the other side of the Fourth Dimension, any event that is at the center of a legal dispute is likely to be preceded and succeeded by other events which in common experience are either consistent with it or in a causal relationship with the central event. Therefore, when one attempts to reconstruct what happened at a moment of substantive importance, it is helpful to focus not only on what may have happened at that moment but also on what may have occurred before and after that moment.

Various reasons suggest why it is helpful to focus on events before and after the moment of substantive importance. Obviously, proof of prior and subsequent events adds credibility. Standing alone, testimony that, "I had an agreement with U.S. Gipsem to purchase 1000 pounds of finished metal." is difficult to evaluate if U.S. Gipsem denies that there was such an agreement. However, if to this testimony there is added evidence of negotiations preceding the agreement and of Gipsem's purchase of enough raw metal to fill a 1000 pound order subsequent to the agreement, the testimony that there was an agreement becomes more persuasive.

Moreover, focusing on "before" and "after" events often expands not only the scope of potential evidence but also the spectrum of available witnesses. The only witnesses to the moment of substantive importance are often the parties themselves, whose versions of events are diametrically opposed. If parties prove nothing more than their opposite versions of what happened at the moment of substantive importance, a factfinder must choose between two witnesses, each of whom is directly interested in the outcome. Courthouse regulars call such situations swearing contests.[1] Naturally, factfinders are often more impressed with evidence from witnesses who appear to be less "interested" than the parties. By looking to events "before" and "after," one often is able to identify a number of potential non-party witnesses. Moreover, one may identify documents which support a party's story.

Consider, for example, a prosecution for rape in which the defense is consent. Typically, the only available witnesses at the moment of substantive importance are the victim and the defendant. If the prosecutor limits his or her investigation to the alleged rape itself, successful prosecution may be difficult. But by focusing on events that may have preceded and succeeded the rape, the prosecutor may identify both additional evidence and witnesses.

For instance, the victim's story may be that at the time of the attack she was on her way to an important business meeting. Using historical reconstruction, one might theorize that there are memos relating to that meeting, people who had met with the victim in connection with the meeting, arrangements for the place of the meeting, and the like. If this theorizing materializes into evidence, one may have important "unbiased" witnesses who support the victim's story. In our common experience, it is unlikely that a person will engage in consensual intercourse while enroute to an important business meeting. Similarly, the prosecutor may consider the likely physical and emotional condition of a rape victim following the attack. Evidence from a doctor as to the victim's bruises and other injuries, or from friends as to her mental state, may likewise be highly probative.

In the example above, the prosecutor at least had the benefit of a favorable witness to the moment of substantive importance. In many situations, however, this is not the case. One's client may be a businessperson injured by a group's allegedly monopolistic practices. The client most likely will never have been present when monopolistic actions were decided upon or taken. The only witnesses to the moment of substantive importance are likely to be aligned with one's adversary. If one is to be successful, then one usually must locate less "hostile" witnesses. Use of historical reconstruction to identify events which may have preceded and succeeded the monopolistic acts will not magically produce friendly witnesses or even the mythical

---

1. Actually, many courthouse regulars use a different expression, but in print a "swearing contest" will have to do.

neutral ones. But even if one does no more than identify a secretary or a clerk in the adversary's office, one has made progress. A person in such a position may be less knowledgeable about substantively critical events than, say, the company president, and therefore less able to conceal information. Particularly when one's client did not observe the moment of substantive importance, the "before" and "after" thought process is a useful aid to developing a broader range of witnesses.

The large number of cases in which the only witnesses to a moment of substantive importance are those aligned with the adversary may be at first surprising. However, mentally run through some categories of standard cases: (1) A plaintiff injured by an allegedly defectively-made product; (2) A manufacturer sued for manufacturing a defective product, who does not know how the purchaser used the product; (3) A prosecutor in a prosecution for murder or for abuse of an infant; (4) A stock purchaser who claims to be the victim of securities fraud. Do you see how in these and in many other common types of cases, the only witnesses to what really happened at the moment of substantive importance are likely to be aligned with the adversary? In all of these types of situations, "before" and "after" may be a useful guide to evidence from more neutral and/or favorable witnesses.

The "before" and "after" method of analysis emphasizes the role of circumstantial evidence in establishing factual hypotheses. Review the descriptive hypotheses sprinkled through Chapter 9. For example, recall that in the hypothetical case of the car that plunged off the mountain road, possible factual hypotheses included a defective steering mechanism, defective brakes, and the driver's "potted" condition. What do these, and the other descriptive hypotheses in Chapter 9, have in common? They all are descriptions of what might have occurred at a moment of substantive importance. This is not merely coincidence. Invariably, descriptive hypotheses do focus on moments of substantive importance. After all, ultimately one needs to prove what happened at such moments if one is to prevail.

However, for the reasons discussed earlier, direct evidence of what occurred at moments of substantive importance is often unavailable. So by expanding the ambit of hypotheses to inquire about what might have occurred before and after critical moments, one automatically moves to the natural solution for the lack of credible direct evidence: circumstantial evidence. Evidence of events occurring before and after the moment of substantive importance is, by definition, circumstantial evidence.

It may now be apparent that the circumstantial evidence one identifies when using historical reconstruction results from using a thought process that is the mirror image of the reasoning process one uses when forming generalizations to analyze circumstantial evidence. In the latter situation, described in Chapter 6, one moves by way of generalization from a specific piece of circumstantial evidence to a conclusion. For example, in the rape hypothetical, evidence that the victim was bruised is circumstantial evidence of the rape. The bruises lead to a conclusion of rape through an inferential chain using generalizations such as, "Women who are bruised are more likely to have been assaulted than those who are not bruised," and "Women who have been assaulted are more likely to have been raped than those who have not been assaulted." [2]

With historical reconstruction, one also uses generalizations, but moves in a reverse direction. One moves from conclusions—i.e., the factual hypotheses—to potential items of specific evidence which might establish the truth of those conclusions. From the hypothesis that the victim was raped, one may generalize that, "Women who have been raped are more likely to have been bruised than those who have not been raped." Of course, when using historical reconstruction, one tries to identify a number of pieces of specific evidence which might prove one's conclusions are accurate. For instance, if one generalizes about victims of rape, evidence one might expect to find after a rape to support the conclusion that a rape occurred include bruises, vaginal injuries, torn clothing, and emotional shock. In any event, since the generalizations one uses during historical reconstruction are the same as those one uses when drawing inferences based on pieces of evidence, historical reconstruction permits one to attempt to make self-fulfilling prophecies. One uses a generalization to identify potential evidence. If unearthed by investigation, that evidence becomes at trial the basis of an inference that the conclusion is true.

4. USING HISTORICAL RECONSTRUCTION

At this point, a short illustration of the use of historical reconstruction may be helpful. In a typical automobile accident case, let us assume that the defendant's factual hypothesis is that at the moment of substantive importance, "Plaintiff was preoccupied and

2. These generalizations perhaps perpetuate the conventional wisdom that rape is an act of violence. Many writers point out that the "rape is violence" notion is often a myth, and that rape is more accurately defined in terms of non-physical coercion, a violation of personal privacy and a woman's sense of self. See, e.g., S. Brownmiller, *Against Our Will: Men, Women and Rape* (1976); C. Mac Kinnon, "Feminism, Marxism, Method, and the State: Toward Feminist Jurisprudence," 8 Signs 635, 646 n. 21 (1983). In adopting any generalization, one must be aware of the potential gap between conventional and empirical reality. In this hypothetical, a prosecutor who focused only on the presence or absence of bruises might well be simplifying reality, thereby failing to identify other important potential evidence.

therefore inattentive to the defendant's car." How might one use this hypothesis to identify potential evidence?

One might first look at the moment of substantive importance itself: the few moments just prior to and perhaps including the collision. Based on our common experience, "generally" what does the world look like when a driver is preoccupied? How is the car driven? What is the driver doing inside the car? What is the driver thinking about at that time?

Next, one might generalize about events which may have preceded the collision. For some reason the driver was preoccupied; had the driver received important information some time before the collision? If so, what might it have been? Or might the plaintiff have been heading for a specific location? If so, where? What was to happen there? Who else was to be there?

Finally, one may think about events which might have occurred after the critical moment. How do preoccupied drivers behave when they realize their minds have wandered? What kind of statements do such people typically make? Whom do they frequently talk with?

Needless to say, there is nothing magical about the above questions. We do no more than suggest a typical way one might use historical reconstruction in the context of a factual hypothesis. Even though one knew nothing specific about the defendant, the use of common experience in conjunction with events occurring before, during and after the moment of substantive importance probably suggested potential evidence that may not have been readily apparent.

If investigation then uncovers such evidence, the evidence uncovered may in turn enable one to carry out a more case-specific historical reconstruction. In the example above, since we knew nothing about the defendant, we could ask only general questions such as, "Might the defendant have been heading for a specific location?" Now, assume that one knows that the defendant is a building contractor who, at the time of the collision, was going to check on a job that was behind schedule. Armed with this information, one can use historical reconstruction to develop case-specific inquiries. For instance, what is a building contractor on the way to check on a job that is behind schedule likely to be thinking about? With whom might a contractor in this situation be in contact just prior to or just after the collision? The answers to such questions identify potential circumstantial evidence not about drivers in general, but about drivers in the more specific group to which the defendant belongs. Hence, that evidence is likely to be highly persuasive to a factfinder. While drivers in general are occasionally inattentive because they are thinking of their destination, contractors may often be inattentive while on their way to a job which is behind schedule. The latter generalization is more likely to be true, for it narrows the connecting premise to the specific group of drivers involved in the case, harried building contractors. It thereby avoids the greater number of exceptions that would adhere to a premise about drivers in general.

To identify evidence which is likely to be persuasive in a specific factual setting, one uses historical reconstruction continuously as evidence is learned. It is occasionally tempting to stop the process at the first sign of success. "Well, I've found out that the plaintiff was a behind-schedule building contractor. That wraps up this case. Guess I'll go fishing, and that'll give me one whole day to gather evidence that the U.S.'s governing document is really the Articles of Confederation, not the Constitution."

Avoid the temptation. Apply the same process of historical reconstruction to identify potential additional evidence. By so doing, one may uncover evidence which is even more case-specific, *and* identify potential witnesses and documents that might otherwise go unnoticed. If a building contractor is behind schedule, what else might be true? Might the contractor have previously tried to catch up? If so, with whom might the contractor have spoken? These questions may suggest potential evidence and witnesses that make one's story about the contractor's state of mind at the time of the collision more persuasive. Think for a moment about what you know about contractors and their work patterns. Can you use whatever knowledge you have to identify other potential witnesses and documents?

Perhaps you have lived your entire life in a community made up entirely of prefabricated igloos and haven't the foggiest idea about contractor practices. If so, what might you do?

5. THE ROLE OF EXPERTS

As igloo-dwellers, and perhaps others, may have recognized immediately, it is difficult to use historical reconstruction in situations in which one lacks experience. This is especially true given that one needs to identify events that might have preceded or succeeded the moment of substantive importance. For example, if one is totally ignorant about the practices of contractors, one will be hard put to identify events that might cause a contractor to be inattentive. Therefore, just as one may need to call upon experts to formulate hypotheses, one may need to knock on their doors as well for help in identifying evidence which might prove those hypotheses. Effective methods of talking to experts about both of these concerns are discussed in Chapter 16. Door-knocking techniques are left to one's own discretion.

By this time, the typical ongoing nature of the professional relationship between litigators and experts should be clear. If one needs an expert's help in formulating factual hypotheses, inevitably, one will need an expert's help to identify potential evidence. Moreover, if one lacks sufficient experience to investigate without the aid of an expert, it is likely that a factfinder too will lack the experience to understand the probative value of evidence at trial without the testimony of an expert. When one employs an expert to help in formulating factual hypotheses, then, one is well on the road to employing an expert at trial.

6. THE "ESPECIALLY WHEN" APPROACH

As has been shown, historical reconstruction is a process of moving from conclusions to specific items of evidence based on generalizations drawn from common experience. However, one need not always state a generalization explicitly to engage in historical reconstruction. Rather, often one need only ask questions such as, "What things might be true if this conclusion were true?"

On some occasions, however, explicitly stating a generalization is a useful aid to identifying potential evidence. Then, by adding to a generalization the words "especially when," one may use experience to identify potential evidence. For example, a building contractor on the way to a job which is behind schedule is likely to be inattentive to traffic conditions, *especially when:*

(a) the contractor may lose a bonus by not finishing on schedule;

(b) the person for whom the contractor is working has previously complained about delays; etc.

The "especially when" technique carries through the "mirror image" metaphor mentioned above, for the "especially when" technique is the mirror image of the "except when" technique discussed in Chapter 6. As you may recall, one may add to a generalization the words "except when" in order to test its probative value. In general, the more exceptions there are to a generalization, the less persuasive it is. The generalization that, "She who hesitates is lost." is not terribly persuasive, because it is subject to numerous exceptions. Conversely, the "especially when" technique identifies evidence that strengthens generalizations by eliminating possible exceptions. For example, "She who hesitates is lost, especially when interest rates are to double the next day."

7. OTHER APPROACHES TO IDENTIFYING POTENTIAL EVIDENCE

Throughout this book, we have attempted to provide a systematic approach to identifying legal theories, factual hypotheses and potential evidence. Our approach suggests that one analyze evidence already on hand in light of what one needs to prove, that one then formulate factual hypotheses supporting one's legal claims, and finally that one use historical reconstruction to identify evidence which supports those hypotheses. Thus, a prerequisite to questioning witnesses is rigorous analysis of known law and evidence.

There are, however, other approaches to identifying potential evidence which do not rely on this sort of systematic and analytical rigor. We describe them briefly, in part for the sake of completeness, and in part because they may prove useful in particular instances. Indeed, they may be particularly useful if combined with our suggested approach.

One possible method is perhaps the reverse of ours. Instead of thinking first about potential evidence and then thinking about possible witnesses who might supply that evidence, one might first think of *sources* of information—potential witnesses. For example, one interviews a tenant whose landlord seeks to evict her from La Casa Apartments because she failed to pay rent. The tenant's story is that the apartment was uninhabitable, and therefore the legal obligation to pay rent was at least partially excused. One may leap directly from this story to thoughts of witnesses with whom one might speak—neighbors or a Health Department inspector.

In fact, some legal literature describes methods of contacting witnesses, separately from considerations of what those witnesses might say.[3] Even if a criminal does not always return to the scene of a crime, the lawyer's job is to do so.[4] One reason is to locate any witnesses who regularly are around the scene at about the same time as the crime was committed, and who therefore might have seen what happened. Lawyers are also advised to run newspaper advertisements and the like in an effort to contact witnesses.

In our view, these suggestions make sense only if one has, in addition, thought through potential evidence systematically. Remember, often one has but a single chance to talk to a witness. Thus, if one does locate a witness, one needs to have made a thorough analysis of potential topics ahead of time. As you know, any question other than a very broad one contains an implicit hypothesis anyway. For these reasons, we suggest that most of the time it is not productive to think primarily in terms of sources of information.[5]

3. See 2 Am. Jur. *Trials* 234–259, 296–407 (1964); F. Bailey & H. Rothblatt, *Fundamentals of Criminal Advocacy* §§ 74–101 (1974).

4. R. Simmons, *Winning Before Trial* 514–518 (1974); F. Bailey & H. Rothblatt, note 2 supra § 41; G. Lowenthal, *A Study of the Fact Investigation Practices of Criminal Defense Lawyers*, 1981 Ariz.St.L.J. 447, 534; 1 Am. Jur. *Trials* 368–370 (1964).

5. Of course, one cannot slavishly follow this or any other rule. Five minutes after one hears a client's initial story, one may get a phone call that an important witness only has one hour to live, but is willing to spend that hour being videotaped about what he saw. Surely a re-

Another investigatory method is to consult published works which attempt to pinpoint specific evidence needed in specific cases. For instance, the series *Am. Jur. Proof of Facts 2d* discusses proof of facts for a variety of causes of action. In Volume 11, one may read about facts needed to prove cases involving "Entitlement to Capital Gains Treatment—Sale of Subdivided Realty?" "Dependency of Child Who Has Attained Majority—Workers' Compensation;" and "Real Estate Brokers' Fraud As To Income From or Earnings of Property." In Volume 30 of that same series, representative titles are "Brain Injuries Due To Trauma;" "Negligence of Landowner as to Contact of Movable Machine with Electric Line;" and "Paint or Lacquer Vapor Explosions."

Unquestionably, such books are helpful if one has a case of the type discussed. However, they can never be more than a starting point for investigation. One still needs to make an analysis of the sort we suggest. As focused as the topics in *Am. Jur. Proof of Facts 2d* are, the reality is that one's cases will always be factually different to a fair degree. On the appellate level, where issues are significantly reduced from trial, it may be possible to speak of one case being "on all fours" with another. At the trial level, cases are so factually diverse that one would have to speak of one case being "on all thousands" with another. Since that will not occur, one needs a general guide to potential evidence that is applicable to most litigated disputes. We hope that Part III of this book provides such a guide.

8. USING HISTORICAL RECONSTRUCTION IN REBUTTAL

Because historical reconstruction is a method of embellishing factual theories with items of potential evidence, one's thought process is the same regardless of whether a factual theory is designed to unearth affirmative or rebuttal evidence. Assume for example that a factual theory is, "Sue-Bob was eating an ice cream cone." No matter whether this theory is intended to uncover affirmative or rebuttal evidence, the process of historical reconstruction is the same. One still asks, "If this is true, what else is likely to be true?" "What would the world be like before, during and after one eats an ice cream cone?"

Thus, whether one's rebuttal theory is of the "denial" or the "admit and explain" variety, one employs "before, during and after" to identify potential evidence. So, if one denies that Sue-Bob was eating an ice cream cone, one asks what the world looks like when a person is not eating an ice cream cone. And if one admits that Sue-Bob was

sponse such as, "He'll have to hang on for a few more hours if he wants to talk to me. Binder and Bergman insist that I develop my hypotheses first." is a most unfortunate one.

eating an ice cream cone, but has as an explanatory theory that five year old Sue-Bob was forced to eat the cone by her father because she did not finish her vegetables at dinner, one thinks about what the world might look like if a five year old is forced by her father to eat ice cream because she did not finish her vegetables.

When one is attempting to identify potential rebuttal in the denial-by-evidence category (as opposed to denial by attacking credibility), one may engage in historical reconstruction from two perspectives. First, one may simply state the converse of the affirmative theory and think about what the world might look like if the converse theory were true. That was the case in the "denial" ice cream cone hypothetical above.

Alternatively, one may identify potential rebuttal evidence by engaging in the identical historical reconstruction thought process as the adversary. One asks, "If the adversary's evidence is true, what else is likely to be true?" [6] As would the adversary, one identifies potential evidence (before, during and after) which in one's experience is likely to exist if the underlying hypothesis is true. Of course, after identifying the potential evidence, one's investigatory goal diverges from an adversary's. The adversary would attempt to prove the existence of the evidence, while one's own task would be to show its non-existence.

9. OUTLINING POTENTIAL EVIDENCE

As you recall, we suggest that one prepare five outlines as a part of case preparation. For those whose memories feature breadth over length, those outlines are as follows:

1. A story outline.
2. An outline of the client's existing affirmative evidence.
3. An outline of the adversary's existing affirmative evidence.
4. An outline of the client's potential affirmative evidence.
5. An outline of the client's potential rebuttal evidence.

At last, we have worked our way to outlines four and five.

The skeletons of both outlines of a client's potential evidence track those of the existing evidence outlines. The skeleton of the outline of potential affirmative evidence is the same as the client's existing affirmative evidence outline, while the skeleton of the outline of potential rebuttal is the same as that of the outline of the adversary's existing affirmative evidence. Make no bones about it, the framework of each is the potentially applicable legal theories, broken into component elements and stated in factual terms. To refresh your recollec-

6. See K. Hegland, *Trial and Practice Skills in a Nutshell* 61 (1978).

tion, we repeat here from Chapter 5 a partial skeleton of Jerry Mason's existing affirmative evidence outline for the Phillipses, unadorned by existing or potential evidence:

Theory One: Fraud (Non–Disclosure of Material Fact)

A. When Landview sold lots 70 and 71 to the Phillipses, the land was subject to slides.

B. When it sold lots 70 and 71 to the Phillipses, Landview was aware that the land was subject to slides.

C. When it sold lots 70 and 71 to the Phillipses, Landview did not disclose that the land was subject to slides.

D. Landview failed to disclose that lots 70 and 71 were subject to slides with the intent to induce the Phillipses to buy the lots.

E. Had the Phillipses been aware that lots 70 and 71 were subject to slides, they would not have bought them.

F. The Phillipses have suffered damages of at least $40,000 because they must install caissons in order to secure a building permit—other consequential damages?

G. Punitive damages according to:

(1) Financial strength of Landview;

(2) Landview's knowing concealment (See 2–C);

(3) Other?

Insofar as potential affirmative evidence is concerned, one simply inserts it under the particular legal element which the evidence might prove. For clarity, one should list factual hypotheses, as well as individual items of potential evidence that might prove them.

Examine a sample outline of potential affirmative evidence. Assume that we are looking at element "B" above in the Phillipses' outline of potential affirmative evidence. What evidence might be out in the world which might prove that Landview was aware that the land was subject to slides? Put to the side possible hypotheses that an expert engineer or geologist might suggest. Based on common experience, one might identify hypotheses and potential evidence and insert them into the outline as follows:

B. When it sold the land to the Phillipses, Landview was aware that the land was subject to slides.

Hypothesis 1. A slide had previously occurred on lots 70 and 71.

Potential Evidence. Earlier photos of the lots; reports by Landview employees; report of Soil Engineers; slides on nearby lots; repair to lots 70 and 71—earth-moving equipment on lots; construction of temporary or permanent supports in Campion Hills.

Hypothesis 2. Previous prospective buyers had discovered that the land was subject to slides and had informed Landview.

Potential Evidence. Names and addresses of previous prospective purchasers in Landview's records; local soil engineering companies would have been out to the lots conducting soil tests; letters and statements to Landview employees from prospective buyers stating why they were not purchasing.

One may of course have numerous hypotheses under any given element. If investigation confirms that an item of potential evidence exists, one crosses it out in this outline and inserts it into the outline of the client's existing affirmative evidence. If an item of potential evidence fails to pan out, one crosses it out in this outline, plays "Taps" and goes on to something else.

Note that the outline is kept as simple as possible. One need not note whether a particular hypothesis is descriptive or explanatory, emotional, or socio-political. Those categories are designed to stimulate the "gray cells" when thinking through potential hypotheses and evidence, not to analytically strangle a useful investigatory tool. Nor need one state the generalization which supports each piece of potential evidence. Given the array of potential items of evidence, to list a generalization for each is simply too burdensome.

Next, examine a sample outline of potential rebuttal evidence, using the same legal element. Landview's attorney, Florence Darrow, of course prepares an outline of the Phillipses' existing affirmative evidence. Assume that Darrow's outline contains the same legal element "B", with the following affirmative evidence for the Phillipses:

Outline of Landview's Potential Rebuttal

Phillipses' Existing Affirmative Evidence	Landview's Potential Rebuttal
B. When it sold the land to the Phillipses, Landview was aware that the land was subject to slides.	
Evidence: City Official Unter La Mesa states there was a slide on lot 71 two years before the Phillipses purchased the lots. (Letter from La Mesa)	
Evidence: Earth-moving equipment on lot 71 was seen by Buzzie Boddie one year before the Phillipses' purchase.	

At this point, Landview's rebuttal column for these pieces of evidence is remarkably clean. Darrow and Landview have to assess whether it is worthwhile attempting to rebut the specific items of affirmative evidence and whether that rebuttal will be by way of denial or explanation. For purposes of this illustration, assume that Landview definitely wishes to rebut La Mesa, but that unfortunately no one at Landview has any clear rebuttal theory. Therefore, Darrow has to consider potential rebuttal of both types. She may use the outline of Landview's Potential Rebuttal to record her thoughts as follows:

Phillipses' Existing Affirmative Evidence	Landview's Potential Evidence
B. When it sold the land to the Phillipses, Landview was aware that the land was subject to slides.	
Evidence: City Official Unter La Mesa states that there was a slide on lot 71 two years before the Phillipses purchased the lots.	1. *Denial Hypothesis* There was no slide on lot 71.
	Potential Evidence: Pictures showing no change in land condition; trees and bushes surrounding the lot were upright and are more than two years old.
	2. *Explanatory Hypothesis 1* After the slide, Landview fixed the land so it would slide no more.
	Potential Evidence: Contracts with repair people; records of repair in Landview maintenance office.
	3. *Explanatory Hypothesis 2:* Informed by an expert once there is one slide on lot, there is never another.
	Potential Evidence: Report from expert; meetings with expert; inspection by expert

In almost all respects, skeletons aside, an outline of potential rebuttal is similar to an outline of potential affirmative evidence. The only difference is that we suggest one separately label "denial" and "explanation." These categories are generally mutually exclusive, and the labels serve to reduce the possibility of confusion when one subsequently looks to the outline for guidance.

Preparing the outlines of potential evidence probably should not be undertaken as a solo activity. Especially since the task of identifying potential hypotheses and evidence is based on common experience, one may better perform that task with some help. One can "brainstorm" potential evidence with other attorneys in one's office or indeed with a sophisticated paralegal. Perhaps less obviously, one can also brainstorm with clients. Though one may have more legal expertise than a client, factually a client may be the far more experienced, especially with regard to the subject matter of the lawsuit. Hence, it is often helpful to sit down with a client, pull out the outlines, and seek the client's help when identifying potential hypotheses and evidence.

If together with one's colleagues and clients one is at all creative, one may well identify more hypotheses and potential evidence that one can reasonably include in outlines, and may fill the outlines with more evidentiary grist than can reasonably be put through an investigatory mill. Naturally, there is no universal point, common to all cases, at which one should stop the creative process. In a particular case, that point will depend upon a variety of things, such as the amount of evidence already on hand, the client's financial resources, the "size" of the case, and the time available for investigation. But since the listing of potential evidence does not demand its pursuit, we encourage one not to skimp at the identification stage. A hypothesis and supporting evidence which at first glance appears "far out" may upon reflection seem less so. And even if they remain far out, their listing may enable one to discern other hypotheses and items of evidence which are a little closer in.

10. OUTLINING CONSIDERATIONS REVISITED

Chapter 3, in first describing the outlines, attempted to respond to potential objections that the time required to record information in the outlines outweighed the benefits of doing so. Now that each outline has been more fully explored, it may be useful to respond again to those potential objections. Recall that there are very tangible benefits to the outlines. The factual complexity of most litigated disputes, the time warp called "litigation time," the limited opportunities one typically has to speak to witnesses, and the likelihood that an associate previously unfamiliar with a case will have to perform some task in connection with it, all militate in favor of systematically recording one's analysis. Moreover, the thinking one does which produces the analysis must be done in any event; the outlines are a way of preserving the fruits of one's mental labors.

To the foregoing considerations, we add one other. The outlines of potential evidence are based on the same substantive framework as the existing evidence outlines. Hence, preparation of the outlines of potential evidence requires almost no additional effort, at least in these days of copy machines. For the outline of potential affirmative evidence, one need only copy the substantive structure of a client's outline of existing affirmative evidence; one need not even include the existing affirmative evidence itself. For the outline of potential rebuttal, one simply copies the outline of the adversary's existing affirmative evidence with the evidence intact. Thus, the additional time expenditure for developing the basic structure of the outlines of potential evidence is quite minimal, especially as compared to the time it takes to prepare Beef Wellington.

Finally, recognize that the preparation time of the story outline and the existing evidence outline can probably be eased substantially by the use of paralegals and computers. Most outline systems are based on a standard form using a combination of numbers and letters. That combination lends itself easily to the use of paralegals and computers. As one receives information, whether it be in the form of memos or witness interviews, depositions, or answers to interrogatories, one may ask a paralegal to list the information in chronological order, noting the source of information. Next, after the chronological summary is returned, one may go through each item of evidence, and using the letters and numbers from the outline indicate the particular element or elements which the item of evidence tends to prove. In addition, where one thought it appropriate, one may jot down the underlying generalization. After this process is complete, one returns the annotated chronology to the paralegal. The paralegal then inserts the various items of evidence into the existing evidence outlines in accordance with the number and letter designations and also inserts the information into the story outline in correct chronological order. Where an office is equipped with computer capabilities (and the right program), this transfer task could be undertaken by a computer operator.[7]

With the foregoing approach, the only time one devotes to outlining existing evidence is when connecting the evidence with an element it tends to prove. Moreover, the only writing one does, apart from noting generalizations, is listing a few letters and numbers. It of course remains the lawyer's task to link evidence with an element it tends to prove.[8]

---

7. See Chapter 3, note 2. The authors are personally aware of litigators who already use computers and paralegals in this manner.

8. Perhaps surprisingly, many litigators depend on paralegals to perform the essentially "lawyer" task of linking evidence to legal theories. See, e.g., Fall 1983 UCLA Extension Career Programs Announcement, Attorney Assistant Training Program, at p. 6: "Among the specific skills taught are how to . . . summarize and index depositions."

11. POTENTIAL EVIDENCE EXERCISES

A. You are the attorney for the Phillipses. In the outline of the Phillipses' existing affirmative evidence, Element "C" of the legal theory of "Fraud-Non-Disclosure of Material Fact," is, "When it sold lots 70 and 71 to the Phillipses, Landview did not disclose that the land was subject to slides." Assuming there is evidence that the land was subject to slides and that Landview knew it, your task is to develop at least three explanatory hypotheses as to why Landview might not have disclosed this fact and to embellish each hypothesis with potential evidence. When you identify potential evidence, remember to keep in mind the concepts of "before, during and after" and "especially when." Write out each hypothesis and its supporting potential evidence in the form in which you would put it in an outline of potential affirmative evidence.

B. You are still the attorney for the Phillipses. In your outline of Landview's existing affirmative evidence, one legal element (stated from Landview's perspective) of Landview's theory that it did not misrepresent the soil conditions of lots 70 and 71 is, "The Phillipses did not rely on statements by Landview that the lots were suitable for building." Your outline of Landview's existing affirmative evidence contains the following pieces of evidence under this legal element:

(a) At the time the Phillipses hired Woody Garvey, the architect, in late September, Mr. Phillips told Garvey, "Better check everything out. You can't trust a thing those damn salesmen tell you."

(b) According to Lotz, at the time the Phillipses signed the final purchase papers, he gave them basic architectural drawings for three home models, each stamped with a notation that, "Revisions may be required because of the conditions of particular lots."

(c) According to Dean Susan, the banker who arranged the Phillipses' bank loan for their purchase of the Campion Hills properties, in a conversation with Mrs. Phillips in early August, Mrs. Phillips stated, "These properties are really a bargain. We'd probably buy them even if they were under water."

For each piece of Landview's existing affirmative evidence, develop rebuttal theories, both "denial" and "admit and explain," on the Phillipses' behalf. Then, identify potential evidence for each theory. Write out your hypotheses and potential evidence in the form in which you would put them in an outline of potential rebuttal.

C. Spell "hypotheses" very quickly, backwards.

*

Part IV

UNEARTHING EVIDENCE

So far the investigatory skills we have asked you to develop primarily depend on little gray cells, legal pads, pencils and perhaps a computer. In this part, we ask you to add two more pieces of equipment—a pair of shoes and vocal cords. Whether one uses the potential evidence as a basis for thinking of witnesses who might supply that evidence, or whether one learns of a potential witness in some other manner, one is ready to stop listing and start listening. Questioning and listening is what Part IV is all about. If the earlier chapters have enabled one to identify *what* one wants to learn, then these ensuing chapters should enable one to identify tactics and techniques for learning it.

Because one's remaining central investigatory task involves conversing with potential witnesses, Part IV focuses mainly on interrogating witnesses. Yet, witnesses are not simply cans of information that may be opened, their contents poured out and then discarded. Or, at least the lawyer who regards witnesses as nothing more than fact receptacles will probably be a less successful investigator than the lawyer who uses interpersonal skills to motivate witnesses, stimulate their memories and facilitate their availability, if necessary. Thus, in the ensuing chapters, considerable attention is devoted to these interpersonal skills.

The chapters focus on informal lawyer-witness interviews: no judge, no adversary, no court reporter, very few rules. In our judgment, many of the suggestions applicable to informal interviews apply equally to more formal questioning settings, such as depositions. Where special considerations seem applicable to formal settings, an attempt is made to point them out. We also devote an entire chapter to written interrogatories. Although this last chapter may have less practical significance for criminal lawyers, it perhaps points out some limitations of oral questioning.

The discussion of information gathering attempts both to develop general principles and to give suggestions for specific situations that arise repeatedly. However, it does not identify every situation that commonly arises and, for those situations which are identified, not all potential considerations are described. Our approach is to illustrate general principles. The permutations of attorney-witness interactions are so great that we can do no more. Nonetheless, we hope that if our descriptions are accurate one may apply the general principles to situations that arise less frequently.

Before turning to the questioning process, we discuss in Chapter 11 a few planning considerations, in addition to building and adorning hypotheses, that one typically considers before questioning witnesses.

Chapter 11

PLANNING FOR INTERVIEWS

---

1. INTRODUCTION

The purpose of this chapter is to expose some aspects of the gap between the essentially sedentary activity of identifying theories and potential evidence and the more physical activity of talking to witnesses. Anyone who has attempted a simple home repair or improvement knows the truth of the old saying, "Before you do anything, you have to do a lot of other things first." If one is painting a room, those "other things" may consist of moving and covering furniture, cleaning and sanding walls, and filling cracks. If one is embarking on interviewing, some of those "other things" are identifying theories, existing evidence, and potential evidence. In some instances, these steps may be sufficient preparation. But often there are more "other things" one must consider before talking to witnesses. This chapter discusses some of these additional preparatory tasks.

No matter how thorough one's analysis of evidence on hand and potential evidence, developing a comprehensive plan to ferret out the latter is an extremely complex task. After all, if re-creating the past is next to impossible, predicting the future is not likely to be any easier. The combination of numerous discovery devices, both formal and informal; unique factual disputes; the need to constantly re-evaluate cases as new information is received; and the vagaries of human behavior in the context of an adversary system is usually enough to overwhelm any grand investigatory plan in which one would plot the entire investigation from start to finish.

Thus, though one may formulate a master investigatory plan for a case, in all likelihood one will be unable to adhere to it. Typically, a grand plan will be abandoned in favor of a series of plans for "the next few investigatory steps." This chapter, therefore, focuses on factors that may help one to plan "the next few steps." However, since if nothing else a grand scheme may make the little schemes more effective, we turn first to overall planning strategies.

2. OVERALL PLANNING STRATEGIES

a. General Decision-Making Strategy

The complexity of investigatory planning is similar to the complexities faced by planners in other fields. All planners try to identify and select options in the face of an uncertain future. Hence, awareness of general decision-making strategy, which probably applies whether one is investigating a legal dispute or deciding where to dine, may be useful.[1]

Organized decision-making is typically thought of as a four step process, in which one asks and attempts to answer the following questions:

(a) What are my objectives?

(b) What are the alternatives?

(c) What are the pros and cons of each alternative?

(d) On balance, which alternative seems best?

The answers generally do not point toward a single, radiant truth. However, the questions produce an approach that allows one to make considered choices.

As for objectives, one may have a number of goals in mind. For instance, one may seek to uncover "all the documents," learn all evidence pertaining to a certain theory of relief, or learn sufficient evidence to support a motion for summary judgment. Moreover, one may have tactical, non-informational objectives in mind. For example, with an eye to negotiation, one may want to learn an adversary's underlying needs and interests,[2] or to demonstrate that one is prepared to expend considerable resources on a case.

After identifying one or more objectives, one then considers alternative ways of accomplishing them. There exist a host of formal and informal avenues for pursuing potential evidence. At the very least, one must be aware of available alternatives. For example, unless one is aware that in civil cases depositions can be taken upon written interrogatories, or that in criminal cases motions to suppress may be used as discovery vehicles,[3] one's awareness of discovery alternatives

1. For a general discussion of decision making theory, See J. March and H. Simmon *Organization* (1958); H. Simmon, The New Science of Management Decision (1960).

2. See R. Fisher and W. Ury, *Getting To Yes* 11 (1981); C. Menkel-Meadow,

"Toward Another View of Legal Negotiations: The Structure of Problem-Solving," 31 UCLA L. Rev. — (1984).

3. See A. Amsterdam, *Trial Manual for the Defense of Criminal Cases* § 184 (3d ed. 1974).

is incomplete. Research, both in a law library and in the offices of more experienced litigators, may be necessary to ensure that no reasonable alternative is overlooked.[4]

Next, one evaluates the alternatives. From both a legal and a practical standpoint, what are the likely advantages and disadvantages of each? For example, for reasons that will be discussed in Chapter 17, interrogatories are useful for learning the identities of witnesses and the existence and location of documents. But they are not well suited to the task of learning the events and details in a party's story. Moreover, sending out interrogatories may alert an adversary to one's theories and areas of factual concern. If nothing else, that knowledge may enable opposing counsel to do a more thorough job of preparing witnesses for later depositions and trial.

Depositions are not without their drawbacks. Though one may compel testimony, opposing counsel has a right to be present, to listen to the evidence, and to ask questions. Moreover, depositions are not an effective way of learning an adversary's legal theories. During depositions, even a party may not be asked for the legal theories on which he or she relies.[5]

Moreover, the timing of discovery is also important.[6] If one conducts discovery of one's adversary before the adversary has had a sufficient opportunity to conduct its own investigation, one may learn little. On the other hand, one needs to find out about an adversary's legal theories and factual contentions, lest one waste time on irrelevancies.

Apart from such standard advantages and disadvantages, considerations of alternatives in a particular case usually involve examining a plethora of assumptions about the future. For example, as a general rule one advantage of interrogatories is that they are cheaper and less time consuming than depositions. But how well does one know the adversaries, both lawyer and client? Are they likely to re-

---

4. For a brief discussion of the various formal civil discovery devices, see D. Karlan, *Procedure Before Trial in a Nutshell*, 177–216 (1972); R. Keeton, *Trial Tactics and Methods* §§ 11.1–11.20 (2d ed. 1973); Fox, *Planning and Conducting a Discovery Program*, 7 Litigation 13 (Summ.1981). For a much more detailed analysis, see J. Underwood, *A Guide to Federal Discovery Rules* (1979); R. Haydock & D. Herr, *Discovery: Theory, Practice, and Problems* (1983). For discussion of discovery in criminal matters, see 8 *Moore's Federal Practice* (Rules Crim.Pro.), Rules 15 and 16; A.B.A. Standards, *Pretrial Discovery and Procedure Before Trial* (2d ed.1978).

5. See, e.g., J. Hogan, 1 *Modern California Discovery* § 5.12 (3rd ed. 1981).

Also compare Fed.R.Civ.Proc. 33(b) with Fed.Rule Civ.Proc. 30. The former provides that an interrogatory which is otherwise proper is not necessarily objectionable merely because an answer to the interrogatory involves an opinion or contention that relates to the application of law to fact. The latter, which governs depositions, does not contain a similar provision.

6. While most commentators agree that interrogatories should generally precede depositions, e.g., R. Simmons, *Winning Before Trial: How to Prepare Cases for the Best Settlement or Trial Result*, 1323 (1974), others feel that the reverse is often wiser. See Fox, *Planning and Conducting a Discovery Program*, 7 Litigation 13, 15 (Summ.1981).

spond in thirty days or to seek an extension? Will a series of follow-up telephone calls and letters be necessary? How about motions to compel answers and impose sanctions? Only by forcing oneself to examine predicted behavior in specific contexts can one fully evaluate likely consequences.

Usually, one lacks the data to make exact predictions. If a decision appears vitally important, one may seek additional predictive data. Otherwise, one makes do with judgments based on experience with the typical consequences of various alternatives, together with the limited specific data available. In many instances, that judgment will be aided by actually writing down the alternatives and their perceived pros and cons. The process of writing down and then staring at choices often leads to more considered judgments.

Finally, perhaps together with a client, one makes a decision. That decision may vary from a clear choice to adopt one alternative to a realization of the need to identify and consider additional alternatives. In the mushy world of investigatory planning, one usually has the comfort of knowing that often there is no single "right" alternative. A variety of tacks may produce good results. Use of the general decision-making approach often enables one to find at least one of those tacks.

b. Preliminary Investigatory Considerations

The task of considering alternative methods of accomplishing objectives is aided by one's undertaking a few preliminary investigatory considerations. These considerations typically give one a sense of the "lay of the land," and thus may facilitate one's choice of an effective alternative to accomplish a particular objective. This section describes some of these more specific considerations. While we discuss the considerations separately for purposes of clarity, in practice they may well be combined.

(i) Connect Potential Evidence with Witnesses and/or Documents

Presumably one has already identified potential affirmative and rebuttal evidence which appears to be favorable to one's client. Before embarking on investigation, one considers sources through which one can convert potential evidence into evidence on hand. Who is likely to have the information? Or, stepping back, who might be able to identify someone else who might have the information? Is the information likely to be included in a document? If so, who might have prepared the document, and in whose possession might it be?

Connecting evidence to witnesses may serve a number of valuable functions. It may indicate that at least for certain potential evidence, one has more than one possible source. Or, if one source keeps popping up, that may help one decide where to begin questioning. And, if one must embark on investigation without possible sources for certain evidence, one is reminded to update the listing as new information is unearthed and additional sources uncovered.

(ii) Consider Whether Potential Witnesses Are Likely to be "Friendly" or "Adverse"

Witnesses are rarely totally helpful or totally harmful. Nevertheless, for one reason or another witnesses are often aligned with one of the parties. Perhaps a witness is employed by one of the parties or is a close friend. Or, perhaps a witness has a socio-political or emotional bias which favors one of the parties.

A number of consequences typically flow from a witness' alignment with a party. If one represents the party adverse to the witness, the witness may not agree to an informal interview. Even if an informal interview is arranged, the witness may be less willing to disclose information than he or she would be under oath, at a deposition. If one imparts information, a "friendly" witness may consider it to fairly reassess an initial story, whereas an "adverse" witness may only report the information to one's adversary (though one may in fact want this to happen.) A "friendly" witness may be more flexible in changing the time of an interview, agreeing to a follow-up interview, or accompanying one to scenes of events. Hence, one should generally make at least a preliminary assessment of a witness' possible alignment.

3. CONCLUSION

After one has identified an objective and considered alternatives for accomplishing it, one will often make a tentative decision that questioning a given witness affords one the best chance of accomplishing the objective. For example, in *Phillips v. Landview*, Mason might think, "I want to learn what Terry Firma knows about Landview's statements about the recreation center. I could send interrogatories to Landview, or I could take Firma's deposition. Maybe I'll talk to Firma informally and save the Phillipses some money."

However, Mason's decision was only tentative, because there are a number of other planning issues one typically considers before actually questioning a witness. The remainder of the Chapter examines these issues. Admittedly, the issues discussed are interrelated and infinitely more complex than can be described. In truth, the law's "seamless web" is as convoluted and sticky when it comes to information-gathering as it is with any other subject. We describe some of the more recurrent planning considerations in the hope that they provide one with a place to start thinking.

4.   AM I READY TO TALK TO THE WITNESS?

a.   *How Important Is It To Talk To The Witness?*

Frequently, certain aspects of cases are more important, or at least more urgent, than other aspects. Therefore, though a given witness might provide information which satisfies one objective, one might compare that objective to others. The comparison may lead to the conclusion that even though one is in other respects "ready" to speak with a witness, one should first pursue more important urgent objectives.

For example, of two legal theories, does one lead to speedier, perhaps injunctive relief? Does one offer the opportunity for greater damages? Are some theories already amply supported by evidence, while as to other theories the factual cupboard is bare? Such questions lead to an assessment of a witness' importance and may suggest that one pursue a goal involving different witnesses.

b.   *Do I Need More Familiarity With Scenes of Events and Tangible Evidence?*

One is routinely advised to be as familiar as possible with physical locations where important events took place and with important pieces of real evidence. However, the ease with which this advice is given should not obscure its purpose. For, in the long run, it is usually a witness' knowledge, not an attorney's, which is critical. One does not view a scene or physical evidence simply to enhance one's own knowledge. Rather, one often does so in order to question witnesses more effectively. For example, a witness may describe something as having happened "sort of off to the right of where I was standing." If one is unfamiliar with the scene, it may be difficult to probe for more exacting detail. But if one has been to the scene personally, one may force the witness to be precise: "You say it was off to the right. Where was it with respect to the bus bench with the tasteful advertisement for Louis the Lawyer?"

If it seems important to see a scene or an item of tangible evidence before talking to a witness, one then decides how to go about doing so. A public location usually presents no difficulty. A "Motion to Produce Mount Diablo" is rarely in order.

But if a physical location or an item of real evidence is under the control of an adversary or a non-party, some awareness of potential alternatives is required. Do not overlook informal discovery. Perhaps whoever has the evidence will share it. A deal is often possible:

"I'll let you see mine if you let me see yours." If this does not work, then resort to more expensive formal discovery may be needed. For example, if real evidence is in the adversary's control, a "Request to Produce" [7] is usually in order. If a non-party has it, a "Subpoena duces tecum re Deposition" [8] or its equivalent is typically used. When a physical location is involved, a "Request to Permit Entry Upon Land" can be considered.

c. Do I Need To Gather Any Documents First?

Ever more frequently, the road to litigation is littered with letters, reports, memoranda, written messages, and other indicia of a highly bureaucratized society. Many disputes concern events that happened over a period of months or even years, and without access to relevant documents a witness may not be able to recall all that occurred. Imagine a witness on the receiving end of this question: "They say that your company's use of various sales forms is an unfair business practice. How did you go about developing those forms?" Most likely that development involved a series of meetings with accompanying memoranda and proposed forms. The witness probably could not meaningfully respond to such a question in the absence of a personal calendar indicating his or her presence at those meetings, the memoranda or reports detailing the development of the forms and the various forms themselves and their predecessors. Hence, one often needs to gather pertinent documents which a witness can review before or during the interview.

Again, if certain documents are under the control of someone other than one's client, one needs to consider formal or informal methods of gaining access to them. If one knows the documents one seeks, and if they are in the hands of the adversary, the appropriate formal discovery device is typically a "Request to Produce." If a known document is in the hands of a non-party, one may need to serve a "Subpoena Duces Tecum re Deposition." Lastly, if one suspects that documents exist but does not know their whereabouts, one may have to take depositions or send out interrogatories before talking to a witness.

7. Fed.R.Civ.P. Rule 34. For a discussion of this much-used discovery device see *Production of Results Under Rule 34*, 5 Am.J.Trial Adv. 253–276 (Fall 1981); J. Underwood, *Discovery According to Federal Rule 34*, 26 Prac.Law. 55, 57–66 (Mar.1980). The criminal equivalent is found under Fed.R.Crim.P. Rule 16 and 18 U.S.C.A. § 3500. For discussion see G. Lowenthal, *A Study of the Fact Investigation Practices of Crimi-*

nal Defense Lawyers, 1981 Ariz.St.L.J. 447, 549–550.

8. Fed.R.Civ.P. Rules 45(b)(d)(1), 30(b) (1). For discussion see R. Haydock & D. Herr, *Discovery: Theory, Practice and Problems* § 4.18 (1983); J. Underwood, *A Guide to Federal Discovery Rules* 63 (1979). This procedure is also available in criminal cases under Fed.R.Crim.P. Rule 17(c).

d. Are There Other Witnesses I Should Talk to First?

Aficionados of the "renvoi" doctrine of choice-of-law particularly enjoy this consideration, as the seamless web truly turns in upon itself. One may desire to speak with a witness—say, an expert who may suggest areas of inquiry with other witnesses. But before one speaks to that witness, one may first have to view a physical location or obtain documents from other witnesses. But to do that one may have to talk to other witnesses, take depositions or send out interrogatories. But first . . . .

If any "master plan" adherents still exist, these possibilities may convince them of the futility of planning beyond a few tasks. Like a drawing by M.C. Escher, everything seems to be preliminary to everything else. Escher had the luxury of stopping at the portrayal of the dilemma—it was enough for him to "spot the issue." Lawyers have to resolve dilemmas by making choices that are less than perfect. All one can do is carefully consider which witness to talk to next, and go from there. Alternatively, become an artist.

e. Should I Use an Investigator?

A witness may be important, amenable to an informal interview, as available as heartburn at a deli, and sensibly interviewed without having to climb Mt. Diablo or to have on hand all documents concerning the national debt. But it does not follow that one's next step is to personally interview that witness. It may be that one should use an investigator.

As with the other considerations mentioned in this chapter, there are few universal principles governing the decision. Indeed, there is not even consensus on who an investigator is. It might be a card-carrying Fenton Hardy-type sleuth, a rank amateur pressed into service, a paralegal or a lawyer other than oneself. But if there are no universal answers, at least there are some useful questions. Do I need to talk to more witnesses quickly than I can talk to personally? Does the witness live in Paris or Beirut? Might a witness be more open with an investigator? Would it be helpful if someone with a personal or professional background similar to the witness' conducted the interview? Will an investigator be sufficiently familiar with the legal theories and factual hypotheses to conduct a thorough interview? Are there cost savings with an investigator? The answers to such questions typically guide one's decision on whether to use an investigator, and if so, whom.[9]

9. See R. Keeton, note 2 supra, at § 9.11; Simmons, note 4 supra, at 403–407.

Moreover, there are ethical considerations that often bear on the decision. For example, attorneys are generally forbidden to testify as witnesses in cases in which they are of record.[10] Thus, if a witness orally tells an attorney, "The light was green," and during trial denies the statement, the attorney may be stuck with the denial. However, no rule prevents an investigator from taking the stand to impeach a witness.[11]

Also, though the rules are something of a morass, the ethical standards governing interviews are apparently not as high for investigators as they are for attorneys.

> Hi! I'm with Channel 3's Happy News staff. You know—the news show that always features closeups of car wrecks. We're doing a consumer survey on traffic safety. There have really been some terrible accidents around here lately, like that one last week. By the way, did you see it?

Assume the statement is false. If the person is an attorney, the attorney's conduct may well be unethical.[12] However, an investigator is apparently not directly subject to such ethical rules, and evidently may use ruses in order to speak to people.[13] Strangely enough courts often uphold the use of ruses by investigators even when an attorney is initially aware that a ruse will be used.[14]

Lastly, it should be noted that an investigator's use of a ruse may raise tactical concerns, if not ethical ones. If a factfinder learns that

10. This rule is not at all absolute. See American Bar Foundation, *Annotated Code of Professional Responsibility* DR5–101 & 102, at 208–221 (1979); *Attorney as Witness for Client in Federal Case*, 9 A.L.R.Fed. 500 (1971).

11. Many commentators suggest that attorneys take along an observer who can impeach a witness if the need arises. 2 Am.Jur. *Trials* 262–264 (1964); R. Keeton, note 2 supra, at § 9.13.

12. See *ABA Code of Professional Responsibility*, DR 1–102(a)(4); DR 7–102(a)(5). But see R. Keeton note 2 supra, at § 9.12. Not only is the practice ethically questionable, more often than not it is counter-productive. See, e.g., K. Hegland, *Trial and Practice Skills in a Nutshell*, 225–228 (1978); R. Keeton, supra.

13. Most investigators are replete with techniques of subterfuge they use in ferreting out information. The Fair Housing Commission's use of "checkers" to identify cases of Housing Discrimination, Smith v. Anchor Building Corp., 536 F.2d 231, 234 (8th Cir.1976), and the skip-

tracing methods for locating delinquent debtors, Rothschild v. Federal Trade Commission, 200 F.2d 39 (7th Cir.1952) are just two examples of investigative subterfuge to which the courts have given sanction. Similarly, in criminal cases courts regularly permit evidence gathered by police undercover agents, who obviously routinely make false statements to carry out investigations.

However, the right to resort to subterfuge is not without its limits. See United States v. Henry, 447 U.S. 264, 100 S.Ct. 2183, 65 L.Ed.2d 115 (1980), holding that use of an undercover informant to gain information from a criminal defendant who was in a holding cell violated the defendant's right to counsel. Indeed, wherever the subject of subterfuge is a party represented by counsel, use of a ruse is ethically questionable. See e.g., A. Golec, *Techniques of Legal Investigation* 28–29 (1976); *ABA Code of Professional Responsibility*, note 10 supra, DR 7–104.

14. See note 10, supra.

a witness has been duped into talking or behaving, the factfinder's sense of justice may be offended. As a result, the factfinder may, for conscious or subconscious reasons, disbelieve the investigator's version.

5. I AM READY!

When the time for interviewing a witness arrives, one wants to use the opportunity to learn as much pertinent information as possible. The next chapter begins an examination of interviewing.

Chapter 12

MOTIVATING WITNESSES

1. INTRODUCTION

This chapter begins the focus on the interaction between lawyers and witnesses. If you have not already done so, disabuse yourself of the notion that because you are a lawyer, people will automatically open up their hearts and minds to you. Lawyer or not, to most people with whom you come in contact, you are a stranger. Thus, even though clients want help, they may be reluctant to disclose intimate details of their lives. And witnesses, be they "friendly," "hostile," or "neutral," may not want to talk. Even if they do, they may either consciously not reveal all they know or subconsciously not probe their memories fully.

Getting witnesses to talk and to be fully responsive requires more than asking the "right questions." Even if one asks the right questions, answers are often less than complete. In nearly every interview, one may have to motivate a witness in order to elicit information. Of course, witness motivation is part and parcel of the entire interview process. One does not, for example, say to a witness, "Before you tell me what happened, let me give you some motivation. You can either listen to twelve compliments, or you can watch this old Knute Rockne film." Nonetheless, motivation is analyzed separately for specific reasons. First, the subject of providing motivation is quite complex. Devoting a separate chapter to it avoids continually interrupting subsequent chapters devoted to question-asking with discussions of motivation. Second, motivation is very important. It is often to an interview what oil is to an engine; without motivation, one is unlikely to go very far. The separate discussion does, we hope, underline the importance of motivation.

This chapter begins by exploring the primary factors that make witnesses reluctant to disclose information. It then examines a second group of factors that tend to motivate people to disclose what they know. Some of these factors are peculiar to lawyer interviews; others probably apply in almost every interviewing context. Finally, since investigative talents rest in part on one's ability to minimize the first group of factors and maximize the second, the last section is devoted to motivational techniques.

2. WHY PEOPLE WITHHOLD INFORMATION

From everyday living, we are all aware that witnesses may be reluctant to disclose what they know. The desire "not to get involved" echoes almost daily from the pages of newspapers. However, this common reluctance is but one of an array of psychological roadblocks to communication. Without entering the realm of deep psychological analysis and treatment, one can learn to recognize and overcome many surface-level psychological barriers to disclosing information.[1] Although these factors are discussed separately, please note that they often work in conjunction with one or more other factors. Fortunately, the authors do not suffer from any of these barriers, or we would not, of course, tell "why people withhold information!"

a. Loss of Self-Esteem

At first glance, it may not be apparent how anything that occurs in a legal interview might affect a witness' self-esteem. Consider, however, that there are two prongs of self-esteem. The first prong is a personal evaluation of what one has done, quite apart from whether anyone else knows about it. For example, we may feel good about making an anonymous gift to charity and bad about pedaling a bicycle over a child's stuffed animal, even if nobody else knows of our actions. The other prong of self-esteem involves evaluation by others. Our self-esteem rises when others compliment us and falls when we are criticized. Below are a number of typical interviewing situations in which a witness might lose self-esteem. In each situation, the risk for the interviewer is that a witness may withhold information rather than suffer the loss.[2]

If a witness believes it is morally wrong to provide information in certain circumstances, the witness may choose not to provide it, even if nobody else will know of his or her actions. For example, witnesses may not provide information that might help a criminal defendant

1. It has been suggested, however, that, in some circumstances, lawyers may need the capacity to deal with subsurface psychological forces that bear on the interviewing dynamic. See A. Watson, *The Lawyer in the Interviewing and Counseling Process* 75–93, 153–154 (1976).

2. The pressure to "save face" influences decision-making by other participants in the litigation process as well, including lawyers and jurors. See R. Traver, *Anatomy of a Murder* 42 (1958).

whom they believe to be guilty or that might get a friend or relative in trouble.

Similarly, moral judgments aside, involvement with lawyers and the litigation process might cause a witness to fear loss of self-esteem. Most of us feel that if we have made it past second grade, we ought to be infallible observers. In the context of a specific event, therefore, some witnesses may fear that their memories are not precise enough to satisfy lawyers or the legal system. Consider the following interview example:

Lawyer: Where was the blue car?

Witness: In the middle of the intersection, heading north.

Lawyer: And at the moment it was in the middle of the intersection, can you describe where the pinky of the driver's left hand was?

Witness: Gulp! I don't know. Oh, dear. Anyway, I didn't really see the blue car.

Witnesses may choose to remain uninvolved and to say they saw nothing, rather than admit they saw only a little.

Moreover, many people fear that as to information they do provide, they will ultimately be brought into court where some tricky lawyer will turn and twist whatever they say and make them end up looking like a fool. They expect that they, instead of the litigants, will be "on trial" and that their failings and shortcomings will be exposed. As a result, some people tend to feel that testifying in court is so fraught with anxiety that it is simply "not worth getting involved."

In other instances, witnesses may fear loss of self-esteem in the eyes of those in the community. For example, if a litigant, such as the A.C.L.U. or the Brotherhood of Right, is unpopular with some sizable segment of a community, witnesses may be afraid to provide even objective information that might aid that litigant.[3] Similarly, if Claude Hopper is an elder in the Church of Strictness, he may be reluctant to provide information about a crime he witnessed while in a gambling den. And Alison Anders Anderson may likewise be reluctant to talk about an auto accident she saw while out shopping, after she had told some friends she could not be with them because she was ill. In all of these instances, rather than risk potential embarrassment in the community, witnesses may withhold information.

3. Consider the cool reception given the A.C.L.U. in Utah when it entered the appeal of convicted murderer Gary Gil- more. See, N. Mailer, *The Executioner's Song* (1979).

b. *Breaching Role Expectations*

Most people have a set of beliefs about what behavior is appropriate when they are in a particular relationship or position. For example, most people think one should behave in certain ways when acting as a parent, a spouse, a coach, a doctor, and yes, even as a lawyer. These role expectations develop from a variety of experiences, both actual and vicarious. Family, friends, associates, news media and societal institutions constantly deliver messages about what constitutes proper behavior for persons in particular positions. Obviously, in different socio-economic strata of our society and in different geographic regions, different messages about appropriate behavior are delivered.

When it comes to giving information to lawyers or legal investigators, society seems to have developed a number of expectations about proper behavior which some witnesses are fearful of breaching. Examine how role expectations may limit disclosure in the following situations.

People who are to testify on behalf of one party often believe it is improper to talk with an investigator or lawyer for the other party. For example, a person who is to be a witness for the plaintiff in an automobile accident case may feel it would be illegal or unethical to talk with a legal representative of the defendant. Or, a witness who might at least talk to a private investigator in this situation may believe that talking with a *lawyer* is always improper.

Compensation also raises issues of propriety. Some people believe any offer of compensation, even if limited to statutory witness fees, is improper. When a person holds such a belief, an offer to pay a fee may be perceived as some sort of a "bribe" and produce a very reluctant witness. In contrast, other people believe that witnesses should always receive compensation, especially for court appearances. If minimal or no compensation is available for such people, the reluctance may be quite pronounced.

Lastly, many people, even neutral and friendly witnesses, believe that they should never reveal more information than is asked for. They feel that the lawyer knows what is important and that they should keep quiet unless specifically asked for certain information.

c. *Etiquette Barrier*

Another hurdle to full disclosure is the "etiquette barrier." Often, witnesses have information which they will freely provide to some persons but not to others. There are things that women tell women, but not men; that blacks tell blacks, but not whites; that students tell students but not teachers. Loss of self-esteem is not necessarily involved. Rather, people may feel that topics they would openly discuss with one person are taboo with another.

For lawyers, the etiquette barrier may cause a witness not to talk to a lawyer at all. More typically, it causes witnesses to avoid topics they believe might shock, embarrass or discomfort the lawyer. (Of course, most do not know that after the first year of law school, almost nothing can shock a lawyer.)

A fascinating example of an etiquette barrier is provided in *After the Fact: The Art of Historical Detection*, which in part describes slavery in America from the slaves' points of view.[4] Because slaves were not generally provided with education, few written accounts by slaves of their experiences exist. Thus, historians had to rely on oral accounts. Those accounts revealed the etiquette barrier at work. With white interviewers, ex-slaves stressed the kindness of their masters. But when interviewers were black, the accounts told of whippings and hardships.[5] Apparently, there were matters that former slaves just would not reveal to whites.

d. *Trauma*

This phenomenon may occur when a person is asked to recall an experience which evokes unpleasant feelings. There are many events which produce negative feelings such as fear, anger, humiliation, or sadness. When people are asked to recall such events, they may re-experience these feelings. As a consequence, people may avoid thinking and talking about these events. For example, a parent being interviewed about a beating administered to his or her child by a babysitter may be reluctant to talk about the incident; the parent may want to avoid re-experiencing the anger, frustration, and sadness which the incident caused.

e. *Loss of Time and Money*

Talking with an investigator and testifying in court take time, and unless a witness is "friendly" with one of the parties, the witness typically will find it more pleasurable or monetarily rewarding to spend time doing something other than providing information to a stranger. There are, of course, exceptions. Some people have nothing to do or do not like what they are doing. In these situations, the opportunity to talk with an investigator or testify in court may be perceived as a real benefit. However, for most people, talking with an investigator and testifying in court costs time.

4. J. Davidson and M. Lytle, *After the Fact: The Art of Historical Detection* (1982).

5. Ibid, Chapter 7 at 169–204.

Moreover, there are losses other than time. If it becomes known that one is the source of certain information, one may be fired from a job, denied a promotion or lose customers or clients. Most of us, for example, are familiar with the frequent newspaper articles concerning governmental employees who have been fired for revealing information about their agencies. In this sense, the mafia stoolie who has been fitted for a cement suit has been subjected to the ultimate communication barrier.

f. Perceived Irrelevancy

If a person believes that information sought has nothing to do with a case, the person may be reluctant to reveal it. In part, the reluctance may be simply a product of the common desire not to engage in pointless acts. And in part, the reluctance may be caused by the cynical belief that if the reason for a question is unclear, probably the real reason is sneaky and underhanded. Rather than be chopped down by an unseen blow, some people may simply not disclose information.

The following example illustrates this factor. Assume that four weeks ago Raye Faye was injured when her car rammed into a highway abutment. Working on the theory that the abutment was known to the county to be a dangerous highway defect, Ms. Faye's lawyer has located a potential witness, Helen Back. Four years ago, Ms. Back struck the same obstruction, although she long ago settled her case and is now fully recovered. Suppose Faye's lawyer were simply to approach Ms. Back and begin to question her about her accident. Is there not some likelihood that she would find the lawyer's questions irrelevant? The lawyer represents Ms. Faye, who was injured only a few weeks ago. What does a case that was settled long ago have to do with Ms. Faye's situation? Might Back's settlement be in danger? Perhaps better to say nothing!

g. Greater Need

The last phenomenon on our list of barriers is "greater need." Often witnesses have a need or desire to talk about a topic other than the topic of most immediate interest to the lawyer. As a consequence, the witness cannot concentrate on the lawyer's topic, and full and accurate information is not forthcoming. For example, a witness to an automobile accident, concerned about whether she must testify in court, or about her own injuries stemming from a different accident, often cannot give full attention to questions about the accident. In such situations, the witness does not perceive the lawyer's questions as threatening or irrelevant. Rather, the witness is simply concerned about a subject which, while perhaps secondary to the lawyer, is primary to the witness.

h. A Hypothetical Case

To conclude this consideration of why people may not want to talk or to disclose information, review the following hypothetical situation and formulate a list of disclosure barriers the investigator might encounter.

Victor Hector is employed by ABC Machinery Company as a punch press operator. Two days ago, Hector lost his left hand while trying to dislodge a piece of metal from a punch press operated by Hector's close friend, Ray Billete. It took over an hour to free Hector from the press.

Tonight, Walter Barbara, an investigator from ABC's insurance carrier, is going to Billete's home to interview him about the accident. Why might Barbara encounter reluctance on Billete's part? List as many reasons as you can think of.

3. WHAT MOTIVATES PEOPLE TO TALK

The foregoing list of barriers may make investigation seem quite short: "Nobody will talk to me. I'll do something else." Yet, we know that people talk to lawyers about cases all the time. Thus, it is safe to conclude that right alongside the reasons why witnesses may not want to talk to lawyers run factors that motivate them to talk. This subsection examines this second group of factors.

a. Empathy

During an early part of an interview, a witness hesitatingly states, "The whole thing was just too much for me. He came home and molested our pet chicken, right in front of the kids. It was just awful." Consider these potential responses:

Attorney A	(The Straight-Ahead Plunger)	"What exactly did he do to the chicken?"
Attorney B	(The Blue-Tailed, Narrowly Focused Fact-Gatherer)	"Did this happen in the family room?"
Attorney C	(The Empathetic Listener)	"That must have been very upsetting. Why don't you tell me as much as you can?"
Attorney D	(The Ever-Searching Defense Pursuer)	"Are you sure the kids saw him do it?"
Attorney E	(The Judgment Maker)	"How could he have done that with the kids there?"

With which attorney might the witness be most motivated to discuss the case further? If, as we hope, you shrewdly selected Attorney C, think about why you did so. The responses of A and B ignore much of what the witness has said, and focus on narrow aspects of the "substantive" point—the chicken incident. Attorney D, too, focuses on this aspect, and seems to probe immediately for a defense—maybe the kids did not see it. Attorney E also focuses on "the incident" by asking for explanations of the perpetrator's "wrongful" behavior. The vice of all of these responses is that they focus on one aspect of the story, to the exclusion of the witness' feelings and other aspects which may be more important legally.

By contrast, Attorney C's response indicates an interest in all that the witness may have to say. It acknowledges that the witness was upset and evidences a willingness to hear the full story. If the witness is like most of us, the witness would probably be more motivated to talk with Attorney C, since C seems more understanding and willing to listen.

A response which demonstrates that one has heard, understood and not passed judgment is empathetic. A person on the receiving end of such a response is usually motivated to talk further. Psychologists have termed the interviewing technique which fosters such responses "active listening." [6] Active listening suggests to a storyteller that one is willing to listen to whatever he or she has to say. It may suggest that the content of a story, and the feelings which accompany it, are both important. Finally, it suggests that one can listen without approving or disapproving of a story. Exactly why active listening motivates people to be forthcoming cannot be stated with certainty. That such empathetic listening does, however, facilitate open and continued communication has often been empirically noted.[7]

For lawyers, active listening may be particularly difficult. We are all products of a legal education which focuses primarily on analysis of doctrine. Doctrine focuses on facts, not feelings.[8] Feelings are made to seem irrelevant.[9] Yet, whether we like it or not, facts are usually not reported in an emotionless vacuum. Experience and common sense bear out the ubiquitousness of feelings. When one sees a parent spank a child, an employer reprimand an employee, or one car collide with another, an emotional response results. Active listening encourages people to allow their feelings to penetrate inter-

6. See T. Gordon, *Parent Effectiveness Training* 49–50 (1970); D. Binder and S. Price, *Legal Interviewing and Counseling: A Client Centered Approach* 25–37 (1977).

7. C. Rogers, *Counseling and Psychotherapy* 131–173 (1942).

8. E. Dvorkin, J. Himmelstein & H. Lesnick, *Becoming a Lawyer* 33–75 (1981).

9. Ibid.

views and thus tends to produce more complete stories. As one legal scholar has noted, in lawyering, both facts and feelings are facts.[10]

Beside the narrowness of legal education, other factors combine to make active listening difficult for lawyers. Any event may produce a mix of emotional responses. A witness to a robbery may be fearful because of the robbery, grateful that a suspect is on trial, nervous because of the need to testify, and angry because the case has dragged on so long. Moreover, emotional feelings may change over time, and during an interview a witness may sometimes report feelings as they existed at the time of an event and other times report feelings as of the time of the interview. A witness' need to tell the whole story may conflict with one's need for an abbreviated interview. Witnesses may actively seek approval of their conduct and disapproval of the conduct of others. Such factors may make empathetic responses at times difficult to give. However, one must learn to be empathetic if one desires to learn whole stories.

b. Providing Recognition

People enjoy receiving compliments and recognition; they increase self-esteem. People, therefore, are often motivated to obtain recognition, particularly when it comes from someone who is not a close friend or relative. You, reader, are quite intelligent and therefore understand this phenomenon.

c. Appeals to Justice

People feel good about themselves when they believe they have done the right, correct and/or just thing, and are motivated to do what they perceive to be fair or proper. For example, many people are motivated to solicit charitable contributions or to provide information which hinders an apparently unsavory individual or group.

This being so, one can often motivate people by pointing out that the revealing of information may produce justice. Because doing justice raises one's self esteem, providing this kind of motivation may take the form of praise from others or arise from the internal satisfaction of doing the right thing.

In many instances, however, it may be advantageous to point out that others will probably not know who provided the information. As your intuition suggests, often people will talk with a lawyer only if they feel that what they saw will remain confidential.

10. T. Schaffer, *Legal Interviewing and Counseling* 3–5 (1976).

d. Expectation

When someone asks a question in a tone of voice that indicates a response is expected, our almost instinctive reaction is to reply. Since birth we have been socialized to answer questions from parents, teachers, store clerks, employers and others. Our analysis of some of the more complex psychological aspects of interviewing should not obscure the simple reality that questions in and of themselves tend to motivate replies. Don't you agree?

e. Concrete Rewards

Thus far, most of the factors discussed provide motivation by giving witnesses some form of intangible psychological reward. For example, empathy, recognition, and appeals to justice are each effective because they tend to make witnesses feel better psychologically.

Sometimes, however, one can motivate witnesses by pointing out that participation can produce rather concrete rewards. Testifying in a deposition or in court usually involves time, energy and expense. Accordingly, one frequently tries to motivate witnesses by noting that by cooperating in an interview or deposition, the witness may aid settlement and thus avoid the time and expense involved in subsequent court proceedings.

Additionally, one may motivate a witness who is in a predicament similar to one's client by pointing out that information which helps one's client may also benefit the witness. For example, assume one represents E. Nuff, who is a defendant in an unlawful detainer action brought by Nuff's landlord, Bill Plenty. Nuff's answer asserts a defense of lack of habitability because of rats in the building. In interviewing A. Katt, who is the neighbor in the apartment next to Nuff, one can perhaps motivate Katt by pointing out how Katt's talking about the rats can help Katt. If Nuff has sufficient information to convince the court that the building does have rats, then Plenty will probably have to do something about the rats. That, of course, will benefit Katt as well as Nuff.

Finally, one may of course give a twenty pound sack of concrete to each witness one interviews.

4. APPROACHES FOR MOTIVATING WITNESSES

When one meets a witness, one will most likely encounter one of the following attitudes:

> (1) an unwillingness to discuss a case at all;

> (2) a reluctant willingness to talk;

> (3) a general willingness to talk openly but a reluctance to discuss one or more specific topics;

(4) a willingness to talk openly and cooperatively throughout the interview.

As one thinks about motivational approaches, it is important to recognize that they are necessary regardless of a witness' attitude. One does not wait for a witness to become non-cooperative to then retaliate with a motivational salvo. Rather, one incorporates motivational approaches into one's interviewing style, so that even witnesses who are otherwise cooperative are encouraged to provide complete responses. The remainder of the chapter illustrates how one may overcome communication barriers with motivational approaches based on the factors identified in the preceding section. We do, however, save for Chapter 13 a discussion of how to motivate witnesses who do not want to be interviewed at all.

a. Be Continually Empathetic

(i) In General

Probably the most effective way to encourage witnesses to talk openly is to be empathetic throughout an interview. One cannot usually convey the idea that one is genuinely empathetic by showing understanding only on occasion, or only when witnesses are emotionally distraught.

For many people, the suggestion that one attempt to be consistently empathetic may be counter-intuitive. After all, must one respond empathetically even to a "hostile" witness? In our view, this is exactly what one should do, unless a climate of openness seems totally beyond reach. Many witnesses who one may term "hostile" merely are people whose stories are adverse to one's clients. And if empathy is a useful approach, its usefulness is not altered by the content of a witness' story. Moreover, if a witness is genuinely hostile, returning the hostility will probably get one nowhere. One might as well try empathy. Though we have stressed throughout the book the goal of learning all information, whether it be favorable to one's client or not, obviously as an advocate one seeks to elicit favorable evidence. An empathetic attitude may encourage "neutral" or "hostile" witnesses to reveal some favorable evidence.

(ii) Active Listening

As you recall, one principally uses active listening to provide empathetic understanding. This technique requires that one listen intently to what a witness says, and then reply by reflecting back the essence of the witness' statement. Please consider this example:

Witness: "I really don't want to testify; I've got to work with all these people."

Lawyer: "You're worried that people at your job will disapprove."

Note that the lawyer does not simply repeat or "parrot" what was said. Rather, the lawyer attempts to reflect back the gist of the witness' remark.

An active listening response demonstrates affirmatively that one has actually heard and understood a witness. One need not "active listen" everything a witness says to be empathetic. Silence; responses such as "I see" and "mm-humm;" a friendly tone of voice; and requests for additional information may also indicate interest in what a witness says. However, an active listening response indicates much more concretely than the other responses that one has actually heard and understood. Active listening responses constitute an explicit form of expression demonstrating genuine comprehension.

Moreover, insofar as "non-judgmental acceptance" is concerned, the active listening response is probably more effective than the other responses. Reflection of a statement in a non-judgmental tone of voice signifies for most people acceptance of what was said. As an empirical matter, responses such as "mm-hmm" and "I see", or even requests for additional information, being less concrete, often leave a witness less sure of one's acceptance.

An active listening response can reflect a witness' observations, a witness' feelings, or both. Assume a witness in a will contest case makes the following statement: "When Ms. Martens asked us to witness the will there were tears in her eyes; it made me sad. Then Bill asked her who was going to get the money; it was terrible." In responding to this statement, one might reflect the factual details of what occurred: "So when you were asked to witness the will, Bill asked about her money." Or one might reflect the witness' feelings of sadness and shock: "It was a depressing moment." Or, one might reflect both the details and the feelings: "It was really depressing when Bill asked about the money." However, since typically a response to feelings is more foreign to lawyers and law students than is a response to content, we discuss active listening primarily in terms of responding to feelings.

(iii) Responding to Expressed Feelings

Witnesses may describe what any of us would recognize as an emotional event without expressly talking about their emotional response. Or, and perhaps more likely, witnesses may include in their stories the feelings aroused by emotional events. This section examines the use of active listening when a witness in some way expresses feelings; the next subsection is devoted to unexpressed feelings.

People may express their feelings in a variety of ways. Often, a feeling is expressed in a vague or obscure manner. When this occurs, one can be most empathetic by reflecting the feelings precisely. By precisely labeling vague feelings, one helps people to understand their own emotional reactions and thereby motivates them to be open.

The following examples illustrate vague expressions of feelings and responses which attempt to identify and label the feelings precisely:

1. Witness: (in an irritated tone of voice) "When I knew he was probably going to die, I felt, you know, real bummed."

    Lawyer: "Realizing he would probably die made you feel depressed."

2. Witness: "I try to never think about what happened that day; poor Ms. Johnston."

    Lawyer: "It makes you sad to think about Ms. Johnston."

3. Witness: "I don't want to testify in court. It would probably be a bad deal—all those questions, people looking at me—I'd probably be so uptight, I'd say the wrong thing."

    Lawyer: "You're worried about getting up on the stand and perhaps embarrassing yourself."

On other occasions, witnesses articulate their feelings quite precisely. "I get angry every time I think about how the police broke into Harry's apartment." When witnesses clearly describe their feelings, one usually has difficulty reflecting back the essence of what was said without merely repeating or parroting the response. The following example is illustrative,

Witness: "I was very disappointed when I found out he didn't pay."

Lawyer: "It really disappointed you."

This kind of "parroting" usually creates a negative reaction. The witness' internal reaction is often something like, "Yes, you dummy, that's what I just said." Outwardly, however, the reply is usually more polite. "Right, I was disappointed." Moreover, using a synonym—e.g. "you felt let down" may not cure the problem. The witness may still experience the "yes, you dummy" reaction.

Since "parroting" is so annoying, what kind of empathetic response can one give when feelings are clearly described? Sometimes a witness describes a situation which is so common that the witness can readily believe that one has been in that same or a similar situation. When feelings arise out of a common situation, an active listening response expressly indicating one's understanding of the feelings usually is effective. Although one's response may use the witness' identical words, the apparent genuineness of the understanding typically creates a positive reaction. Consider this example:

Witness: "It really makes me angry every time I think of how she always ignores her children; they are only four and five, and they need a mother's care."

Lawyer: "I can understand how it'd make you angry to see her neglecting her kids; they're so young."

Given our societal norms about parental duties, it is believable that the lawyer's response represents genuine empathy.

In a few situations, however, a witness may expressly verbalize a feeling which one finds inappropriate, or even abhorrent. In such cases, unless one has won three Oscars for acting, the witness is likely to regard an "I understand" response as artificial and insincere. Assume this sort of witness remark: "When I saw those Braille Society collection boxes stacked six feet high in the middle of the store, I got so angry I had to pull them down. What right do they have to collect money in a store?" A response, "I understand how that would make you angry," is quite likely to backfire and to cause one to feel insincere. Simple, passive acknowledgment such as "I see" may be the best one can muster.

Finally, note that to use active listening one is not called upon to play amateur psychologist. It is enough that one identifies a feeling; attempting to identify the reason for the feeling is likely to be irrelevant and outside a lawyer's sphere of competence. Please consider this dialogue:

Witness: Every time I think of that woman rushing over to her dog after it was hit by the car, my eyes get misty.

Lawyer: That's probably because you were imagining it could have been your own pet. Perhaps you were even thinking it could have been a child, not a dog.

Psychological reasons for the witness' sadness probably have little relevance to the story. And most lawyers are simply not qualified to make these kinds of extrapolations. Fortunately, to be an active listener, one need not do so.[11]

(iv) Responding to Non-Expressed Feelings

Thus far, the discussion has focused on witnesses who in some way articulate their feelings. Sometimes, however, feelings are neither precisely nor vaguely stated. Rather, witnesses discuss situations which for most individuals would be emotionally charged without expressing any emotion.

---

11. But see A. Watson, note 1 supra.

Consider this example:

Witness: "There is always supposed to be a doctor in the recovery room. His blood pressure began to drop. I looked for the doctor, but she wasn't there. I went into the hall; no doctor."

Lawyer: "What happened then?"

Witness: "I went back and checked the pressure; it was dropping. I tried the phone page; there was no response. The pressure leveled off but it was extremely low; the heart rate became uneven. I again tried the page; no doctor."

Without verbalizing any emotion, the witness has described a situation which most people would find extremely stressful. Even though one has never been in that precise situation, one's analogous and vicarious experience gives one the strong sense that the witness was probably feeling, at the least, fear, frustration and anger.

When one recognizes that a situation probably produced emotion, one can use active listening even though the witness' feelings are unstated. For instance, in the above example one might have responded along the following lines, "I imagine you were quite scared when you couldn't find a doctor to help you."

(v) Phrasing Responses

Active listening neophytes tend to concentrate too heavily on getting an empathetic response "just right". They often feel, "If I state the wrong feeling, a witness will think I'm a fool." Or, "I'm forced to use specific words. I want to concentrate on the witness, not on a memorized script." Or, "The cost of Indian food in restaurants is too high." At least we can allay two of these concerns.[12]

First, there is no single, correct way to phrase active listening responses. A witness may say, "Milo was crying out, 'I've been shot! I've been shot! The robber was staring right at me." In this situation the following responses, among others, would seem in order:

"I imagine you were frightened."

"I guess you were frightened."

"What a scary situation to be in."

"You felt frightened."

"It must have been frightening."

"I can understand your being really scared."

12. For other possible objections to active listening see D. Binder and S. Price, note 6 supra, at 32–36.

"You must have been scared for both Milo and yourself."

"You felt very helpless."

Moreover, if, as in the above example, a witness does not expressly articulate feelings, one need not fear disrupting an interview by identifying the wrong feeling. If one is paying attention to a witness, the feeling one identifies is bound to be in the ballpark. If the response is somewhat off-the-mark, it typically will, at most, draw a correction, not hostility. For example, assume one's response to the witness above was, "I imagine you felt helpless." If this response does not accurately capture the witness' emotional state at that time, the witness may well clarify. "Well, not helpless—all I can remember is fear." That clarification probably helps the witness label feelings precisely and thus aids the sense of empathy. Of course, a witness' reaction may be different if one's response could not touch a witness' emotion with a 10-foot pole: "That must have been really funny."

Finally, we remind you again that although empathy should typically permeate an entire interview, one does not "active listen" everything witnesses say. Even if one tried to active listen only emotional portions of stories, a few emotional witnesses might consume the better part of one's legal career. Also, if there were a world empathy champion, even he or she would not acknowledge every feeling that arose in the course of an interview. To try to do so would be insincere, and probably at the expense of understanding the content of a story. Hence, think of active listening as a useful device for demonstrating empathy, not as a mandated rule to obey slavishly at every opportunity.

(vi) Conclusion

Many people routinely use active listening in everyday life, if only subconsciously. Others are at first very self-conscious of using a "technique." There may be the same sort of internal discomfort that is felt upon hearing one's voice played back on a cheap tape recorder. However, just as one's recorded voice rarely sounds as strange to other listeners as it does to oneself, so will witnesses be unaware that one is using a learned technique. Active listening tends to induce interviewers to focus more intently on witnesses. What begins as a learned technique to demonstrate empathy becomes a part of one's natural style, and one becomes an interviewer to whom witnesses genuinely desire to talk.

b. Show Personal Interest in Witnesses

Most of us are more willing to talk with someone who is interested in us as individuals than we are in talking with someone who is only interested in what we may know. For example, court clerks are usually more willing to provide information to lawyers who, when things are quiet, take the time to inquire about what the clerk is doing or thinking than they are in talking with lawyers who only want to find out when their cases will be called.

Interest in a witness encompasses more than empathizing with the witness' feelings about the topics one is exploring. It means taking the time to inquire into what the witnesses are doing, and how life is treating them. It perhaps means inquiring about little "Infant Witness" whose picture is on a desk. It means inquiring about these matters even though they may have nothing whatsoever to do with a case.

Interviews that take place outside the law office usually provide many opportunities to show interest in a witness. Since the witness is typically approached at home or work, one can very naturally move into a conversation about the witness' surroundings and/or activities. Thus, an interview with a governmental employee concerning agency records can focus normal conversational attention on the nature of the employee's job and his or her feelings about it:

Lawyer: Hi, Mr.Bureau. I'm Ms. Law. I'm interested in learning about records your department keeps on oil slicks.

Witness: Uh, huh.

Lawyer: Sounds like you must get a lot of requests like mine.

Witness: Well, we get lots of requests but not exactly like yours.

Lawyer: What do you mean?

Witness: Well, it's not so much what they want, it's when they want things. We can never act fast enough to suit most people.

Lawyer: Everybody seems to need something yesterday.

Witness: Exactly.

Lawyer: How do you handle this situation?

Witness: We just do our best.

Lawyer: Do you use any kind of priority system?

Witness: Well, not exactly.

Lawyer: Well, how do you work it out? To tell you the truth, we have those same problems in my office.

Witness: . . .

Similarly, interviews in a witness' home can focus on areas such as the residence, items within it and the witness' family. Thus, it is common to hear lawyers inquire about unique objects displayed in a witness' home.

As with any other approach, this one must be undertaken with sincerity. Also, one must be careful not to give the appearance of prying into personal matters, and one must be sensitive to the witness' time needs. People are typically delighted when someone is sensitive enough to show interest in them, but, like most of us, witnesses usually have other things to do.

When interviews take place in a law office, even without the formality of a deposition, it may be more difficult to move naturally into personal discussion. Most lawyers' offices lack atmospherical props of personal concern to witnesses. As a consequence, conversations about the witness may have fewer natural lead-ins. Moreover, a witness has come to talk about a case and expects to do so. They are often under time pressure and therefore want to "get down to brass tacks" rather quickly. Accordingly, an early discussion of any length about the witness rather than the case may create suspicion and suggest insincerity.

Even in a law office, however, a conversation may extend beyond the facts of a case. Some small talk about the witness is usually appropriate; and road conditions near one's office, a notable sporting event, or epistemological inconsistencies in a popular writing of Herodotus are possible icebreakers.

c. *Provide Recognition*

Praising witnesses for providing information at various times during an interview increases their self-esteem and motivates them to provide additional information. To provide recognition, one need do no more than sincerely thank a witness for being cooperative or for supplying useful data. The following examples illustrate this approach. "Mr. Higgenbottom, all those details about how Mr. Washbottom ended up in the creek without a paddle give me a clear picture of what happened; you're really being helpful." "Ms. Higgenwash, I can see you are really trying to remember what happened; I really appreciate that."

As with empathetic understanding, one uses recognition to motivate witnesses throughout entire interviews, not merely at trouble spots. Again, how often to give praise must be left to one's judgment. Unctuous fawning will result in a witness' perception that one is insincere. However, most of us do not give praise as often as it is deserved, and therefore we must consciously set out to provide recognition.

d. *Expect Replies*

Motivation is also aided if one consistently shows that replies to questions are expected. Remember, if one's words, tone of voice and accompanying manners convey expectation of a reply, witnesses frequently try to live up to the expectation. Although this concept is difficult to put into words alone, please compare the following questions:

1. "Please think back to the moment you touched the detonator, and describe everything that happened."

2. "I don't know what you can remember; I guess it was a long time ago; is there anything maybe you can tell me about the detonator incident?"

The first question places the witness at a specific moment in time, and asks a direct question in a way that almost demands a reply. Assuming the questioner's demeanor and tone of voice match the words, the witness will have little doubt that an answer is expected. With the second question, one can almost imagine the interviewer cowering and being grateful if the witness can recall nothing.

Conveying that one expects information is sometimes difficult. When a witness seems to be experiencing difficulty coming up with data, one's tendency is to empathize with the difficulty. After all, it frequently is arduous to remember exactly what happened at some earlier time with the precision a lawyer requests. Therefore, to build rapport it is tempting to acknowledge the problem—e.g. "I know it's difficult to think back that far"—and not press the witness too hard.

But this inclination should be followed only to a point. Empathize with the witness' difficulty, but then indicate that an answer is nevertheless expected: "Mr. Bottomhiggen, I know it's difficult to try to remember what happened six months ago. But I'm pretty sure that if you think about it and really concentrate for a while, you'll remember some more of what occurred."

One can also convey the expectancy of a reply by asking a witness to picture herself or himself at the scene of an event. A mental image tends to stimulate recall; requesting a witness to form a mental image demonstrates one's genuine desire for additional thought. Picture yourself at a witness interview; can you see yourself conveying expectancy?

Of course, one can push too hard and cause resentment, falsification or both. Nonetheless, the natural tendency to let the witness off because remembering is difficult often must be jettisoned. Otherwise, a witness is too likely to rely on, "I don't remember."

e. Provide Information

Recall that if people do not perceive the relevance of requested information, they are less likely to provide it, and indeed may be suspicious of the request. For witnesses, questions may appear irrelevant even in situations with obvious legal implications. A witness may observe another shout "Fire!" in a crowded theatre and realize that the person may incur legal difficulties. But what if the questioner inquires about a second person, who as far as the witness knows only sat and watched the picture? The witness may well wonder, "Why the interest in that person? Who is interested? Am I in trouble?" If a witness is thinking of such questions, she or he is unlikely to be thinking about giving full and complete responses to questions.

Therefore, one may often motivate witnesses by giving them some bits of information about a case. The information not only provides context but also may flatter the witness' self-esteem. After all, giving the information implies that the witness has some legal sophistication, and perhaps has even been given "inside information."

How much information one supplies is an issue that often requires serious thought, in part because disclosure may carry ethical consequences. One may usually provide information that is general or a matter of public record: the nature of a case (civil or criminal), names of parties, remedies sought and procedural status of a case. However, disclosing even such general matters may cause a witness to tell a story that favors one party over another. The potential tactical and ethical ramifications of disclosing information that may produce a biased response is explored in Chapters 13 and 14.

f. *Respond to Reluctance*

Ideally, one uses each of the above approaches independently of any apparent reluctance on the part of witnesses. They are an interviewer's stock in trade because they tend to motivate full disclosure and prevent reluctance.

Even with an interview already underway, however, the most skillful use of motivational techniques will not always elicit full disclosure. Witnesses may be reluctant to discuss certain topics, or they may wish to terminate interviews prematurely. Hence, it is appropriate to consider approaches that may overcome indications of reluctance.

Reluctance may manifest itself in a number of ways, ranging from point blank refusal for no stated reason ("I do not want to discuss the events of September 22") through refusal for an articulated reason ("I've already talked to the police about that"; "I can't talk about Charlie with the moon in the seventh house of Venus") to vague, subtle evasions (terse answers; rapid change of subjects).

When a witness appears reluctant, one may of course choose not to pursue the apparently troublesome topic. Or, one may temporarily shelve the topic and move to greener pastures. Perhaps later in an interview, or even during a later interview, the reluctance may dissolve. The level of rapport may then be higher, and additional information already disclosed may make a topic less threatening.

If, on the other hand, one chooses to deal with the reluctance, one does so carefully. If a witness advances a reason for the reluctance, one uses common sense and creativity to try to surmount it. Because one's response depends largely on a witness' specific reasons, no sure fire, universally applicable ethical persuaders can be given. However, a general approach which is often helpful may be described.

First, whatever a witness' reason for reluctance, one can begin by letting the witness know that the concerns have been heard and understood. An active listening response is superb for this purpose. Following the empathetic response, one may:

(a) ask the witness to elaborate on the stated concern, so one gets a more exact idea of its nature;

(b) respond with reasons showing the concern is ill-founded or unrealistic;

(c) respond with reasons that may outweigh realistic and legitimate concerns;

(d) try something else.

Assume one represents a mother in a child custody dispute. Seeking information on the parents' parenting skills, one interviews a neighbor, Jerry Lopez. Mr. Lopez is generally cooperative and informative, but when asked about a violent quarrel that occurred the night of March 12, states, "I'd rather not go into that—it'll seem like I'm taking sides."

To press for disclosure of what happened that night, one might first active listen: "You're concerned about your friendship with Mr. and Mrs. Kramer." Then, if one felt more elaboration might be useful, one might ask, "Why do you feel that talking about that night would be taking sides?" Alternatively, one might try to show that the concern is unrealistic, by responding, "Given that what you've told me so far is fair and balanced, I'm sure that the Kramers will see you as a person who is just objectively saying what he knows." Or, one might indicate that though the concern is legitimate, it is outweighed: "Although your friendship is very important, isn't it the children whom you and the court are most concerned about?"

What approach might one take when witnesses do not state reasons for reluctance? As mentioned above, this situation might arise either when a witness does not state a reason or when the reluctance is evidenced largely by subtle, often non-verbal behavior. In both situations, counterpunches, no matter how deft, are usually premature.

Until one has some understanding of the source of reluctance, one cannot surmount it.

For example, in the child custody case, assume that when asked about the night of March 12, Lopez replied only, "I really can't talk about that." In the face of this answer, one might speculate, "Hmm—he's probably trying to protect Mrs. Kramer," and then respond, "No matter what Mrs. Kramer has done, for the sake of the kids it's important for you to disclose what happened."

If one guesses accurately, well and good. But an erroneous assumption may be quite disruptive. Now the witness has two possible reasons for not talking—the witness' own and the questioner's. Perhaps the witness will find the questioner's reason more convenient and be convinced that disclosure would be wrong! Alternatively, the witness may become angry that a false, and even arguably improper motive, has been attributed to him. Perhaps all Lopez meant was that he did not know anything at all about a March 12 argument. If one's guesses were invariably accurate, the disruption danger would be minimal. But given that guessing at unstated motives is a risky business, one should first make inquiry: "Mr. Lopez, might we take a moment to discuss why you prefer not to talk about the night of March 12?"

When reluctance is evidenced only by non-verbal behavior, attempts to "psyche out" and overcome the reluctance without first identifying the reasons are especially perilous. Assume that when asked about the night of March 12, Lopez becomes tense, hesitant, and evasive. Now, one cannot even be sure that Lopez is being reluctant. Thus, to attempt to ferret out both the reluctance and the reason for it, one may state as follows:

"Mr. Lopez, many people feel uncomfortable talking with a lawyer; it's a very common reaction. It's also very understandable, especially when the situation doesn't even involve them directly. However, if people let the lawyer know what's bothering them, often the problem can be remedied. I wonder if you'd feel more comfortable if you'd tell me why you seem so concerned about March 12. Maybe we can talk about your concerns."

Often, this kind of approach elicits a reason for reluctance with which one can deal as though the reason had been stated initially. However, occasionally it may produce a denial of any problem, along with a feeling on a witness' part that he or she has been "accused." Nonetheless, one may try to salvage rapport: "I'm glad I've misread the situation, and I hope I haven't offended you. But if I do touch on something that is troublesome, please let me know and we can talk about it."

In sum, one may respond to different forms of reluctance in a variety of ways. At least, our suggestions may give one a sense of how to approach problems as they arise.

g. A Few Final Words

Too many beginning lawyers believe that interviewing is just something one does naturally, and that one's interviewing success is determined by one's personality. However, as this chapter suggests, there are techniques that one can learn and use to motivate witnesses. A pleasant personality might have gotten one elected Hall Monitor in third grade, but that by itself is usually not enough to motivate people who are essentially strangers. The approaches described may not always be successful, and undoubtedly there are others one might employ. However, these approaches should enable one to interact successfully with most witnesses.

Chapter 13

COMMENCING INTERVIEWS

1. INTRODUCTION

Although most lawyers do not consciously break interviews into set stages, effective legal interviewers certainly attempt to elicit information in an organized fashion. During interviews, questions are not asked in random sequence as a witness' story suggests first one topic and then another. Whether one provides information or asks questions, and if the latter, the kinds of questions, depends very much on what stage of an interview one is in. Hence, we discuss evidence-gathering by identifying and analyzing what may be thought of as four interviewing stages. As one might imagine, these stages are set more in gelatin than concrete. Certain of the stages may be unnecessary with some witnesses, and impossible with others. However, what generally differentiates legal interviews from other social interactions is organized purposefulness, and that is what we begin to explore in this chapter.

The four stages we identify are as follows: [1]

(a) *Introductory Stage.* This stage is typically devoted to putting witnesses at ease and giving them a sense of what will occur during the later stages.

(b) *Chronological Time Line Stage.* During this phase, one attempts to obtain a sequential narration of the events which comprise the witness' story. One's questioning encourages the witness to select and relate the various events comprising her or his story.

(c) *Theory Development Stage.* This stage is one's reward for allowing a witness' sense of importance to dominate during the

---

1. In Chapter 16, we explore why interviews of experts may be organized differently.

Chronological Time Line stage. One selects and thoroughly examines, pursuant to the parties' legal and factual theories, events which seem to be the most important.

(d) *Conclusionary Stage.* During this stage, one cements informational gains. One perhaps secures a signed statement, arranges a follow-up interview, takes steps to obtain documents, or relocates a witness to a "safe house." [2]

This chapter concentrates on the introductory phase of informal interviews and depositions. We assume that a witness is to some degree willing to talk. This is entirely realistic. In a deposition, a witness has little choice but to say something. And informal interviews are usually pre-arranged by a client or by the attorney so that one knows at the outset that a witness will talk. Hence, we examine how one typically commences interviews in these common situations. We recognize, however, that occasionally one must attempt to persuade a reluctant witness to talk. Therefore, the chapter concludes with some suggestions for getting one's foot in the door of recalcitrant witnesses.

2. COMMENCING INFORMAL INTERVIEWS

Assuming a witness' willingness to talk, one's major concern at the outset is to make a witness comfortable, both with the attorney and with the format and content of an interview. For these reasons, one generally starts the introductory phase by beginning to establish rapport and explaining one's purpose for seeking information. One may then explain how the interview will proceed and give a witness an opportunity to ask preliminary questions.

Please examine the following introductory phase of an interview of Lou Purvisor, the Landview maintenance superintendent. The interview was arranged by Landview's Vice-President, Paul Lade, and is conducted by Landview's attorney, Florence Darrow, in Purvisor's

2. In the case of non-party witnesses, one may also be tempted at this point to dissuade them from cooperating with the opposition (provided one gets there first). This practice is almost certainly ethically improper. ABA, *Opinions of Committee on Professional Ethics and Grievances*, Opinion 131 (March 15, 1935); R. Keeton, *Trial Tactics and Methods* § 9.17 (1973). However one can, quite ethically, ask a witness to notify one whenever he or she is contacted by the opposition so that one can arrange to be present at any interview. R. Simmons, *Winning Before Trial: How to Prepare Cases for the Best Settlement or Trial Result* 218 (1974).

office. As you read the dialogue, please consider the extent to which Darrow uses the motivational techniques described in Chapter 12.

1. L   Mr. Purvisor, I'm Florence Darrow, a lawyer for Landview. I believe Mr. Lade told you I'd like to talk with you.

     W   Right.

2. L   Nice office you have here; you've got a good view of the development.

     W   Well, it's not bad.

3. L   Is that a picture of your family?

     W   Yep, my wife and the two kids; only one of the kids still lives with us.

4. L   Well, both of my children are still at home, but I know it won't be long before they're out of the house. Which one of your children is still at home?

     W   The boy; the girl moved out about a year ago. She's got an apartment in San Francisco and is working for the Bank of America. I think she is doing pretty well although we don't hear from her much.

5. L   Sounds like you'd be happier with a little more contact.

     W   Yep, and my wife, too.

6. L   Has this been a cause of any problem?

     W   Well, not really; the usual stuff, I suppose.

7. L   Did Paul Lade explain why I wanted to talk with you?

     W   Something about a lawsuit filed by the Phillipses against Landview.

8. L   Right. They claim their land is subject to slides and that Landview knew about the condition but failed to warn them. I'd like to find out what you know about the situation.

     W   I'll tell you what I can.

9. L   Good; I appreciate that. I'm interested in what you know about the Phillipses' purchase of their two lots and also about the conditions of the land in Campion Hills before the Phillipses bought their lots.

     W   I know very little about the Phillipses.

10. L   Well, do your best to tell me whatever you know. I find it's easiest for people if they start in at the beginning and then move forward step by step, event by event, telling me whatever they can remember. If I

have some questions, I'll ask them, but basically at the outset I'd like to hear the story pretty much in your own words from the beginning. After that, I'll probably have some specific questions I'll want to ask you. I hope we can get this done in an hour or so. Do you have any questions?

W   No. Where should I start?

11. L   Let's start with the Phillipses' purchase of their lots. As you talk, I'll probably take a few notes. Start wherever you feel your knowledge about the Phillipses begins and move forward sequentially one step at a time.

W   Well, the first time I saw the Phillipses . . .

Before turning to the "substance" of the introduction, consider the very beginning. In segments 1 through 6, Darrow attempts to use various motivational techniques to "break the ice." While not all attorneys subscribe to the social chit chat that characterizes this portion of the interview, those who do feel that such an approach helps build rapport by demonstrating that one is a human being who is genuinely interested in the witness. Those who oppose this sort of a chit chat beginning argue, however, that the approach produces the opposite impression. To these lawyers the approach represents an obviously phony technique, because the witness knows the lawyer is there to get information about a case and not to discuss personal interests. Whether either camp is completely correct is doubtful; perhaps all one can do is make a judgment according to an individual witness.

Even assuming that Darrow used good judgment in deciding to "break the ice," how good was her ice-breaking? In the light of Chapter 12, which techniques does she appear to use, and how effectively does she appear to use them?

Turning to the remainder of the introduction, consider first Darrow's explanation of why she seeks information. In 8–L, Darrow explains that she wants information because the Phillipses have filed a law suit claiming that "their land is subject to slides and that Landview knew about the condition and failed to warn them." As indicated in Chapter 12, one usually provides some explanation about why one desires information, at the potential risk of biasing a response. For example, if before getting the story of a witness favorable to a client, one explains in detail the elements of a claim for relief or a defense, one may practically be begging the witness to tailor a story to those elements.[3] Here, Darrow does not merely tell

3. For an interesting example of the subtlety of this process, see R. Traver, "Anatomy of a Murder" 34–49 (1958). For those unfamiliar with the novel, which was written by a state Supreme Court Justice, it involved a successful

Purvisor, "I'd like to know what you know about the Phillipses purchase of their two lots." Rather, Darrow explains the Phillipses' contentions. With this information, Purvisor may be more likely to slant his story to help his employer than if he were unaware of the contentions.

Typically, biasing witnesses to some degree is probably unavoidable. As an advocate for a party, one selects topics and the order in which they are pursued at least partially to further the client's interests. The very process of selection is likely to influence responses. Also, the fact that a witness knows that one is an attorney for a particular litigant may bias replies.[4]

Some writers have suggested that it may be appropriate to go beyond the unavoidable biasing aspects of interviews, and that one may consciously ask questions at times and in ways that help produce favorably-biased answers.[5] Undoubtedly, some lawyers adhere to this practice. In the end, one must decide for oneself, with such guidance as is available, upon a comfortable dividing line between zealous advocacy and unethical conduct.[6]

Consider next Darrow's statement to Purvisor regarding the subjects upon which she seeks information. After telling him why the Phillipses have sued Landview, Darrow could have broadly asked, "Tell me anything you know pertaining to the Phillipses that might be helpful." But in 9–L, Darrow calls Purvisor's attention to two specific topics: the Phillipses' purchase of the two lots and soil conditions in Campion Hills before the Phillipses' purchase.

Because witnesses often know little about issues in dispute, at the outset one usually needs to guide witnesses' attention to specific topics. This early guidance stands in sharp contrast to most client interviews. With a client, one often begins to elicit a story by saying, "Tell me whatever you think I ought to know." Since clients are ad-

homicide defense of diminished capacity with the defendant supplying the requisite "facts" only after having been educated by his attorney as to what type of facts might constitute the defense.

4. Recall the phenomenon of etiquette barrier.

5. For an exposure to some of these writers and a discussion of this subject see G. Bellow & B. Moulton, *The Lawyering Process: Materials for Instruction in Clinical Advocacy* 364–392 (1978).

6. It is not clear to what degree, if any, the canons of legal ethics regulate questions that are purposefully biased. See American Bar Foundation, *Annotated Code of Professional Responsibility* 290, 314–320 (1979). It is clear however, that the pressure to gain a story with a favorable slant inclines one to flirt with perjury more often than one may care to admit. For a discussion of the tensions between "truth" and the client's interests, see M. Freedman, "Professional Responsibility of the Criminal Defense Lawyer: The Three Hardest Questions," 64 Mich.L.Rev. 1469 (1966); M. Frankel, "The Search for Truth: An Umpireal View," 123 U.Pa.L.Rev. 1031, 1055–1059 (1975); H. Uviller, "The Advocate, The Truth, and Judicial Hackles: A Reaction to Judge Frankel's Idea," 123 U.Pa.L. Rev. 1067 (1975); E. Abramson, "Attorneys, Clients, 'Ethics,'" 52 Notre Dame Law. 797 (1977).

dressing their own problems, one can fairly expect them to have a sense of what is important. Since witnesses often lack this same sense, however, they typically need and appreciate topic selection.

There is a risk, however, in selecting topics for witnesses. First, if one omits to mention a topic, there is a good chance that even the friendliest witness will overlook it. For example, if Darrow had asked Purvisor only to "tell me about soil conditions", probably he would not on his own mention what he knows about the Phillipses. Moreover, with regard to the topics one broaches, one must take care not to frame the topics too narrowly. As a general rule, the narrower a topic, the less information a witness will provide. Thus, if Darrow had asked Purvisor to "tell me about any slides that occurred in Campion Hills before the Phillipses' purchase," probably she would get less information than from the broader topic which referred to the "condition of the land in Campion Hills." As one might imagine, the more adverse a witness the greater the danger of choosing a narrow topic.

Darrow asked Purvisor to tell a story about two topics: the Phillipses and the condition of the land. Does Darrow expect him to discuss the two simultaneously, or should he tell as much as he knows about one before moving to the other? While there is no universal answer, often witnesses find it helpful to track one topic from beginning to end before beginning another. This varies, however, according to the witness and the interrelationship of topics. Perhaps one can ask a witness in what way he or she would feel most comfortable recounting the events.

Next, please note that Darrow uses the introduction to explain how the interview will proceed. Such explanations tell witnesses how to relate their stories, and perhaps relieve their uncertainty over what one expects. In 10–L and 11–L Darrow mentions that the interview will last about an hour and that she will take notes. Witnesses are often anxious, or at least curious about such matters, and Darrow may aid rapport by anticipating the dormant questions.

In another part of the explanation, Darrow tries to affect the content and organization of Purvisor's story. In 10–L Darrow explains that she wants a sequential narration: "Start in at the beginning and then move forward step by step, event by event, telling me whatever (you) can remember .   .   .   . If I have some questions, I'll ask them, but basically at the outset I'd like to hear the story pretty much in your own words from the beginning." These instructions tell Purvisor to relate his story chronologically, one event at a time. In the next chapter, we explain the importance of getting a chronological time line. Here, note that providing such instructions at the outset may not be sufficient to keep a witness on a chronological track. With some witnesses, even repeated instructions are no guarantee of

chronology. However, many witnesses will describe events chronologically, once they understand that it is expected.

Finally, note that in 10–L and 11–L, Darrow also tells Purvisor
where to begin his chronology: ". . . from the beginning . . .
Wherever you feel your knowledge of the Phillipses begins." By so
stating, Darrow identifies the topic for Purvisor's story, but leaves it
to Purvisor to decide when his version of the Phillipses' saga begins.
When first conducting legal interviews, one often experiences difficulty giving witnesses such free rein. Based on common experience
and prior knowledge, one may form a mental picture of the point at
which a witness' story probably begins and ask the witness to start at
one's imagined beginning. But if one miscalculates the "true" beginning, one may lose important information. For example, had Darrow
asked Purvisor to start his story "when you first met the Phillipses,"
Darrow might miss whatever Purvisor knew about the Phillipses before he actually met them. Remember that hearsay is not in-
admissable during discovery.

Of course, instructions do not guarantee that witnesses will start
at the "true" beginning. At least, however, one can encourage witnesses to do so. One may doubt a witness' choice of starting points.
For example, from prior investigation one may be aware of earlier
events which a witness either does not connect with a story, or which
the witness does not care to mention. One may explore such omitted
events during the Theory Development stage.

Any introduction is to some extent a compromise between providing witnesses with adequate instructions and larding up the front end
of interviews with so many instructions that witnesses pick up
magazines while one speaks. As one becomes familiar with typical
witness concerns, the temptation is to cover each with a few remarks.
For example, if during one's practice one has interviewed a number
of witnesses who are concerned about testifying, one may begin to
say something about giving testimony during one's standard introductions. We can do little more than caution one against the dangers
of long-winded introductions. On the other hand, we now illustrate
the benefits of speedy conclusions. Proceed to the next section.

3. COMMENCING DEPOSITIONS

One is undoubtedly familiar with the formal trappings of most
depositions: court reporters, oaths, opposing counsel and polished ta-
bles. However, depositions have less obvious informal aspects as
well. Thus, before illustrating a "standard" deposition introduction,
we focus briefly on the informal period that often precedes a deposition.

Assume, as commonly happens, that one is to take the deposition of a witness aligned with one's adversary. Before the deposition, opposing counsel will probably have spoken with the witness to review the expected deposition testimony.[7] And, in addition, opposing counsel may have told the witness how brutal depositions can be, and how deviously one may phrase questions.[8] A witness could thus be excused for regarding a deposition subpoena as equivalent to a summons to Dracula's castle. Thus, if before the deposition begins one chats informally with the deponent, one may start to put the witness at ease and overcome the witness' hidden reservations. No special "deposition rapport builders" are needed. Whatever works during informal interview introductions is appropriate prior to depositions. If one continues the rapport-building effort in the deposition and during breaks, one may convince the witness that one, and therefore perhaps one's client also, is a nice person. As a result, one may get a more complete, even a more favorable, story.

The introductory portion of depositions itself is quite ritualistic. It shares one purpose with introductions to informal interviews—putting witnesses at ease and telling them what will occur. Additionally, it has a second purpose—to cut off likely explanations for changed testimony at trial.

To give you a sense of a basic approach for beginning a deposition, we set forth below pre-deposition remarks and the introductory portion of a deposition of Lou Purvisor. Purvisor's deposition is taken by the Phillipses' attorney, Jerry Mason, at Mason's office. Purvisor is accompanied by Florence Darrow, attorney for Landview.

(Pre-Deposition Dialogue)

1–L	Hi. I'm Jerry Mason.
(Darrow)	I'm Flo Darrow; glad to meet you finally. This is Mr. Purvisor.
2–L	Glad to meet both of you. The reporter, Ms. Quesnel, should be here soon. Mr. Purvisor, I hope this

7. Most commentators agree that witnesses should be prepared for depositions as thoroughly as they would be for trial. See 14 Am.Jur. *Trials* 61–62 (1968); R. Keeton, note 2 supra, at §§ 2.10–2.14, 11.4; P. Bergman, *Trial Advocacy in a Nutshell* 377–384 (1979); H. Bodin, *Trial Techniques Library: Final Preparation Before Trial* 10–19 (1946). For those who agree with Solomon that ". . . the writing of many books is endless and excessive devotion to books is wearying to the body," The State Bar of California Commission on the Continuing Education of the Bar offers several taped lectures by prominent lawyers and judges on this subject (and many others). Try CEB, *Preparing Your Client to Testify: A Half-Hour Discussion* (1971); or CEB *Preparing Witnesses for Deposition and Trial: A Two-Hour Discussion* (1981).

8. By "role-playing" the opposition, one may help prepare a witness for the "ordeal." 5 Am.Jur. *Trials* 617–618 (1966).

	deposition isn't coming at an inconvenient time for you.
W	Not really; although there is plenty else I could be doing.
3–L	Sounds like you're pretty busy.
W	Well, there are always things that need my attention.
4–L	And I guess you'd rather be working on those things than having your deposition taken.
W	Well, I don't know.
5–L	Did anyone see the article in this morning's paper about the robbery at Bergman's Bank? They apparently got away with two million; I didn't think they had that much.
W	I saw that. They were inside the bank before the first employee got there. Sounds like an inside job.
6–L	Oh, here is Ms. Quesnel. Ms. Quesnel, this is Flo Darrow, who represents Landview Corp., and this is Mr. Purvisor, whose deposition I'll be taking. I guess we'll have to put the robbery on ice for a while. Ms. Quesnel, after you get settled, can you swear in Mr. Purvisor?

Deposition Transcript

	(Oath)
7–L	Mr. Purvisor, will you state your full name please.
W	Louis Purvisor.
8–L	Mr. Purvisor, I assume that Ms. Darrow has reviewed with you what will take place here today, but just so there won't be any misunderstanding, let me briefly describe what will happen. My clients, James and Joan Randolf Phillips, have filed a lawsuit against your employer, Landview Corporation, and certain of its employees concerning the Phillipses' purchase of two lots in Campion Hills. My purpose here today is to ask you questions to learn information that might be relevant to that suit. My questions and your answers will be taken down by the court reporter on this machine that you see in front of you, and then they will be transcribed into a booklet which is known as your deposition. That booklet will be sent to you, and you will be asked to read it

over and sign it. In that regard, I would like to caution you about several things.

9–L   Do you understand that these proceedings have the same solemnity and dignity as though we were in a court of law?

W   Yes.

10–L   Now with regard to your deposition, when you get it you will have an opportunity to correct it—that is, to make any corrections that you deem necessary. But in that connection, you should be advised that if you do make any corrections, it might happen at the time of trial if you were called as a witness by someone, that an attorney for one of the parties would have an opportunity to ask you why changes were made in your sworn testimony between today and the time you make the changes in the deposition. Do you understand?

W   Yes.

11–L   Similarly, if you testify at trial differently than you testify here today, again someone may have an opportunity to ask you why there were changes in your sworn testimony; okay?

W   Yes.

12–L   Now I am only interested in what you know. Subject to the limitations that I will explain to you in a minute, I do not want you to guess. Let me tell you about two kinds of guessing. No. 1, you cannot understand my question and you guess at what I am asking and then base your answer on it; that guesswork, I don't want you to do. The second type of guessing is where you can understand my question perfectly well, but do not know the answer and then guess at the answer. I don't want either type of guessing; okay?

W   Okay.

13–L   Now, it may come to a point where you can understand my question, and the only fair answer you can give me is a guess; if so tell me that in this particular case you have to be guessing at the answer, and your answer would be such and such; okay?

W   Okay.

14–L   Thus, we can assume that if you answer a question, that you understood the question and that you know

	the answer, unless you have told us otherwise; all right?
W	All right.
15–L	And if you don't know, just tell us you don't know; if you don't understand my question, just tell me you don't understand and I will either rephrase it or in some way make it understandable; okay?
W	Okay.
16–L	Do you have any questions about what I've said so far?
W	No.
17–L	Is there anything that you would like explained to you before we start with the questioning?
W	No.
18–L	Are you ill today?
W	No.
19–L	Are you under any medication?
W	No.
20–L	Is there anything at all preventing you in any way from giving accurate testimony today?
W	No.
21–L	If you do get tired, please tell me so we can take a break. Will you do that?
W	Yes.
22–L	Have you reviewed any documents in preparation for your testimony here today? [9]
W	No.
23–L	How long have you been employed by Landview Corporation?
W	A little over six years.
24–L	What is your position with the company?
W	I'm the supervisor in charge of the maintenance of the public areas and the undeveloped property in Campion Hills. I've been there since it opened two and a half years ago.

9. This is a standard question. Part of properly preparing a witness for examination is to have the witness review any previous statements, depositions, letters or other documents with which the witness should be familiar. McCormick, *Evidence* 14–19 (2d ed. 1972). The opposing party may have a right to inspect any papers or memorandum used by a witness to refresh his recollection. See Fed.R.Evid. Rule 612.

25–L   Do your responsibilities include supervision over the maintenance of lots which have been developed but not sold?

W   Yes.

26–L   I'd like to start by having you tell me what you know about the history of lots 70 and 71 in Campion Hills. What is the first thing you can recall that specifically touches upon or involves either or both of these lots?

W   I really can't recall anything specific at all.

27–L   Well, in July of last year, didn't you have a conversation with Mr. and Mrs. Phillips about those two lots?

W   Oh yeah; you mean the time we talked about how nice those two lots were?

28–L   Correct. Now, before that conversation, what's the first instance you can remember regarding either or both of those lots?

W   Well, I do remember another couple being interested in one of those lots; I think it was lot 71. I don't know their name.

29–L   Tell me what you can about this couple.

W   They were an elderly couple; that's about all I remember.

30–L   Can you tell me about the first time you saw them?

W   I was up in the area of lot 71 and they came over to me; I was standing by my truck. They said they were interested in lot 71 but wanted to know if there were any other lots in Campion Hills that had similar views.

31–L   Tell me a little more about that conversation.

W   They said they liked lot 71 but they weren't sure they wanted a house on a lot that would put them close to the type of drop off that lot 71 has.

32–L   You're giving me just the kind of information that I'm looking for. I appreciate that. What I'd like you to do now is to go forward step by step, telling me in sequential order about each specific occurrence or event that you can recall that in any way involves or concerns either lot 70 or 71. What's the next thing you can recall after talking with this elderly couple?

W   . . .

Compare the dialogue (pre-deposition and deposition) to the introductory remarks of Darrow when she went to Purvisor's office for an informal interview. To what extent do their attempts to put Purvisor at ease and to motivate him differ? To what extent do Mason's comments serve to put Purvisor at ease or to raise up his guard? How might these comments cut off explanations for changed testimony? What potential explanations do they attempt to cut off?

Motivational efforts and explanatory comments aside, note that Mason gets into Purvisor's story somewhat differently than did Darrow. Darrow called Purvisor's attention to one of two topics and asked him to "start at the beginning." Mason, on the other hand, asks some background questions of Purvisor before he gets into the story. (23–L and 24–L) One may attribute this solely to personal preference. There is nothing inherent in informal interviews or depositions that makes one approach correct for one and not for the other. Some attorneys prefer to ask more background questions than did Mason, on the theory that background questions, being easy to answer, put a witness at ease. Also, frequently background questions turn up tidbits of relevant information that may alter the plausibility of the witness' story. Other attorneys feel that beginning with extensive background questioning appears prying and puts witnesses off. Still others, like Mason, hew to the middle.

Finally, note that Mason gets into chronology in a somewhat different way from Darrow. They both define the topic on which they want a story. For Mason, it is "the history of lots 70 and 71," whereas for Darrow it was "the Phillipses' purchase of their two lots." But when Purvisor is unable to recall any particular event, Mason supplies one that he already knew something about: Purvisor's discussion with the Phillipses in July. Using that event to trigger Purvisor's memory, and realizing that Purvisor may have had some dealings with lots 70 and 71 prior to the Phillipses, Mason tries to move the story to the "true" beginning: "Correct. Now before that conversation, what's the first instance you can remember regarding either or both of those lots?" (28–L) Only after learning of the earlier incident (i.e. the elderly couple) does Mason ask Purvisor for a sequential narration. (32–L)

Again, neither Darrow's nor Mason's approach is invariably correct, nor is either especially suited to informal interviews or depositions. In both settings one wants a time line that begins at the earliest relevant time, and whatever approach one uses, one must be careful not to substitute one's assumed beginning for the "true" beginning.

4. GETTING A FOOT IN THE DOOR

Although in most instances witnesses are willing to talk, on many occasions this is not true. Whether one telephones first to set up an appointment or appears unannounced at a person's residence or place of work, witnesses often refuse to become involved. Particularly for attorneys who represent criminal defendants and poor people, a refusal may be a double whammy. Not only are witnesses in these cases often less inclined to become involved, but also depositions are typically not an available alternative.[10]

Perhaps the best repositories of methods of overcoming reluctance are door-to-door food freezer salespeople.[11] However, in the context of two possible foot-in-the-door approaches, we illustrate how lawyers might use various motivational techniques to overcome initial reluctance. If nothing else, these suggestions should enable one to fend off the next freezer salesperson who comes calling.

Sometimes, one is aware before speaking to a witness that he or she is inclined not to talk. Perhaps one has spoken to a witness' friend, who states, "Miriam knows something about that but forget it—she'll never talk to you." One cannot help but feel some trepidation approaching Miriam's door, especially if one hears loud barking coming from behind it. In such instances, seeking the witness' agreement to talk, then or at a later time, may be useless. As an alternative, one may *just start in talking*. A witness may get into the flow of an interview without ever consciously deciding to do so. An approach of this kind might go something like this:

1–L	Good afternoon. I'm Edward Graham. You're Miriam Walker?
Miriam	Yeah, but why do you want to know?
2–L	I've been talking to Sue and Brian about the burglary that occurred next door, and they say you might be able to help me. They're really friendly, aren't they?

---

10. For a discussion of when depositions are available in a criminal action under the Federal Rule of Criminal Procedure, Rule 15, see C. Wright, *Federal Practice and Procedure: Criminal* 2d, §§ 241–242 (1982). As for the poor, the prohibitive costs of litigation are well documented. See, e.g., T. Willging, "Financial Barriers and the Access of Indigents to the Courts," 57 Geo.L.J. 253 (1968). The relative failure of ameliorative measures is also no secret. R. Cramton, "Promise and Reality in Legal Services," 61 Cornell L.Rev. 670 (1976).

11. If one can't get tips from one of these personable people first-hand, one of their manuals ought to help get one started. Try J. Ernest & G. DaVall, *Salesmanship Fundamentals* 214–231 (3d ed. 1965); or A. Smith, *How to Sell Intangibles* 33–71 (1958). Knowing a few salesmanship techniques may often come in handy and if the law business ever goes soft, there always are vacuum cleaners.

(*Comment:* Note how the crafty Edward tries to take himself out of the "stranger" category, by using the names of Patty's neighbors. Moreover, Edward perhaps minimizes hostility by not disclosing that he is an attorney.[12] He suggests to Miriam an expectancy that she will help and also tries to break the ice by talking about the folks next door.)

Miriam

They really are nice people, but I really don't know anything about the burglary.

3–L

Well, I'm just trying to clear a few things up. As I understand it, you were washing your car at the time. That's a beautiful car you have—just where was it parked?

(*Comment:* Edward ignores the apparent reluctance, shows interest in the witness, and asks a question which can be easily answered. Moreover, he provides information about Miriam's story that he already knows, so Miriam is not faced with giving away any secrets at the outset.)

Miriam

Well, it was right over there, near the garden hose.

4–L

You sure take good care of your car. How do you keep that kind of shine on it?

(*Comment:* With one answer in the bank, Edward shows more interest and switches topics to keep the conversation going.)

Miriam

Believe me, it takes a lot of work.

5–L

I know it does—I wish I took as good care of my car. By the way, when you were working on your car, what drew your attention to the burglary?

(*Comment:* Edward shows some empathy and interest and then returns to the case with another question that can be easily answered.)

Miriam

I saw the guy jump the fence, but I don't really want to get into that. Please excuse me.

6–L

I understand you don't want to get involved—that's a common reaction. But maybe if you tell me what's bothering you specifically, we can

12. Neighbors may often prove a fertile source of information if approached properly. R. Simmons, note 2 supra, at 412–416. Recall that one need not routinely disclose that one is an attorney.

work around the problem. After all, we all want to make sure the right guy is punished.

(*Comment:* If Miriam will not talk about the burglary, she might talk about why she won't talk, aided by Edward's "appeal to justice.")

Miriam   Look, I'm sorry, I just don't have the time.

(Slams door)

(*Comment:* No technique is always successful.)

On other occasions, one will approach a witness and, in a more typical manner, initially seek the witness' agreement to talk. If the witness seems reluctant to speak, one may deal with the reluctance as one would at any other point in an interview, when it arises.

Such an approach might occur as follows:

1–L   Hi. I'm Bill Klein. I'm a lawyer representing Patrick Knapland, the guy who was arrested here last week for shoplifting. Are you Carol Ambrose, the store manager?

Ambrose   I am. What can I do for you?

2–L   I'd like to talk to you for a few minutes about what happened. Would this be a convenient time?

(*Comment:* Bill assumes no reluctance, and without wasting time on ice-breakers tries to get the manager to commit to "a few minutes.")

Ambrose   Look, I'd be glad to talk but I really don't have the time.

3–L   I understand that. Everyone seems short of time these days, and I'm sure this case is not your first priority. I'd be glad to come back at a more convenient time. What can you suggest?

(*Comment:* Bill is empathetic and offers a solution to the stated reason for reluctance. Had Ambrose not stated a reason, Bill would probably have had to ask for one.)

Ambrose   Frankly, it's more than time. The company has a policy against our making statements in these kinds of cases. We're just not supposed to do it.

(*Comment:* This is a common response. Most working people today are part of large organizations, typically consisting of more than 100 employees.[13] There may

13. P. Samuelson, Op. Ed. Page, Los Angeles Times, July 22, 1981.

be an actual "company policy," or the witness may just be setting it up as an excuse for not talking.)

4–L   I can understand you're wanting to be careful. But as long as I'm here, maybe we can get a waiver or figure out some other way around the policy. Knapland might lose his job over this, and he's told me some things I'm anxious to check out because this case may not be one that belongs in court. He's never been in trouble before. I really do need just a few minutes of your time.

(*Comment:* Bill empathizes with the manager's desire to act properly, but treats the "company policy" as less than absolute. He then makes an appeal to Ambrose's sense of justice, at the same time suggesting subtly that if Ambrose speaks now, she may save time later by keeping the case out of court.)

Ambrose   I don't like getting anybody in trouble, but he did walk out of here with a jacket he didn't pay for.

5–L   I appreciate that you don't want to get a person in trouble, and you're quite right that if a person does intentionally take something without paying for it, he should be punished. But I don't want to waste anyone's time by dragging people into court unnecessarily. Can I tell you a little bit of Knapland's version of what happened and get your reaction to it?

(*Comment:* Bill praises Ambrose's attitude and empathizes with it. He then makes a not-so-subtle time saving pitch. Bill continues to minimize Ambrose's concern about becoming involved by indicating he will take only a short time in telling Ambrose "a little bit." Finally, Bill offers to provide information to Ambrose as a knowledgeable insider whose views are important.)

Ambrose   Well, how much time will it take?

(*Comment:* Success! "Company policy" this time was just an excuse.)

Though Bill's approach is different from Edward's, they each incorporate a variety of motivational statements into their remarks. Moreover, both Bill and Edward refuse to accept the witnesses' initial reluctance as final. In a friendly and professional manner, they pursue the witness. Often one needs to be part terrier to get a foot in the door.

On those occasions when a terrier seems ineffective, one may need to rely upon bulldog instincts. By making "threats," one may cajole witnesses into realizing that their best interests lay in informal discussion. Return to Bill's dialogue with Ambrose, changing Ambrose's last response to, "Look, I'd like to cooperate, but I just don't have the time." With Bill the Bulldog now in place, the dialogue might proceed as follows:

6–L   Frankly, you may find it much less time consuming to talk with me now in private. If the case proceeds to trial, you will be subpoenaed to testify in open court. As a matter of fact, a trial date is already set, and I have a subpoena in my briefcase that I will be forced to serve on you if we cannot talk. If I can find out what you know, there's a good chance trial can be avoided. Even if we do talk, I may still have to subpoena you, but I think talking gives us a good chance to avoid a trial.

        (*Comment:* Bill makes a variety of threats here: a subpoena, testimony in open court, consumption of more time. Note, however, that the threats rely in part on a standard motivation: saving time.)

Ambrose I just think I'd better not.

7–L   I'm sorry. Here's a subpoena. If you change your mind, my phone number is on the subpoena.

        (*Comment:* See you in court, sucker.)

Might Bill or Edward have gotten a foot in the door by way of the telephone? Undoubtedly, many witnesses prefer to talk with someone who calls in advance to arrange an interview at a convenient time. Moreover, if a witness agrees to set aside time for an interview, the witness is more likely to be free of distractions during the interview.

There are some disadvantages to phoning ahead, however. Witnesses often find it much easier to refuse to speak to a voice on the phone than to a person on the doorstep. For another thing, the lack of physical proximity makes it more difficult to motivate a witness. For still another, most of us find it easier to hang up on someone than to close a door in somebody's face. Lastly, some witnesses are suspicious of unseen, unknown telephone callers, and they will refuse almost any telephone request.

Perhaps these factors could be safely ignored if, after one's phone attempt failed, one could simply show up at a witness' doorstep as though nothing had happened. However, once a witness has refused to speak over the phone, the witness will usually find it easier to maintain that refusal should one appear personally. Hence, while it is perhaps more courteous and professional to phone ahead, one must evaluate the likely reaction of each individual witness.

At this point, assume that one has gotten not just one's foot, but one's entire body through a witness' door and has concluded any introductory remarks. One is now ready to seek a chronological narrative of the witness' story.

Chapter 14

OBTAINING A CHRONOLOGICAL
TIME LINE

1. INTRODUCTION

Stories, as you recall, are chronological narratives of events and surrounding details.[1] In earlier chapters, it was sufficient to state the goal of "learning full stories" without describing how one should set about learning them. This chapter initially discusses why it is important to devote initial information-gathering to encouraging witnesses to narrate, in their own words, a "time line" of events. A time line consists of all relevant events known by a witness arranged sequentially. The chapter concludes by suggesting questioning techniques which encourage witnesses to provide time lines.

Focus on techniques is necessary because witnesses do not typically gush forth with time lines whenever one asks, "What happened?" In response, instead of a sequence of discrete events one often may get an answer which is the equivalent of "Once upon a time three bears went for a walk; they came home and lived happily ever after." Such a conclusionary response is as unsatisfactory to a lawyer as it is to a child.

Consider this same problem in a legal context. If a witness who observed a collision from a street corner is asked, "What happened?" the witness is likely to respond, for example, "Well, a white car smashed into a blue car that was turning left. The driver of the blue car had to be pulled out—the white car just drove away." This response narrates a story of a sort, and one's instinctive reaction may be to flesh it out immediately with detailed questions. But examine the "story" more carefully. It consists of two or three conclusions,

---

1. However, stories need not be so defined. See Chapter 2, note 6.

not a series of individual events.[2] One knows there was a collision but has no idea what really happened. Moreover, the story gives one just the barest sense of chronology. One cannot tell in which order events may have occurred, the length of time between events, or whether other events might have occurred during the same span of time.

Because witnesses are unlikely on their own to describe discrete events sequentially, one must consciously urge them to do so. Compare how events in the street corner witness' story might look if they were laid out in time line fashion. Please note that the time line is for illustrative purposes only. We do not suggest that one need actually prepare such a time line during interviews.

1	2	3	4	5
Witness leaves George's Luncheonette after having "Mushroom Yoghurt Surprise" for lunch	Blue car, going East in intersection on green light, signaling left turn	Signal changes from green to red	Blue car starts left turn	White car going West enters intersection

6	7	8	9	10
White and Blue collide	Driver of White car leaves scene	Wit. calls police	Police arrive	Police talk with Blue driver

11	12	13	14	15
Police pry Blue driver out of car	Police talk with wit.	Wit. leaves	Lawyer contacts wit. to arrange interview	Today

Whether or not one "maps out" a story as above, a time line usefully portrays a story as a succession of discrete events.

2. For further discussion of the distinction between events and conclusions, see Chapter 4, p. 51.

2.　THE IMPORTANCE OF BEGINNING WITH TIME LINES

a.　*Identifying Events*

If one accepts learning complete stories as an investigatory goal, then a primary purpose for which one first seeks a witness' time line is simple efficiency. Even if one has already gathered much evidence, one's predictions about what portions of a witness' story will be important to probe may prove very wrong. Thus, if one begins to ask detailed questions before eliciting a time line, one may waste time on events or topics that, in the context of a witness' whole story, are insignificant. By first piecing together a time line, one has a guide to the areas where specific questioning is needed.

Time lines promote efficiency another way. At some point, one normally has to arrange a witness' information into sequential events. If one ploughs ahead with questions without regard to the sequential order of events, one may (though for reasons stated below, one is less likely to) learn most of what a witness knows. But then, on some other occasion when one could more pleasurably be reading about the historical antecedents of the Rule Against Perpetuities, one will have to wade through one's notes and try to organize the information sequentially.[3] Often it will even be necessary to re-interview the witness. Better to get the story straight the first time, when seeking a time line can help accomplish efficiency and other goals.

What are some of these other goals? The primary one is stimulating memory. Focusing witnesses' attention on specific events usually enables witnesses to remember details that otherwise might go unnoticed. Try this yourself. Assume that upon returning home one evening, you discover your wallet is missing. No obvious moment when it was lost leaps to mind. How do you go about thinking where you might have left it? Probably, you do not abstractly think about the wallet. Instead you reconstruct the day's events, one at a time. You picture yourself engaged in each event, recalling the details to see if they include the wallet. By mentally placing oneself at the scene of an event, one is usually able to recall more details than through abstract, random thought. In a manner of speaking, events are the gates through which one pursues details.

A time line also stimulates memory in a somewhat different fashion. Not only does a time line's focus on events enhance the recall of detail, but it also tends to sprout more events. Return to the lost wallet. If one thinks of the wallet in abstract fashion, one may well forget some events during which one might have used it. But if apart from the wallet, one tries to reconstruct the day moving se-

---

3.　See section 2(b), infra.

quentially from one event to the next, one is less likely to overlook an event.

Finally, accumulating a list of events enables one to engage in thorough probing during the subsequent Theory Development stage. Return from the missing wallet to the more legalistic world of car collisions. One is interviewing the street corner witness and wants to trace the witness' movements during the period in question. This task would be difficult to do if one had not first isolated specific events. But with those events as a guide, one can ask precise, focused questions: Where were you at the time of the collision? At the time the white car drove away? After the white car drove away, where did you go? Through such questions, one may elicit the details that help to produce persuasive stories at trial.

b. Sequential Order

First, as you know, chronology is a powerful evaluative tool. The sequence of events often determines inferences one draws. Change the sequence, and perhaps reverse the inference:

1. The blue car entered the intersection; the light turned red.

2. The light turned red; the blue car entered the intersection.

Similarly, changing the time gap between events may well change inferences. Compare the following stories:

1. I had two martinis, and thirty minutes later I drove the car.

2. I had two martinis, and three hours later I drove the car.

In each pair of examples, chronology is a key determinant of the inferences one may draw.

But more than an evaluative tool, chronology is an important memory aid. Events are a more powerful memory stimulant when they are considered sequentially along a time line than when they are considered randomly. In the lost wallet hypothetical, would one not consider the day's happenings from daybreak through lights out? Is that thought process not more natural than thinking about getting up, then about afternoon tea, then about a morning stop at a gas station, and so forth? By trying to get witnesses to relate events sequentially, one tries to use the very natural thought process of chronology to maximize recall.

Interestingly, chronology seems to work best in a forward direction. In other words, when one is trying to recall a series of events, it is usually easier to recall succeeding events than preceding events. This point too may be illustrated by an example drawn from everyday life. Try to recall everything you did yesterday. You will probably find it easier to recall events if you start from the morning and go forward. Of course, what is "typically" true may not be true if the preceding event is particularly noteworthy. If one event in the sequence is, "Got into lifeboat," it may be easier to remember that the preceding event was the "Sinking of the Titanic" than to remember any succeeding event.

Lastly, arranging events along a time line reminds one to watch for chronological gaps. Certainly one need not account for a witness' every waking breath. But if one is attuned to chronology, one may be more likely to see periods of time during which a witness is silent about events. By probing these gaps, one may uncover additional events.

c.   Learning Complete Stories

Obviously, during most interviews a primary concern is to unearth evidence which supports one's legal theories and factual hypotheses. The primacy of that concern is exemplified by chapters 9 and 10: one develops hypotheses and potential evidence that support one's client; one does not conjure up potential evidence for the adversary.

But one cannot confine questioning to previously-identified theories and hypotheses. Often, witnesses have their own ideas as to what information is pertinent. On some occasions, this information will not in fact be relevant. On other occasions, however, it may suggest hypotheses and evidence that one has not yet identified. (Or at least, it may contain juicy, scandalous tidbits!)

Moreover, frequently one is concerned with information known to witnesses which supports an adversary. Sometimes, this concern takes center stage. For example, when deposing the opposing party, one may be less interested in developing favorable evidence than in learning the true scope and extent of the unfavorable evidence.[4] And even when interviewing a witness other than the party opponent, one has some interest in learning unfavorable evidence. As we have stated before, one cannot adequately counsel a client or prepare for trial in blissful ignorance of evidence that favors an adversary.

Pursuing a time line rather than merely seeking to confirm pre-existing hypotheses enhances one's chances of learning a complete story. Whether the data be helpful or harmful, commonly a witness' complete time line takes one beyond the theories one initially intended to pursue.

4.   See R. Keeton, *Trial Tactics and Methods* § 11.2 (2nd ed. 1973); R. Haydock and D. Herr, *Discovery: Theory, Practice and Problems* § 2.6.2 (1983); California Civil Discovery Practice § 5.16 (CEB 1975).

3. TIME LINES IN CONTEXT

Time lines are but one way of stimulating memory. Returning witnesses to the scenes of events, showing them pictures and documents, and disclosing portions of other witnesses' stories are among the other ways. For those witnesses whose sense of chronology rivals that of mollusks, such alternatives may even be superior, at least until one can begin to piece together a rough chronology.

Moreover, many stories contain information that does not fit into a neat, or even messy, chronology. Recall that portions of stories may not be events. For example, typically evidence relating to a witness' background or the organizational hierachy of a corporation does not involve an event that occurs at a particular time in a story. Similarily, in personal injury cases, conditions such as pain may continue over long periods. That one often elicits information about nonevents does not defeat the usefulness of time lines. Usually, nonevents grow out of or are related to events in a time line, and one may fit them in alongside these events as often as seems useful. For example, in the personal injury action, one may include "pain" at the time of the injury and at later times when the injured person was visited by relatives and attempted to return to work.[5]

4. ADAPTABILITY OF TIME LINES

The adaptability of time lines may be illustrated by an example in which use of a time line at first glance seems unrealistic. Assume one represents a parent in a child custody dispute and is to interview a witness who has lived next door to the family for a number of years. The information one seeks concerns the fitness of the parents. Surely, one could not develop a time line consisting of all the events the witness has observed over a period of years. But more limited time lines are possible and useful. For example, one may limit the witness to a period of time—say, the most recent three months—and develop a chronology of events during that span. Or, one might ask the witness to relate qualities of each of the parents— say, their disciplining the children—and then develop for each parent a time line of disciplining incidents. The latter organization may produce multiple time lines—one for discipline, one for sharing time and so forth. Other approaches are of course possible. Time lines are quite adaptable, and they help produce stories at trial which are organized and detailed, and therefore understandable and persuasive.

5. Recall that when making a story outline one is also confronted with the problem of including non-story events. See Chapter 4, pp. 52–53.

5. TIME LINE QUESTIONING TECHNIQUES

a. *Minimize Specific Questions*

After one has heard a client's initial story, one tends to approach every interview with a burning desire to ferret out specific information with probing questions. First, as an advocate, one usually has a sense of particular information that would help one's client. The process of identifying investigatory theories and possible additional evidence has undoubtedly filled one with a host of important questions. Moreover, gaps in stories often raise a number of specific questions to which one desires answers. Finally, as a witness begins to speak, ambiguous references and significant "nuggets," or perplexing omissions from a narrative, also prompt one to probe for specifics immediately. Not suprisingly, one is often champing at the bit to probe quite specifically.

By way of example, consider the witness who saw the blue and white cars collide. The witness' initial description of the accident was, "Well, a white car smashed into a blue car that was turning left. The driver of the blue car had to be pulled out—the white car just drove away." If one is interviewing this witness, some of the specific probes one might feel an urge to make include, "How fast was the white car going?" "What were you doing on the street corner?" "What color was the light for the blue car?" "In your opinion what was the cause of the collision?" [6]

However, by and large, until one has fashioned a time line (or at least has made a valiant effort to do so), one should resist the siren call of immediate specific probes. One may believe that specific questions will produce information a witness would otherwise omit. But quite the opposite is often true. For a variety of reasons, constant probes of witnesses' stories before the events in those stories have been laid out are quite apt to bury potential evidence. First, recall that cases with similar legal issues are quite likely to be factually diverse. Even in cases which appear straightforward, the possibility of unique facts always lurks. One cannot possibly think and inquire about all potential events and details that may have occurred. If one wants to end up with complete stories, one must initially rely on witnesses' narratives, not on one's experience in "these kinds of cases." Remember, there is almost always the possibility that a witness' story will provide evidence that triggers a theory that no previous evidence has suggested.

6. Most of us have developed through social conversation the unconscious habit of unnecessarily restricting the scope of our questions in an effort to control the dialogue. We need, therefore, to learn the value of delimiting the scope of our inquiries. R. Gordon, *Interviewing Strategy, Techniques and Tactics* 203–205 (1969).

Second, specific questions almost inevitably take a witness off track. When a witness is asked to tell a story about historical events, the witness frequently has a chain of association in which recall of one event triggers recall of another. The chain of association is typically chronological. An event that happened at time "B" triggers recall of an event at time "C". But the chain may also be topical: recall of the topic "car" may trigger recall of the topic "repairs." But whatever the chain, it is the witness' chain, not the attorney's. Specific probes are likely to break that chain.

Moreover, even if after a break one returns the witness to the pre-probe topic (and one is likely to forget to do that), events which may have surfaced but for the probe often remain submerged. Once a chain of association is broken, a witness may not regain the initial thought pattern. We have all experienced the frustration of an interruption which forever drives a thought from our minds. Of course, there are those times that immediate probes are necessary: "Might I inquire why you are now standing 50 feet in front of that speeding locomotive?"

Third, listening to a witness' story with few interruptions aids rapport. If one constantly poses specific questions, a witness may well sense that one is more interested in one's own questions than in everything the witness knows. Encouraging a witness to narrate a story in his or her own words, accompanied by other empathetic behavior, conveys genuine interest in the whole story.[7]

Refraining from asking probing questions may aid rapport in another way. If a witness is allowed to narrate a story, the witness has substantial freedom to decide what events and details to report. The witness can downplay or omit topics with which he or she is uncomfortable. But, after rapport is established, the witness may be more willing to discuss troublesome topics.

Finally, and quite significantly, allowing for initial narration relatively free of specific probing greatly enhances the likelihood that a witness may disclose information that the witness would otherwise be inclined to slant or withhold. When one asks witnesses to simply relate "what happened," the specific purpose of the inquiry is almost always more obscure than when one asks a specific question. Compare the following two questions in terms of the apparent purpose of the inquiry: "What happened next?" "Did other cars traveling in White's direction stop rather than enter the intersection?" It is much easier for a witness to assign a potential purpose to the question about whether other cars stopped than to the question about what happened next. If a witness were inclined to conceal information

7. See D. Binder & S. Price, *Legal Interviewing and Counseling: A Client-Centered Approach* 41, 73 (1977).

about other cars, the witness will be more likely to do so in response to the specific question.

In summary, getting a chronological time line first is one's chance to start smart by playing dumb. One may want to begin by impressing a witness with a stream of insightful, creative questions. But there are likely to be costs to that practice, in terms of time, rapport, and the amount of information one gets. Allow witnesses some free rein. One need only wait for the theory development stage to demonstrate how clever one really is. It is during theory development that one probes events throughly according to legal theories and factual hypotheses.

b. Ask Open Questions

If one minimizes specific probes while seeking a time line, how then does one elicit time lines? Primarily, assuming during the introduction one has encouraged a witness to "tell your story sequentially from beginning to end," one simply asks open questions. Completely open questions allow witnesses to decide what events to talk about and what aspects to describe when talking about them.

"Please tell me what you know."

"Is there anything else you can think of that pertains to this case?"

More typically, open questions set some limits by calling attention to a particular time period or topic:

"What happened next?"

"After he climbed the Empire State Building, what happened?"

"Please tell me about the car."

"Why do you think Ms. Medea is a good mother?"

Each of these questions does little more than indicate a topic. In discussing the topic, a witness has wide freedom. For example, with the Empire State Building question, the witness can discuss:

(a) a variety of *actors:* himself or herself; others; animals

(b) a variety of *activities:* talking; doing; feeling

(c) a variety of *places:* on the building; in the building; on the ground; in the air.[8]

The only restriction imposed on the witness is time: "after he climbed." Similarly, with regard to the car question the witness is invited to discuss anything so long as it concerns the car. Thus, open

8. R. Gordon, note 6 supra, at 205.

questions allow one to exert some control over an interview while allowing witnesses substantial freedom to narrate their stories.[9]

To develop a time line, one typically uses one or more of three types of open questions each time a witness describes a new event. If one wants to learn more about the event, one typically uses open probes such as, "Tell me more about that" or "Can you describe that for me in a little more detail." Such questions ask a witness to stay with the point just revealed, and to elaborate on it in more detail.

If one wants to learn about potentially omitted events between the most recent event and an event which preceded it, one uses questions like the following: "What else happened between the time you first saw the signal (the preceding event) and the time you saw it change to red (the most recent event)?" By selecting this type of probe, one chooses to move the witness back in the story to search for intervening events.

Finally, if one wants a witness to move a story forward, one can select questions such as, "What happened next?" or "Tell me about the next incident you recall?"

In sum, one can use open questions to orchestrate the development of a time line by asking a witness, at each point in a story, (1) to stand still and elaborate an event in more detail, (2) to move back and search for intervening events between a new event and a predecessor, or (3) to move forward to later events.

Of course, depending on the witness, one typically varies questions to develop time lines. Witnesses vary in their ability to narrate, their sense of chronology, their inclusion of detail, and their cooperativeness. With one witness, one may struggle to get the witness to narrate a story, while with another one may wonder how to turn off the bubbling detail machine. Thus, there can be no standard formula for eliciting a time line. However, to obtain the flavor of how one might develop a time line, consider the lawyer's attempt below. In the hypothetical case of the blue car/white car collision, the interviewer represents the defendant, the owner of the white car, Andrea Sossin. Andrea's defense is that her car had been stolen and that she

---

9. There is a broad spectrum of questions, ranging from narrative questions which exert almost no control over a witness ("Tell me anything you think I ought to know") to leading questions ("You did it! You did it! You did it, correct?"). Between these extremes lie a variety of forms of questions with which one may control the scope of a witness' response. As just noted, a question may be open, in the sense that it allows a witness to describe a topic or event in his or her own words, while it limits the scope of the answer: "Tell me everything you can about the gun." Narrow questions ask for specific pieces of information, or often for only "yes" or "no": "Please tell me who else was there." "Were you present when the chicken crossed the street?"

For a further discussion of forms of questions see P. Bergman *Trial Advocacy in a Nutshell* 86–106 (1979); D. Binder & S. Price, note 7 supra, at 38–48.

was not driving it at the time of the collision. Andrea suspects that the car was stolen by Melinda, the teenage daughter of Andrea's neighbor, Sally Adelson. In light of this defense, consider the following dialogue between Andrea's lawyer, Chris Chross, and police officer Pat Downe, who came to the scene of the mishap. The dialogue begins with their meeting at the Chatam Restaurant and continues through Chross's efforts to develop a time line:

1–L Officer Downe?

W Yes.

2–L I'm Chris Chross; it's nice of you to meet me here. I sure appreciate your giving me some of your time.

W Well, the chance for some coffee and a few minutes out of the patrol car sounded good.

3–L Great; let's sit over here. How much time during a shift do you usually spend in the car?

W Too often too much time, sometimes 6 to 8 hours. It can get really boring.

4–L I didn't realize you would ever spend so much time with very little happening.

W It happens all the time.

5–L I guess I'm used to television, where the police are always chasing someone in dangerous situations. I'm glad you can spare me a few minutes. I think the waitress will take our order in a moment. From our brief phone conversation, you know what I'm here about. Probably we could get through this most easily if you could start from the beginning and describe for me sequentially everything that happened thereafter step by step.

W Well, I'll try, but I think most of it is in the accident report. About five minutes before I arrived at the scene, I got a call to check out an accident at Lime and Lemon. I must have gotten to the scene just after 10:00 p.m.

6–L Could you tell me a little bit more about the call to go to the scene?

W It was brief; I was told to check out an injury accident at Lime and Lemon.

7–L Okay, between the time you got the call and the time you arrived did anything else happen?

W Well, I got another call saying the accident might involve a 11359. I got out my book to see what the heck that was. Why do they have to talk in code?

8–L   Anything else happen before you arrived?

W   No.

        (Interruption to order two coffees, a double cheeseburger with fries and a salad. Dessert comes later.)

9–L   Okay, what happened when you got to the scene?

W   I saw this blue car up against a power pole on the northeast corner and a crowd gathered around the car. I exited my vehicle, went over to the blue car and saw the driver was still inside. When the car door wouldn't open, I began talking with the guy inside. People in the crowd then began closing in and shouting all kinds of suggestions. I had to ask them to move back.

10–L   I guess you didn't like taking time to do that.

W   It was aggravating, but you come to expect such things in a job like mine.

11–L   I imagine you do, but I'm sure it's still aggravating at times. By the way, how did you know the door wouldn't open?

W   The left door was wedged against the pole, and the right door had been bashed-in in the accident. I could see that as I walked over to the car from the police vehicle. I gave it a try, but it wouldn't budge.

12–L   That really gives me a clear picture of what the situation was. What happened when you began trying to talk with the driver?

W   He said he wanted out but was having trouble with his left arm. He had a shoulder harness belt and I asked him if he could release the belt. He did that and then I asked him to try to roll down the left window. He tried to do so but couldn't.

13–L   What happened next?

W   The ambulance arrived.

14–L   Between the time of your conversation with the driver and the arrival of the ambulance, what else happened?

W   Not much; a couple of people came up and said they had seen the accident; I asked them to wait and talk with me later.

15–L   Could you tell me a little bit more about these people and what they said?

W   Well, one of them was a man whose name I never got who said he got a good look at the driver of the white car; after that conversation, I never saw him again. The

	other one was a woman who waited and talked with me. Her name is on the police report.
16–L	Mrs. Schwartz?
W	Yeah, I think that's it.
17–L	Could you tell me some more about what the man said?
W	It wasn't much; I remember he said she looked too young to drive.
18–L	Okay, what happened after you asked these people to wait?
W	Really nothing until the ambulance arrived; it couldn't have been more than a minute or so.
19–L	What happened when the ambulance got there?
W	Well, the two attendants and I got the driver out of the car.
20–L	Did a tow truck arrive before you got the driver out?
W	Yeah; I'd forgotten about that.
21–L	Okay, can you tell me what happened just between the time the ambulance arrived and the time the tow truck got to the scene?
W	The two ambulance attendants came over to the car and I described the situation. Then the three of us tried to yank open the passenger door but it wouldn't budge. We then began discussing the possibility of breaking out the front window on the passenger side. We didn't have any equipment for that purpose and were talking about what we might use when one of the attendants spotted the tow truck.
22–L	That must have been a relief!
W	It was.
23–L	Did the driver of the car participate in the discussion about breaking the window?
W	No, we stood away from the car.
24–L	Okay, what happened when the attendant spotted the tow truck?
W	I went over and described the situation to the tow truck driver.
25–L	What happened then?
W	He got out a crowbar and then together with the ambulance attendants we got the driver out.
26–L	What happened next?

W   The ambulance attendant started working with the driver, and I talked with Mrs. Schwartz.

27–L   How much time elapsed between the time you got to the scene and you began talking with Mrs. Schwartz?

W   About 25 minutes.

28–L   Can you tell me about that conversation?

W   She said the driver of the white car appeared to be a young woman. She probably had dark hair, but Mrs. Schwartz couldn't say that for sure. She said the white car backed up and left the scene quite quickly. She also gave me the license number.

29–L   After you talked with Mrs. Schwartz, what's the next thing that occurred?

W   Not much. I looked for other witnesses and couldn't find any, and then I took some notes for my report.

30–L   Between the time you talked with Mrs. Schwartz and the time you made notes, did anything else happen in addition to looking for witnesses?

W   Not that I can recall.

31–L   Did you complete your report at the scene?

W   No. I finalized it back at the station.

32–L   What occurred next, after you had written up your notes?

W   I went by the hospital and got a statement from the driver of the blue car.

33–L   What time was that?

W   About 11:30.

34–L   Is that the statement in your report?

W   Right.

35–L   What's the next thing that happened after you got the statement?

W   I went back to the station and wrote up my report.

36–L   What time did you finish?

W   About 1:30.

37–L   What happened next?

W   I filed my report and I never heard anything else about this until you called me.

38–L   What's the next incident you recall about the case be-
           tween the time you filed your report and the time I
           called?

W   None that I remember.

At this point, Chross has apparently secured a time line from Officer Downe, and presumably Chross will next probe the most significant events. However, before turning to the probing inquiries that
characterize theory development, examine how Chross elicited the
time line. Consider first the introduction. After 38–L, would Officer
Downe expect further inquiry, or would Downe expect the interview
to conclude? Should Chross have mentioned during the introductory
stage that detailed probes might follow the time line? (See 5–L) Or
would it have been a sufficient clue if Chross had suggested that
Downe order a lot to eat?

Next, consider how Chross orchestrates Downe's story. Lest one
regard Chross' approach as a standard which one must adhere to or
court disaster, in a moment we discuss alternative questions Chross
might have asked. For now, however, focus on the questions Chross
used to elicit the events.

Initially, please note that though Chross had evidently read
Downe's accident report, the interview proceeded nearly independently of it. Reports, agreements, other documents, and prior information frequently foul efforts to develop a time line. For example, a
witness may produce a document, and suddenly an entire interview
consists of narrow randomly-sequenced questions triggered by the
document. Although Chross may well have questions pertaining to
the accident report, they are deferred until after the time line stage.

Chross uses each of the three types of open questions. Sometimes, Chross asks Downe to elaborate after an event is mentioned.
(See e.g., 6–L "Could you tell me a little bit more about the call to go
to the scene," and also 15–L and 17–L). At other points, Chross
probes for the possibility of other events between events already
identified. (See e.g., 7–L "Okay, between the time you got the call
and the time you arrived, did anything else happen?" and also 14–L
and 21–L). Finally, some questions move the story forward from one
event to another. (See e.g., 13–L "What happened next?" and also
25–L and 29–L).

The time line stage is not, however, limited to open questions
which move witnesses back and forth in time. For reasons that will
soon be apparent, one may ask some specific questions as well.
Here, Chross uses specific questions to clarify a name of a witness in
the report (See 16–L) and to pin down the time that certain events
occurred. (See e.g., 27–L, 33–L and 36–L). Furthermore, Chross
uses motivational statements. (See 10–L, 12–L, and 22–L). Such spe-

cific questions and statements are encompassed in Chross' main goal of securing a time line through open questions.

If the above description is straightforward, it should not conceal the primary issue which is likely to confront one during the time line stage. That issue is the extent to which one seeks elaboration while developing a time line.

6. PROBING FOR ELABORATION

Remember that a major purpose for securing a time line is to enable one to decide which events are worth probing during the theory development stage. If during the time line stage a witness responds to one's open questions with full narrative answers, then one may do little probing during this stage. But if during the time line stage a witness' answers are terse and sketchy, one may need to seek further elaboration if one is to have a meaningful basis for deciding where to probe further during theory development. The frequent result is a "detail dilemma." Some elaboration is necessary to flush out events in the time line, but if one seeks excessive elaboration, one may lose the benefits of having a time line prior to theory development.[10]

As one might imagine, there are no fixed rules which can be called upon to resolve this dilemma. In individual instances, one must exercise judgment when inquiring into detail during the time line stage. In the final analysis, perhaps what is most important is learning to distinguish questions that ask for elaboration of an event from those which move a story to other events, and to choose between them intelligently. From this perspective, please look at Chross' question 12–L: "What happened when you began talking with the driver?" Is Officer Downe asked to elaborate on the conversation with the driver, or to move on to the next event following it? Either interpretation is possible, and either may well comport with Chross' purposes. However, unless Chross is aware that a choice needs to be made in light of those purposes, the time line may be partly the product of fortuity. See also 9–L.

There are times when the need for elaboration is obvious. If one is having difficulty understanding events, then specific probes may be called for. For example, if a witness is describing a conversation involving seven people, and says "she said . . . then he said . . . ," immediate probes to find out who said what are warranted.

Unfortunately, most lawyers are capable of finding ambiguities as easily as teenagers find fault with their parents. In order not to

10. Sometimes distinctions are made between probes for elaboration and probes for clarification. See Binder & Price note 7 supra at 73–75. Here we treat any request for more information about an event the witness has disclosed as a quest for elaboration.

cloud a time line with too many interruptions for detail, restraint is needed. In this regard, return to the interview of Officer Downe. In Downe's response to 15–L, the officer mentioned a conversation with a woman whose name is on the police report. In 16–L Chross, perhaps attempting to clarify an ambiguity, responds, "Mrs. Schwartz?". The propriety of 16–L is doubtful, at best. The witness is narrating freely, and there seems little need for Chross to clarify at that moment the name of the woman. Of course, one may regard 16–L as innocuous, and alone it probably will not upset Downe's chain of association or otherwise affect the time line. Repetitive probes of this nature might be destructive, however, and they are better left to theory development.

When a witness describes an event which seems particularly important, one is tempted to seek immediate elaboration. For example, in the hypothetical interview, Officer Downe has told Chross that Downe had a conversation with Mrs. Schwartz when the ambulance attendants were helping the injured driver. This conversation is ripe with potential importance—after all, Mrs. Schwartz apparently is a "neutral" eyewitness who perhaps saw the driver of the white car. Nevertheless, the event—the fact of a conversation—has been elicited, and its location on the time line is clear. Thus, Chross could have forgone elaboration of it until theory development. However, in 28–L Chross asks, "Can you tell me about that conversation?"

Though Chross' question is an open one, the decision to ask it during the time line stage is questionable. For one thing, how much elaboration does Chross seek? Note that after Downe gives some initial description of the conversation, in 29–L Chross moves the officer forward to "what happened next." Given the potential importance of Mrs. Schwartz's information, Chross will probably have to probe it further during theory development. Indeed, its importance militates in favor of deferral: no further details are needed to show this to be an event to explore. The piecemeal probing may well be confusing and break a witness' chain of association. Moreover, when during theory development the attorney returns to the event for thorough probing, the return may even make a witness angry: "This again?" Finally, if Chross were to pursue the conversation fully in the time line stage, Chross would inevitably consume time with narrow questions and move far off the time line. For all of these reasons, 28–L was perhaps ill-advised.

By contrast, note that when in response to 32–L the officer mentions talking to the blue car driver in the hospital, Chross does not ask for elaboration of that conversation. Perhaps one cannot insist that Chross be consistent. However, at the least one can demand that Chross be aware of the inconsistency and be able to justify it.

In this light, please examine other questions by Chross which seek elaboration. Such questions include 11–L, "By the way, how did you know the door wouldn't open?" and 15–L and 17–L. On the rather limited information given, do you have a sense of their wisdom?

If our advice to defer elaboration to theory development seems excessively cautious, perhaps we over-compensate because of our empirical sense that new lawyers are too inclined toward immediate elaboration. On the other hand, for at least one purpose other than understanding the story, one should be aware of the value of seeking elaboration during the time line stage. Recall the concept of oblique searches for evidence (affirmative or rebuttal) that a witness might not reveal if the witness clearly understands the purpose of a question. Despite the fact that one understands a story, if one senses that an event described by a witness may contain evidence that might not be revealed in response to a question whose purpose is apparent, one may ask for seemingly innocuous elaboration. "Tell me a little bit more". When this kind of probe is rather routinely inserted into the quest for the witness' time line, its purpose is often more obscure than when the event is singled out during theory development. Return to the automobile accident hypothetical. Assume that Officer Downe had nothing in the written report of the accident about the possible identity of the hit and run driver. Assume further that one sensed that the officer had more knowledge of the driver's identity than mentioned in the report, but sensed also that specific questions about that topic might make the officer reluctant for fear of looking incompetent. In such a situation, one might well ask for elaboration at each point in the time line where one sensed the officer had perhaps obtained information about the driver's identity. Arguably, such probing would make less apparent one's purpose than any questions asked during more specific theory development probing.

7. EXPANDING TIME LINES BY DISCLOSING SIGNPOSTS

The discussion thus far has been devoted to developing and elaborating a witness' time line. Since the time line is the primary basis for the probing that will occur during theory development, one normally wants to make a time line as chronologically complete as possible. Can one inquire about potential unmentioned events while remaining loyal to the notion of a witness' freedom to determine the subject matter during this stage?

First, recognize that a variety of factors may contribute to incomplete time lines. Especially when a witness' story covers a considerable span of time, a witness, no matter how hard he or she may try, may be unable to provide a very complete time line. Assume, for example, in a case involving the alleged negligent design and manufacture of a brake system, one is to interview the defendant manufacturer's chief engineer to obtain the story of how the system was designed. Assume further, that the time interval between the idea for the manufacture of the system and its release to the public was two and one-half years. In such a case, anyone trying to obtain a complete time line from this witness would almost certainly have to suspect that the engineer might overlook some events.

But time spans are not the only enemy of complete time lines. Sometimes, witnesses omit events because they just do not see their relationship to a case. On other occasions, of course, witnesses may simply forget that certain events occurred, or they may intentionally conceal their knowledge.

Prior to interviewing a witness, one often knows of events which a witness omits from his or her story. One usually does not start an interview with a blank slate. From the client's story, the stories of other witnesses and various documents, one frequently begins with an idea of some of the events that probably will compose part of a witness' time line.

Another way that one may identify unmentioned events is through "normal course" events. From one's knowledge of everyday life, one can often identify routine events that are probably part of a witness' complete story, though they are not mentioned. Events that are repetitive and routine may escape a witness' conscious attention when a story is told. If a witness verifies that a "normal course" event did occur, one's time line is more complete. Perhaps more importantly, recall of the "normal course" event may spur recall of additional details or other omitted events. Officer Downe, for example, following the "normal course" of events in a police officer's life, probably took street measurements before leaving the scene and put out a call for a hit-and-run suspect. Chross might consider inquiring into such matters while developing the time line of Downe's story.

Events from "prior knowledge" and "normal course," then, may be considered "signposts" which may expand a witness' time line. There are, of course, some potential disadvantages of suggesting signposts when developing a time line. Open questions are not well suited for the purpose. If a witness initially omits an event, a question such as, "Do you recall anything else?" is not likely to stimulate recall. Thus, one will almost certainly have to use narrow questions,—e.g. "Did you take street measurements?"—which one seeks to minimize at this stage.

On balance, however, our reservations about probing for omitted events are less than they are about probing for elaboration. One's need for a fairly complete time line generally outweighs one's immediate need for detail. Also, most witnesses, including adverse witnesses, probably omit entire events more out of lack of recall than conscious choice. Finally, recall of an omitted event often triggers recall of still other events. For all these reasons, time line inquiries often introduce signposts to probe for omitted events.

To consider the propriety of disclosing signposts to witnesses, return to the interview of Officer Downe. Assume that before interviewing the officer, Chross had interviewed Kevin Hillary, a tow truck driver who came to the accident scene. Assume further that in the interview Hillary had stated that he had arrived in time to assist Downe and some ambulance attendants pry open the blue car to remove the driver. You cannot observe the nonverbal behavior of either Downe or Chross and hence cannot fully appraise the rapport between them. Nonetheless, from what you can see of the interview so far, to what extent do you believe Chross' decision in 20–L to bring up the suspected event—"Did a tow truck driver also help getting him out?"—was sound? Examine 19–L through 25–L. From Chross' prior conversation with Hillary, the lawyer undoubtedly suspected that before the driver was taken from the blue car, the tow truck driver had arrived on the scene and had participated in removing the driver. In response to 19–L, however, Downe states that the sequence of events was (1) arrival of the ambulance followed by (2) removal of the driver. The officer omitted the suspected event of the arrival of the tow truck and the details of the truck driver's participation in prying open the car. What arguments support Chross' decision to raise the suspected signpost of the tow truck's arrival?

8. DIVISIBLE TIME LINES

For both analytical and practical purposes, one normally thinks of the time line stage as a single entity preceding theory development. However, in lawyering perhaps no quality is more prized than flexibility. Sometimes it makes sense to elicit a time line in more than one stage. One may elicit part of a time line, subject that part to theory development questioning, then get more of a time line, and so forth. By doing so one of course runs the previously identified risks—for example, wasting time on insignificant events, breaking chains of association through narrow questions, or plunging into discomforting topics before rapport is established. But in some situations, one may want to run those risks.

For instance, a story may cover a considerable span of time. Remember the chief engineer, whose story about the design and manufacture of allegedly defective brakes covered two and one-half years. Or, a story which spans a relatively short period of time may teem with important events. An allegedly mangled brain surgery may take only a few hours, but the operating surgeon may have numerous important events to relate.

In such cases, one may consider getting a time line in stages. Otherwise, both attorney and witness may expend so much energy on a lengthy time line that neither has the mental agility for theory development. When the end of the time line has been reached, recollection of earlier portions may be hazy. One may then have to consume time and risk annoying the witness by having to reestablish early portions of the time line. Of course, when one does so, and subjects that portion to detailed theory development questioning, then later portions of the time line may have vanished from memory, and the cycle repeats. One may break the wasteful cycle by eliciting the time line in stages.

Multiple stories also may call for multiple time lines. Recall the witness in the child custody proceedings, whose story might concern a number of different parenting traits. Rather than attempting a single time line encompassing all events, one may elicit a time line regarding a single trait, subject that time line to theory development, and repeat the process for other traits. This approach might have been used by Darrow during her interview of Lou Purvisor. She identified two topics for him: the Phillipses' purchase of the lots and soil conditions in Campion Hills prior to their purchase. Darrow might get a time line on one topic and then ask detailed theory development questions before moving to the next topic.

Breaking time lines into stages may also be useful in a number of specific instances. Available time may dictate one's approach. If an interview is slotted into several non-consecutive days, different approaches are possible. Perhaps each day one may both elicit a portion of a time line and then ask detailed theory development questions. Or, one may elicit a time line one day and ask for detail the next. Or, if a witness is disorganized and simply impervious to the discipline of a time line, one may be better off with a series of short time lines. Occasionally, one may thereby mold a scatter-gun witness into one able to tell a logical and chronological story.

There is no magic formula one can apply to identify occasions when a time line is best elicited in stages. More than anything else, the above comments should alert one to the opportunity to consider the method by which one will conduct an interview separately from the information one seeks. Aware of the choices, one hopes to choose wisely.

9. NOTE–TAKING

Advising new lawyers to take notes during interviews is as unnecessary as reminding law professors to assign gobs of reading over holiday breaks. If anything, new lawyers are apt to bury their head in legal pads during interviews, feverishly attempting to write down everything. However, extensive note taking may block rapport and so obscure the forest with the trees that one does not know where to follow-up during theory development. Worse yet, one's wrist may get very sore. Hence, consider a few suggestions for effective note-taking.[11]

During the time line stage, typically one need do no more than jot down key events and details. One tries to write down the same words spoken by a witness. The witness' own words usually stimulate recall during theory development better than one's paraphrased language. Moreover, one can note, with an asterisk or other marking, events which appear particularly important or apparent gaps in the time line which one wishes to probe during theory development.

For an example of key word notes, examine a portion of Chross' interview of Officer Downe. Opposite the dialogue are the notes Chross might have made.

Interview	Notes

9–L	Okay, what happened when you got to the scene?	
W	I saw this blue car up against a power pole on the northeast corner and a crowd gathered around the car. I exited my vehicle, went over to the blue car and saw the driver was still inside. When the car door wouldn't open, I began talking with the guy inside. People in the crowd then began closing in and shouting all kinds of suggestions	Blue against power pole—N/E Crowd gathered Officer gets out Driver inside Door won't open
	I had to ask them to move back.	Asked crowd to move back.
10–L	I guess you didn't like taking time to do that.	(* witnesses in crowd?)
W	It was aggravating, but you come to expect such things in a job like mine.	
11–L	I imagine you do, but I'm sure it's still aggravating at times. By the way, how did you know the door wouldn't open?	
W	The left door was wedged against the pole and the right door had been	Left door—pole

11. For further discussion of note taking, see, e.g., A. Watson, *The Lawyer in the Interviewing and Counseling* *Process* 34–36 (1976); C. Rogers, *Counseling and Psychotherapy* 242 (1942).

> bashed-in in the accident. I could see   Rt. door—bashed
> that as I walked over to the car from
> the police vehicle. I gave it a try, but
> it wouldn't budge.

During theory development, one will typically take more extensive notes. At that time, one elicits the details that are transferred into a memorandum of the interview, the various outlines and ultimately used at trial. During the time line stage, however, the above notes are usually sufficient.

Note that even if one secures a witness' permission to record an interview, noting key events and details is probably still necessary.[12] The notes guide the follow-up questioning that will occur. Thus, recording is not a substitute for note-taking.

10. TIME LINES MEET THE REALITY MONSTER

We recognize that some of the distinctions drawn in this chapter are artificial, and perhaps they state ideals that are often unattainable. For instance, though the time line stage is primarily a search for events rather than details, as mentioned in Chapter 4, it is often difficult to decide when an event stops and a detail begins. Also, practical concerns such as one's need to work on other cases and a witness' perceptual frailties and need to carry on daily life usually combine to make a time line less than totally complete. For some witnesses, the time line theory development progression is too confining; whatever the event/detail distinction means, they will not be bound by it. Or, benefits of time lines aside, one may need detailed information from a witness *now*, perhaps to draft an affidavit in support of a motion for a temporary restraining order.

But do not therefore conclude that the time line concept is meaningless. As a general rule, time lines are useful. Importantly, they aid one to identify events that occurred before and after substantively critical events. Moreover, the closer one comes to obtaining complete time lines, the firmer basis will one have for theory development questioning. "There are already more shoemakers practicing law than there are shoemakers making shoes." [13] If one uses the

12. Recording an interview without a witness' permission may well be unlawful. See West's Ann.Cal.Penal Code § 632; People v. Belkota, 50 A.D.2d 118, 377 N.Y.S.2d 321 (1975); People v. Patrick, 46 Mich.App. 678, 208 N.W.2d 604 (1973). Moreover, one should recognize that it usually requires from three to twelve hours to transcribe one hour of recorded dialogue. See R. Gordon, note 5, supra at 175–176. Finally, one commentator has suggested that where a witness is "hostile" or "neutral," it may be wisest to keep the pencils at bay during the initial run-through of the story, or at least through several preliminary questions. J. Tracy, *The Successful Practice of Law* 33–36 (1959).

13. From a conversation with Peter Katsufrakis, former judge of the Los Angeles Municipal Court.

admitted limitations of time lines as an excuse to overlook them completely, one may easily slip from the category of lawyer to that of shoemaker.

11. LIMITED STORY INTERVIEWS

If there are some occasions when complete time lines are unattainable, there are other occasions when they are unnecessary. Time lines are appropriate when one seeks to learn everything a witness may know about historical facts. However, interviews at times have more limited goals.

On some occasions, one may seek only to find out what a witness knows about a specific event, or about events that happened during a limited time period in an overall story.

In other instances, one may be interested more in what a witness is likely to say at trial than in what the witness knows. In these latter instances, one typically starts with a strong view of what "the facts" probably were and primarily seeks to learn whether the witness is likely to support or contradict them. And, in other situations, one interviews witnesses not so much to learn what they know or will say about the historical facts, but to identify avenues for "getting at" the historical facts. For example, one might interview an expert to identify potential hypotheses and evidence. Likewise, an interview might be conducted primarily to identify potential witnesses or potential documents, to learn the background of one or more persons or entities involved in a case and/or to learn the common practices of one or more such persons. For instance, where the other party is a corporation, one might seek to learn its past and present organizational hierarchy—who reports to whom, what records it normally maintains, and where such records are kept. There are, of course, other limited purposes for which one might interview. In all the foregoing situations, one needs to think through whether a time line will be helpful.

Chapter 15

THE THEORY DEVELOPMENT AND CONCLUDING STAGES

1. INTRODUCTION

If after the time line stage there remains any notion that a legal interview is just so much social chit-chat, questioning during the theory development stage normally puts it to rest. During theory development, one uses a combination of open and narrow questions to thoroughly probe aspects of stories which, in light of parties' competing theories, seem important. Though one attempts to question in a professional manner that maintains or even furthers rapport, there is little doubt that the lawyer controls the agenda.

This chapter explores techniques for thoroughly probing stories. In general, one is thorough if, with respect to the parties' theories, one (a) gives witnesses sufficient opportunity and encouragement to recall additional events and details on their own; and (b) makes specific inquiry for potential evidence which witnesses do not mention. Both of these criteria are particularly dependent upon effective preparation, and we begin by examining that topic.

2. PREPARING FOR INTERVIEWS

Admittedly, discussion of "preparation" at this point to some degree violates the chronology concept stressed in the preceding Chapter. After all, preparation precedes an interview; one does not gain preparation time by asking a witness to read *War and Peace* after the time line stage has concluded. However, preparation is discussed out of sequence because it connects so intimately with theory development questioning.

Preparation is the key link between the analytical emphasis of Parts 2 and 3 of this book and the methodological emphasis of Part 4.

From the interviewing standpoint, the reason one breaks theories into separate elements stated in factual terms, and ultimately analyzes potential additional affirmative and rebuttal evidence, is very simple: one learns what to ask. As you know, no matter how much rapport one has with a witness, one cannot rely upon open questions to produce all the relevant information the witness might know. Almost inevitably, one must ask specific questions and employ other techniques to pull out information that might otherwise be unreported.

Hence, before an interview, commune with the outlines, and perhaps with other sources of information. The outlines serve to generate topics for specific inquiries, not merely to record information. Review of a story outline may indicate chronological gaps which a witness might be able to fill with intervening events. Outlines of a client's potential affirmative and rebuttal evidence enable one to refresh one's memory of legal theories and factual hypotheses and to identify specific helpful evidence which a witness may provide. Review of one's outline of an adversary's existing affirmative evidence reminds one to probe for evidence helpful to the adversary. Under an outline of existing evidence, one's car keys may often be found. After this review, and based upon what one knows in advance about a witness, make a list of topics to probe during theory development.

In our experience, forcing oneself to make a list of topics to explore based on the outlines is the best method of leaving interviews with complete information. Inexperienced litigators frequently fail to press witnesses to reveal information. In part, that failure may be attributed to unfamiliarity with probing techniques. But in part, the failure is often due to insufficient pre-interview preparation.

Recognize, at the same time, that no amount of preparation will avoid the necessity to question spontaneously. Witnesses often broach topics for which one is not prepared. For example, a witness might mention an unforeseen event which provides affirmative evidence for one's adversary. On the spot, one will have to consider and then formulate questions to test credibility and seek out potential rebuttal evidence. However, like "possession," preparation typically determines nine-tenths of the outcome.

Preparation, of course, encompasses more than listing topics to probe. One makes sure that documents and other records that will be useful during an interview are in one's possession. One also searches the record for the witness' prior statements, if any. And, perhaps one checks into the witness' background. Is the witness likely to disclose information willingly? Does he or she have a financial or an emotional stake in an outcome? Are there particular topics about which the witness may be especially sensitive? Answers to such questions help one think through how to motivate the witness.

Of course, answers to such questions are not always available. But often a list of personal information can be cheaply gleaned. One's client, or a client's close associate, may know a great deal about a witness.

3. EXPANDING STORIES BY UNCOVERING ADDITIONAL EVENTS

During theory development, one expands a witness' story primarily by uncovering additional events and by probing selected events for detail. Depending on the circumstances, this expansion may be for the purpose of supporting one's own hypotheses or for the purpose of examining the strength of the adversary's hypotheses.

Recall from the previous chapter that during the time line stage, one often seeks to expand a witness' spontaneous story by searching for further events. For example, if one believes that there are gaps in a story, one may inquire about intervening events. To the extent, however, that one has not sought to uncover additional events during the time line stage, one often does so during theory development. Remember that events provide context and thereby stimulate recall of details. Accordingly, a substantial portion of theory development may be devoted to uncovering additional events.

One may uncover additional events by asking about "events" or by inquiring about "topics." If the distinction between "events" and "details" is fuzzy,[1] that between "events" and "topics" is no less so. An "event" inquiry typically concerns an occurrence at a discrete moment in time; a "topic" inquiry typically calls attention to a certain subject matter and searches for moments in time when that subject matter occurred. In a sense, a topical inquiry initially divorces an event from the moment of its occurrence. For instance, topical questions might be, "Did you ever talk to the manager about the sparks coming from the sink?" or "Did your company suffer any losses as a result of your supplier's failure to send the explosives?" If a witness answers either question affirmatively, one may then expand the story by uncovering the specific event or events giving rise to the response. For example, if the witness responds that losses did occur, one may then ask the witness to identify specific incidents of loss.

That one may expand a story with questions about events or topics illustrates that an essential purpose of theory development questioning is to stimulate a witness' memory as fully as possible. It really does not matter whether one defines the subject matter of a question as a "topic" or an "event." What is important to recognize

1. See Chapter 4, pp. 50–52.

is that witnesses' memory cells may be activated in different ways, and that one may come at the same subject from different directions.

For example, if Chross wanted to ask Officer Downe about statements made to the officer about the age of the driver of the white car, Chross might ask,

> (a) A topically-focused question: "Did you ever speak to anyone about the approximate age of the driver of the white car?";

or

> (b) An event-focused question: "When you talked to Mrs. Schwartz, did she say anything about the age of the person driving the white car?"

In the abstract, neither question is superior to the other. Witnesses respond differently to different questions, at different times. The event question places the officer at a specific moment in time and asks whether a particular subject arose during that moment. The topical question mentions a particular subject and asks whether it ever occurred. Many times, of course, both types of inquiry are needed to uncover all pertinent events and thus ultimately to elicit details.

4. PROBING STORIES FOR DETAIL

Uncovering additional events aside, the bulk of theory development consists of asking witnesses to elaborate portions of their stories. Obviously, one does not probe every event a witness mentions. Instead, one selects for elaboration those events which seem most important in light of the parties' theories.

Details, as you know, are the veritable lifeblood of persuasive stories.[2] Details transform lackluster statements such as, "They conspired to fix prices." into a story that portrays, for example, three men from Rapacious Steel Co. meeting in a room with two women from Stealing Steel Co. and discussing half-inch and three-quarter inch rebar. One Rapacious representative, Vice-President Alloy, states that Rapacious desires to have the lowest rational prices for rebar in the San Francisco Bay Area. A Stealing representative, Vice-President Ingot, replies that Stealing will consider the proposal if it can set the lowest rational prices in the St. Louis market.[3] These kinds of details make clearer exactly what happened because they present specific evidence rather than conclusions. Moreover, the details make the story vivid; they allow the factfinder to visualize the

2. See Chapter 2, p. 12; Chapter 8, pp. 141–142.

3. For those who believe this sort of dealing to be entirely apocryphal, see "American Air, Its President Get Trust Suit Voided," The Wall Street Journal, September 14, 1983, page 2; "Baxter's Suspicions of Price Fixing," The Wall Street Journal, February 25, 1983, p. 25.

actual events. Hence, details provide specific evidence and make stories credible and persuasive.

a. Areas to Probe

Depending upon the parties' theories and the events in a witness' time line, one decides which portions of a witness' story to probe for detail. It is rare that a witness describes any event in so much detail that no probing is needed. More than rare, substantial detail might be a sign of falsity. Spontaneously, a witness in a medical malpractice case may say, "She examined him on the 24th of August in her office. She had him remove his shirt, and under a lamp she checked the lump on his shoulder. She said that it was probably a simple cyst and that it should come off." If a witness adds to this description a plethora of details such as the instruments the doctor used, statements the doctor did *not* make, and the signing of a consent form, one may well wonder whether one is hearing a story or a script. Hence, for reason of too little or too much detail, any event in a witness' story that touches upon a relevant theory may be an area ripe for probing.

In addition, one must be particularly sensitive to the need to probe various forms of conclusions. Conclusions often appear to provide facts. But if they do so, it is only by way of a listener filling in missing details on his or her own.[1] A statement that an incident occurred at an "intersection" appears to supply a fact until one recognizes how many kinds of intersections there are. Upon closer questioning, the details often do not support the initial mental image one has formed. Therefore, one must develop the ability to recognize conclusions and probe them. Examine briefly typical types of conclusions.

One type of conclusion consists of statements relating to conditions or behaviors that persist over a period of time. "He was in terrible pain for at least a year." "She was always coming home very late." "He usually was the one who had to discipline the children." "The lots were subject to slides." Typically, there are events underlying these conclusions. For example, undoubtedly there were specific moments when the first chap felt terrible pain and when the last person noticed the condition of the lots. But their statements lump events into conclusions.

Conversations are frequently described in conclusionary terms. "They agreed to ship 5000 pounds of aluminum billets f.o.b. our plant." "She was yelling and screaming." "We spoke three or four times about it, and he finally said we could keep the dog." While

4. See P. Bergman, *Trial Advocacy in a Nutshell*, 47–51 (1979); D. Binder and S. Price, *Legal Interviewing and Counseling*, 45–46, 49–50 (1977).

each of these statements conveys some information, not one contains a single detail as to what somebody actually said.

There are, of course, non-conversation conclusions as well. "I got a good look at the robber." "I was skydiving very carefully." "She was stewed to the gills."

Lastly, an area that resembles conclusions, but is perhaps analytically different, may be termed "clumped events." Witnesses often combine what in reality is a series of occurrences into a single clumped event. "Our union negotiated with management vigorously over the contracting-out provisions." "We put together a group of 10 investors." "She was taught martial arts." Though each statement seemingly conveys a single happening, a witness is actually describing a series of events.

Whatever the type of conclusion, one must be aware that a witness has conveyed only potential information. The techniques discussed later in the chapter will aid one's ability to probe for detail. However, those techniques will be of no avail unless one is alert to conclusions.

Finally, note that expanding stories by adding events, eliciting details and piercing conclusions encompasses almost all the kinds of probing one typically engages in during theory development. For example, one is typically advised to inquire into foundational elements required by various rules of evidence. Thus, if a witness reports that a bystander to a collision stated, "My word! The guy on the unicycle was doing at least 90!," one should inquire into the requirements for a spontaneous exclamation. In doing so, of course, one merely probes for the events and additional details surrounding the making of the statement, albeit events and details required by a rule of law. Similarly, if one must show that a hearsay declarant is "unavailable," the inquiry is a probe into the conclusion, "He's not around."

b. Risks of Probing

Probing for details is not without its potential risks. For one thing, such probing may damage rapport. If thorough questioning is unfamiliar to novice lawyers, it is equally so to witnesses unfamiliar with lawyers' thirst for detail. To such witnesses, theory development questions may seem unfriendly and convey distrust. However, it is usually much more important to get details than to be put at the head of a witness' party invitation list. If one is ultimately forced to choose between detail and rapport, scrap the latter almost every time. If one senses that the rapport loss may be so great that a witness will become uncooperative, one may attempt to deal with the problem through the motivational techniques suggested earlier.

At the other end of the scale, probes for detail may produce too much recollection. When subjected to probes for specifics, some witnesses feel they *ought* to be able to remember everything. In order to satisfy the attorney and build their own egos, these witnesses "remember" details they feel they should recall even if their memories are blank. Again, this risk does not outweigh one's need for detail. After all, even a single open question such as "What happened?" may produce a mass of fictional detail. Probing questions may occasionally stimulate a witness' inventiveness, but without them one is unlikely to unearth evidentiary detail and build credible stories.

5. TECHNIQUES FOR EXPANDING STORIES

A litigator's appetite for detail has not, of course, been lost on generations of advice-givers. Novice interviewers are frequently advised to "get details," or "find out everything a witness knows." This advice and best intentions notwithstanding, novice lawyers nonetheless frequently complain that their interviews overlook what in retrospect are important details. One reason for the complaint undoubtedly is that pursuit of detail requires mental discipline and learned techniques. A general bromide such as "get details" is no more helpful to a beginning interviewer than the advice "just move your arms and legs" is to a would-be swimmer.

Perhaps another reason for overlooking details is that it seems socially impolite to press people for information. For most people, the experience of purposefully and methodically extracting from witnesses a great deal of detail is brand new. It does not occur in normal conversation and therefore does not come naturally. But whatever the reasons for the failure, the probing techniques to be discussed may help one to overcome them.

Our discussion is necessarily incomplete. It focuses only on major methods of oral interrogation that stimulate memory. There are certainly other stimulation techniques which do not relate to the questions one asks. For example, interviewing witnesses together,[5] taking them to the scene of events, and hypnotizing them[6] are other ways of expanding stories. However, our focus here is on fundamental questioning techniques.

5. R. Keeton, *Trial Tactics and Methods* § 9.16 (2d ed. 1973). But see, F. Bailey and H. Rothblatt, *Fundamentals of Criminal Advocacy*, § 108 (1974).

6. Note, however, that in some jurisdictions a witness may not be allowed to testify after he or she has undergone hypnosis for the purpose of restoring memory of the events in issue. See, e.g., People v. Shirley, 31 Cal.3d 18, 181 Cal. Rptr. 243, 641 P.2d 775 (1982).

a. Techniques for Uncovering Additional Events

There are a number of methods of uncovering those events which a witness does not spontaneously mention during the time line stage. Two methods, already described in Chapter 14, are questions drawn from (1) "prior knowledge" and (2) "normal course of events." From reports and discussions with other witnesses, one may know of events of which a witness may be aware. If a witness has not mentioned such an event, one may ask the witness about it in relatively open fashion ("Can you tell me anything about a tow truck that came on the scene?") or perhaps with a more leading question ("Now, a tow truck arrived after you did but before you got the driver out of the car, is that right?") When mentioning an event from prior knowledge, one may even include the source of the knowledge. "According to Elliott Millstone, a tow truck came on the scene just after you did. Is that about right?" If Millstone is the noted town drunk, mention of the source may accomplish little. On the other hand, if the witness perceives the source as authoritative, mention of the source may well bias the response. A witness will be more likely to agree with an authoritative source if the witness' actual recollection is dim.

When one attempts to uncover occurrences by using "normal course" events, again there is no single form of question that is always proper. Thus, depending on the circumstances, one can use open questions ("Can you tell me about any street measurements you took?"); narrow questions, ("Did you take street measurements?"); or leading questions ("I take it you took street measurements?").[7]

A third method of uncovering additional events is to question according to *topics* which one's preparation suggests are important. Topical inquiries are useful when one seeks to uncover additional events supporting a particular theory.

A topical question is typically put to witnesses in the form of "Did you ever . . . " For example, Officer Downe might have been asked, "Did you ever investigate body work done by local auto body shops after the collision?" In an anti-trust case, a witness may be asked, "Did Bailey and Barnum ever discuss the price of the elephants?" If a witness responds affirmatively, one may then ask about the event(s) to which the topic is related. For instance, one may ask the Barnum and Bailey witness, "Can you tell me when they discussed the price of elephants?" According to one's preference, one may seek to learn of all events relating to discussion of the price of elephants before inquiring into the details of any single event or seek details of an event as soon as a witness mentions it.

Regardless of whether a topical question elicits mention of an event, it is important *not* to regard a witness' response as final. The

7. See Chapter 14, note 8.

human mind is not yet like a computer. In response to a "Did you ever" type question, a witness is unable to systematically search through all relevant time periods and spit out each instance in which the topic arose. In the "Barnum and Bailey" example, perhaps the witness was present at many discussions between Barnum and Bailey. If the witness were asked only, "Did they ever discuss the price of the elephants?" probably the witness would be unable to think through each discussion separately, searching for mention of elephant prices. More likely, the witness will consider the question in some quite unfocused way and respond affirmatively only if for some reason one or two such conversations stick out in the witness' mind. Hence, if one wants to be thorough, one should follow a "did you ever" question by mentioning known events from the witness' time line where the topic might have arisen. "Earlier you mentioned a discussion between Bailey and Barnum in a tent. Was there any mention of the price of elephants during that discussion?" "How about a week later when they were leaving the ring, any mention of it then?" A witness who is unable in the abstract to recall an event, or to recall no more than one or two, may recollect more fully in the context of previously described events.

Finally, that favorite question of the two year old,—"Why?"—is also useful. With our strong belief in cause-and-effect we often perceive of one event as caused by or causing other events. Yet, the "related" event may lie dormant until uncovered by a "why" inquiry. For example, returning to Barnum and Bailey, the witness may state that the topic of elephant prices arose when they were all shopping for peanuts. By asking the witness "why" the topic arose at that time, one may uncover significant additional events.

b. Techniques For Eliciting Details: T-Funnels

Assume now that whether an event was included in a witness' time line story, or whether it was uncovered through subsequent questioning, one decides that it relates to one or more theories and that therefore more details about it are needed. This section focuses on techniques for uncovering details. However, please do not assume that it is either realistic or desirable to try to flush out all possible events before inquiring into details. Interviews are too complex and rich in interaction to structure and compartmentalize totally. Initially, obtaining a time line prior to probing for detail is useful, and depending upon the nature and extent of an initial story one *may* seek to expand the time line horizontally before probing for detail. Beyond that, however, order is a phantom goal. One may well uncover additional events while discussing details. Pursuing the details of the latest events, one may either stumble upon or consciously decide to pursue more events. It is impossible to describe completely in words the dynamics of interviewing. We ask only that you not be intimidated by the orderliness with which written words tend to cloak descriptions into believing that the description mandates a sequence to be enforced in actual interviews.

How, though, does one go about probing events for detail? One might, of course, ask in random fashion as many questions as one can think of that seem important. Usually, however, a technique which has been described as resembling a "T-funnel" [8] will be more effective. The term "T-funnel" refers not to tornadoes but to an orderly process of dissecting events. One begins probing by asking witnesses to recall as much about an event on their own as they can. This is the horizontal portion of the "T", and it is normally accomplished through a series of open questions. For example, assume that Officer Downe has told Chross about a conversation with witness Mrs. Schwartz but as yet has told Chross few details of what was said. To probe this event, Chross might begin by asking, "Tell me please about your conversation with Mrs. Schwartz."

In response, Officer Downe will probably mention a number of topics; for example, the officer might mention how the accident occurred, when the white car left and what the driver looked like. However, before exploring those topics, *or* asking specific questions about the original topic (the conversation with Mrs. Schwartz), one should tarry awhile on the upper bar of the "T". Encourage a witness to recall more on his or her own before suggesting additional potential topics. "What else did you talk about?" "O.K., what else can you remember?"

When a witness' independent recollection of an event is exhausted, one moves to the lower portion of the "T". Based on theories that seem connected to an event, one searches for additional, specific items of evidence that may be part of the event. At this point, one's role in the interview becomes more active. From the possible additional evidence listed during preparation, which items might have occurred during the event that might establish those theories? Such considerations are the foundation for the questions one asks in the lower part of the "T".

The preference for first encouraging witnesses to recall as much as they can about an event free from specific probing questions is based on a number of factors. First, the T-funnel method tends to be efficient. A few open questions usually produce information more quickly than numerous narrower ones. Even witnesses who switch topics as quickly as hummingbirds change direction are often responsive to open questions when their attention is focused on a discrete

8. See D. Binder and S. Price, note 4 supra, at 92–99.

event. Second, it often facilitates rapport. Although one controls the agenda by selecting an event that is important in light of the parties' theories, one shows interest in a witness' own version of the event. Third, just as with open questions in the time line, the T-funnel method may elicit information a witness would be inclined to slant or withhold if asked a more specific question. Finally, if one takes upon oneself the onus of inquiring into all potential details connected with an event, one is more likely to overlook certain details. Life is sufficiently complex that one can never think of all the factual possibilities. Therefore, to maximize the chances of getting all details, first use several open questions; let witnesses work at exhausting their recall.

Because of the benefits of the "witnesses first" approach, one should not automatically accept a witness' first pleas of "that's about all I can remember." If one believes that a witness has been lazy in thinking through a response, or has consciously or subconsciously failed to provide some details, one should press the witness for additional revelations. There are, of course, traditional forms of pressure: the bright light in a witness' eyes, or repeated playing of the last act of "Tosca." However, those methods have largely given way to more subtle conversational gambits employing motivational statements. For example, recall that a witness' memory is often stimulated if the witness can mentally return to an event, and picture the event in progress. "There you are; you're alone on the raft, about 5 feet away from Killer Falls. What else can you remember?" Or, one may empathize with a witness' difficulty and then state reasons why the witness should disclose everything. For example, if one is taking the deposition of an adverse party, one might state, "I know it is difficult to remember everything that happened at that meeting three years ago. But this is the time to remember everything you can, for if later you go into court and add additional details, I will be able to comment on your failure to remember them during your deposition." In addition to tugging at a witness' memory, such a comment also tends to discomfit opposing counsel, who has often cautioned the witness to "say nothing unless you're specifically asked." [9]

While figuratively in the upper part of the "T", seeking all a witness can recall through open questions, one may sound a bit like a metronome if one does little except to repeat, "Anything else you can remember?" Vary the pattern: use active listening; praise the witness' recall ability; perhaps summarize details the witness has previ-

9. For examples of such instructions to witnesses, see, R. Haydock, and D. Herr, *Discovery: Theory, Practice and Problems* p. 381 (1983); J. Kelner and F. McGovern, *Successful Litigation Tech-* *niques*, Student Edition, § 509 (1981); G. Kornblum, "The Oral Civil Deposition: Preparation and Examination of Witnesses" 17 The Practical Lawyer 11, May 1971.

ously given. Even such simple gestures help to convert an interview from an interrogation into a two-way conversation.

Moving to the lower portion of the "T", one typically asks narrow questions which emanate from specific evidence one seeks. The narrow questions are often of the "Did x happen?" variety. For example, assume witness Fats Gram joined the later defunct "Inch a Day Health Spa" and is interviewed by deputy county attorney Steve Ellis in connection with possible fraudulent conduct of the health spa operators. Assume further that two theories being pursued by Ellis are that the health spa employees misrepresented the availability of (1) medical supervision and (2) other health spa locations. In the interview, Ellis has completed the horizontal part of the "T" by asking Gram to recall everything he can about his initial membership discussion with two Spa employees. Assuming Gram did not mention the topics of medical supervision and other locations at that time, questions in the lower portion of the "T" derived from Ellis' theories might be, "Did they tell you anything about medical supervision?" "Did they mention how many locations they would have?"

After one's supply of potential additional topics has been exhausted, one may then pursue any topic mentioned by the witness for further details. To do so, one employs the identical T-funnel format. That is, one begins with open questions which seek a witness' spontaneous recall, and then shifts to narrow questions to search for evidence in support of particular theories.

Thus, in the health spa example above, suppose that all topics that arose during the initial membership meeting have been exhausted and that Gram has stated that the employees did mention other locations. Since this topic is important, Ellis may then ask Gram to "Tell me all you can about what they said about other locations." After Gram's independent recollection is exhausted, Ellis may follow up with narrow questions searching for specific details about what was said about other locations. In turn, when this inquiry is completed, Ellis might then apply the T-funnel to other details Gram recalled: "What did they say about the Rats Alley location?" In this manner, the formation of T-funnels may continue ad infinitum, or to Judgment Day, whichever comes first. As one parses an event, every new detail a witness mentions is a potential candidate for T-funnel treatment. However, in the context of actual interviews, one need not worry about approaching infinity. There is no need to extend the technique beyond its limit of usefulness.

Due to the great disparities in witnesses and factual situations, one may at times be unable to adhere strictly to the T-funnel format. But do not be beguiled into believing that because total organization is impossible, lack of organization is desirable. That interviews are somewhat unpredictable furthers the need for an organized approach.

At least, one then can make conscious choices about deviating from one's plans.

In at least one respect, however, one should not stray from the suggested format. After one has asked an initial open question or two and gotten some information in return, one often is tempted to explore bits of that information before journeying all the way through a funnel. In other words, before completing the open search for all relevant topics, one may be tempted to probe in depth one or two topics a witness initially mentions. In principle, there is nothing wrong with this procedure. But in actual interviews, if one quickly abandons the initial topic in favor of newly mentioned ones, a return passage to the initial topic is often difficult. Enmeshed in a new topic, one forgets to return to the abandoned topic. Hence, for the sake of thoroughness try to finish one topic before moving to another.

Use of complete T-funnels is debatable when exploring events favorable to an adversary. Of course, uncovering such events is part and parcel of theory development. And one may use the upper part of the "T" to learn whatever details of an event a witness can remember on her or his own. After all, the adversary will be likely to learn of those details too. But should one engage in the memory-stimulation questioning in the lower portion of the "T"? Lower-T questioning may suggest unfavorable evidentiary possibilities, and perhaps carry one beyond a proper adversarial role. Once the upper part of the "T" is concluded, one may instead test credibility or probe for rebuttal, as described in sections (6) and (7), infra.

Though the "T-funnel" has gained fame primarily as a method of probing for detail, note that its format may also be used to uncover additional events. If one believes there are events which a witness has not mentioned, one may attempt to uncover them with an open inquiry: "Between the first and second meetings, did anything else happen?" If that inquiry proves fruitless, one may search for specific potential events: "Did you meet with Johnson?" "Did you talk to anyone at the bank?"

c. Techniques for Piercing Conclusions

As noted earlier, conclusions often masquerade as evidence. In general, how one pierces conclusions to arrive at evidentiary detail depends upon whether a conclusion relates to a single event or to more than one event.

If a conclusion relates to a single event, one pierces it through T-funnel questioning. "She agreed to fix the plumbing." "He was furious." Assume, as is typically the case, that a witness makes these remarks with reference to a particular event. One then asks open questions of the "Tell me more" variety to exhaust the witness' recollection of the event, and if required follows them up with specific questions based on relevant theories. For example, after a witness states, "She agreed to fix the plumbing," one may ask, "Can you please tell me as accurately as you can what each of you said during that conversation." If after a few open questions the witness' recall seems exhausted, one then slides to the vertical portion of the "T": "Did she say anything about putting handles on the faucets?"

But when a conclusion appears to be drawn from more than one event, as is the case with clumped events or conditions over time, one typically attempts to break the conclusion into its constituent events before pressing for detail. For instance, assume that in an action for rescission of the purchase of a dog food plant, a witness during the time line stage had stated, "We inspected the plant before we made an offer." This assertion appears to be a clumped event. The inspection probably took a lengthy period of time, covered a variety of physical locations, perhaps included different people, and may well have taken place on more than one day. In such a circumstance, one probably first wants to develop a mini-time line of events constituting the inspection, and then subject important events to T-funnel questioning.

On other occasions, a witness' conclusion may relate to conditions over time. "Gillig is a wonderful mother." "Palm was in pain for at least a year after the accident." With such statements, one may be unable to secure a time line of individual events. Often the events that produce such conclusions are so numerous and routine that witnesses cannot possibly remember them individually. However, if the conclusions are accurate, witnesses ought to be able to support them with some specific examples. Hence, to pierce such conclusions one searches for supporting examples. "Can you recall any specific instances when Palm was in pain?" The witness may state, "I remember he was in pain when we drove to Phoenix and when he had to sit down all day at a seminar." But whether or not the witness recalls one or more examples, to be thorough, one may want to search for other instances in much the same manner as one follows up topical "did you ever" questions. Thus, one might want to ask the pain witness if he or she can recall specific examples in connection with various incidents in the witness' time line. "Can you think of any instances around the time Palm came home from the hospital?" Of course, for each incident the witness can recall, one will want to locate it as accurately as possible along the time line. "Okay, the time he had trouble lifting the shopping bag, was that before or after the Saturday you took him to have his car repaired?" Finally, as to any specific event, one may want to flush out the details as one would with any other event.

6. TESTING CREDIBILITY

Given the infinite variety of events and evidentiary details that may arise in connection with lawsuits and the only slightly less infinite theories that may apply to those events and details, there exist few "standard" specific inquiries that one makes when expanding stories. But an exception concerns credibility. Because credibility issues arise repeatedly, and because the credibility factors themselves are perhaps somewhat finite in number, some description of routine inquiries into credibility is possible. Whether the purpose of an inquiry is to buttress or to undermine a witness' credibility, the credibility probes discussed below are usually in order.

At some point during many interviews, one inquires into a witness' personal background. Personal background may relate to credibility either because something in the background gives a witness expertise in a particular relevant subject or because it may affect a listener's perceptions of a witness. In the former situation, witnesses are likely to be cooperative since the purpose of the inquiry is relatively clear. But in the latter, one may appear to be snooping. A witness' reaction may be along these lines: "I just happen to see a robbery, and now this xxxxx wants to know where I've lived for the last ten years. Forget this!" If a witness is likely to recoil from personal background questions, the motivational factors discussed earlier need to be brought into play.

Another typical focus is on a witness' perceptual abilities. As mentioned earlier, witnesses are not like cameras, able to depict accurately any event. Instead, witnesses' perceptual abilities are affected by a variety of factors, both within the observer and in the environment. Typical of the factors are the following:

(a) *Physical Setting:* How close to the event was the witness? What were the lighting and noise conditions? Did anything obstruct the witness' vision?

(b) *Attentiveness:* Was the witness paying attention to an event, or was the witness' attention on other things going on in the vicinity?

(c) *Physical and Mental Condition:* Did the witness trip over the coatstand on the way into the office? Can the witness hear what you say? Was the witness intoxicated or under stress while an event was occurring? Is the witness' perception clouded by bias or prejudice?[10]

These are but a few of the physical, psychological and physiological factors that impair witnesses' abilities to observe objectively. Be-

---

10. A classic list of factors that may cloud perceptual ability is found in F. Wellman, *The Art of Cross-Examina-* *tion,* Ch. 8 (4th ed. 1936). See also D. Binder and S. Price, note 4 supra at 48–52.

cause many of these factors operate on the subconscious level, one cannot expect open questions such as "Please describe the scene for me" to prompt complete responses. Typically, one must use narrow questions to probe fully perceptual factors such as those described above.

A third type of credibility test relies upon that familiar question, "Why?" Just as we tend to be impressed when witnesses state why events occurred, so are we when they state why they are able to recall events. A plausible causal relationship helps to convince one that a story is accurate. Hence, a standard credibility test is to inquire if there is any particular reason why a witness can recall an event or detail. Here, because of the variety of potential reasons, one may be confined to open questions. The "why" may be a personal birthday or anniversary, Vasco de Gama's birthday, or the fact that it was the first or the hundredth time the witness had seen such an event. Beyond the most obvious "why's", one may have difficulty framing narrow questions.

Fourth, one may test a witness' conduct in the light of common experience. Was the witness' behavior consistent with what the witness claims to have seen or heard? What did the witness do after the event was concluded? Here a T-funnel approach may be helpful. After the witness responds to the open questions, one can ask about possible behaviors that would be consistent with having seen or heard the reported fact. For example, if the witness saw a crime, did the witness call the police?

Fifth, one may inquire into other statements a witness may have made concerning an event. Has a witness discussed it with someone else, be it opposing counsel or a personal friend? Has the witness made any written statements? If so, one can perhaps check for any variations between the witness' current version of events and earlier ones.

During interviews one will often encounter facts which seemingly detract from a witness' credibility. For example, an aspect of a witness' behavior may appear implausible, or a witness' current account may in some respects conflict with an earlier one. Recall that if a helpful story lacks credibility, one is apt to despair; if the story is harmful, one tends to gloat. However, both reactions are mistaken, or at least premature. Regardless of whether a witness helps or hurts one's client, one probes for possible explanations of the apparent implausibility or inconsistency. Perhaps a witness can explain it away: "You asked me how I could see the robber's face while hiding behind the bench. I could see it reflected in the window behind me." Or, perhaps the apparent implausibility is simply a result of faulty communication: "I did tell the defense attorney I couldn't see the robber's face. But I thought she was talking about before the gunshot." A credibility test is not complete without a search for explanations of possible implausibilities.

Unfortunately, we cannot state with any confidence how often or as to which parts of stories one should probe for credibility. One should remember, however, that credibility may have a "spillover" effect. That is, if one part of a story is believed to be particularly credible or implausible, that conclusion may color other portions of the story. Hence, one typically does not probe the credibility of everything a witness says. But just where the probes end must be left to one's individual judgment.

7. PROBING FOR REBUTTAL

Probing for rebuttal evidence is, of course, also a routine part of theory development questioning. In the outline system, one outline is devoted to potential evidence which might rebut the adversary's affirmative evidence. During preparation for an interview, one reviews that outline and develops questions which seek out rebuttal.

However, what may be less apparent is that one may also ask questions with respect to the adversary's rebuttal of one's own affirmative evidence. Beyond mentioning earlier that one may well have to reveal affirmative evidence to learn of rebuttal,[11] the text has paid little attention to the subject of how one thinks through an adversary's potential rebuttal. For example, while one records the adversary's existing rebuttal and one's own potential rebuttal in different outlines, one does not usually consider an adversary's *potential* rebuttal. Nevertheless, during theory development one may want to inquire into that latter subject.

To do so, one may explore both "denial" and "admit and explain." For example, in *Phillips v. Landview*, assume that one piece of affirmative evidence for the Phillipses is that, "Lotz was aware that there were caissons installed on other lots prior to the Phillipses' purchase." Mason, attorney for the Phillipses, may ascertain whether Lotz admits to the knowledge: "You knew in July that caissons had been installed on other lots, correct?"

Even if Lotz admits that he knew, this response does not end Mason's search for rebuttal. Lotz's admission furnishes evidence that he knew the Phillipses' lots might be subject to slides only through the operation of an underlying premise(s). From Mason's standpoint, the operative premises might be something like the following: "Real estate salespeople who know that caissons have been installed in one area of a tract usually are aware that that area is subject to slides." And, "Real estate people who are aware that one area of a tract is subject to slides usually are aware that other areas of the tract are

11. See Chapter 7, pp. 123–126.

also likely to be subject to slides." However, Lotz may have an explanation that constitutes an exception to these generalizations. Hence, to learn of a possible explanation, Mason should *juxtapose the evidence with the conclusion:* "How could you have been aware of caissons on lots 20 and 84 without being aware of possible slide conditions on lots 70 and 71?" If Lotz does have an explanation, such a question should ferret it out.

Note that one may seek rebuttal from witnesses who do not have first-hand knowledge. In the above example, assume Mason were questioning Lade, Landview's Vice President, about Lotz's knowledge. In the denial category, Mason might ask Lade, "Do you have any information which might suggest that Lotz was not aware that caissons had been installed on lots 20 and 84?" And in the explanation category, Mason might ask, "How could Lotz have been aware of those caissons yet have been unaware that lots 70 and 71 were subject to slides?" Though the question clearly "calls for speculation," it is calculated to lead to the discovery of admissible evidence, and hence proper.

When searching for explanations, one might use the T-funnel approach. If a witness cannot think of an explanation, one could theoretically suggest a few. But perhaps at this point, one would again do well to recall that ours is an adversary system. Suggesting a bevy of possible explanations to adversary witnesses perhaps goes beyond one's goal of learning the evidence that might be produced at trial.

8. TAKING NOTES

The notes one takes during theory development are likely to be far more extensive than those taken during the time line stage. After all, during theory development one typically unearths a plethora of details, and the details are likely to be important because they are tied to theories that seem critical.

Nevertheless, one need not bury one's head in a legal pad. One may take extensive notes while maintaining eye contact and a conversational attitude. Moreover, especially during theory development, the questioner typically controls the agenda and the pace of an interview. If one needs time to take proper notes, one can pause to do so. In so doing, one can explain the delay: "I'm jotting down what you told me. I want to make sure I record what you've said correctly."

Notes are important both during and after an interview. During an interview, notes call attention to events and details which merit further questioning. For example, remember that when using T-funnel questioning, one attempts to uncover all important topics which are part of an event before probing selected topics. By noting the topics as a witness mentions them one is less likely to overlook a topic. Because notes serve as helpful reminders during interviews, recording machines are not an adequate substitute for notes.

One's notes should state accurately, in a witness' own words, the events and details of the story. Take care not to submit to the tendency merely to summarize a story. To summarize is often to cast into oblivion the details that one has so carefully attempted to elicit during an interview. Hence, careful notes enable one to preserve the fruits of one's oral labors.

Usually, raw notes themselves do not suffice as a permanent record of an interview, since they typically lack organization and completeness. Hence, following an interview one usually prepares a "Memo to File," which sets out a witness' story in some complete and sensible fashion. How quickly should one prepare a Memo to File following an interview? That will of course vary according to one's schedule and the complexity of a story. However, as the chart below suggests, one's memory of a story diminishes rapidly with time:

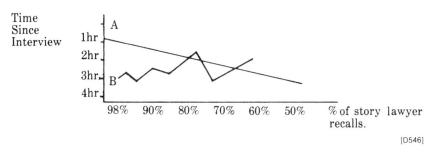

[D546]

Line "A" clearly demonstrates that one's memory diminishes over time. Line "B" depicts seasonal variations in Columbia's coffee crop, and is not important to readers of this book.

Among other things, a "Memo to File" enables one to review a witness' story, and subsequently a memo may be given to the witness to help prepare the witness to testify.[12] Additionally, the notes serve as the source of data that is transferred to appropriate outlines. Thus, by taking proper interview notes, one extends the life of details through an entire case.

9.   FROM THEORIES TO DETAILS

As to any individual witness, the questioning techniques in this chapter essentially complete the investigatory analysis that began

12. Since the memo will have refreshed the witness' recollection, opposing counsel may be entitled to have access to the memo if the court in its discretion determines it is necessary in the interests of justice. See Fed.Rules of Evid., Rule 612.

with the formation of legal theories stated in factual terms. To demonstrate how that analysis ultimately leads to many of the questions one asks, this section traces selected theory development questions to their sources, two legal theories drawn from *Phillips v. Landview*.

In that case, one of Mason's legal theories on behalf of the Phillipses is that Landview induced them to purchase by fraudulently misrepresenting a material fact—that a recreation center would be built in Campion Hills within 18 months. One element of that legal theory, stated in factual terms, is, "Prior to selling lots 70 and 71 to the Phillipses, Landview represented that a recreation center would be built in Campion Hills within 18 months." Mason would include this element in the outline of the Phillipses' potential additional evidence. Assume that through the use of historical reconstruction, Mason has listed the following in his outline of potential additional evidence for that element:

1. Scale model of the recreation center was in the sales office.
2. Site of recreation center was staked out, graded, posted or otherwise identifiable.
3. Other potential purchasers were told about the recreation center.
4. Landview had contacted a financial institution to secure money to build the center.
5. Landview had gotten a building permit for the center.
6. Landview had contacted architects, general contractors or others for bids on the design and construction of the center.
7. Brochures contained drawing or verbal description of center.
8. Salespeople in addition to Lotz stated to prospective purchasers that a center would be built in 18 months.

A second legal theory of Mason's is that Landview fraudulently failed to disclose to the Phillipses that lots 70 and 71 were subject to slides. One element of that legal theory, again stated in factual terms, is that "Lots 70 and 71 were subject to slide at the time of the Phillipses' purchase." After talking with Doug Under, an expert in soil engineering, Mason has included the following indicia of land subject to slide in his Outline of Potential Affirmative Evidence for this element [13]:

1. Settlement of portions of roadways.
2. Bulges on portions of roadway.
3. Broken pipes.

13. See *Landslides: Analysis and Control*, Special Report 176, National Academy of Sciences (1978), p. 71 (edited by R. Schuster and R. Krizek).

4. Broken power lines.

5. Minor Scarps—soil slippages confined to limited areas.

Aided by these two portions of the Outline, Mason has made a few notes in preparation for an informal interview of Bernard Sydney, who purchased a lot in Campion Hills from Landview about two weeks after the Phillipses. With respect to the theory concerning a recreation center misrepresentation, Mason has made in part the following notes:

(a) Model of recreation center

(b) Sites staked or graded

(c) Statements by Landview about recreation center

    1. had financing

    2. had building permit

    3. had contractor

(d) Brochures

With respect to the theory that lots 70 and 71 were subject to slide, Mason has made in part these notes:

(a) Roadway conditions—settlement or bulges

(b) Broken pipes or power lines

(c) Scarps

(d) Statements by Landview concerning previous slides.

The introductory and time line portions of Mason's interview with Sydney have concluded. Here is a portion of the time line which Mason developed based on events which Sydney has mentioned:

Mid-May	**Late May**	**Early June**
Friend mentioned subdivision in Campion Hills	Set up meeting with salesperson, Terry Firma	Drove around subdivision with Firma

Mid-June	**Late June**	
On phone, salesperson Dale talked about future plans for subdivision	Drove to lots 37 and 38 and walked over them alone	

Against this background, Mason may turn to theory development questioning pursuing the above theories. Below are set out excerpts from that questioning which exemplify the techniques discussed earlier. Please note that the only purpose here is to illustrate theory development; the order of the excerpts has no particular significance.

a. *Uncovering Additional Events*

Assume that, in addition to those events described in the time line, Mason wants to learn of other possible events when the recreation center might have been mentioned. Mason has no prior knowledge of additional events, and in this excerpt he proceeds topically.

Q: Mr. Sydney, do you recall ever discussing a recreation center with a Landview representative?

A: Well, yes, that time I talked on the phone with Dale.

Q: O.K., that was in mid-June, as I recall. Any other times that you can remember?

A: Hmm—no, not right off, anyway.

Q: How about Bob Farrell and other office staff people—did you ever discuss it with them?

A: No, I'm sure I didn't.

Q: How about Paul Lade?

A: Now that you mention it, I do remember talking about it briefly with him.

Q: You're doing fine. When, approximately, was that?

A: Well, let's see. Sometime in September, about a week before I bought the lot.

Q: Did you discuss the recreation center when you set up the meeting with Terry Firma?

A: No, that was a very brief phone call.

Q: How about that time in early June, when you drove round the subdivision with Firma?

A: Yes, Firma did say something about it, as we were getting back to the sales office.

Q: How about your mid-June phone call with Dale?

A: Yes, that's right. Then too.

Q: All right, any other times you can recall?

A: No.

Q: Did you ever talk to anyone at Landview, aside from Dale, about future plans for Campion Hills?

A: No, I didn't.

In this T-funnel dialogue, Mason gives Sydney the first opportunity to recall possible events on his own. Thereafter, he suggests a variety of persons who might have mentioned the recreation center, and a variety of events spanning the time line during which the topic may have arisen, hoping to uncover additional evidence. In so doing, Mason recognizes implicitly that Sydney's mind does not work like a computer. Sydney is unlikely to be able to scan each event in his time line to determine if the topic of "recreation center" arose. Hence, Mason prompts him by mentioning events where the topic might have arisen. Finally, Mason does not confine the questioning to a single topic, the center. With his last question, Mason asks about a separate topic, "future plans." Perhaps this broader topic will ultimately lead to the recreation center.

b. *Eliciting Details*

Sydney's mid-June conversation with Dale seems rife with evidentiary possibilities:

Q: You mentioned speaking to Dale in mid-June about plans. Could you please tell me more about that conversation.

A: O.K. I remember he talked about how many people would eventually be living there, a new highway that was going to be built, and I remember something about trails for horseback riding.

Q: Can you remember anything else he talked about?

A: Hmm . . . yes, he talked about a recreation center, and the possibility that there might be a lake built in the development.

Q: You're doing fine. Anything else you can remember?

A: I don't think so.

Q: Try to think back to your conversation with Dale. You're in your office, you told me, and you're talking to Dale on the telephone. If you picture that scene, does that help you to remember anything else?

A: (A few moments pass.) I'm sorry, I'm sure there were some other things, but my mind's a blank.

Q: Well, did he say anything about a golf course?

A: That I don't remember.

Q: Anything about soil conditions?

A: I'm sure we didn't talk about that.

Q: O.K., let's go back to what Dale said about the recreation center. Please tell me about that.

A: As best as I can recall, he told me they were planning a center with a pool, a couple of tennis courts, a croquet lawn, and some barbecue areas. He said it would be a nice social center.

Q: Sounds real nice. Do you remember anything else?

A: Let's see—there was something about the design—two story, wood and brick. That's about it, I guess.

Q: Well, did Dale say anything about when the center might be built?

A: Oh yes, he said . . .

Mason, apparently a student of the suggestions in this chapter, uses a classic T-funnel approach. There are in fact three "T's": (1) the conversation as a whole, (2) the recreation center, and (3) the time for building the center. Mason does not move to the lower portion of the first "T" when Sydney's memory first falters. Instead, Mason uses, though unsuccessfully, the "mental image" device described earlier. Also, Mason asks Sydney about whether Dale spoke of soil conditions. That topic obviously relates to the theory that the land was subject to slides, and Mason therefore mentions it before turning away from the conversation as a whole—horizontal part of the "T"— to the narrower topic of the recreation center. Of course, if Mason believed that topics relating to still other theories might have cropped up in the conversation as a whole, Mason would also ask about these before moving to the narrower subject of the recreation center. Lastly, note the unbearable suspense created by our not telling what, according to Sydney, Dale said about when the center might be built.

c. *Probing Clumped Events*

As good fortune would have it, Sydney's time line also contains a clumped event. Hence, we may illustrate Mason's breaking it down into a mini-time line:

Q: Now, if I recall correctly, some time in early June you inspected the development with Firma, correct?

A: Yes, that's right.

Q: I'd appreciate it if you could think back to that inspection, and tell me step-by-step everything that occurred during the inspection.

A: Good grief! Is this necessary?

Q: Well, it may be. It's very possible that important things were talked about during the inspection, and in my experience it's easier to find out about them if we go through this part of your story slowly. Why don't you just go through it sequentially, telling me as much as you can remember.

A: Well, I was supposed to meet a salesman named Guy Lotz, but when I got there this other salesperson, Terry Firma, said Lotz was out sick but Firma could show me around. We talked for awhile in Firma's office, and then we walked to an area where there was a three dimensional layout of the subdivision. Then we drove around the perimeter of the development and returned to the office.

Q: O.K. Other than talking in Firma's office and looking over the layout, did you do anything or talk to anyone else before going for the drive?

. . .

Mason's questions would continue in this manner as Sydney describes the inspection. As is evident, the questioning pattern is the same as that followed when one develops an initial time line: open questions; chronological order; and an eschewing of immediate probes for detail.

After the mini-time line is developed, Mason may then proceed to elicit details with respect to the constituent events that seem significant. Assume now that Mason wants to learn more about one event, Sydney's and Firma's drive around the perimeter. Mason could use a T-funnel to probe this event for details as follows:

Q: Mr. Sydney, can you tell me what happened when you and Firma drove around the perimeter?

A: Not too much. He pointed out the various sections of Campion Hills, told me the price range of lots in each section, and the approximate number of lots in each area that were available.

Q: Anything else you can recall?

A: Not really. We didn't stop. The drive was only about half an hour.

Q: Was there any discussion of a recreation center at this time?

A: No, I'm sure of that.

Q: During this drive, did you happen to notice any bumps or lumps in the road?

A: No, not at that time. But I did other times, on some of the inner roads.

Q: O.K., I'll ask you about those lumps later. That's very helpful. For the moment, let's return to the perimeter drive. Did you happen to notice anything special about the power lines?

A: Can't say that I did.

Q: How about something which, since I've been handling this case, I've found out that geologists call "scarps." Do you know what a scarp is?

A: Nope—I've never heard the word.

Q: Well, a scarp is a place on a hillside where soil has slipped away and left a hollowed-out impression. Scarps can be large, or rather small. Still referring to that drive around the perimeter, did you notice any scarps?

A: Well, funny you should mention it. There was something like that, on the roadway right outside Firma's office.

Q: Can you describe this scarp for me?

. . .

Note that in this example, Mason treats the perimeter drive as a single event. Depending on a witness' ability to recall details and the kind of detail one seeks, one might of course treat the "perimeter drive" as a clumped event, and attempt to break it into still further events. Molecular scientists and computer chip manufacturers seemingly automatically strive for the smallest possible unit. However, attorneys do so only when doing so seems productive. What arguments support the notion that Mason should have broken the drive into constituent events—e.g., "driving through the west portion?"

d. Probing Conditions Over Time

Assume that in response to an earlier question, Sydney had stated that a portion of a road in Campion Hills was "always rough." Mason here probes that conclusion for details:

Q: Earlier you said that a portion of Bolas Street was always rough. Can you tell me what you mean by that?

A: Well, real lumpy—there were a lot of little lumps in the road. If you didn't go really slow, you'd shake your fillings out.

Q: Where was this part of the road?

A: I guess about fifty feet west of where Bolas intersects with Hanley Avenue.

Q: Can you tell me about a specific occasion when you remember the road was lumpy?

A: Well, one time in particular when my wife Carrie and I went to look at our lot. I guess she had never been on that piece of road before, and I remember her remarking how lumpy it was.

Q: Can you tell me a little bit more about what happened that time that you and your wife drove over that portion of the road?

A: All right. There's not much to it. Bolas Street is smooth, then there are four or five lumps in a row. The third one is the biggest, almost a foot I'd say. Bolas around there just looks all wrinkled.

Q: Do you recall anything else about that occasion?

A: Oh—I do remember Carrie saying that we should tell someone at Landview about the road. I told her that they already knew, because Dale had told me there were a couple of places where the road was like that, and that they'd be doing repair work soon.

Q: Can you please describe the lumps in a little more detail?

. . .

(Sequence of detail questions omitted)

Q: O.K., Mr. Sydney, this time you and your wife were driving on Bolas, about when was that?

A: About early September, I'd say. We'd pretty much made up our minds to buy a lot.

Q: Can you tell me about any other time that you remember noticing the lumps?

. . .

Mason's tack here is probing the "rough road" conclusion in the context of specific events. He elicits the details of a single event before inquiring about other events, though another order, such as first identifying a number of discrete events before getting details, might well be followed.

e. Testing Credibility

Recall that when Sydney described his inspection in early June, he mentioned that Firma showed him a three-dimensional layout of the subdivision. Following Sydney's helpful response, Mason tests Sydney's credibility:

Q: While you were at the layout, was there any mention of the recreation center?

A: There was. It came up sort of funny. I was on one side of the layout, and some couple was on the other side. The woman pointed to a small building on the layout and said something like, "I wonder if that's the recreation center." Firma, who was standing next to me—but you know these salespersons, they're always selling. Has that ever happened to you? One I met a few years before, walked up to me in Rome and tried to sell me some Florida swampland. Wanted me to see a film about it, eat lunch on them, even get a tour of some catacombs or something. I'll never forget it.

Q: Sometime I'd like to hear more about that—it sounds like a truly memorable experience. For the moment, you were saying a woman mentioned the recreation center?

A: Yes. Firma said, "It's just a model now, but in a year and a half that baby's going to be built. It will be a beautiful recreation center you'll be proud of."

Q: You definitely remember that statement?

A: Well, I can't swear to it word for word, but that's pretty much what Firma said.

Q: That can be pretty important, and if you'll bear with me I'd like to ask you just a few questions. Could you describe the area around the layout as it was that day for me?

A: Sure. It was nothing fancy. Just a small room off to the side of the main offices. The layout was on top of a table; it seemed like it was on a standard 4 by 8 foot sheet of plywood.

Q: Anything else you remember about the room?

A: A bunch of boxes piled up against a couple of the walls. Like I said, nothing fancy.

Q: Beside you, Firma, and this other couple, was anyone else in the room?

A: No, I don't think so.

Q: Was anything else going on while Firma was talking?

A: No, it was pretty quiet.

Q: Is there any particular reason you remember Firma making this remark about it being built in one and a half years?

A: Well, you might say so. When this woman made the remark about that little model building, I was wondering exactly the same thing myself.

Q: That's really helpful, but I'm just a bit confused. A few days ago I talked to Florence Darrow, who represents Landview in this matter. According to her, you told her investigator, Mike Hidden, that Firma never said anything to you about the recreation center. Is there an inconsistency there?

A: I don't think so. I was just trying to be cute—you attorneys don't miss a thing. Both statements are true—Firma did not make the statement *to* me. I just overheard it, as I told you.

Q: Yes, that does seem to clear things up. Now, about this other couple . . .

A: Wait. Before we get into that, how'd you like to buy a nice piece of property in Florida? . . .

In this excerpt, Mason tests Sydney's credibility immediately, in the context of Firma's significant remark. One often probes the credibility of a witness with respect to a particular event in the immediate context of that event, when it is fresh in everyone's mind. However, one may choose not to do so, if for example a witness might interpret credibility probes as a hostile act. Similarly, one often groups questions relating to a witness' general credibility (e.g. personal background) at the beginning or the end of an interview, rather than in connection with particular events.

f. Probing for Rebuttal

Sydney's testimony as to Firma's recreation center statement provides circumstantial affirmative evidence for the Phillipses that Landview represented that a recreation center would be built within 18 months. During a later deposition of Paul Lade, Landview's Vice-President, Mason may probe for rebuttal of this evidence as follows:

Q: Mr. Lade, according to a witness, a Landview salesperson, Terry Firma, told prospective purchasers in early June that the recreation center would be built in a year and a half. Have you discussed this matter with Firma?

A: I don't know that we've discussed that particular incident.

Q: So at this time you cannot deny that Firma made that statement?

A: That's true.

Q: Are you aware of any information by having been told, or perhaps seeing it in a document, suggesting that Firma did not make this statement?

A: No.

Q: Can you think of any reason why Firma might deny making the statement.

A: Well, as I've told you, at that time plans for the recreation center were very indefinite. Our entire sales staff was aware of that, and they were aware that they were to make no promises regarding it.

Q: O.K. But if Firma made this statement to one prospective purchaser, can you think of any reason other salespeople might not have similar statements to other prospective purchasers?

A: Other than the statement I have just made, no. I think it is most likely that your witness is simply mistaken.

Q: Any other reason?

A: No.

Although it is Firma's conduct which is the source of Mason's affirmative evidence, Mason here inquires into rebuttal from Lade. A potential inference Mason might seek to have a trier of fact draw is that if one salesperson makes a statement to a prospective purchaser, other salespeople may make the same statement to others. Mason searches for potential rebuttal of this inference by juxtaposing the evidence with the inferred conclusion. Mason does not, however, go so far as to suggest potential rebuttal explanations.

10. CONCLUDING STAGE

Aside from the social conventions one engages in at the conclusion of conversations, the concluding stage of interviews is a time to cement gains and make specific future plans. In terms of cementing gains, one typically considers securing a signed statement from a witness. Such a statement normally contains a narration of one or more parts of a witness' story and may also contain a declaration that it is accurate.[14]

As for the future, one wants to wrap up ends that are often left loose during interviews and make sure that helpful information is available in the event of trial. Often, witnesses say things like, "I've got that information on a piece of paper at home" and "I can get her to give you a call." Or, a witness may have information at an interview ("I've got his address and phone number in my wallet"), but at the time one did not want to interrupt the interview while the witness looked for the information.

In these sorts of situations, one gets as much specific information as possible during the concluding stage or at least makes definite arrangements to get it. Is a follow-up interview necessary? Who will perform a task, be it making a phone call, writing a letter or securing documents? By what date is it to be done? How will the other person know it has been done? Might the witness learn of information in the future which one wants to know about? What if a witness changes phone numbers or moves? Has a written summary been prepared which indicates the attorney's and the witness' respective tasks? Do not shy away from or thumb your nose at these seemingly "ministerial" details. Much important information can be lost merely because of inadequate follow-up.

Finally, it is almost always a good idea to ask an open question or two near the end of an interview. "Can you think of anything that I may have overlooked?" sometimes miraculously produces important evidence.

14. See R. Keeton, *Trial Tactics and Methods* (2d ed. 1973) § 9.13 for a discussion of the characteristics of a good written statement. See also I. Goldstein and F. Lane, *Goldstein Trial Technique* Vol. 1 §§ 2.10 and 2.11 (2nd Ed.1969); H. Bodin, *Marshalling the Evidence* 21–23 (PLI, 1966).

Chapter 16

EXPERT WITNESSES

1. INTRODUCTION

Thus far, this book has described three general areas in which one repeatedly uses expert witnesses. Experts may identify the probative worth of evidence on hand, identify investigatory hypotheses and possible additional evidence, and testify. Recall that in each of these areas, one turns to an expert because the expert has experience which non-experts do not have. For example, one may represent a contractor who has been unable to collect the remainder of a fee due for installing a brick patio. The person for whom the patio was installed claims that the work was improperly done. The contractor's story is that before installing the bricks she leveled the area to allow for a four inch drop, set the patio circumference bricks in concrete footings, laid in plastic sheeting, and watered and hand packed the sand in which the remaining bricks were set. Unless one is a brick mason, one probably would need the aid of an expert. Which parts of this story furnish evidence that the patio was properly installed? Which parts indicate the contrary? Why? What other evidence might one gather to prove the installation was proper? To answer such questions, one generally needs the training and experience that only an expert can provide.

2. SELECTING EXPERTS

a. *What Kind of Expertise is Needed*

One of the first considerations in selecting an expert is to identify the specific area of expertise required. As human culture becomes ever more complex, areas of specialization tend to become narrower and more well defined. Generic titles such as "cardiologist" and "civil engineer" often conceal a multitude of sub-specializations. Thus, while any cardiologist may technically qualify as an expert in a case involving a child born with heart problems, one is likely to obtain more pertinent experience from a pediatric cardiologist. In short, unless an expert's training and experience precisely "fit" specific issues, the expert's opinions may be of little value during investigation and at trial.

Of course, the less information one has about a general subject, the harder it becomes to define the sort of expert one needs. With familiar medical issues, honing in on a narrow speciality may be relatively simple. But what if the issues revolve around citizens' claims that airport noise unreasonably interferes with the enjoyment of their homes? What types of experts might one need—psychologists, engineers, geologists, others? And which specialists within each field should one consult? Might a lay person—say, a long term resident— qualify as an "expert" with regard to certain of the issues?

These are not easy questions, and they suggest that one often needs to do preliminary research before making a selection. To conduct this research, one might read materials relating to the broad subject matter; perhaps the materials will help one identify the specialties one needs. Consider also the specialties of the experts who have authored those materials. Appellate cases are sometimes a source. In their opinions, appellate courts often identify the kinds of experts who testified at trial.

Of course, one may supplement or supplant one's reading with a variety of personal contacts. If one personally knows someone who by training and experience is even tangentially knowledgable about a given subject matter, that person often can help identify the type of expert one requires. Other attorneys—including those whose names are listed as attorneys of record in a relevant appellate opinion—are often another fertile source of suggestions. So too are university professors. Through some combination of these sources, one can nearly always identify the type of experts with whom one should consult.

Assume that a relevant and sufficiently precise field of expertise has been identified. One's thoughts then turn to the names of experts. And as one might imagine, sources for identifying particular experts are legion. Other attorneys are perhaps the most frequent sources of recommendations. Usually one need not personally know an attorney to seek a recommendation. Most practitioners are quite willing to speak with another professional and share their knowledge about experts. Attorney organizations are a related source of recommendations. State and local bar associations and their sections often maintain lists of experts according to fields of expertise.

No less organized are the experts themselves. Nearly every field of expertise has at least one professional organization to which experts in that field belong. By contacting the national or local office of such organizations, one can usually learn of experts in one's geographical vicinity.

There are also a wide variety of proprietary consulting firms, which typically advertise their services in law journals and legal newspapers. Among the many types of consulting firms are those that provide economic testimony, do accident reconstruction, make appraisals, and relate human behavior to the design of products.

This listing only scratches the surface of sources of expert witnesses. Universities, trade associations, appellate opinions and jury verdict reporting services are among the many other possibilities.[1] Finally, if one seeks the services of a "lay" expert, who may not belong to any sort of professional organization, one may have to make a personal visit to the factory, farm, auto body shop or other colorful locale where a person with the requisite training and experience may be found.

b. Which Expert Will Wear the Glass Slipper?

Given the foregoing array of sources, locating potential experts is not often a concern. But, by contrast, locating the best possible expert is a repetitive concern. All experts in a given field are by no means fungible; two experts in the same subject matter may differ markedly in their effectiveness. Accordingly, consider some of the major criteria that account for varying degrees of effectiveness. By and large, these criteria are the same whether an expert advises an attorney during investigation or a trier of fact at trial. In both instances, there is need for an expert who can identify pertinent information and clearly explain why it supports the expert's opinion.

Perhaps the most important criterion concerns an expert's training and experience. It is largely on the basis of this background that one typically evaluates the validity of an expert's opinions. Consider why this is so.

Since experts are not usually percipient witnesses, the information they normally provide consists not of historical facts, but rather consists of opinions about evidence together with their explanations for such opinions. As you know, one typically needs such opinions and explanations because one's reservoir of common experience does not give one the knowledge to know what conclusions, if any, to draw from evidence. Accordingly, to render an intelligent judgment about

1. For a more detailed discussion of sources of expert witnesses, see, e.g., R. Kennedy, *California Expert Witness* *Guide* pp. 60–70 (CEB, 1983); 2 *Am.Jur. Trials* 293–356, also 1983 Supplement, Chapter 4.

whether an expert has drawn an accurate conclusion (utilized valid premises) one looks in large part to the expert's training and experience. If it is substantial, one is inclined to conclude that the expert has an adequate reservoir of experience upon which to base his or her opinion.

A second and related criterion is an expert's standing in the relevant community of experts. Is an expert an author, a teacher, or a member of one or more professional societies with grandiose titles such as "The National Academy of . . . ?" Has an expert garnered any titles or awards? Has an expert's work concerned matters of public interest or particular complexity? Can he or she recite the "Pledge of Allegiance" backwards? The more professional achievements an expert has, the more will one infer that an expert is particularly qualified to render an opinion.

A third criterion concerns an expert's neutrality or objectivity. Nowadays, "forensic experts" specialize in courtroom testimony. And many of these experts are oriented toward plaintiffs or defendants. For example, in large metropolitan areas it is not unusual for an association of plaintiffs' personal injury lawyers to have one list of experts, and a defendants' association to have an entirely different list. The seeming lack of neutrality typically comes out at trial during cross examination:

Q: Dr. Bryant, how many times have you testified as an expert witness?

A: 247.

Q: And on how many of those occasions have you testified on behalf of the defendant?

A: 246. Once I broke my own toe.

Thus, one must carefully evaluate an expert's objectivity. When doing so, one is in a position very similar to that of the trier of fact. If one has doubts, a factfinder is likely to share them.

A fourth criterion is an expert's ability to communicate opinions and explanations. Witnesses who cannot explain complex aspects of their speciality in ways that laypeople can understand are unlikely to be helpful.

There are of course other criteria that one considers when selecting experts. For example, demeanor is as important an aspect of an expert's credibility as it is for a lay witness. Fees too are important. However, if an expert has sufficient experience and standing, appears objective and communicates well, the expert is quite likely to be effective both during investigation and at trial.[2]

2. For a further discussion see, R. Kennedy, note 1 supra at 71–81; H. Spellman, *Direct Examination of Witnesses*, Chapter 9 (1968); R. Keeton, *Tri-*

3. TALKING TO EXPERTS DURING INVESTIGATION

a. *Organizational Considerations*

There are both differences and similarities in the way one interviews lay witnesses and experts. The general organizational format that earlier was suggested for interviewing lay witnesses depicts attorneys as somewhat passive during the time line stage, and then more active during theory development. To a large extent, this general format is reversed when one interviews an expert. Since most experts are not percipient witnesses, there is usually nothing they can tell one without knowing about issues and evidence. Hence, at the outset one is usually not concerned with developing a time line of events;[3] instead one normally needs to supply information to an expert. When this is done, the expert will then become a more active conversationalist as he or she seeks further information and begins formulating ideas.

If the overall format of an interview of an expert usually differs markedly from that of a lay witness, the introductory phase is often quite similar. Of course, one is apt to begin with an exchange of social pleasantries. Moreover, experts, like lay witnesses, generally appreciate and profit from an explanation of what will occur during an interview and what one hopes to accomplish. For example, assume that Florence Darrow, attorney for Landview, is talking to Mel Practice, a soil engineer. The following sort of explanation might be appropriate:

> As I told you on the phone when we set up this appointment, my client has been sued for fraudulently concealing the soil condition of a couple of lots in a development just outside of town. My clients are confident they have done nothing wrong. Long before they developed the land they had a soil study done which gave the development a clean bill of health. By the way, I'm happy to tell you that my client has indicated there is no problem with the fee you quoted over the phone.

> Today I'd like to tell you a little bit more about the facts of the case and some of the legal issues involved, and get your opinion on a few matters. In particular, it would be very helpful if you could tell me the significance, from your point of view, of the evidence I have so far, and if you could suggest other evidence I could look for. If you eventually conclude that the land might be subject to slides, I'll be especially interested in your views as to whether the previous soil engineering firm should have unearthed

---

al Tactics and Methods 319–322 (2nd Ed. 1973).

3. Of course, to the extent that an expert is also a percipient witness, an interview of an expert may be organized similarly to that of a layperson.

(pardon the pun, Mel) the condition and disclosed it in its report. To tell you the truth, as of now, I don't know much about soil engineering. So maybe at some point, you can suggest some reading material that would help me understand more about the specific soil condition issues we face in this case. From what you know so far, is there any particular place I should begin?

As this explanation indicates, and as is typically the case, the interview was preceded by a phone conversation in which certain details such as the nature of the case and fees were discussed. During the explanation Darrow appeals to Practice's sense of justice by suggesting that Practice is on the "right" side; Darrow explains early on that her client is innocent of any wrongdoing. Undoubtedly, Darrow hopes that the suggestion will encourage Practice to be enthusiastic and creative on her client's behalf. Finally, compare the question with which Darrow concludes the explanation with the instruction typically given to a lay witness early in an interview. One often tells a lay percipient witness to, "Start at the beginning, go step-by-step . . ." But with an expert, one wants and needs the benefit of the expert's training and experience. Hence, Darrow asks Practice if there is any particular place Darrow should begin.

Unless the expert suggests a different starting place, one usually begins with a concise and precise statement of what a case is about. One typically gives a succinct summary of the evidence and explains the legal and factual issues. Even if an expert has testified concerning the relevant issues on many occasions, it is usually important to take some time explaining the current legal standards. In particular, one may want to discuss the extent to which the legal standard differs from standards employed by those in the expert's specialty. For example, many commentators have pointed out that one of the legal tests of insanity, "ability to understand right from wrong," is not a standard that psychiatrists recognize in their professional practices.[4] Also remember, just as one encourages an expert to avoid jargon in favor of everyday terms, so too must one take care to avoid, or at least define, legalese for the expert.

To enable an expert to tailor her or his comments to specific issues, one must do more than provide the expert with an abstract soliloquy on applicable law. Recall from Chapter 5 that in the outlines one states legal theories in factual terms. So too should one convert general legal principles to factual terms when speaking with an expert. For example, Darrow might abstractly explain to Practice that a legal element involved in the *Phillips* case is whether Landview "fraudulently concealed" information from the Phillipses. But her odds of getting useful information from the expert are much greater

4. See United States v. Brawner, 471 F.2d 969 (D.C.Cir.1972); A. Brooks, *Law,* *Psychiatry and the Mental Health System* 111 (1974).

if she explains the legal element as involving "conditions that Landview probably was aware of which indicated that lots 70 and 71 were subject to slides."

Once an expert generally understands the factual and legal issues, the order, and to some degree the content of the remainder of an initial interview, will often depend in large part upon the expert's views. One usually takes up topics in the order suggested by the expert.

As to the concluding stage of an expert interview, it is likely to resemble that of a lay witness interview. Primarily, one wants to conclude with definite arrangements for the next steps that each participant will take. Also, one typically contemplates continuing contacts and exchanges of information. Thus, one may want to set up a series of future appointments as an impetus to activity.

b. Discussing Existing Evidence

When one turns to an expert's evaluation of existing evidence, one should generally provide the expert with the evidence of both parties. Suppressing unfavorable information in an effort to gain a favorable opinion is often short-sighted. An expert's opinion is no better than the information upon which it is based. If the facts on which an opinion is based are inaccurate or incomplete, so too will be the opinion. Hence, though as an advocate one will tend to emphasize favorable evidence, disclose the adversary's evidence as well. Leave it to the expert to decide which items of evidence are important.

Existing evidence may be supplied to experts in a variety of ways. One may describe it orally, send a written memorandum, or even simply dump one's complete file, outlines and all, on an expert's desk.[5] Usually, experts develop their own preferences, and one does well to follow them.

To the extent one sends an expert something less than one's entire file, one may be faced with a bit of a dilemma. On the one hand, an expert must be made aware of existing evidence pertinent to rendering an opinion. On the other hand, the reason one has come to the expert in the first place is probably that one lacks the experience to know what evidence is pertinent. Hence, by selecting evidence one runs a real risk of unintentionally omitting pertinent evidence. To overcome this risk, one may consciously send more information than one believes necessary. Alternatively, and perhaps more simply, one

---

5. For a discussion of the application of rules of confidentiality and work product as they apply to lawyer-expert communications, see R. Kennedy, note 1 supra, at 88–101, 111–117; J. Underwood, *A Guide to Federal Discovery Rules* 23–27 (ALI–ABA 1979).

seeks the expert's advice as to what sort of information would be useful.

One should be aware that the flow of information back and forth between attorney and expert raises issues of confidentiality and discoverability. We do not treat these issues in depth as they are beyond the scope of this book, and their treatment varies tremendously from one jurisdiction to another. Suffice it to say that under many circumstances, neither the attorney-client privilege nor "work product" rules will prevent an adversary's access to an expert's opinions.[6]

Once an expert has examined existing evidence and rendered an opinion, regardless of whether that opinion is favorable or unfavorable, one inquires into the foundation for the opinion. Normally, the foundation of an opinion is a focus of attention at trial, as that foundation is the sum total of the experience, training and skill that underlies the premises adopted by the expert. But during an interview, one should also inquire about evidence which detracts from an opinion, as well as evidence which supports it. By so doing, one may learn of evidence which supports one's adversary. Moreover, as one personally becomes familiar with the expert's subject matter area, one can compare the reasons the expert cites with one's own knowledge of the subject area. As a result, one can perhaps begin to evaluate more critically the accuracy of the expert's opinion.

c. Discussing Hypotheses and Potential Evidence

When interviewing an expert, one typically seeks the expert's advice with respect to investigatory hypotheses and potential additional evidence. To maximize an expert's effectiveness, one generally describes directly and precisely what information one needs and why. General inquiries such as, "In what ways might Soil Engineers have been been negligent?" often do not adequately guide an expert to factual issues in a particular case. By contrast, assume that Darrow wanted the expert soil engineer, Mel Practice, to provide some hypotheses under which Soil Engineers would be liable to Landview if the land were found to be subject to slides. In such circumstances, Darrow might express herself in a manner such as the following:

> You recall that earlier I mentioned that if the land is subject to slides, Soil Engineers might bear the ultimate responsibility if it could be shown that Soil Engineers was negligent in not discovering and reporting the condition. Although this is somewhat of an oversimplification, someone is negligent if they don't perform a task, for example examine property and prepare a report, the way people who operate in that industry normally complete such tasks. What I would like to have your help on is coming up with some theories about things that Soil Engineers might have done or

6. Ibid.

failed to do in examining the land in Campion Hills and preparing a report that would account for their failure to discover that the land was subject to slides. Also, maybe you can tell me whether any such things would have constituted, in your opinion, negligence by Soil Engineers. Can you think of anything that they might have done or failed to do that would account for their failure to report that the land was probably subject to slides?

In providing this explanation, Darrow adheres to the suggestion that legal principles not be explained merely in abstract terms. Note how she enriches the concept of negligence by providing examples of what kind of conduct might constitute negligence on Soil Engineers' part.

Darrow would use this same approach when seeking explanatory hypotheses. Assume that Practice has suggested that Soil Engineers might be considered negligent if it failed to inspect aerial maps of Campion Hills. Darrow might ask, "If Soil Engineers did fail to check aerial maps, do you have any theories about why they might have failed to do so?" By searching for hypotheses that add explanatory force to a particular descriptive theory, Darrow may get maximum use of the expert's experience.

Similarly, a specific approach is usually the most effective when one seeks potential additional evidence. Assume again that Practice mentioned that a professional inspecting soil conditions would normally inspect aerial maps of the Campion Hills area. If Darrow were seeking guidance to potential evidence showing that Soil Engineers did not make such an inspection, Darrow might inquire as follows:

You told me a few moments ago that one thing Soil Engineers might have failed to do is to look at aerial maps of the area. If they had failed to do this, what evidence could I look for that would indicate this kind of an omission? I know proving a negative is hard, but can you think of, say, things that might be missing from their files if in fact they failed to check aerial maps?

Lastly, note that one's specificity is well calculated to lead to specificity by the expert: "I think my fee in this case may be $250 an hour rather than $100."

Chapter 17

WRITTEN INTERROGATORIES

1. INTRODUCTION

This chapter explores briefly the effectiveness of written interrogatories in pursuing the major investigatory objectives described in this book. Our discussion assumes a general familiarity with interrogatories. But for those who have successfully avoided the topic until now, we mention a few basic concepts. Interrogatories are written questions served by one party to an action upon another party. Subject to appropriate objections, the questions must be answered in writing under oath. Although interrogatories can only be submitted to parties (not to individual witnesses), a party answering questions must include information known to the party's agents, including the party's attorney. Thus, if the party's attorney has gathered certain information from witnesses and a question calls for such information, the party's answer generally must disclose such information even if it is personally unknown to the party. In lawyer's parlance, answers to interrogatories must give the party's "corporate knowledge."

2. USES OF INTERROGATORIES

Interrogatories are used for a large number of purposes. Although we discuss their uses primarily in connection with the major evidentiary categories described in this text, recognize that interrogatories are often used to gather preliminary information needed to learn various parts of a story. In other words, interrogatories may be used to uncover a variety of *sources* of stories.

Among the typical preliminary "source" uses of interrogatories are the following:

a. Identifying and Locating Documents

Interrogatories are frequently used to learn of the existence, title, location and basic contents of documents. When ground through a written interrogatory machine, requests for suspected documents usually look something like this:

No. 379

Since November 1 of last year has there been in existence any written or electronic document of any type whatsoever which refers in any way to the sympathetic qualities of Marie Antoinette?

No. 380

If the answer to Interrogatory 379 is "Yes," please state for each such document:

     a.   The document's nomenclature, if any;

     b.   The date the document bears, if any;

     c.   The document's description, with sufficient clarity that it can be identified;

     d.   The name and business and residence address and telephone number of each person having custody and control of the document;

     e.   Whether you would be willing to make a copy of the document available to counsel for the Serfs without the necessity of a formal motion to produce.

b. Identifying Witnesses

One may ask whether the adversary is aware of any lay or expert witnesses [1], and seek each witness' name and other identifying data. Of course, one is also frequently interested in the information each witness may have provided to the adversary. Although in most jurisdictions the contents of statements given by witnesses to an adversary's lawyer are often protected by a qualified work product privilege, one can often learn of information revealed by such witnesses through techniques suggested later in this chapter. Interrogatories to learn the identities of witnesses are commonly phrased along the following lines:

No. 381

For each witness having any knowledge of the sympathetic qualities of Marie Antoinette, please state the witness' full name and last known business and residence address and telephone number.

---

1. See Federal Rules of Civil Procedure, Rule 26.

c. Learning Organizational Hierarchy

If an adverse party is an organization, one may send interrogatories calculated to uncover its past and present organizational hierarchy. The response may uncover potential witnesses to depose or interview, and also indicate how decisions were normally processed through the organization. Such interrogatories might be phrased as follows:

No. 13

For the period during which the "Waterproof Sponge" was developed and first marketed, did any employees, consultants, agents and/or other representatives of your company, paid or unpaid, participate in any decisions concerning the planning, development and/or marketing of new products?

No. 14

If your answer to Interrogatory No. 13 is "Yes", please state for each such employee, consultant, agent, or other representative his or her

(a) Full name and last-known business and residence address and telephone number;

(b) Current and previous positions with your company;

(c) Position(s) with your Company during the period that the "Waterproof Sponge" was developed and first marketed;

(d) Duties during the period that the Waterproof Sponge was developed and first marketed;

(e) Immediate supervisor(s) during the period the "Waterproof Sponge" was developed and first marketed, including such supervisor's name, current position and last known business and residence address and telephone number.

d. Learning A Witness' Background

As you know, background often affects the substance of a witness' evidence as well as the credibility of that evidence. Accordingly, even if one intends to depose or interview a witness, one may first send out interrogatories concerning such witness' personal and professional history.

As one might well imagine, the foregoing list is not intended to be complete but merely suggestive of the types of preliminary data one often seeks to learn.[2] Depending upon the particulars of a case, the list of preliminaries may be expanded almost without limit. For ex-

2. For a more extensive list of preliminary uses of interrogatories, see R. Haydock and D. Herr, *Discovery: Theory, Practice and Problems* § 3.2.1 (1983).

ample, in some cases the existence and extent of liability coverage may be a vitally important preliminary, yet be completely irrelevant in other cases.

The remainder of this chapter concentrates on the use of interrogatories to learn (1) an adversary's story (2) an adversary's theories (3) one's own as well as an adversary's affirmative evidence and (4) an adversary's rebuttal evidence.

3. LEARNING AN ADVERSARY'S STORY

a. *Adversary's Overall Story*

Interrogatories are a remarkably poor vehicle for discovering an adversary's overall story. There are a number of reasons why this is so. For one thing, the cry of "work product" presents a significant obstacle. Remember, a party's overall story is not merely the assemblage of all facts known to the party's witnesses. Rather, the party's attorney shapes the overall story by selecting which witnesses will testify, what portions of their stories will be included in their testimony and the emphasis given to different portions of the stories. Therefore, interrogatories seeking to learn an adversary's overall story ask in part, "Counsel, tell us how you are going to select and organize your evidence." But since one is supposed to propound interrogatories to learn facts, not an adversary's legal reasoning, interrogatories seeking counsel's ideas for presenting evidence are generally deemed an improper inquiry into work product.[3]

Even when interrogatories attempt to focus only on events and details known to the other side, rather than the story the adversary intends to tell based upon such events and details, interrogatories remain a largely ineffective discovery tool. Such an effort might be attempted through broad open questions centered on limited time periods in an overall story. "Describe all events and details which occurred between July 1 and September 30 concerning the contract." Such an interrogatory, however, would run into trouble on a number of fronts. First, it is vague, especially to a legally-trained eye and ear. After all, where does an event stop and a detail begin? Do the details include what the parties ate when they met to discuss the contract? Does the question exclude the actions of non-parties? Vague interrogatories generally meet the same fate that befalls vagueness throughout the legal system: "Objection sustained."

---

3. Although contention interrogatories, discussed *infra*, are probably an exception, in general an attorney's impressions, conclusions, opinions, legal research or theories are not discoverable. C. Wright and A. Miller, *Federal Practice and Procedure: Civil* § 2026 (1970); *California Civil Discovery Practice* § 1.47(c) (C. Brosnahan, C. Jones and J. Rantzman, eds. 1975).

Moreover, many judges and litigators would be of the opinion that to permit such questions would be tantamount to undermining traditional values perceived as inherent in the adversary system. One such value is akin to the notions of work product: each side must be responsible to prepare and present its own case without the aid of the other side. The value finds expression in the child's game of "Go Fish." Even if one is entitled to information held by an adversary, one can get it only through a proper question at the proper time. If one were able to find out the total story known to an adversary merely by asking, in essence, "What happened?", why bother to force the question at all? Surely, the logical next step would be an adversary's obligation to disgorge all events and details known to its witnesses without one having to ask for them. In view of the broad philosophy that lies behind modern discovery statutes ("eliminate surprise; obtain fullest possible knowledge" [4]), this logical next step might be well suited to the statutes' goals. However, in the struggle between the values of the adversary system and the philosophy of the discovery statutes, the former often prevail. In this era, at least, courts are unlikely to force counsel to reveal everything they know, even about limited aspects of a case, in response to open-ended interrogatories.

A final reason that open-ended questions are unlikely to be effective is that the responses are drafted by opposing counsel. Typically, opposing counsel reveal information about as willingly as families reveal their skeletons. Thus, a broad interrogatory such as, "Tell us what happened" is likely to be met with a conclusionary response such as, "You breached."

b. Stories Regarding Discrete Events

Given that open-ended interrogatories pursuing an overall story are not well suited to the task, one might wonder about the utility of open-ended interrogatories which have a more limited goal of uncovering the details of discrete events in an overall story. To frame such interrogatories, one usually must be aware of an event in the first place. Then, one might ask open questions such as the following:

> 1. "Please describe in detail the meeting which took place in early June between Bernard Sydney and Terry Firma."

> 2. "Please relate everything that occurred on June 10 after you entered the intersection of 1st and 10th Streets."

Though such interrogatories focus an adversary's attention upon a particular (albeit perhaps "clumped") event, they still are unlikely to

---

4. See Hickman v. Taylor, 329 U.S. 495, 67 S.Ct. 385, 91 L.Ed. 451 (1947).

elicit a complete story about that event. They suffer many of the infirmities that afflict interrogatories which search for an overall story. Even if they are not vague, the adversary's response is likely to be couched in conclusionary terms, and judges are unlikely to force fully detailed responses.

Moreover, recall that our discussion of interviewing indicated that even cooperative witnesses are usually not able to provide fully detailed responses to open questions. One normally must ask a multitude of follow-up questions which probe initial and often conclusionary responses. Opposing counsel, of course, is the antithesis of a cooperative witness. To learn the details of even a single event, therefore, one would have to include in one's interrogatories both initial and follow-up questions. This task seemingly is impossible. Usually, one cannot frame follow-up questions until one has seen the initial answer. You cannot use a T-funnel until you know where to pour!

Accordingly, if one is to learn details about specific events through written interrogatories, one is consigned to additional and probably multiple sets of interrogatories. However, multiple sets of interrogatories become expensive for clients, and they severely test one's endurance. Additionally, they often send opposing counsel scurrying to court for protective orders seeking relief from burdensome interrogatories. Not only do the resultant court appearances increase costs and sap energy further, but also judges, who tend to favor "economical" litigation, frequently grant at least partial relief. In general, then, open question interrogatories are unlikely to ferret out the details of even a single event.

Still, resolute pursuers of stories through interrogatories are not yet at an impasse. Perhaps narrowly-framed interrogatories are the answer. Unfortunately, such is not often the case. If one were interested in the details of a meeting between Pennoyer and Neff, one could posit specific interrogatories such as the following:

1. "On what day and at what time and place did the meeting between Pennoyer and Neff take place?"

2. "How long did the meeting referred to in Interrogatory No. 1 last?"

3. "Who was present during the meeting referred to in Interrogatory No. 1?"

4. "At the meeting referred to in Interrogatory No. 1, was there mention made of a Sheriff's Deed?"

5. "If the answer to Interrogatory No. 4 is "Yes", did Pennoyer state that he received the deed?"

A reasonably responsible adversary may well provide adequate responses to such narrowly-framed questions. But as even these few interrogatories suggest, it is nearly impossible to learn all the details of an event through narrow questions. To succeed, one would have to conjure up every important topic and detail that might be part of an event and frame a question for each. For instance, in the Pennoyer and Neff hypothetical, one would need to frame a multitude of specific questions about matters such as (1) what all participants in the meeting might have said; (2) what documents might have been reviewed or drafted; and (3) what factors might have been present that affect the credibility of the participants. Even if one could think of all the pertinent questions, the time involved in, and monetary costs of, framing them would be prohibitive. Moreover, their sheer number undoubtedly would prompt opposing counsel to object that they were "unduly burdensome." Since many courts tend to disfavor numerous interrogatories, a lengthy set of questions, narrow though they be, is unlikely to meet with judicial favor.[5] Finally, such specificity might go a long way toward suggesting to the adversary potential evidence that he or she might not have considered. In such instances, the answers one receives may be written on a "Thank you" note.

c. Learning Details

One may infer from the foregoing discussion that, preliminary matters aside, interrogatories are a useless procedure created by an Evil Being to punish litigants, litigators, paralegals and secretaries. However, if interrogatories are generally ineffective for learning a complete story, or the full details of single events, they may be used to elicit specific details. Thus, the reason that interrogatories are so frequently used to elicit "preliminary" information is precisely because preliminary facts are typically specific details. For example, the titles, dates and whereabouts of documents evidencing a particular transaction are the sorts of preliminary, specific details that may be efficiently elicited through interrogatories.

Similarly, if one is aware of a specific event—e.g. that a conversation occurred—interrogatories may be used to discover specific details such as the date it took place, and witnesses to it. Hence, some details about specific aspects of stories can be gotten through interrogatories.

---

5. Some courts and commentators suggest limiting the number of interrogatories (see D. Segal, *Survey of the Literature on Discovery from 1970 to the Present: Expressed Dissatisfactions and Proposed Reforms* (1978), pp. 49–50) and many courts will limit the number of interrogatories either by sustaining objections to the interrogatories as unduly burdensome or by issuing protective orders. R. Haydock and D. Herr, note 2 *supra*, at § 3.5.1; 4A *Moore's Federal Practice* §§ 33.08, 33.27 (2nd ed. 1981).

d. Conclusion

Interrogatories that attempt to develop details of stories by focusing on specific aspects of stories are likely to be effective only to the extent that they seek limited specific information.

However, lawyers do not exclusively focus their interrogatories on specific aspects of stories. Often, interrogatories focus on an adversary's contentions and the evidence supporting such contentions. The next section considers the effectiveness of "contention interrogatories" in eliciting the details of an adversary's case.

4. LEARNING AN ADVERSARY'S THEORIES AND AFFIRMATIVE EVIDENCE

Just as one usually marshals one's own affirmative evidence according to one's legal theories and factual hypotheses, so too may one frame interrogatories which seek out an adversary's affirmative evidence in relation to its contentions regarding specific theories. It should come as no surprise that such interrogatories are often referred to as "contention interrogatories."

In the years prior to the 1970 amendment to Rule 33 of the Federal Rules of Civil Procedure, there was some doubt as to whether interrogatories could properly request contentions or legal conclusions. Since that amendment, however, there is no doubt that one may propound interrogatories which compel an adversary to disclose his or her legal contentions and the evidence which the adversary contends supports such contentions.[6]

Thus, in a breach of contract action, if the plaintiff wants to know whether the defendant contends that there was no contract between the parties, the plaintiff may submit interrogatories of the following sort:

1. Do you contend that on May 4, defendant True Blue did not enter into the contract attached as Exhibit "A"?

2. If the answer to Interrogatory No. 1 is "Yes," please state all facts upon which you base this contention.

Certainly, if the defendant responds affirmatively to Interrogatory No. 1, the plaintiff will learn that the defendant intends to make an issue of the element of formation. However, how effective is Interrogatory No. 2 likely to be? The question is another broad open-ended one to which opposing counsel will draft the answer, and the results are likely to be less than spectacular. Conclusions are quite likely to pervade the answer to the exclusion of most, if not all, de-

---

6. See Federal Rules of Civil Procedure, Rule 33(b); 4A *Moore's Federal Practice*, note 5 supra, at § 33.17[2].

This rule obviously is an exception to general notions of attorney work product.

tails. For example, the answer to No. 2 might be something like, "Wes Ipsa had no authority to sign the contract."

However, one might try to circumvent the adversary's opportunity to provide conclusionary responses by narrowing the scope of the information sought. To narrow the search, one may include in contention interrogatories potential factual grounds upon which the adversary might base a legal contention. The following sample interrogatories illustrate this kind of approach.

1. Do you contend that True Blue did not enter into the contract attached hereto as Exhibit "A"? (hereafter "the contract").

2. If the answer to Interrogatory No. 1 is anything other than an unqualified "No," do you contend that the contract was not signed by an authorized agent of True Blue?

3. If your answer to Interrogatory No. 2 is anything other than an unqualified "No," please state each and every fact upon which you base your contention that the contract was not signed by an authorized agent of True Blue.

4. If the answer to Interrogatory No. 1 is anything other than an unqualified "No," do you contend that the contract was not authorized by True Blue's Board of Directors?

5. If your answer to Interrogatory No. 4 is anything other than an unqualified "No," please state each and every fact upon which you base your contention that the contract was not authorized by True Blue's Board of Directors.

6. If your answer to Interrogatory No. 1 is anything other than an unqualified "No," do you contend that the contract was signed subject to an oral agreement that it would be binding only if ratified by True Blue's Board of Directors?

7. If your answer to Interrogatory No. 6 is anything other than an unqualified "No," please state each and every fact upon which you base your contention that the contract was signed subject to an oral agreement that it would be binding only if ratified by True Blue's Board of Directors.

8. If your answer to Interrogatory No. 1 is anything other than an unqualified "No," please state each and every fact upon which you base your contention that True Blue did not enter into the contract, which fact is not already listed in your answers to Interrogatories Nos. 3, 5 and 7.

In contrast to the initial set of interrogatories propounded to True Blue, this set does not limit the search to the single broad contention (theory) that there was "no contract." After asking the general question in Interrogatory No. 1, this set moves on to ask about possible factual grounds on which the broad contention might be based.

As you might guess, narrowing contention interrogatories in this fashion is not foolproof. First of all, no matter how carefully one thinks through potential grounds for a legal contention, one often may be unable to think of each ground upon which an adversary might rely. Imagine, for example, trying to come up with every ground that a plaintiff might be relying upon in an automobile accident case in which the plaintiff's claim is based on negligence. In the example above, the questioner recognizes that he or she might not have thought of all the possibilities, and concludes the interrogatories with a request for facts not brought out in responses to Interrogatories Nos. 3, 5 and 7. See No. 8.

Secondly, one runs a substantial risk of suggesting potential contentions that, left to its own devices, an adversary might have overlooked. A client may be peeved to learn that an adversary's case emanates from one's own interrogatories. However, the risk may be worth taking. Because one's investigation may be guided in large part by an adversary's contentions, one is often stuck in neutral when unaware of those contentions. Against this very real impediment must be balanced the potential risk of suggestion. Often, the scale tips in favor of asking.

Of course, even if one does come up with the ground(s) upon which an adversary bases a legal contention, one still is faced with the problem of getting the details of each ground upon which that contention is based. Nos. 3, 5 and 7 ask the adversary to "state each and every fact upon which you base your contention." This is standard contention interrogatory language. However, as one can tell from our earlier discussion, this kind of request is typically satisfied with a conclusionary response. For example, No. 3 might be answered with a phrase such as, "Wes Ipsa was not an employee of True Blue." Hence, while the latter set of interrogatories perhaps increases the chances of identifying the factual grounds of a contention, it does not guarantee that one will receive evidentiary detail.

There are other reasons why contention interrogatories may not uncover specific evidence. If contention interrogatories (or indeed any others) are sent out early in a case, an adversary may not yet have identified the theories or uncovered the evidence it will ultimately advance at trial.[7] Also, particularly if opposing counsel has not marshalled evidence according to contentions during investigation, one may not get evidence which is in the adversary's file simply because the adversary is unaware of its existence or significance.

Drafting to overcome these stumbling blocks to detailed responses is, frankly, difficult. Sometimes, one may attempt to coax evidentia-

7. As a general rule, a party is under no obligation to supplement responses to interrogatories with information thereafter acquired. But see Fed.Rules Civ. Proc. Rule 26(e).

ry detail from an adversary *by explicitly requesting* all evidence which might support a legal contention. Thus, this form of follow-up interrogatory is common:

> "If the answer to Interrogatory No. 3 is 'Yes,' please state each and every act, event, statement, or document which you contend, directly or indirectly, supports your contention that the contract was not signed by an authorized agent."

Is the additional language likely to be effective? If you were bent on revealing as little information as possible, would the subtle threat of the "legalese" overcome your predilection?

A second possible approach is to narrow the search for underlying evidence in the same way that one narrows the search for the underlying bases of legal contentions. That is, one may include in interrogatories potential evidentiary details that would support a particular ground. In the following example, plaintiff in the True Blue case asks for specific details which would support the contention that there was no contract because it was not signed by an authorized agent:

> 3. If your answer to Interrogatory No. 2 is anything other than an unqualified "No," do you contend that the contract was not signed by an authorized agent because Wes Ipsa was not an employee of True Blue at the time the contract was signed?

> 4. If your answer to Interrogatory No. 3 is anything other than an unqualified "No," please state each and every fact upon which you base your contention that Wes Ipsa was not an employee of True Blue at the time the contract was signed.

> 5. If your answer to Interrogatory No. 2 is anything other than an unqualified "No," do you contend that the contract was not signed by an authorized agent because plaintiff was aware that Wes Ipsa was not authorized to enter into contracts?

> 6. If your answer to Interrogatory No. 5 is anything other than an unqualified "No," please state each and every fact upon which you base your contention that plaintiff was aware that Wes Ipsa was not authorized to enter into contracts.

> 7. If your answer to Interrogatory No. 2 is anything other than an unqualified "No," please state each and every fact upon which you base your contention that the contract was not signed by an authorized agent, which fact is not already listed in your answers to Interrogatory Nos. 4 and 6.

The specificity of these interrogatories is no doubt reminiscent of the narrow interrogatories illustrated in Section 2 of this chapter as a potential method of learning details about events. And, these latest interrogatories suffer from the same deficiencies. To develop evidentiary details which might support an adversary's legal contentions, one would have to spend time identifying the adversary's potential evidence. That is a task which one ordinarily does not take on. Moreover, by so doing one of course runs a great risk of suggesting evidentiary possibilities to an adversary. Finally, propounding a voluminous set of detailed interrogatories is likely to be costly and to invite objections. For all of these reasons, one does not normally include in a set of interrogatories questions that suggest potential evidentiary detail for the adversary.

In combination with Requests for Admission,[8] contention interrogatories are the principal vehicle through which one narrows issues in civil cases. When an adversary's response denies that it is making a particular contention, one may use a Request for Admission to formally eliminate that potential contention as an issue. In summary form, the process looks something like this:

(a) *Interrogatory No. 1349.* Do you contend that True Blue entered into the contract attached hereto as Exhibit "A"?

(b) *True Blue's Answer.* Yes.

(c) *Plaintiff's Request for Admission No. 7.* For purposes of this action only, please admit that True Blue entered into the contract attached hereto as Exhibit "A."

If True Blue admits Request No. 7, it is foreclosed from contending at trial that it did not enter into the contract.

5. LEARNING ONE'S OWN AFFIRMATIVE EVIDENCE

From time to time we have pointed out that much of one's own affirmative evidence often rests in the hands of one's adversary. For example, in securities fraud cases, if one represents the plaintiff, a full story of "what happened" is likely to be known primarily by witnesses employed by, or aligned with, the adversary. More generally, in most litigation, one often seeks evidence which is in an adversary's possession to support one's affirmative case. For instance, in a child custody case in which a mother alleges that the father abuses their children, the father may want to seek evidence from the mother regarding his reasonable use of discipline. In criminal cases, this principle has evolved into an aspect of due process. A prosecutor has a duty to make known to defense counsel evidence which tends to exculpate a defendant.[9]

Although we are aware of no cases discussing the point, perhaps courts will not generally permit one to ask directly for affirmative evidence on behalf of one's own client. Such an interrogatory is in theory quite tempting. For example, in a typical personal injury

---

8. Fed.Rules Civ.Proc. Rule 36; see also R. Haydock and D. Herr, note 2 supra, at 265 et seq.

9. See ABA Code of Professional Responsibility, DR 7–103(B) and EC 7–13.

case, a defendant, Shackle, who is alleged to have driven negligently, would dearly love to pose the following interrogatory:

> "Please state each and every fact known to you that tends to establish, in whole or in part, directly or indirectly, that just prior to the accident Shackle was not speeding."

Probably courts would be reluctant to permit such interrogatories on the ground of work product. Arguably, they require one party's lawyer to marshal evidence so as to help to prove an adversary's case, and as such run afoul of the notion that each party is responsible for preparing its own case.

If contention interrogatories are not well-suited to discovering one's own affirmative evidence, one may nonetheless seek potential *sources* of affirmative evidence through "witness interrogatories." Courts tend to be less troubled by interrogatories which are limited to sources of information, perhaps because the interrogator has to follow up the interrogatories by contacting the witnesses. All the information is not provided cheaply through the opponent's efforts.

For example, in the negligence hypothetical above, assume that one of defendant Shackle's theories is that the plaintiff Potted negligently ran out into the street from between two parked cars just before Shackle's car hit Potted. Attempting to uncover affirmative evidence to support this story, defendant Shackle might propound the following interrogatory:

> "Please state the name of each and every person who has knowledge (whether obtained through sight, hearing or other sensory source) of any fact (including but not limited to any act, event, statement or document) indicating, evidencing, and/or demonstrating, directly or indirectly, that just prior to being struck by the car driven by Shackle, plaintiff Potted entered Kurby Avenue from between two parked cars."

This interrogatory seeks the source of potential affirmative evidence rather than the potential affirmative evidence itself. Hence, it is likely to withstand any objection an adversary might make.

Though we illustrate "witness interrogatories" only in the context of discovering one's own affirmative evidence, please note that they are also useful in connection with the discovery of an adversary's theories and evidence. See sections 4, supra and 7(b) infra. By the same token, the forms of interrogatories used to learn adversarial stories, described in section 3, supra, may be used in connection with the discovery of one's own evidence. See in particular section 3(d).

6. LEARNING REBUTTAL EVIDENCE

Though interrogatories are not often consciously used for the purpose of discovering rebuttal evidence, one might consider using them for this purpose. When seeking to discover an adversary's rebuttal, one may pursue both "denial" and "explanation." Remember, however, that a usual precondition of discovering rebuttal is disclosing one's own affirmative evidence.

Assume that in *Potted v. Shackle,* an item of affirmative evidence for Shackle is that on March 13, two days after the collision, Potted told a nurse, Linda Charles, "Now I know why J-walking is illegal." Here are alternative interrogatories that Shackle's counsel might propound seeking to learn whether Potted *denies* this piece of affirmative evidence: [10]

Interrogatory No. 15. On March 13, did Jill Potted say to Linda Charles, in essence, "Now I know why J-walking is illegal?"

Interrogatory No. 16. (Alternative A): If your answer to Interrogatory No. 15 is anything but an unqualified "Yes," please set forth each and every fact indicating evidencing and/or demonstrating, directly or indirectly, that on March 13th Jill Potted did not say to Linda Charles in essence "Now I know why J-walking is illegal," and with respect to each such fact, please identify the following:

a. the full name and business and residence address of each person having knowledge of such fact.

b. the date and location of the occurrence of such fact.

c. the identity of each document or electronic recording which evidences, pertains to, refers to and/or records such fact. Thus, your answer to this interrogatory should be set forth in the following form for each such fact:

(1) the fact . . .

(2) the full name and business . . .

(3) the date . . .

(4) the identity of each and every document . . .

Interrogatory No. 16. (Alternative B): If your answer to interrogatory number 15 is anything but an unqualified "Yes," please state the name of each and every person who has knowledge (whether through sight, hearing, taste and/or smell, hearsay or otherwise) of any fact (including but not limited to any act, event, occurrence, incident, reason, statement, and/or document) indicating, evidencing and/or demonstrating, directly or indirectly, that on March 13th Jill Potted did *not* say to Linda Charles, in essence, "Now I know why J-walking is illegal."

---

10. Of course, even if Shackle's counsel has some evidence indicating that Potted made the J-walking remark, Shackle's counsel might also propound other interrogatories seeking to learn of additional affirmative evidence indicating that Potted did make the remark.

Interrogatory No. 17. With respect to each person set forth in your answer to interrogatory No. 16 (alt. B) please state:

a. The person's full name and business and residence address.

b. Each and every fact of which such person has knowledge and with regard to each such fact:

(1) the date and location of its occurrence and,

(2) the identity of each and every document or electronic recording which evidences, pertains to, refers to and/or records such fact.

Approaches "A" and "B" above are definitely alternatives; one would not submit both in the same set of questions. Both ask for evidence of denial. The distinction is that Alternative "A" is a direct request for evidence, followed by requests for information about witnesses who can supply the evidence. As previously pointed out, however, requests for "all evidence" are apt to be treated cavalierly by opposing counsel. Alternative "B", which emphasizes information about witnesses, might often be more effective. Attorneys are more used to disclosing the identities of witnesses, than they are to revealing "all evidence." Thus, an adversary may well respond fully at least to the witness portion of alternative "B." One should expect, of course, that the "each fact" follow-up questions in Interrogatory No. 17 will be less than totally successful.

At the same time, if Potted does not deny making the statement, Shackle's counsel will want to know what explanation, if any, Potted intends to offer. Through an inferential chain, Shackle would like a trier of fact to infer from the March 13 statement that on March 11 Potted stepped into Kurby Avenue from between two parked cars. To learn whether Potted has an *explanation* that might persuade a trier of fact not to reach this conclusion, Shackle might propound the following interrogatories. (Note: we repeat Interrogatory No. 15 for purposes of clarity):

Interrogatory No. 15. On March 13, did Jill Potted say to Linda Charles, in essence, "Now I know why J-walking is illegal?"

(Interrogatories 16 and 17, "denial" interrogatories, omitted)

Interrogatory No. 18. (Alternative A): If your answer to Interrogatory No. 15 is an unqualified "Yes," please identify each and every fact which indicates, directly or indirectly, or explains why on March 13th Jill Potted said to Linda Charles, in essence, "Now I know why J-walking is illegal." With respect to each such fact please identify the following:

(1) the fact . . .

(2) the full name and business . . .

(3) the date . . .

(4) the identity of each and every document . . .

Interrogatory No. 18. (Alternative B): If your answer to Interrogatory number 15 is an unqualified "Yes," please state the name of each and every person who has knowledge (whether through sight, hearing, taste and/or smell, hearsay or otherwise) of any fact which indicates directly or indirectly, or explains why, on March 13th Jill Potted said to Linda Charles, in essence, "Now I understand why J-walking is illegal."

Interrogatory No. 19. With respect to each person set forth in your answer to Interrogatory No. 18, please state:

   a. the person's full name and business and residence address.

   b. each and every fact known to such person which indicates directly or indirectly, or explains why on March 13th Jill Potted made the aforesaid statement to Linda Charles *and* with regard to each such fact:

   (1) the date and location of its occurrence and,

   (2) the identity of each and every document or electronic recording which evidences, pertains to, refers to and/or records such fact.

Again, approaches 18A and 18B illustrate alternatives; they would not be used together in the same set of interrogatories. Number 18A requests evidence of explanations, whereas 18B together with 19 emphasizes information about witnesses who might know of potential explanations.

7. DRAFTING CONSIDERATIONS

The previous sections have purposely attempted to phrase interrogatories in a variety of ways. The variety is realistic; though "form" interrogatories are available in formbooks, office form files, and even through court rules in some areas, there are, as of yet, no mandated or perfect methods for always phrasing questions. Nonetheless, there are drafting considerations of which one should be aware. This section addresses a few of those considerations.

In general, one's questions should be clear and precise. Remember, opposing counsel who are perfectly adept at surviving in a complex world may be suddenly overwhelmed by purported ambiguities in the simplest of questions. For example, in one notorious case an attorney did not produce a "letter" from an expert because he did not consider it an "interim report." [11] Through careful drafting, one might convince an adversary that the best course is simply to answer. If that fails, and the adversary shows up at trial with omitted evidence known at the time the interrogatories were answered, careful drafting may foreclose an excuse for not answering and thus impel a judge to impose some type of sanction.[12]

a. Minimizing Evasion

The sample interrogatories in this chapter were drafted in part to overcome some common types of evasion. A standard type of evasion is to purport to read a word in the most narrow way possible. Thus, a "letter" is not an "interim report." A document which refers to a fact does not "evidence" it. A request for "facts" is interpreted so as to exclude "statements."

One method commonly used to overcome such nit-picking is to phrase interrogatories in the alternative by using synonyms. For example, if one wants all facts supporting a contention, one asks not simply for "facts supporting the contention," but rather for "all facts indicating, evidencing and/or supporting the contention." However, even the synonyms may not be adequate protection against an adversary stricken with Terminal Ambiguity. Thus, one might ask for "all facts indicating, evidencing, suggesting and/or supporting, *directly or indirectly*, the contention."

A second approach often used to prevent overly narrow interpretations of words is to preface interrogatories with a series of definitions. The definitions attempt to define, typically through synonyms, the meaning of important terms that are repeatedly used in a set of interrogatories. Defining terms separately saves one the time and trouble of repeating phrases every time a term appears. On the other hand, an adversary may find it quite awkward if compelled to flip back and forth constantly between questions and definitions. Moreover, many trial judges when ruling on motions to compel answers to interrogatories containing a preface of definitions will agree that having to move continually from question to definition is "too burdensome" and, on that basis deny the motions. In any event, here is a portion of a typical "Definitions" section of a set of interrogatories:

Definitions:

As used here the following terms shall have the following meanings:

    1. "Complaint" means and refers to the complaint filed by the plaintiff in this action.

11. See Walter Kiechel III, "The Strange Case of Kodak's Lawyers," *Fortune,* May 8, 1978, p. 188.

12. See C. Wright and A. Miller, note 3 supra, at §§ 2182, 2050 (1970).

2.　"Person" means and includes a natural person, corporation, partnership, association, agency and/or any other kind of entity, and all of his, her or its agents, servants, employees and/or representatives.

3.　"Document" means and includes the original and all copies of any kind of written, typewritten, printed, graphic and/or any other tangible means of recording any form of communication or representation including specifically, but without limiting the generality of the foregoing, reports, memoranda, letters, telegrams, telexes, books, accounts, photographs, inter-office communications, reports, drafts of documents, calendars, appointment books, diaries, notes of meetings or conversations, written agreements, checks, receipts, invoices, bills, accounting reports, and/or financial records.

4.　"You" and "your" means and includes Mellow Yellow Gas and Electric Co. and its agents, servants, employees and/or representatives, including its attorney.

5.　"Accident" means the plaintiff's coming in contact, through his picking pole, with electrical wires and being thrown to the ground as alleged and described in paragraph VII of page 3 of the complaint and paragraph IV of page 5 of the complaint.

6.　"Property" means the real property referred to in paragraph VII, page 3 of the complaint.

To dedicated nit-pickers, using synonyms and prefacing questions with definitions just whets the evasive appetite. Hence, one often inserts the phrase "and/or" in a set of synonyms. Consider item # 4 from the list of definitions above: " 'You' and 'your' means and includes Mellow Yellow Gas and Electric Co. and its agents, servants, employees and/or representatives, including its attorney." To some nit-pickers, if the last "and" were standing alone, a person or entity would not be included as an agent, servant, employee or representative unless the person or entity satisfied each individual criterion. Similarly, if the "or" stood alone, an adversary might omit the names of those persons or entities who satisfied two or more, but less than all, criteria. The "and/or" phraseology attempts to overcome both types of nits.

Another character trait of nit-pickers is a seeming congenital inability to answer questions definitively either "yes" or "no". If a nit-picker reads a simple question such as, "Did Skip eat a peanut butter and jelly sandwich for lunch?" the thought of responding simply "yes" or "no" may produce cold chills. After all, "yes" might imply that a sandwich was *all* that Skip had for lunch, while in actuality Skip also had a glass of milk. Similarly, even if Skip did have a peanut butter and jelly sandwich by itself, maybe Skip was only having a snack, not really a lunch. Even given our adversary system, one would hope that many attorneys would respond "yes" in either situation, but then go on to qualify the answer with the additional facts that make it accurate. Undoubtedly, however, there are nit-pickers at large who would capitalize on the somewhat less than total accuracy of "yes" to respond "no."

To attempt to prevent these sorts of nit-pickers from sowing false discovery information, we have demonstrated how one may phrase questions to ferret out qualified responses. One interrogatory was, "On March 13, did Jill Potted say to Linda Charles, in essence, 'Now I know why J-walking is illegal?'" Even if the quote is substantially accurate, a nit-picker might respond "no." Perhaps Jill Potted said other things to Linda Charles. Perhaps the statement was made at 12:01 A.M. on March 14. Or perhaps Potted contends her statement was, "Now I know why J-walking is against the law," thereby encouraging a nit-picker to narrow greatly the meaning of "in essence."

To prevent an adversary from hiding behind such potential qualifications, one may follow-up a yes/no question with an explicit inquiry for evidence (or, alternatively, for witnesses who can provide evidence) which would qualify the initial response. If Potted does *not unqualifiedly answer "yes,"* then Potted is asked to state the facts that prevent an affirmative response.[13]

b. Obtaining Complete Information

Quite apart from problems caused by evasive adversaries, one should form the habit of making requests for information complete. If one asks for the identity of people or entities, one also asks for information that enables one to contact them. If one asks for the identity of a document, one asks also for information that will enable one to describe and locate the document sufficiently to support a Motion to Produce if an adversary will not willingly turn it over. And if one asks for evidence, one asks for witnesses and documents that are the source of any evidence supplied. One may also ask when the evidence arose, in order to expand one's time line.

As with definitions of terms, one may include requests for complete information in a prefatory portion of interrogatories, as follows:

General Instructions:

A. Whenever you are requested to identify or state the identity of any "person", state the following with respect to such person:

     1. The full name of the person;

---

13. Although this example discussed "other than an unqualified yes," please note that using similar reasoning, one may ask for "other than an unqualified no." One chooses the language which seems best suited to the circumstances.

2. The last known business and residence address of the person;

3. The last known business and residence telephone number of the person;

4. Occupation of the person.

B. Whenever you are requested to identify any document, state the following with respect to such document:

1. A description of the document in sufficient detail so that it may be readily identified by its custodian;

2. The date appearing on the document;

3. The name of any person signing the document;

4. The present location of the original of the document;

5. The names and addresses of the person or persons having custody or control of the original, and any and/or all copies of the document;

6. Whether you will make it available to counsel for _____ without the necessity of a Motion to Produce.

C. Whenever you are requested to identify any fact state the following with respect to each such fact:

1. The full name and business and residence address and telephone number of each person having knowledge of such fact.

2. The date and location of the occurrence of such fact.

3. The identity of each document or electronic recording which evidences, pertains to, refers to and/or records such fact.

Instead of lumping these requests together at the beginning of a set of interrogatories, one may include them as applicable in specific interrogatories. See, for example, Interrogatories 18–A and 19, supra.

8. CONCLUDING THOUGHTS ABOUT INTERROGATORIES

We cannot conclude the chapter without personal comment on the all-too-typical behavior of some attorneys during discovery. The avowed philosophy of our highest courts that prior to trial litigants should be knowledgable with respect to each other's evidence is often disregarded.[14] In some respects, the contentious behavior which was in the years before the discovery statutes reserved primarily for

---

14. See W. Brazil, "Civil Discovery: How Bad are the Problems?" 67 A.B. A.J. 450 (1981); W. Lundquist, "In Search of Discovery Reform," 66 A.B. A.J. 1071 (1980). See also 4 *Moore's Federal Practice* § 26.02[3] (2d Ed. 1981), ar-guing that abuses of the discovery rules "for the most part . . . can be met under the Rules as they now stand by a more deft, appreciative and firm application of the Rules."

courtrooms has been pushed back into discovery procedures.[15] Litigators dedicate pretrial months to concealing as much evidence as possible, for as long as possible. To some extent, trial judges foster this attitude by failing to impose sanctions on attorneys who hide behind hypertechnical interpretations of discovery requests.[16] We are not proud of the legalistic verbiage we have suggested including in interrogatories. However, that language may be necessary as long as so many judges and attorneys view discovery as a game, not a time to exchange information responsibly.

Many authors have a difficult time concluding books. We do not.

15. R. Lempert and S. Saltzburg, *A Modern Approach to Evidence* 118–19 (2d ed. 1982).

16. See note 14, supra.

Index

ETHICAL CONSIDERATIONS
Disclosing evidence to adversary, 123–126.
Disclosing evidence to witnesses, 240, 247–248.
Disclosing purpose of interview, 247–248.
Duties as counselor, 30.
Identifying potential rebuttal, 114–115.
Interviewing subterfuges, 219–220.
Investigating prior to suit, 75.
Learning harmful evidence, 30.
Preventing access to witness, 245 n. 2.
Probing for detail, risks of, 293.
Pursuing emotional evidence, 180–181.
Topic selection, bias of, 248.

EVENTS
As signposts, 280–282.
Before and after, evidence, 14.
Clumped, 52, 292, 300, 310–312.
Conclusions distinguished, 51, 263–264.
Details distinguished, 52.
Disclosure in depositions, 256.
Distinguished from topics, 289.
Interrogatories to learn, 330–332.
Non-events, 53–54.
Substantively critical, 14;
    See also, Moments of Substantive Importance.
Time line as sequence of, 263.
Time lines to identify, 265–266.
Uncovering during theory development, 289–290; 294–295.

EVIDENCE
Attorney as shaper, 2–3, 5, 13, 30, 162.
Marshalled around theories, 61–62.
Need for recording, 36–38.
Probative worth, 35.
Relevance, 84.
Sprinkled throughout testimony, 17, 59.
Uncovering adversary's, 30–31.

EXPECTANCY, 147–148

EXPERTS
Crediblity, 145–146, 319–320.
Criteria for selection, 319–320.
Defined, 146, 173.
Disclosing data to, 323–324.
Discussing existing evidence, 323–324.
Discussing hypotheses & potential evidence, 324–325.
Identifying factual hypotheses, 172–174.
Identifying speciality, 317–318.
In historical reconstruction, 197–198.
Methods of locating, 318–319.
Ongoing involvement in case, 198, 317.
Organizing interview, 321–323.
Physical appearance, effect on credibility, 153.

EXPERTS—Cont'd
Supplying experience, 97–99, 317, 319–320.
Three uses of, 317.

EXPLANATORY EVIDENCE
See also, Theories, Explanatory.
Defined, 14.
Effect on credibility, 140–141.
Establishing moral culpability, 141.
Testing credibility, 302.
Why persuasive, 21.

EXPLANATORY HYPOTHESES
See Theories, Explanatory.

FACT ANALYSIS
"Admit and explain," effect of, 117.
Credibility evidence, role of, 82.
Jurors, when begun, 151.
Marshalling evidence, 59–60.
Role of experts, 97–99.
Role of premises, 83.

FACTUAL HYPOTHESES
Activating legal theories, 169.
Adversary's, 187.
Beyond initial story, 170.
Defendant perspective,
    Derailing legal stories, 175.
    Identifying responsible party, 175–177.
Defined, 162.
Evidence to bolster, see Chapter 19.
Experts to develop, 172–173.
How to develop, 171–172.
In closing argument, 121–123.
In evidence-marshalling outlines, 66–67.
Joy of building, 183–184.
Learning adversary's, 333–337.
Legal theories distinguished, 163.
Multiple, 66–67, 170–171, 182–183.
Rebuttal theories,
    Denial and explanation, 185.
    Except when, 185.
    Nature of, 184–185.
Selecting among, 181, 205.
Using intuition, 174.

FILLING, 147–148

GENERALIZATIONS
Affecting credibility, 135.
Approximating probative value, 97, 131.
Basis of, 85–86.
Case-specific, 196–197.
Defined, 84–85.
"Especially when," 96, 198.
"Except when," 90, 95–96, 154, 198.
How to formulate, 93.
Identifying rebuttal, 90.
In existing affirmative evidence outlines, 102–105, 131.

PLANNING—Cont'd
Use of investigator, 218–220.
Witness' importance, 216.
Preliminary considerations, 214–215.

POTENTIAL EVIDENCE
See Historical Reconstruction, Outlines.

PREMISES
Bases of, 83–85.
Express articulation, 93–94.
In closing argument, 120–121.
Role of, 82–83.

PREPARATION
See Planning.

PREPARING FOR INTERVIEWS
See Planning.

PRIMACY, 151–152

PROBATIVE VALUE
Analysis of circumstantial evidence, 89–
    92, 94–97.
Approximating, 97.
Clarified by outlines, 131.
Common experience,
    Uniformity of, 94.
    Use of, 91–92.
Credibility evidence, 152–153.
Direct and circumstantial evidence, 80.
Generalizations, need to articulate, 93.
Item by item analysis, 90–91.
Meaning of, 89.
Reasons to determine, 89–92.
Strengthening through "especially
    when," 96.

PSYCHOLOGICAL EVIDENCE
See Emotional Evidence.

QUESTIONING
"Did you ever," 294–295, 298, 308–309.
Discomfort of,
    Active listening, 235.
    Probing, 293.
Experts, 321–325.
Probing clumped events, 292, 300, 310–
    312.
Probing for details, 290–293, 309–310.
Probing for rebuttal, 303–304, 315.
Probing implausibilities and inconsisten-
    cies, 302–303.
Testing for credibility, 301–303, 313–314.
T-funnel method, 295–299, 309–310.
Theories as basis, 163–164.
Thoroughness defined, 287.
Topical, see Theory Development.

REBUTTAL BY ARGUMENT
By denial, 121–122.

REBUTTAL BY ARGUMENT—Cont'd
By explanation, 122.
Forms of, 120–123.
Outlining, 130–131.

REBUTTAL EVIDENCE
As affirmative evidence, 15, 118, 120.
Categories of, 111.
Defined, 13–15, 110.
Denial, 118–120.
Disclosing affirmative, to learn, 123–126,
    339.
"Except when" to identify, 90, 96, 185.
Explanation, 116–118.
Factual hypotheses for, 184–187.
Identification precedes questioning, 111–
    116.
In potential evidence outlines, 201–204.
Interrogatories to learn, 338–341.
Need for categories, 111–116.
Outlining, 126, 130–132.
Probing for during theory development
    303–304.
Using argument to identify, 123.
Using historical reconstruction to identi-
    fy, 200–201.

RETURN TO THE SCENE, 199, 216, 268,
    293

SIMILARITY, 151–152

SOCIO–POLITICAL ATTITUDES
Effect on credibility, 143–145.
Factual hypotheses chosen for, 179.
Overcoming, 144–145.

STATES OF MIND
Circumstantial evidence to prove, 82.
Motive, 146–150.

STATUS, 150–151

STORIES
Credibility evidence meshed into, 133,
    154.
Defined, 11, 263.
Evidence embedded in, 17, 59.
Expanding with new events, 272, 277,
    282, 289–290.
Feelings in, 228–229.
Legal stories,
    Defendants derailing, 175, 179.
    Defined, 171, 175.
    Factual hypotheses for, 171–172.
Parameters set by elements, 58, 162.
Party's overall, 12.
Selectively told, 2–3, 5, 13, 30, 162.
Spontaneous, limitations of, 29, 112–113.
Substantively critical events, 14.

†